John Knox Laughton

State Papers Relating to the Defeat of the Spanish Armada

John Knox Laughton

State Papers Relating to the Defeat of the Spanish Armada

ISBN/EAN: 9783743392632

Manufactured in Europe, USA, Canada, Australia, Japa

Cover: Foto ©ninafisch / pixelio.de

Manufactured and distributed by brebook publishing software (www.brebook.com)

John Knox Laughton

State Papers Relating to the Defeat of the Spanish Armada

STATE PAPERS

RELATING TO

THE DEFEAT OF

The Spanish Armada

ANNO 1588

EDITED BY

JOHN KNOX LAUGHTON, M.A., R.N.

Professor of Modern History in King's College, London

VOL. I.

PRINTED FOR THE NAVY RECORDS SOCIETY

MDCCCXCIV.

THE COUNCIL

OF THE

NAVY RECORDS SOCIETY

1893-4-5

ADVERTISEMENT.

It having been found necessary to extend this work to two volumes, the second volume will be issued this year, in immediate sequence to the present. The letters of Lord Hood are thus unavoidably postponed till next year.

August, 1894.

INTRODUCTION.

The defeat of the Spanish Armada in 1588 has been rightly described by Sir Edward Creasy as one of the decisive battles of the world, speaking of it as one continued battle lasting for nine days, rather than as a succession of battles. It marks alike the approaching downfall of Spain and the rise of England as a great maritime power. England had indeed always believed in her naval power, had always claimed the sovereignty of the Narrow Seas; and, more than two hundred years before Elizabeth came to the throne, Edward III. had testified to his sense of its importance by ordering a gold coinage bearing the device which is now reproduced on the title page and cover of this volume, a device showing the armed strength and sovereignty of England based on the sea. It was no mere coincidence which led to the adoption of such a device in 1344, four years after the most bloody battle and decisive victory of western war—the battle of Sluys—which, by giving England the command of the sea, determined the course of the great war which followed; determined that Crécy and Poitiers should be fought on French soil, not on English; determined that the

English—not the French—armies should consist of trained soldiers ; that the French armies—not the English—should consist of raw levies of half-armed peasants.

The device thus adopted was continued by Edward's successors, and was still in use under Elizabeth, telling to those who could understand it that the might and majesty of England rested on her navy. That this was fully proved in the summer of 1588 is a familiar story, but the following pages show that few indeed of her statesmen, or warriors, or seamen, had realised the fact. They could believe that the fleet of England was capable of withstanding that of Spain ; that the armada, of itself, was not a thing to be feared ; but they never quite succeeded in getting rid of the notion that the Duke of Parma's army was still terrible. Wynter, indeed, with nigh fifty years' experience at sea, and memories of former expeditions to guide him, was sure that the enemy must find very great difficulty in the transport of the army, and that if the squadron in the Narrow Seas was kept up at its actual strength, ' the Prince's forces, being no other than that which he hath in Flanders at this time (20th of June), dare not come to the seas' (p. 214). Wynter's opinion is eminently practical. It was supposed that Parma might attempt a landing at Sheppey, Harwich or Yarmouth, places where ' a small charge will make a sufficient strength to withstand any sudden attempt; but in these princely actions a man cannot be too provident ; and no wisdom were it to put things to an even balance, when more weight may be added ' (*ib.*).

Drake's experience was, in its nature, altogether different from Wynter's. His fighting had been brisker, more adventurous, less systematic. He had seen less of fleets, little of the transport of troops. He had made attacks and found the enemy helpless to prevent him. It would almost seem that he imagined Parma might try to do for London what he himself had done for Nombre de Dios or Cartagena. And yet he fully realised the difficulties in Parma's way. He must have a spring tide to bring his ships out; he must have fair weather, his ships being small and pestered with soldiers; and if the Duke of Medina should return with the fleet, 'he is like, God willing, to have unquiet rest.' 'We ought,' he adds, 'much more to have regard unto the Duke of Parma and his soldiers, than to the Duke of Sidonia and his ships. . . . My opinion is that the Duke of Parma should be vigilantly looked upon for these twenty days, although the army of Spain return not this way; for of them I have no great doubt; although there be great cause for us all to watch carefully' (vol. ii.— Drake to Walsyngham, August 23). That in the face of a strong squadron Parma could not cross he quite well understood; but not so well that—with Medina-Sidonia defeated and fled—he could not attempt to do so; that the merest threat of interference was sufficient to prevent him.

But when even Drake did not see this clearly, it is not strange that the action of the fleet was for long misunderstood, and that the failure of the Spaniards should have been represented—as it often is even now—as due to a Heaven-sent storm.

Flavit Deus et dissipati sunt was accepted as at
once a true and pious explanation of the whole
thing. It was, too, a flattering and economical
belief. We were—it has been argued—a nation
peculiarly dear to the Almighty, and He showed His
favour by raising a storm to overwhelm our enemy
when the odds against us were most terrible.

From the religious point of view such a
representation is childish ; from the historical it is
false. False, because the Spanish fleet, after being
hounded up Channel, had sustained a crushing
defeat from the English, a defeat in which they lost
many ships and thousands of men before they fled
to the north ; a defeat so terrible that nothing could
induce them to turn on their pursuers ; a defeat
which forced them to a headlong flight into the unknown dangers of the northern seas, rather than
face the more certain and now known danger of the
English shot. Childish, because in affairs of State
Providence works by recognised means, and gives
the victory not by disturbing the course of nature
and nature's laws, but by giving the favoured
nation wise and prudent commanders, skilful and
able warriors ; by teaching their hands to war and
their fingers to fight.

But, in fact, much of the nonsense that has been
talked grew out of the attempt, not unsuccessfully
made, to represent the war as religious ; to describe
it as a species of crusade instigated by the Pope, in
order to bring heretical England once more into the
fold of the true Church. In reality nothing can be
more inaccurate. It is, indeed, quite certain that
religious bitterness was imported into the quarrel ;

but the war had its origin in two perfectly clear and wholly mundane causes.

The first and chief of these was the exclusive commercial policy adopted and enforced by the Spanish Government in respect of its West Indian and American settlements. That such a policy should give rise to smuggling, that the smuggling should be met by violent repression, and that, again, by bloody reprisals, was all a matter of course. Now amongst the smugglers were two men—kinsmen— who by force of character, by genius curiously well adapted to the circumstances of the age, and by undaunted courage, were destined to achieve a foremost place in the roll-call of English seamen. Their names were John Hawkyns and Francis Drake. In September 1568 these two men, with some few companions and a little squadron of five vessels, whilst carrying on a lucrative though illicit traffic with the Spanish settlements, were caught, in the harbour of San Juan de Lua, by a vastly superior Spanish force and were overwhelmed. Hawkyns and Drake, in two of the smallest vessels, alone escaped. Ordinary men, under the circumstances, would have digested their loss as they best might ; but these, not being ordinary men, determined by fair means or foul to exact compensation for the injury which they conceived had been done them. Hawkyns, with the cunning as well as the courage of the fox, entered into a simulated negotiation to hand over a considerable part of the navy of England to King Philip, on condition of having the men who had been taken prisoners set free, and of receiving money compensation for his loss. The

intrigue forms a curious episode in the history of
the Ridolfi plot in 1571. Drake, on the other
hand—a man of bolder and more generous character
—finding compensation not forthcoming, resolved
to seek it for himself; and after some preliminary
cruises, made that wonderful and adventurous
voyage in which, with a mere handful of men, he
took Nombre de Dios, sacked Venta Cruz, captured
a convoy of mules laden with silver, and returned
home with more treasure than any one ship had
previously brought to England. His achievement
was to be speedily surpassed, but by himself. Four
years afterwards he started on a voyage for the
South Sea, and, capturing Spanish ships by the
score and Spanish towns by the dozen, put a girdle
round about the earth, and returned to England,
again bringing back an enormous quantity of
treasure, to the amount, it was said, of a million and
a half sterling.

The outcry of the friends of Spain was very
loud. Drake, they said, was a pirate, and unless he
was punished, war was inevitable. Elizabeth had
probably made up her mind that, in any case, war
was very likely. She positively and in the plainest
language refused to admit the Spanish claim to the
whole of the islands and continent of America. She
herself sympathised, she knew that all England
sympathised, with Drake, and held his achievements
to be not only heroic but lawful. Besides, she had
got the money; and to return money which she
had once clutched was to her a constitutional
impossibility. She kept the money and she
knighted Drake. Spaniards naturally took a very

different view of Drake's conduct. It is quite certain that the King of Spairf, and not only the King, but every one of his subjects, considered Drake as a pirate who ought to have been hanged, and maintained that the approval and support which he received from the English crown was a distinct and valid reason for an appeal to arms.

The other and perhaps equally valid reason was the countenance and assistance which had been given by the English to the King's rebellious subjects in the Low Countries ; and though many English, whether for pay or principle, had served in the Spanish armies against the Dutch, it was not doubted that the general opinion of England and of England's Queen was in favour of the rebels. There were, of course, many other grounds of ill-will, beginning, it may be, with Elizabeth's refusal to marry Philip. The quarrel had been growing all along : Elizabeth had seized the Duke of Alva's treasure ; had allowed Dutch privateers to shelter in English harbours ; had supported the claimant to the crown of Portugal. Philip, on the other hand, had stirred up and fomented rebellion in Ireland, and had been a party to many plots in England— plots against the Queen's sovereignty, plots against the Queen's life. He had behaved with the utmost insolence to the Queen's ambassador, and had placed many offensive restrictions on the commercial intercourse of the two nations and on English residents in Spain.

It was said, too, and universally believed, that unoffending English subjects, visiting Spain on their lawful occasions, were on the most shadowy pretexts seized by the Inquisition, imprisoned, tortured, and burnt at the stake. That these stories had a very great effect on popular opinion is certain : it is as certain that they were much exaggerated and frequently grossly misrepresented. Englishmen in Spain were, of course, subject to Spanish laws ; and if they went to Spain for their own profit they were bound to submit to such laws as were there in force ; but the known instances of Englishmen residing for many years at the Spanish ports, and carrying on a lucrative business there, are too numerous to permit us to believe that the English, as such, were subject to any undue and irregular oppression ; though as aliens in blood, in customs, and in religion, they were not looked on with much favour. On the other hand, transgressors met with little consideration. On both sides sharp measure had been dealt out to pirates : the hanging of Oxenham and his fellows was a smaller analogue of the butchery at Smerwick, and both executions were quite in accordance with the custom of the age. Even prisoners in recognised war might be, and not uncommonly were, put to death, if they were judged not worth keeping for a ransom. It will be seen that, in the surrender of the Nuestra Señora del Rosario, it was especially stipulated that the lives of the prisoners were to be spared, and that when the ship was taken to Torbay the sheriff of Devon thought it a pity that the men had not 'been made water spaniels' (vol. ii.—Don Pedro to the King, August 21 ; Cary to Walsyngham, August 29). In the case of the San Mateo, no conditions were made, and whilst 'the best sort were saved, the rest were cast overboard and slain' (vol. ii.—Borlas to Walsyngham, August 3). Of course, when prisoners were a source of danger, there was no hesitation. The action of Henry V. at Agincourt was a commonplace of mediæval war, and in 1588 a similar measure was meted out to the Spaniards who were thrown, naked and destitute, on the coast of Ireland.

There would thus, according to the ideas and practice of the age, have been nothing out of the way in summarily slaying the men who, in 1568, were captured at San Juan de Lua, or were afterwards put on shore by Hawkyns. In Spanish law, as indeed in English law, smugglers forcibly resisting the king's authority were pirates, and might be put to death without more ado. It is probable that many of them were so put to death, but more seem to have been enslaved ; and in after years some few returned to England with stories of Spanish tyranny and Spanish cruelty which made a great impression on their countrymen. Prisons in the sixteenth century were nowhere luxurious abodes, and Spanish prisons are not likely to have been better than those of other nations. Howard, the philanthropist, has left a description of English prisons two hundred years later, when they were presumably less barbarous than in the days of Queen Elizabeth ; and from this we may understand that, without any special malice or design on the part of the Spaniards, Englishmen, and especially Englishmen of a respectable position —merchants, or masters of merchant-ships—who had the misfortune to get into a Spanish prison, did experience grievous sufferings.

Nor were the horrors of the prison-house necessarily the worst part of their lot. The Spaniards, as also the French and Italians, had no scruples about making their prisoners useful ; and an able-bodied man was as likely as not to find himself helping to tug an oar in one of the king's galleys, without the slightest regard paid to his personal dignity or his nationality, or the cause of his imprisonment (cf. p. 181).

That many Englishmen did thus rot in Spanish dungeons, or break their hearts in Spanish galleys, is very well established, but the reason why is not so clear. As a general rule it is attributed to the Inquisition, and is assumed to have been on a charge of heresy. It seems, however, not impossible that there has always been a confusion of names. *Inquisicion* means equally the Inquisition and a judicial inquiry : *inquisidor* might be an inquisitor, or a magistrate, or, in the armada, the provost-marshal ; and men reported to be lingering in the dungeons of the Inquisition may have been in some other and perhaps fouler prison on a charge of smuggling or piracy, brawling or contempt of court. And magistrates were not immaculate, even in England. Even in England alleged criminals were sometimes allowed to lie for months without a hearing, and when heard, were sometimes wrongfully condemned. It is not to be supposed that similar blunders—blunders of ignorance, carelessness or prejudice—did not occur in Spain.

Still there is no doubt that many fell into the hands of the Inquisition, as we understand the word, the Holy Office. Always on the watch to detect and punish heresy, which, in Spain, was held to be as dangerous to the State as popery was in England, the Holy Office did not professedly exercise jurisdiction over foreigners who kept their religious opinions to themselves ; but the man who openly and noisily preached his false doctrine or denounced the dogmas of the Church, be he Englishman or Spaniard, was arrested with as little ceremony as ever was a popish recusant in England, and racked, imprisoned, or put to death, even as if he had been a Mayne, a Sherwood, or a Campion. When we recollect the atrocities that were practised in England against the Papists under Elizabeth, or, a hundred years later, in Scotland, against the Covenanters under Charles II. ; that Burghley advocated the use of the rack, and that the burning of women as witches was common even in the seventeenth century, we may allow that the Spanish Inquisition, abominable institution as it was, and aggravated by political conditions and the death-struggle with the Moors, was a disease of the age, and common alike to Papist and to Protestant.

But as to the wrongs and sufferings of English prisoners in Spain, a point which does not seem to have been duly considered is that we seldom have any account of them except that given by the men themselves. Miles Philips, for instance, and Job Hortop, two of the men who were landed by Hawkyns after the rout at San Juan de Lua, are credible witnesses when they describe how the Spaniards 'hung them up by the arms upon high posts, until the blood burst out of their finger ends,' and punished them severely for attempting to escape, breaking out of prison, or conspiring to seize the

a 2

ship. We know from such narratives as that of Captain O'Brien, how, two hundred years later, the French treated prisoners of war who committed such offences; and according to Garneray,[1] who professes to write from personal experience, the life of a French prisoner on board a hulk at Portsmouth was wretched beyond the power of words. But when these two men—smugglers and pirates in the eye of Spanish law—describe themselves and their mates as being brought before the Inquisitors, and as being racked, burnt, or imprisoned because they could not say the Lord's Prayer in Latin, or give satisfactory answers to abstruse questions on the Real Presence, their statements require corroboration.[2]

So, too, the story of Robert Tomson, who, after residing for several years in Spain and Mexico, was, he says, dragged before the Inquisition and sentenced to a term of imprisonment for entering on a religious argument at a supper party, and denouncing images, pictures, and the invocation of saints before a mixed company. During a long residence in Spain, Tomson must have outwardly conformed to the Catholic religion; as he afterwards married a Spanish woman, he must have again conformed; so that his untimely display of Protestant zeal was a relapse such as the Inquisition always judged severely, and for which it would have inflicted a heavier punishment than three years in prison, with permission to marry a rich heiress at the end of the time. The story is therefore suspicious, and—as the other—needs corroboration.[3]

[1] *Mes Pontons*, par Louis Garneray.
[2] Hakluyt's *Principal Navigations*, iii. 469, 487.   [3] *Ib.* iii. 447.

It is not often possible to subject such stories to a critical examination ; but the case of Thomas Cely, which has been put prominently forward, admits and is deserving of a fuller discussion. In 1575 (vol. ii. App. A.), Dorothy, the wife of one Thomas Cely, a Bristol trader, petitioned the Council, setting forth that ' her husband upon most vile, slanderous, spiteful, malicious, and most villainous words uttered against the Queen's Majesty's own person by a certain subject of the King of Spain, not being able to suffer the same, did flee upon the same slanderous person and gave him a blow ; hereupon her said husband, no other offence in respect of their religion there committed, was secretly accused to the *Inquisidores* of the Holy House and so committed to most vile prison, and there hath remained now three whole years in miserable state with cruel torments.' [1]

Dorothy Cely certainly believed that her husband was in the dungeons of the Inquisition, and petitioned the Lords of the Council and the Queen to institute reprisals specially directed against foreign Papists. Mr. Froude, too, accepting the petition as sufficient authority, has lately repeated and emphasised the narrative. He says :—

' Thomas Cely, a merchant of Bristol, hearing a Spaniard in a Spanish port utter foul and slanderous charges against the Queen's character, knocked him down. To knock a man down for telling lies about Elizabeth might be a breach of the peace, but it had not yet been declared heresy. The Holy Office,

---

[1] *S.P. Spain*, xvi. ; Froude's *History of England*, cab. ed. viii. 22, where the petition is assigned the impossible date of 156?

however, seized Cely, threw him into a dungeon, and kept him starving there for three years, at the end of which he contrived to make his condition known in England.'[1] He thinks, however, that it was to no purpose, and that Cely was 'one of the many hundred English sailors who rotted away in the dungeons of the Inquisition, or were burnt to please the rabble of Valladolid.'[2]

Whether the fate of the 'many hundred English sailors' rests on a more solid foundation than that of Cely does not appear; but Cely lived to command a ship against the Armada, to write the quaint letter (p. 262), to plunder the Spanish prisoners (vol. ii. Index), and to be granted a pension of 30*l.* a year (May 5, 1590). He was still alive and in good health in July 1591.

But Cely's letter is specially interesting from the naïve confession of the cause of his punishment, which was very different from that alleged in the petition, or the paraphrase of it: to knock a man down in a Spanish port, presumably on the wharf, for uttering foul and slanderous charges against the Queen's character can scarcely be considered the same thing as 'striking their secretary as I was before the *Inquisidores*, they sitting in judgment.' It might be well, before speaking too strongly of the cruelty to which Cely was subjected, to ask what would have been the fate of a foreign sailor in England who, in open court, struck the judge's secretary? As to why Cely was, in the first instance, before the magistrates or *Inquisidores*, or whether the Holy Office had anything to do with the matter, there is

[1] *Longman's Magazine*, August 1893. [2] *Hist.* viii. 23 *n*.

no evidence. It may have been for smuggling, or for brawling, or possibly for contempt shown to the Host in its passage along the street.

Much more might be said on this moot point; but political affairs commonly depend on belief rather than on fact, and, whatever the actual truth, it appears fairly certain that, to the English, the real or supposed cruelties of the Inquisition were a principal cause of the very strong feeling against the Spaniards and Papists; whilst, to the Spaniards, the aggressions of the English smugglers and pirates, and the assistance rendered by the English to Dutch rebels, were direct causes of the war. The breach was by no means a one-sided one, and though we are naturally accustomed to lay most stress on our own grievances, real and sentimental, we cannot but admit that the Spaniards also had suffered very substantial injuries. What brought matters to a climax were the embargo laid on English shipping in Spain in May 1585, and the dread of Spain, which could now only be considered as a hostile power, obtaining the command of the Dutch ports.[1]

The war between the two countries, which avowedly began in 1585, anticipated, in a very curious manner, the lines of the war of the French Revolution two centuries later. In both cases the immediate cause of war was the dread of a hostile power fortifying itself in the sea-ports of the Netherlands; to prevent this a levy of men was ordered; the newly-raised army was sent abroad under an incompetent general, whose sole title to command was royal favour—it matters little whether

[1] *S.P. Dom. Eliz.*, clxxx. 35.

he was called Earl of Leicester or Duke of York—
and the result was ignominious failure. But meantime the English fleet swept the West Indies, and
Drake's expedition of 1585–6 may be considered
the precursor and prototype of Jervis's campaign of
1794. It will be seen that this correspondence was
not only in the commencement of the wars, but also
in their more advanced stages; that the flat-
bottomed boats at Dunkirk were imitated by those
at Boulogne; and that the destruction of the
enemy's ships at Cadiz in 1596 presents a very
exact analogy to the final overthrow of Bonaparte's
schemes at Trafalgar.

Drake's brilliant raid through the West Indies
determined Philip on a decided course. For the
past fifteen years the invasion of England had been
mooted, as a thing desirable and not impossible.
It had been proposed by the Duke of Alva in 1569,
after the seizure of his treasure. It had been
spoken of in 1579, after the exploits of Norreys in
the Low Countries had rendered the services of the
English volunteers notorious; and in 1583, after
his victory over Strozzi and his scratch fleet at
Terceira, the Marquis of Santa Cruz had urged it
as a necessary step towards the reduction of the
rebellious Netherlands.[1] The Duke of Parma had
written to the same effect, repeating that English
soldiers were of little count in presence of the

---

[1] *La Armada Invencible*, por el Capitan de Navío C. Fernandez
Duro, i. 241. In the book here referred to, Captain Duro has
done, from the Spanish point of view, what is now attempted, in
the following pages, from the English. The two works are, in a
measure, complementary of each other, and both must be studied
for a full understanding of the events of the year.

Spanish veterans, and adding a statement, which
seems to have obtained general credence among the
Spaniards, that the English ships at Terceira had
been the first to fly; had, in fact, played a part
somewhat resembling that of the Egyptian ships at
Actium. It is quite possible that there were some
English ships at Terceira, though it is doubtful; if
there were, they rightly declined to imitate Strozzi's
ill-judged and suicidal manœuvre of closing with the
Spaniards, and—small blame to them—effected their
escape. True or not, however, it appears certain
that this reported flight of the English ships did
have very considerable weight with many of the
King's advisers; and so advised, and at the same
time impelled by wrath, Philip determined on the
attempt. The Marquis of Santa Cruz was called on
for his scheme, which extended to gigantic proportions. Everything was to be done from Spain.
The whole shipping of the empire was to be
collected. Every available soldier was to be
mustered. According to the very detailed project
submitted by Santa Cruz on the 12th of March,
1586, the numbers amounted to :—

—	Nos.	Tons	Sailors	Soldiers
Great ships of war . .	150	77,250		
Store ships . . .	40	8,000	16,612	55,000
Smaller vessels . .	320	25,000		

besides—

—	Nos.	Sailors and fighting men	Rowers
Galleasses	6	720	1,800
Galleys . . .	40	3,200	8,000

giving a total of 556 ships of all kinds, and 85,332 men,[1] to which were to be added cavalry, artillery-men, volunteers, and non-combatants, bringing up the number of men to a gross total of 94,222.

Philip could not approve of a project so vast and so costly; he resolved on the expedition, but conceived the idea of doing it at a cheaper rate by utilising the army in the Low Countries. From this grew up the scheme which ultimately took form. The Duke of Parma, in Flanders, was to prepare an army of invasion, and a number of flat-bottomed boats to carry it across the sea. The Marquis of Santa Cruz was to bring up the Channel a fleet powerful enough to crush any possible opposition, and carrying a body of troops which, when joined with those under Parma, would form an army at least as numerous as that which Santa Cruz had detailed as sufficient.

The necessary preparations were extensive, and it is not quite clear that, as they became more definite, Philip's ardour did not somewhat slacken. The cost was certain; the issue was doubtful; and even if successful, the result might perhaps not be exactly what was desired. Philip had always posed as a supporter of the Queen of Scots; but the doubt must have suggested itself whether it was worth while, at this great cost, to conquer a kingdom for her—a kingdom which, with her French blood and French proclivities, would become virtually a French province. The death of the Queen of Scots, on the 8th of February, 1587, removed this difficulty. Even if the conquered kingdom was to be handed

[1] Duro, i. 253, 274.

over to James, James was not bound to France as his mother had been. Placed on the throne of England by Spanish arms, he might be expected or even constrained to hold it virtually as a Spanish fief. But it might not be necessary to give it to James at all. Elizabeth was, of course, outside the reckoning ; once dispossessed, she was merely the illegitimate offspring of an abominable and incestuous concubinage. But Philip himself was lineally descended from John of Gaunt, and had a theoretical right to the throne of England distinctly superior to that which, in the case of Henry VII., had been held sufficient. As an abstract problem in genealogy, Philip's claim was by no means absurd. Whether it could become something more, and take a practical form, might very well depend on the fortune of war.

Preparations were therefore now hurried on in earnest. Ships were collected at the several ports, and especially at Lisbon and Cadiz. It seemed probable that the invasion would be attempted in the summer of 1587, when some months before, Drake, with a fleet of twenty-four ships, all told, appeared on the coast. The orders under which he sailed from England, on the 2nd of April, were to prevent the different Spanish squadrons from joining, and where he found their ships, to destroy them. It was a grand and masterful step, but it had scarcely been ordered before the Queen repented of it. Counter orders were sent post-haste to Plymouth, but Drake had already sailed. They followed him, but never found him ; and Drake, acting on those first given, went down to Cadiz and there sank, burnt, or brought away thirty-seven of the enemy's ships. They were as yet unarmed, unmanned, and, when the forts were once passed, could offer no resistance. Other damage Drake did, insulting Santa Cruz in the very port of Lisbon, offering battle, which Santa Cruz was in no position to accept. Ships he had in numbers, but they too were neither manned nor armed ; and before the guns were ready, Drake had stretched off to the Azores, where he captured the San Felipe, a very large and rich East Indiaman, whose treasures are said to have first opened the eyes of our English merchants to the capabilities of Eastern trade, and to have led to the foundation of the East India Company.

The destruction of shipping and stores at Cadiz necessarily delayed the equipment of the Spanish fleet ; the year passed away, and it was not ready. In the following January the Marquis of Santa Cruz died. The loss to Spain was incalculable, for he was the only man who by birth was entitled, and by experience was competent, to command such an expedition as that which he had set on foot. His name was encircled with a halo of naval victory. He had held a high command at the battle of Lepanto, and in the action at Terceira was accredited with having put to ignominious flight these very English who were now the object of attack. The King and his court, however, do not seem to have realised their loss, and with a light heart appointed Don Alonso Perez de Guzman el Bueno, Duke of Medina-Sidonia, to the vacant command. Medina-Sidonia, now in his thirty-eighth year, was a man with no qualification for the post except his distinguished birth and a gentleness of temper which,

it was perhaps thought, would fit better with the idea
of making him subordinate to the Duke of Parma.
It had, indeed, appeared that Santa Cruz was not in
the least disposed to accept this inferior part; and
it may very well be that the King was almost relieved
by the solution of the difficulty which his death had
offered. His successor was utterly ignorant of naval
affairs, had but little experience of military, and none
whatever of high command. Personally brave, as
became his long line of ancestry, his total want of
experience and knowledge rendered him, as a com-
mander, timid, undecided, and vacillating. His
answer to the King, on being ordered to take on
himself the command, is in itself a curiosity. The
business, he wrote, was so great, so important, that
he could not conscientiously undertake it, being, as
he was, without experience or knowledge of either
the sea or of war.[1] His objections were, however,
overruled; and in an evil hour for his reputation,
he consented. The equipment of the fleet was
pushed on, and by the middle of May it was ready
to sail from the Tagus. It did actually sail on the
20th of May.

It may here be said that the name 'Invincible,'
so commonly given to this fleet, was not official.
In Philip's numerous letters there is no trace of it.
By him, by his secretary, by Medina-Sidonia and
other officers, and by all the contemporary chroniclers, the fleet is spoken of as the Grand Fleet—a
name constantly used in England during the eighteenth century for what we now call the Channel
Fleet. In a semi-official list printed at Lisbon it

[1] Duro, i. 415.

was called *La felicísima Armada*—the fortunate fleet. The ' Invincible' probably sprang out of the idle talk of some of the young adventurers (cf. p. 175), braggarts as became their age, or out of the silly gossip of the Lisbon taverns.[1]

None the less, the power of Spain was everywhere recognised as gigantic. The Spanish soldiers were numerous, well-disciplined, inured to war; Spanish galleons, navigating the most distant seas, brought to the Spanish treasury the riches of India or Peru ; and Spanish galleys had curbed the ambition of the fierce conquerors of Constantinople. Spanish statesmen were known to be most crafty and sagacious ; and nineteenth century historians had not yet discovered that the Spanish king, who ruled one half of continental Europe and controlled the other, was ignorant and incapable, childish if not imbecile. In the sixteenth century he was believed to be a far-seeing, prudent, ambitious man, slow in council, swift in execution. His accumulated wrath against England tempted him to listen to the voice of his counsellors, who urged on the war, and of his ambition, which invited him to seize the inheritance of his forefathers ; but, whilst yielding to the temptation, he endeavoured, so far as in him lay, to deserve that success which he hoped to win. He had no practical familiarity with war, but he had heard enough of English soldiers and English sailors to be convinced that they were not the dastards they were represented to be : he knew that if they had fled from Terceira, they certainly had not fled from Rymenam ; the brilliant skirmish of

[1] Duro, i. 50.

Zutphen had then a reputation not unlike that of the light cavalry charge at Balaclava forty years ago; and he was not ignorant of Drake's exploits in the West Indies, in the Pacific, or at Cadiz only the year before. He knew that the enterprise on which he was bent would not resemble a military promenade, and all the available forces of his vast empire were collected in this Grand Fleet. He hoped, too, for assistance from outside, and that, at any rate, a subsidy from the Pope would lessen the financial burden.

France, it was evident, might do much to forward his project, or to render it abortive; but already Philip exercised great influence over the party of the Guises, which his attitude as the champion of the Church and the avenger of their cousin, the Queen of Scots, confirmed. No politician has better understood the value of the maxim *Divide et impera!* and by the financial aid and moral support which he gave to the Guises, he rendered it certain that France would not take any active part against him, and not improbable that she might become a powerful auxiliary. To the last this remained a matter of doubt. It will be seen that Burghley and Walsyngham thought it not impossible, that Howard was fully convinced that a French fleet and a French army would join with the Spanish (pp. 203, 227). They knew that the French king was naturally antagonistic to the designs of Spain, but they had no trust in his steadfastness (p. 49); they could not gauge either the strength of his party or the pressure that might be brought to bear on him, and the 'day of the barricades' seemed to prostrate him before the Guises and Philip.

In England, as elsewhere, there prevailed an exalted opinion of Spanish power and of Spanish prowess. The prestige of Spanish arms stood high, and may be fairly compared with that of the Grand Monarque before Blenheim, or of Napoleon after Austerlitz or Jena. In forming a lower estimate of them the English sailors were almost alone, but their experience was exceptional. For the last twenty years they had been, in their own irregular way, fighting the Spaniards on every sea where they were to be met, and had come to the conclusion that, whatever the Spaniard might be ashore, afloat he was but a poor creature: the experiences of Drake, Hawkyns, the Fenners, and scores of others had proved that, even with great apparent odds in their favour, Spaniards were not invincible. Of all the panic-stricken accounts of the great armada which have come down to us, not one was written by a seaman or by any one who had practical knowledge of the Spaniards by sea. We are all familiar with the exaggerations of contemporary historians. The Spanish ships were so huge that ocean groaned beneath their weight ; so lofty that they resembled rather castles or fortresses ; so numerous that the sea was invisible—the spectator thought he beheld a populous town. What English sailors thought of them may be judged from a letter written by Fenner, who was with Drake when he burnt the shipping at Cadiz. 'Twelve of her Majesty's ships,' he said, 'were a match for all the galleys in the King of Spain's dominions.'

Still, not even Drake or Fenner could feel perfect confidence whilst ignorant of the magnitude of the task before them.   They had no fear of the fleet (pp. 229, 241); of the army they were not so sure.   And then, too, the known power of Spain, the tavern gossip and braggadocio of Lisbon, and the reports of spies who felt in honour bound to give full value for their hire, grossly exaggerated the size, the might, the armament, and the equipment of the fleet as it sailed from Lisbon.   Some of these reports (pp. 90, 122) may have been honestly meant.   They appear to be based on the first proposal of Santa Cruz, the details of which may have been allowed to leak out.   But the actual numbers were very different, and as to the equipment, it was so far from being perfect that by the time the fleet reached Cape Finisterre vast quantities of provisions were found to be bad, putrid, fit for nothing but to be thrown overboard.   The ships were short of water, probably because the casks were leaky.   The ships themselves were leaking—strained, it was said, by the heavy weather, but really from being over-masted.   Several of them were with difficulty kept afloat, some were dismasted, and the distress was so general that Medina-Sidonia determined to put into Corunna to refit.   This he did, but without taking any precautions to let his intention be known through the fleet.[1]   The Scilly Isles had been given out as the rendezvous in case of separation, and some dozen or more of the ships, finding they had lost sight of the admiral, did accordingly go to the neighbourhood of the Scilly Isles, where they were duly seen and reported at Plymouth (p. 221).   Their recall, the collecting the fleet at Corunna, the

[1] Duro, i. 57.

refitting, the reprovisioning, all took time. The damage was so great, the number of sick so large, the season getting so advanced, that a council of war urgently recommended postponing the expedition till the next year. The King's orders were, however, imperative, and the fleet finally sailed from Corunna on the 12th of July.

The main part of the English fleet was meantime mustered at Plymouth, under the command of Lord Howard of Effingham, the Lord Admiral of England, with whom were Drake and Hawkyns as vice- and rear-admirals; several noblemen, including Lord Thomas Howard, the admiral's cousin—his first cousin's grandson; Lord Sheffield, his sister's son; Sir Robert Southwell, his daughter's husband; and most of the seamen whose names make up the maritime history of the century: Frobiser, Thomas Fenner and his cousins, Fenton and Luke Ward, Raymond, Lancaster, Richard Hawkyns, and many more. Large numbers of merchants' ships, levied by the Queen, or by their own towns, had joined the fleet, which as it lay at Plymouth consisted of about 80 sail all told. From the time of his return from the coast of Spain in the previous summer, Drake had been urgent that he should be sent out again, with a still more powerful squadron, to repeat the blow (pp. 124, 148, 166, 238). Hawkyns (p. 60), Frobiser, Fenner (p. 238)—all the seamen of experience—were of the same opinion. Howard, guided by their advice, repeatedly pressed the importance of the step (pp. 192, 200, 203), but Elizabeth steadfastly refused. It may be that she hoped for peace; but it is difficult to believe that she was entirely hoodwinked by the false protestations of the Duke of Parma and by the negotiations carried on in Flanders. She was herself too well versed in the arts of dissimulation to be snared by such evident pretences. It is, perhaps, more probable that she believed the war might still be carried on in the same cheap and desultory fashion as during the last three years, and was unwilling to set Philip the example of more sustained efforts. It is very possible she had persuaded herself that the preparations in Spain were merely a threat, which, however, any aggressive action of hers might convert into a reality. And thus, notwithstanding the prayers and entreaties of Howard and Drake, backed up by every man of experience, no further attempt was made on the Spanish ports. It can scarcely be doubted that, if Drake had been permitted, he would have kindled such a blaze in the Tagus or in the harbour of Corunna as would have effectually prevented even the threat of an invasion.

It has been repeatedly stated[1] that the Duke of Medina-Sidonia was ordered by Philip to hug the French coast, so as to avoid the English fleet and to reach the Straits of Dover with his force intact. This is contrary to the fact. The Duke's instructions were to the very opposite effect. They ordered him, if he should meet Drake near the mouth of the Channel, to fall on him and destroy him ; it would be more easy to destroy the English fleet piecemeal than after allowing it to collect in one. And, so far from directing him to hug the French

[1] Monson's *Naval Tracts* in Churchill's *Voyages* (edit. 1732), iii. 149.

coast, they advise the Scilly Isles or the Lizard as a rendezvous, and suggest the propriety of seizing on some unfortified port in the South of England.[1] As a matter·of fact, a position south of the Scilly Isles was given out as a rendezvous in the first instance ; in the second, on sailing from Corunnà, the rendezvous was Mount's Bay.[2]

In crossing the Bay of Biscay the armada experienced some bad weather, and was a good deal scattered ; barely two-thirds of the ships were in company when Medina-Sidonia sighted the Lizard on the afternoon of the 19th of July. There, whilst waiting for the fleet to collect, he hoisted the royal standard at the fore, and at the main a sacred flag, showing a crucifix between the figures of Our Lady and St. Mary Magdalene. Other flags there were by the score. The fleet was organised by provinces, and the ships of each squadron presumably wore the flag of its province—Andalusia, Guipuscoa, Naples, &c.—as well as the flags of the nobles and knights on board, and probably also the flag of the particular saint to which they were dedicated. But the flag which they appear to have worn in common as the flag of the empire was, strictly speaking, the Burgundian flag, which had been adopted by Spain in the time of the Emperor Charles V.—white, a saltire raguled red ; and it may be noted that, amongst the great number and diversity of flags, the one flag which was not worn, and could not be worn, was the red and yellow ensign of the present day, a flag which was not invented till the year 1785.

[1] Duro, ii. 8.   [2] *Ib.* ii. 27, 168.

The English flag at this time was the plain St. George's flag—white, a cross red—and this was worn by every English ship. The Ark, Lord Howard's ship, flew also the royal standard, the flag of the Queen's arms, and, probably at the fore, a flag of Howard's arms. Some of the other ships were also supplied with 'flags of the Queen's arms' and 'ensigns of silk' distinct from 'the flags of Saint George.' Many had streamers 'small and great,' and one, the Elizabeth Bonaventure, had 'a bloody flag,' the plain red flag which down to the end of the eighteenth century continued to be the signal to 'engage the enemy' (vol. ii.—September 25, Reports of Survey). That some of the ships, and especially those sent forth by the coast towns or by private individuals, wore also local or private flags, is not improbable, but the State Papers make no mention of such.

On Saturday, the 20th of July, the Spanish fleet was collected off the Lizard and moved slowly eastwards. Medina-Sidonia wrote to the King that he intended to proceed as far as the Isle of Wight, where he hoped to have word of the Duke of Parma. At present he had no intelligence, and was quite in the dark as to the enemy's movements. In passing Plymouth he hoped he might pick up some pinnace from which he could get information. In the afternoon, however, many ships were seen, though thick weather and mist prevented his counting them; and towards midnight an English boat was brought in, with four men on board, from whom he learnt that the English fleet, commanded

by the Admiral of England and by Drake, had put
to sea that afternoon.[1]

Medina-Sidonia's statement is perfectly clear,
connected and intelligible, and, being written on the
very day, has high claims on our belief. It describes,
too, conduct which is quite in keeping with the
character of the man. He avowedly knew nothing
of the art of war, and had now come on the enemy's
coast, and was about to proceed leisurely through
the enemy's sea, without taking any trouble to find
out where the enemy's fleet was. His frank ac-
knowledgment, whilst it proves him a fool, argues
that he was, at least, a truthful one. On the other
hand, the letter of Don Pedro de Valdes to the King
(vol. ii.—August 21) speaks of a fisherman being
captured on the Saturday, of a council of war
being held to consider his intelligence that the
English fleet was at anchor at Plymouth, and of the
resolution come to, to ' make to the mouth of the
haven and set upon the enemy, if it might be done
with any advantage,' a design which was prevented
by their discovering the English fleet at sea, some
two hours later. Captain Duro accepts a still
different story, according to which the council of
war was held on the Friday afternoon, and they
then knew that the English fleet was at Plymouth.
At this meeting Recalde, Leyva and Oquendo, more
particularly, urged that the destruction of the
enemy's fleet was the first object, and that the
opportunity ought not to be neglected ; to which
Medina-Sidonia replied that the King's orders did

[1] Medina-Sidonia to the King, July 20–30 ; Medina-Sidonia's
Journal, Duro, ii. 222, 229.

not permit him any latitude, and compelled him to proceed without delay to join the Duke of Parma.[1] But the reference which Captain Duro gives for this story not only does not sanction it, but confirms the statement of Medina-Sidonia ; and as Don Pedro's letter was written a month after the date, it is quite possible that his memory deceived him as to the sequence of events.

About the result, however, there is no difference of opinion. During the Friday evening the English warped out of the harbour ; on the Saturday they beat out of the Sound, ' very hardly, the wind being at South-West. About three of the clock in the afternoon they descried the Spanish fleet, and did what they could to work for the wind ' (p. 288). The wind, by veering to the West-North-West,[2] and the Spaniards, by sailing large through the night, assisted their efforts. On Sunday morning, when the two fleets were first in presence of each other, the English were to windward, and by their practical skill and the weatherly qualities of their ships, had no difficulty in keeping the advantage they had gained.

And now, before the fighting begins, it will be well to examine the comparative force of the opposing fleets. We have all known from our infancy that the Spanish ships, as compared with the English, were stupendous in point of size, marvellous in their strength ; in guns and in number of men beyond all proportion. As to the numbers, the first proposal of Santa Cruz has already been given. It was never anything more than a proposal. The

[1] Duro, i. 67.   [2] *Ib.* ii. 230.

actual numbers when the fleet sailed from the Tagus
on the 20th of May were :—[1]

Ships	Tons	Guns	Men
130	57,868	2,431	8,050 seamen 18,973 soldiers 1,382 volunteers, &c. 2,088 rowers
		Total . .	30,493

These numbers, however, had suffered a marked
decrease before the fleet left Corunna, and a still
further decrease before the fleet came into the
Channel. Of the ships left behind there is no
exact account. Some, and some large ships
amongst them, certainly did not come on. Some,
again, appear to have parted company on the
voyage ; and of four galleys, from which much had
been expected, one was driven ashore and wrecked
near Bayonne ; the other three, making very bad
weather of it, put into different French ports, and
eventually returned to Spain.[2] Allowing for these
losses, it is doubtful whether more than 120 ships
of all sizes came into the Channel ; the number
of men did certainly not exceed 24,000 ; and in the
council of war held at Corunna it was estimated
as low as 22,500.[3] Of the ships, about half were
transports or victuallers pure and simple, and took
no part in the fighting ; many, too, were pinnaces,
or despatch boats, unfitted for fighting ; but they
all carried men, sailors or soldiers, who must be
deducted from the gross numbers. The effective

[1] Duro, ii. 66, 83. [2] *Ib.* i. 65. [3] *Ib.* ii. 142, 199.

total of fighting men in the. Spanish fleet can thus scarcely have been more than from 10,000 to 12,000.

On the other hand, the total number of English ships, of all sizes and qualities, registered as in the Queen's service during any part of the season was 197, bearing 15,925 men; to which must be added the many recruits sent off from Plymouth on the 21st of July (p. 289), or who joined as volunteers in the passage up Channel. It is difficult to estimate the gross total at less than from 17,000 to 18,000 men. Of the 197 ships, however, by far the greater number neither had, nor were meant to have, any part in the fighting; many of them were not even present when the fighting was going on. Seymour, for instance, with all his squadron, did not join the Admiral till the 27th of July. The fifteen victuallers which went west, under Burnell, in June, were probably discharged at once, and their men pressed for the great ships. Four of the coast ships with Seymour were sent away to convoy the Stade fleet; six others were discharged during June, for want of victuals (p. 255). The eight London ships under Gorges (p. 311) and the ten under Bellingham (p. 339) did not leave the river till after the 29th of July, and joined Seymour only after his return from the north (vol. ii.—Seymour to Walsyngham, Aug. 1). The galley Bonavolia was, at the last moment, judged unseaworthy, and was sent into the river; on the 29th of July she was lying at the Nore-head (p. 338). These which are certainly known to have been absent from the battle of Gravelines account for 2,650 men, a number not affected by the burning of eight ships at Calais. Of the rest, whether present or not cannot be determined, 37 had crews of not more than 30 men, and 900 in all. No one will suppose that these pinnaces added to the effective strength of the fleet on the day of battle, any more than the Pickle or Entreprenante did at Trafalgar. They had their use in the fleet, but that use was not engaging the enemy's great ships. And many others of the English vessels were scarcely of greater value as men-of-war, so that the number of men who, even in appearance, took part in the battle of Gravelines can scarcely have been more than from eight to nine thousand.

Our idea of the size of the Spanish ships has been also somewhat exaggerated. According to Barrow,[1] 'The best of the Queen's ships placed alongside one of the first class of Spaniards would have been like a sloop-of-war by the side of a first rate.' In point of tonnage they were, in fact, the same. The largest Spaniard, the Regazona, of the Levant squadron, is given as 1,249 tons. The largest English ship, the Triumph, is described as of 1,000 or 1,100 tons, and many circumstances seem to show that, whilst the reckoning of tonnage was everywhere extremely vague, the English method gave a smaller result than the Spanish. The San Salvador, for instance, was classed by the Spaniards as of 958 tons; when she fell into English hands, she was described as, by estimation, of 600 (vol. ii. Aug. 24). There is no doubt, however, that the Spanish ships looked larger. Their poops and fore-castles, rising tier above tier to a great height, towered

[1] *Life of Drake*, 270.

far above the lower-built English. Not that the large
English ships were by any means flush-decked ; but
they were not so high-charged as the Spanish. The
difference offered a great advantage to the Spaniards
in hand-to-hand fighting; it told terribly against
them when their enemy refused to close ; it made
their ships leewardly and unmanageable in even a
moderate breeze, and, added to the Spanish neglect
of recent improvements in rig—notably, the introduction of the bowline—rendered them very inferior
to the English in the open sea.[1]

And not only was there this inferiority of the
ships ; there was at least a corresponding inferiority
of the seamen. The Spaniards, and still more the
Italians, were to a great extent fair-weather sailors.
Some there doubtless were who had been through
the Straits of Magellan or had doubled the Cape
of Good Hope, but by far the greater number
had little experience beyond the Mediterranean,
or the equable run down the trades to the West
Indies. To the English, accus-
tomed from boyhood to the Irish or Iceland fisheries ;
in manhood to the voyages to the north-west
with Frobiser or Davys, or round the world with
Drake, and semi-piratical cruises in the Bay of
Biscay or in the track of the homeward-bound
treasure-ships, the summer gales of the Channel
were, by comparison, passing trifles—things to be
warded off, but not to be feared. Even if the men
had been equal in quality, the Spanish ships were
terribly undermanned. The seamen habitually gave
place to the soldiers ; the soldiers commanded ; the
seamen did the drudgery, and not one was borne in

[1] Cf. Monson, in Churchill, iii. 312, 319.

excess of what their soldier masters thought necessary. The absolute numbers speak for themselves,
and one comparison will be sufficient. The San
Martin, of 1,000 tons, the flagship of the Duke of
Medina-Sidonia, had 177 seamen and 300 soldiers.
The Ark, of 800 tons, the flagship of Lord Howard,
had 300 seamen and 125 soldiers.

More important, however, than even this inferiority of the Spanish ships and sailors was the
inferiority of their guns and gunners. It was long
believed in this country, and has been repeatedly
stated, that the Spanish guns were both numerous
and large. They were, in fact, neither one nor the
other ; as a rule they were small—4, 6 or 9-pounders ;
they were comparatively few, and they were very
badly worked.

The guns at that time in use on board ship were,
roughly speaking, the same in the English and
Spanish navies ; and as everything was rough, as
the minimum windage prescribed was one-fourth of
the bore of the gun and as much more as pleased
the gunner, the Englishmen felt no difficulty in
assigning English names to the Spanish guns, as
shown in the following tables. The weight of the
shot is approximate, but sufficiently accurate for
purposes of comparison (vol. ii. App. C).

I. Cannon . . .	Perhaps a 60-pounder, but more probably 42.
II. Demi-Cannon .	A 30-pounder.
III. Cannon-Pedro .	A very light 24-pounder.
IV. Culverin .	A long 18-pounder.
V. Basilisco .	A 15-pounder.
VI. Demi-Culverin .	A long 9-pounder.
VII. Saker . . .	A 6-pounder.
VIII. Minion . . .	A 4-pounder.

And smaller pieces under the ħames of fowler, falcon, falconet, &c., throwing balls of from 3 pounds to 8 ounces.

COMPARISON OF ARMAMENTS

Ships names	Tons	Men	Number of guns	Approximate weight of broadside in lbs.	I.	II.	III.	IV.	V.	VI.	VII.	Small pieces
Spanish												
S. Lorenzo	—	386	50	330	4	8	—	6	—	6	10	16
N.S. d. Rosario	1,150	422	41	200	—	3	6	4		1	6	20
San Salvador	958	396	25	185	4	—	4	5		1	—	11
Anunciada	793	275	26	60	—	—	—	—		8	—	18
Sta Maria d. Vison	666	307	24	50	—	—	—	—		6	—	18
English												
Triumph	1,100	500	44	340	4	3	—	17	—	8	6	6
Ark	800	425	44	330	4	4	—	12	—	12	6	6
Nonpareil	500	250	40	230	2	3	—	7	—	8	12	8
Foresight	300	160	31	96	—	—	—	—	—	14	8	9
Tiger	200	100	30	106	—	—	—	4	—	8	8	10

With the exception of the Tiger, whose armament is taken from an order [1] by Sir William Wynter in 1586, the English armaments are given from a table dated 1595–9, printed by Derrick.[2] The comparison shows that the change between 1586 and 1595 had been rather to decrease the weight of the guns. Wynter's order of 1586 also gives the armament of two ships which he distinguishes as galleon P. Pett at Deptford, and galleon Ma. Baker at Woolwich. In 1588 they were known as the Rainbow and Vanguard. Two papers [3] of 1595 give estimates for the armaments of three ships 'now in building,' the ordnance for the first two being described as 'answerable to the pieces that are in the

[1] *S.P. Dom. Eliz.*, clxxxvii. 65.
[2] *Rise and Progress of the Royal Navy*, 31.
[3] *S.P. Dom. Eliz.*, ccliii. 114 ; ccliv. 43.

Mer Honour,' whose armament is here given from
Derrick's table :—

Ships' names	Tons	No. of guns	Approximate weight of broadside in lbs.	Description of guns				
				II.	IV.	VI.	VII.	Small pieces
Galleon Pett, 1586 } Galleon Baker, 1586 }	500	54	300	8	10	14	2	20
Ship, September 1595	?	44	300	4	16	18	4	2
Ship, October 1595, I.	?	44	280	—	20	20	4	—
Ship, October 1595, II.	?	36	220	—	16	12	8	—
Mer Honour . .	800	41	280	4	15	16	4	2

and comparing the armament ordered in 1586 for
the Rainbow and Vanguard, two ships which may
be classed with the Nonpareil given in the former
table, the necessary inference is that the armaments
of 1595 were not so heavy as those carried in 1588.

Another estimate, which, though inexact, is entitled to credit, is that given of the armament of the
Revenge, also a ship of 500 tons, taken by the
Spaniards in 1591, and reported by them to have
43 brass guns : 20 on the lower deck of from 4,000
to 6,000 pounds weight, and the rest from 2,000
to 3,000.[1]   The greater weights correspond to the
cannons, demi-cannons, or culverins ; the smaller to
the demi-culverins and sakers.

Of the Spanish armament we cannot speak with
the same absolute knowledge ; but it seems admitted that the galleasses were the most heavily armed
ships in the fleet, and of these the San Lorenzo,
which was taken at Calais, was the largest and
heaviest.   The report of her armament given by our

[1] Duro, i. 76.

people (p. 349), who had possession of her for some
time, corresponds fairly well with the official statement.[1] The Nuestra Señora del Rosario was the
large ship captured by Drake and sent into Torbay.
Her armament is given from the official inventory
taken at Torquay (vol. ii. August 29, November 5).
She is spoken of by Duro as one of the most powerful
and best ships of the fleet.[2] The San Salvador was
the ship partly blown up and sent to Weymouth (pp.
9, 301); her armament is also given from the official
inventory (vol. ii. Aug. 24). Some of her small guns
were very likely thrown overboard by the explosion.
Duro tabulates her as carrying 25 in all. The
inventory accounts for 19, including four old minions
and one old fowler. The missing six were probably
fowlers or falcons. The two remaining ships have
their armament given by Duro.[3] They do not
seem in any way distinguished from others of the
same size; they belonged to the Levant squadron,
and are classed with the San Juan de Sicilia, of
800 tons and 26 guns, which took a prominent part
in the battle of the 29th of July. There is no published account of the armament of the great ships of
the Portuguese squadron, and amongst them the
San Martin, San Felipe, and San Mateo, of which
all were in the thickest of the fight, and the two last
were driven on shore in a sinking state. It was
probably not very different from that of the N. S.
del Rosario. There is here, of course, no sugges-
tion that the more powerful ships were armed like
the Anunciada or Santa Maria de Vison ; but it

---

[1] Duro, i. 390. [2] *Ib*. i. 83 *n*.
[3] Tom. i. 389.

appears a fair presumption that many of the ships which have been counted as effective were so armed.

It should also be noted that whereas the Spanish ships of below 300 tons burden carried only four or six small guns, English ships of 200 tons had a very respectable armament, and ships still smaller were not altogether despicable. Of the way in which the English merchant ships were armed we have little knowledge. The larger ones, under the command of men like Lancaster or George Fenner, may certainly be classed as efficient men-of-war. The Margaret and John, of 200 tons, is named as having rendered good service on more than one occasion; and considering that many of the others had probably been on privateering cruises, and that the Pelican or Golden Hind, in which Drake went round the world— a ship of nominally 100 tons—had 14 guns, it is allowable to question Barrow's judgment that, 'looking at their tonnage, two-thirds of them, at least, could have been of little, if any, service, and must have required uncommon vigilance to keep them out of harm's way.'[1] They were not, indeed, the ships that were to be looked for in the forefront of the fight—no more was the Euryalus or the Naiad at Trafalgar—but there is no reason to doubt that they did, in their own way, render good and efficient service.

It was not only in the number and weight of guns that the English had a great comparative advantage; they were immensely superior in the working of them. According to Captain Duro,

[1] *Life of Drake*, 270.

whose statement is fully corroborated by original writers and by known facts, 'the cannon was held by the Spaniards to be an ignoble arm ; well enough for the beginning of the fray, and to pass away the time till the moment of engaging hand to hand, that is, of boarding. Actuated by such notions, the gunners were recommended to aim high, so as to dismantle the enemy and prevent his escape ; but, as a vertical stick is a difficult thing to hit, the result was that shot were expended harmlessly in the sea, or, at best, made some holes in the sails, or cut a few ropes of no great consequence.' [1]   On the other hand, the gun was the weapon which the English sailors had early learned to trust to. Their practice might appear contemptible enough to an Excellent's gun's crew, but everything must have a beginning. With no disparts or side scales, with no aid beyond a quadrant or marked quoin to lay the gun hori-zontal, and with shot which—a good inch and a half less in diameter than the bore of the gun—wobbled from side to side, or from top to bottom, leaving the gun at any angle that chance dictated, the hitting the object aimed at was excessively doubtful.

Thoroughly trained gunners might perhaps have done better. In the opinion of William Thomas, master gunner of Flushing, 'Had her Majesty's ships been manned with a full supply of good gunners, it would have been the woefullest time or enterprise that ever the Spaniard took in hand, and no otherwise to be thought or doubted of but that the most noblest victory by the sea that ever was heard of would have fallen to her Majesty.

[1] Duro, i. 77.

What can be said but our sins was the cause that
so much powder and shot spent, and so long time in
fight, and in comparison thereof so little harm?'
(vol. ii.—Thomas to Lord Burghley, September 20).
But it does not appear that Mr. Thomas had any
experience on board ship; and, as a matter of fact,
there were gunners on board each of the Queen's
ships—about 8 per cent. of the ship's company—
sufficient for the captains of the guns.   The guns'
crews were, of course, seamen, and, with no special
training, but firing a great many shot, they did
manage to get home with sufficient to do a good
deal of damage.   The Spanish accounts, speaking
of the quickness of the English fire, estimate the
English expenditure of shot as about three times
their own.

But the Spaniards were fully warned of the
peculiar strength of the English.   On this point, the
King's instructions to Medina-Sidonia before he
left Lisbon are quite clear.   'You are especially to
take notice that the enemy's object will be to engage
at a distance, on account of the advantage which
they have from their artillery and the offensive fireworks with which they will be provided; and on the
other hand, the object on our side should be to close
and grapple and engage hand to hand.'[1]   And the
determination to do so, without understanding that
the choice of closing or not closing might not lie
altogether with them, may partly explain the comparatively small quantity of shot per gun provided
for such a vast undertaking; a quantity so small
that, notwithstanding the slowness of their fire,

[1] Duro, ii. 9.

they ran short even after the skirmishes in the Channel.

In estimating the opposing forces, this great superiority of the English armament must be taken into account. Of Spanish ships of 300 tons and upwards, the number that left Lisbon was officially stated as eighty : but of these, eighteen were rated as ships of burden (*urcas de carga*) ; and though they carried troops and some guns, could not be counted as effective ships of war. Of the remaining sixty-two, many ought to be reckoned in the same category. An armament such as that of the Anunciada or Sta Maria speaks for itself. From the number of soldiers they carried, and from their lofty poops and forecastles, such ships would be dangerous enough in a hand-to-hand fight, but would be perfectly harmless as long as they were kept at a distance. But counting all these, we have the following comparison of the fleets :—

	Spanish		English	
—	Nos.	Tons Average	Nos.	Tons Average
Of 300 tons and upwards	62	727	23	552
Of 200 to 300 tons . .	—	—	26	210
			49	

The English ships of 200 tons being included, as unquestionably superior as fighting machines to many of the much larger Spanish ships.

We may assume that these forty-nine ships were all more or less engaged during the nine days, and especially in the battle of Gravelines. The fact

c 2

that Captain Coxe, of the Delight, a pinnace of 50 tons, was slain by a round shot, is a proof that all the small ships did not keep out of harm's way; but we may fully accept the statement in Wynter's letter to Walsyngham (vol. ii.—August 1), that on the 29th of July the greater number of the merchant ships were of little use, 'otherwise than that they did make a show.' It must have been so. Ships of 150 tons and less carried no guns bigger than the saker (cf. p. 339), a 6-pounder, and their armament consisted for the most part of minions, fowlers, &c., throwing shot of four or three or two pounds, very effective against bodies of men or boats or small vessels, quite useless against the thick sides of the Spanish galleons. But when the Spaniards were driven from their anchorage at Calais, the English were left with the weather-gage. The wind was blowing fresh, and the armada streamed off before it. When their weathermost ships were attacked, those to leeward could render no assistance. It was a condition of naval warfare which had been and has been repeated over and over again, from the battle of Sandwich in 1217 to that of the Nile in 1798, and always with the same inevitable result. The weathermost of the Spanish ships were, indeed, the largest and the best, but not more than thirty-two seem to have been actually engaged (Wynter, August 1), and the brunt of the battle fell on some fifteen.[1]

It is unnecessary here to describe the fights of that eventful week. The official papers which follow tell how on Sunday morning, the 21st of

[1] Duro, ii. 390.

July, the English, having gained the wind, fell on
the ships of the Spanish rear-guard, under the
command of Don Juan Martinez de Recalde, in the
Santa Ana, and without permitting them to close,
as they vainly tried to do, pounded them with their
great guns for the space of three hours, with such
effect that Recalde sent to Don Pedro de Valdes for
assistance, his ship having been hulled several times
and her foremast badly wounded; how Don Pedro's
ship, the Nuestra Señora del Rosario, in going to
his assistance, fouled first one and then another of
her consorts, lost her bowsprit, foremast, and main-
topmast, and was left by Medina-Sidonia, who,
whether from spite and malice, as Don Pedro believed, or from gross ignorance and incompetence,
resolved to push on to Dunkirk, even at the sacri-
fice of this large and powerful ship, which was
taken possession of by Drake the next morning,
and sent into Torbay; how another ship, the San
Salvador, of 958 tons, was partially blown up and
was similarly left, to be taken possession of by
order of the Admiral, and to be sent into Weymouth; how on the Tuesday there was another
sharp action off Portland, and again a third on the
Thursday off the Isle of Wight, when Recalde's
ship, the Santa Ana, of 768 tons, received so
much further damage that she left the fleet and ran
herself ashore near Havre; how the English, joined
as they passed along by many small vessels full of
men, but finding their store of shot running short,
were content for the next day with closely following
up the Spaniards, who on Saturday afternoon anchored off Calais, whilst the English anchored

excess of what their soldier masters thought necessary. The absolute numbers speak for themselves,
and one comparison will be sufficient. The San
Martin, of 1,000 tons, the flagship of the Duke of
Medina-Sidonia, had 177 seamen and 300 soldiers.
The Ark, of 800 tons, the flagship of Lord Howard,
had 300 seamen and 125 soldiers.

More important, however, than even this inferiority of the Spanish ships and sailors was the
inferiority of their guns and gunners. It was long
believed in this country, and has been repeatedly
stated, that the Spanish guns were both numerous
and large. They were, in fact, neither one nor the
other ; as a rule they were small—4, 6 or 9-pounders ;
they were comparatively few, and they were very
badly worked.

The guns at that time in use on board ship were,
roughly speaking, the same in the English and
Spanish navies ; and as everything was rough, as
the minimum windage prescribed was one-fourth of
the bore of the gun and as much more as pleased
the gunner, the Englishmen felt no difficulty in
assigning English names to the Spanish guns, as
shown in the following tables. The weight of the
shot is approximate, but sufficiently accurate for
purposes of comparison (vol. ii. App. C).

I. Cannon . . .	Perhaps a 60-pounder, but more probably 42.
II. Demi-Cannon .	A 30-pounder.
III. Cannon-Pedro .	A very light 24-pounder.
IV. Culverin . .	A long 18-pounder.
V. Basilisco . .	A 15-pounder.
VI. Demi-Culverin .	A long 9-pounder.
VII. Saker . . .	A 6-pounder.
VIII. Minion . . .	A 4-pounder.

And smaller pieces under the names of fowler, falcon, falconet, &c., throwing balls of from 3 pounds to 8 ounces.

COMPARISON OF ARMAMENTS

Ships names	Tons	Men	Number of guns	Approximate weight of broadside in lbs.	I.	II.	III.	IV.	V.	VI.	VII.	Small pieces
Spanish												
S. Lorenzo . .	—	386	50	330	4	8	—	6	—	6	10	16
N.S. d. Rosario .	1,150	422	41	200	—	3	6	4	1	1	6	20
San Salvador .	958	396	25	185	4	—	4	5	—	1	—	11
Anunciada . .	703	275	26	60	—	—	—	—	—	8	—	18
Sta Maria d. Vison	666	307	24	50	—	—	—	—	—	6	—	18
English												
Triumph . .	1,100	500	44	340	4	3	—	17	—	8	6	6
Ark . . .	800	425	44	330	4	4	—	12	—	12	6	6
Nonpareil . .	500	250	40	230	2	3	—	7	—	8	12	8
Foresight . .	300	160	31	96	—	—	—	—	—	14	8	9
Tiger . . .	200	100	30	106	—	—	—	4	—	8	8	10

With the exception of the Tiger, whose armament is taken from an order[1] by Sir William Wynter in 1586, the English armaments are given from a table dated 1595-9, printed by Derrick.[2] The comparison shows that the change between 1586 and 1595 had been rather to decrease the weight of the guns. Wynter's order of 1586 also gives the armament of two ships which he distinguishes as galleon P. Pett at Deptford, and galleon Ma. Baker at Woolwich. In 1588 they were known as the Rainbow and Vanguard. Two papers[3] of 1595 give estimates for the armaments of three ships 'now in building,' the ordnance for the first two being described as 'answerable to the pieces that are in the

[1] *S.P. Dom. Eliz.*, clxxxvii. 65.
[2] *Rise and Progress of the Royal Navy*, 31.
[3] *S.P. Dom. Eliz.*, ccliii. 114 ; ccliv. 43.

enemy's great ships was espied to be in great distress by the captain [Robert Crosse] of her Majesty's
ship called the Hope, who, being in speech of yielding unto the said captain, before they could agree on
certain conditions, sank presently before their eyes '
(vol. ii.—Abstract of Accidents, August 7).

The actual loss of life was certainly very great—
how great was never known, for the pursuit of the
English and the disastrous passage round the west
of Ireland prevented any satisfactory attempt at
official returns.   One set of depositions (vol. ii.—
September 12) outlines the early losses and suggests
the causes of those that followed.   It is incorrect
to attribute everything to the bad weather.   Bad
weather in August is comparative, and is seldom
such as to be dangerous to well-found ships; nor,
indeed, do the accounts from Ireland or Spain tell
of any wholesale losses from storm.   The ships were
lost partly from bad pilotage, partly from bad sea-
manship, but principally because they were not well
found; because they were leaking like sieves, had
no anchors, their masts and rigging shattered, their
water-casks smashed, no water, and were very short-
handed; and that they were in this distressed condition was the work of the English fleet, more
especially at Calais and Gravelines.

An exhaustive account of these losses among the
Isles of Scotland and on the coast of Ireland has
not been attempted: a few of the Irish papers will
serve as indications, and amongst them, or the pages
of *La Armada Invencible*, the fuller narrative must
be sought.   The English story ends when the
Spanish fleet passed the Firth of Forth; and for

the rest, it is sufficient to say that, according to the
official Spanish reports, which, in such an over-
whelming disaster, are rather mixed, about half of
the original 130 got home again ; some apparently
by the simple process of not going farther than
Corunna, some by turning back before they crossed
the Bay of Biscay.

A point of more immediate naval interest regards
the statements that have been made of the wholesale death of the English seamen from starvation, or
from the unwholesome nature of the victuals which
the Queen's shameful parsimony compelled them to
eat.   Such statements have been put forward, in an
authoritative manner, by our best and most popular
historians, as established by sufficient evidence,
which, as it appears, has been misunderstood, and,
taken apart from its context, has been misinterpreted.
The full evidence is now before us, and permits us
to say positively that, from first to last, the Queen
had nothing to do with the victualling of the fleet.
No doubt she insisted on rigid economy in everything ; no doubt Burghley, and Walsyngham, and
Howard knew that their accounts would be subjected
to a strict, probably an unsympathetic, scrutiny, and
that no item would pass which could be objected to ;
but with this general knowledge, the management
of the business was left entirely in their hands.

And almost every page of these volumes tells of
the unceasing care with which it was conducted.
Money is freely ordered ; bills are passed and paid ;
letters are written to Darell directing him to provide
for the victualling, and by Darell, explaining what
is being done and how : again and again Burghley

adds up the totals of men and money, or translates items and results into the Roman notation,[1] so as to have a clear idea of what was going on. To any one examining the evidence, there can be no question as to the victualling being conducted on a fairly liberal scale, as far as the money was concerned. It was in providing the victuals that the difficulty lay. What victualling yards or stores there were were still in their infancy, and of little use in a great emergency. The beef had to be salted, the biscuit to be baked, to meet the requirements of the day. When a fleet of unprecedented magnitude was collected, when a sudden and unwonted demand was made on the victualling officers, it would have been strange indeed if things had gone quite smoothly. Even in this present age, with an organised but inexperienced commissariat, the troops in the Crimea suffered grievous privations, and died by hundreds. In 1588 there was no commissariat at all, and the whole burden of the business fell on the shoulders of Darell, to whose energy, ability, zeal and goodwill Howard repeatedly bears witness (p. 197).

Howard, on his part, was very anxious that the ships should be victualled for six weeks at least, so that, by completing at frequent short intervals, they might always be ready for service. He wrote that King Henry VIII. 'never made a less supply than

[1] Arabic figures seem to have conveyed no definite meaning to him. In all his own memoranda the calculations are made in the Roman notation ; and on the margin of every paper he translated the numbers into that notation. It is thus not surprising that his arithmetic is frequently inaccurate. Even a practised accountant might have some difficulty in subtracting xix^m v^c iij^{xx} x from xxi^m ij^c ix (p. 298), or in finding the total charge of mm ix^c iiij^{xx} x men for xviij days at xvi^s iiij^d *per mensem.*

six weeks' (p. 137)—a statement wildly incorrect. It may be hoped that the early organisation of the navy will be elucidated in some future volume; at present little is known beyond the fact that in 1513 Sir Edward Howard complained most bitterly that some of his ships were provisioned for only a fortnight;[1] and though it is very possible that ships going on a foreign expedition, carefully arranged beforehand—such perhaps as the expedition to the Forth in 1544—were provisioned for six weeks, and were also accompanied by victuallers, we may be quite certain that for home service—as, for instance, in 1545—they were provisioned from hand to mouth, on the same system as in 1588. No other was, indeed, possible where there were no stores, and where, from the nature of the service, the necessity could not have been foreseen and prepared for in advance.

No doubt such a system was as bad as it well could be, and especially bad in the case of a great fleet which might at any moment be called on to put to sea, to meet or to follow the enemy. As early as the 3rd of March, Fenner called Walsyngham's attention to the danger. ' I fear,' he wrote, ' when we shall be hastened to go, our provision of victual needful will not be ready in a month, in which time it will be no small matter, the waste in doing nothing' (p. 92); and on the 8th of April, Howard, writing to Burghley, put it still more clearly. ' I thought good to put your Lordship in remembrance how necessary it is to have a better proportion of victual than for one month, considering

---

[1] Ellis's *Original Letters*, 3rd series, i. 145.

the time and the service that is likely to fall out,
and what danger it might breed if our want of victual
should be at the time of service. We shall be now
victualled unto the 18th of May, and by the advertisements that giveth the largest time for the
coming out of the Spanish forces is the 15th of May.
Then have we three days' victual. If it be fit to be
so, it passeth my reason' (p. 137).

The particular danger which Howard thus
pointed out did actually occur. On the 21st of July,
when Howard received intelligence of the Spaniards
being off the Lizard, the ships at Plymouth were
employed in completing their victuals to the 10th
of August ; 'only,' wrote Darell on the 22nd (p. 294),
'the haste of my Lord Admiral was such in his
setting forth upon Saturday morning, as that divers
of his ships had not leisure to receive the full of
their last proportions.' Even so, however, things
were not so bad as they seemed, for, ' by placing of
more than four men to a mess and also by the
mortality which hath been amongst them, the ships
(having been from time to time furnished by me
with their due proportions, as if that had not been)
have all in them a store, which no doubt will serve
them a good time after their ordinary victualling be
expired.'

We must suppose that Burghley and Walsyngham were quite able to see that such a danger was
no vague fancy, but to alter the system at a moment's
warning was impossible. The provisions were not
ready ; there were no government establishments to
fall back on ; and from the 23rd of May, when the
Lord Admiral went to Plymouth, Darell was scour-

ing the country round, buying up what he could, more like a mess-steward with a market-basket than the agent-victualler of a great fleet. Every available means had to be used to eke out the supplies. A Hamburg ship laden with rice coming into the Sound, was summarily stayed and the rice bought for the use of the navy (p. 189). The 'scantyings' referred to by Howard (p. 219) was another means. The men were put at five or six in a mess instead of four. To many writers this has seemed an atrocious measure specially invented by the Queen in her rage for economy. It was—they say—stealing the men's victuals. As a matter of certain fact, the Queen had nothing to do with it. It was the established custom in the navy and continued to be so for the next 250 years. When the stowage of ships was very limited, when there were no stores in distant parts of the earth, any ship going on a long voyage or being thrown on her own resources for any length of time, placed her men at 'six upon four' as a matter of course;[1] so much so, that it is unusual to find it mentioned in naval Memoirs. Unquestionably it was an evil. Putting the men on insufficient food lowered their vitality and made them a ready prey to scurvy and the many other diseases then supposed to be incidental to sea life ; but it was not considered by either officers or men more than a passing hardship, to be endured, not merely for the necessity, but for the convenience of the service ; though latterly convenience alone was held not to warrant it, and at the present time it could scarcely

---

[1] Cf. *Memoirs relating to the Lord Torrington*, 183 ; Thomas's *Journal of a Voyage to the South Seas*, 3.

be done except on extreme emergency. In putting the ships' companies on short allowance, Howard was adopting the most ordinary precaution, in view of a possible scarcity of provisions, and the indignation which has been expressed about it by writers ignorant of naval custom is altogether uncalled for; the more so, indeed, as the short allowance complained of was two-thirds of two pounds of beef and of a gallon of beer.

But this beer, it is said, was sour. That also was not unusual. It was nasty, it was unwholesome; but so long as beer continued to be the authorised drink on board ships of war, so long were the never-ending complaints of its being sour. Hawke's correspondence in 1759 is unusually full of such complaints, and especially of the West country beer. ' Our daily employment,' he wrote on the 4th of August, ' is condemning the beer from Plymouth '; to which the Admiralty replied that they were sorry to hear of the beer being bad, ' but the Commissioners of Victualling informed them that the uncommon hot weather this summer has occasioned the beer to spoil upon moving.' Howard's complaint, also in August, is of the beer from Sandwich. Both the man who supplied it and Darell declared that it was good when it was put on board ; a survey showed that it had gone sour within a month, which Howard thought must be the brewer's fault (vol. ii.—August 26). The brewer excused it by the want of hops, a matter which Howard did not concern himself with, but wrote. ' I know not which way to deal with the mariners to make them rest contented with sour beer, for nothing doth displease them more.' Nevertheless, Howard's letter does not authorise the paraphrase of it given by Mr. Froude :—' Notwithstanding the disorder was traced definitely to the poisonous beer, it continued to be served out. Nothing better was allowed till it was consumed.'[1] What Howard says is ' The mariners have a conceit—and I think it true, and so do all the captains here—that sour drink hath been a great cause of this infection amongst us. . . . Mr. Darell makes trial to brew the sour beer again, and so to mix it with other new beer, which I hope will do well.' Between the 'mariners' conceit' of Howard and the 'definite tracing' of Mr. Froude, there appears nearly as much difference as between ' brewing the sour beer again' and 'continuing to serve it out . . . till it was consumed.'

But in such cases sailors and their officers have sometimes had very queer ' conceits,' as when, for instance, in Anson's celebrated voyage across the Pacific, the commodore and Michell and the surgeons, discussing the terrible scurvy that was raging, came to the conclusion that—' the steams arising from the ocean may have a tendency to render the air they are spread through less properly adapted to the support of the life of terrestrial animals, unless these steams are corrected by effluvia of another kind, and which perhaps the land alone can supply;'[2] whereupon Anson administered to the sick ' the pill and drop of Mr. Ward,' two abominable quack medicines[3] which seem to have been both emetic and

---

[1] *History*, xii. 432.
[2] Walter's *Voyage round the World* (1748), 294.
[3] *Gentleman's Magazine*, 1798, ii. 739.

cathartic in a high degree. The fancies of Howard
and his men may be considered as in a similar
category, for there can be no doubt that the sickness
which so terribly scourged our ships' companies was
of the nature of typhus, and had been busy in some
of the ships—especially in the Elizabeth Jonas—
before the Spaniards came into the Channel. It is
very possible that the pestilence was aggravated by
scarcity and bad provisions, but it was primarily and
chiefly due to infection from the shore and from
ignorance or neglect of what we now know as sani-
tary laws; and it seems an interesting point, that
the ships commanded by the experienced old salts
escaped comparatively lightly. The ships named as
most heavily scourged are the Elizabeth Jonas, the
White Bear, and the Lion, commanded by Howard's
kinsmen, men splendid in the day of battle, but of
no experience in the very necessary art of keeping
a ship clean and sweet. A similar infection continued occasionally to scourge our ships' companies,
and still more frequently and more severely French
or Spanish ships' companies, till near the close of
last century. In our service, at least, it is now
happily almost forgotten.

The want of ammunition experienced by our
ships even after two days' fighting is another point
which has been brought forward as illustrating the
niggardly behaviour of the Queen. As before, it
was a detail with which the Queen had nothing to
do, and—also as before—there was no available
store in the kingdom. Anticipating the want,
Walsyngham had directed his agent to buy powder
in the Low Countries (p. 312), though little seems

to have been forthcoming from that quarter. But the full explanation of the want seems to lie in the rapidity of the fire which has already been mentioned. The ships had the usual quantity on board, but the expenditure was more, very many times more, than anyone could have conceived. Drake, indeed (p. 125), and perhaps others of the more experienced sailors, men who had been at Cadiz when the King's beard was singed, or who had, for years past, been settling their personal quarrels with the Spaniard in their own irregular way, might have some idea that a great deal of powder would be burnt; but they were probably alone in that belief.

It has not been remembered, it needs an effort to remember, that the off-fighting then practised by the English was an essentially new phase of naval war. The only thing that had at all resembled it, and that on a very small scale, was the distant interchange of shots between the English and French fleets at Spithead in 1545. But at Lepanto, the memory of which was still fresh in men's minds, the fighting was, for the most part, hand to hand, as it also was in the still more recent action at Terceira, from which the English were reported to have fled so ingloriously; and beyond question, not only the Spaniards, but many of the English officers and most—perhaps all—of the Queen's ministers expected that it would be so again. It was thus that when Richard Drake was sent to the Lord Admiral by the Council, he was directed to inquire how it was that none of the Spanish ships had been boarded (p. 355). Sir Walter Ralegh, who must have

talked with Howard and Drake and Hawkyns while
the business was fresh in their memories, has left us
what we may consider very direct testimony on this
point.   He says :—

'Certainly, he that will happily perform a fight
at sea must believe that there is more belonging to
a good man of war upon the waters than great
daring, and must know that there is a great deal of
difference between fighting loose or at large and
grappling.   To clap ships together without consideration belongs rather to a madman than to a
man of war ; for by such an ignorant bravery was
Peter Strozzi lost at the Azores, when he fought
against the Marquis of Santa Cruz.   In like sort
had the Lord Charles Howard, Admiral of England,
been lost in the year 1588, if he had not been better
advised than a great many malignant fools were,
that found fault with his demeanour.   The Spaniards
had an army aboard them and he had none ; they
had more ships than he had, and of higher building
and charging ; so that, had he entangled himself with
those great and powerful vessels, he had greatly
endangered this kingdom of England.   For twenty
men upon the defences are equal to a hundred that
board and enter ; whereas then, contrariwise, the
Spaniards had a hundred for twenty of ours, to
defend themselves withal.   But our admiral knew
his advantage and held it ; which had he not done,
he had not been worthy to have held his head.' [1]

But this off-fighting and this rapid and continuous
fire quickly exhausted the supply of ammunition
which had seemed sufficient ; and though some was

[1] *Historie of the World*, edit. 1736, ii. 565.

sent from the Spanish prize in Torbay, some also from the shattered prize at Weymouth, some from Portsmouth by the Earl of Sussex, some from London by Walsyngham, and more, perhaps, that has not been recorded, the magazines of the principal ships were almost depleted on the evening of the 29th of July (vol. ii.—Wynter to Walsyngham, August 1), and the pursuit of the next three days was strictly, as Howard called it, 'setting on a brag countenance' (vol. ii.—August 7).

Another stock complaint against the Queen is that the men were not paid their wages. This again was a detail with which the Queen was not concerned. The money was sanctioned by the Council and ordered by the Lord Treasurer. It was presumably paid to the Treasurer of the Navy, and if he had kept it at usance for his own advantage, he would only have been doing what was and continued to be the custom, both in the navy and the army, to the end of the eighteenth century. The prompt payment of naval officers and seamen is, indeed, a thing of the present day. But in fact, the Elizabethan seamen were very much better off in that respect than their successors under the Commonwealth, or the Restoration, or even George III. When the ship was paid off, these got a ticket which they could cash at whatever discount the Jew-agent chose to abstract. In Elizabeth's time they were paid in cash, and apparently at the end of every three months (p. 296). It may, of course, be represented as an abominable injustice that they were not paid down every Friday night, as the hands in a modern factory ; but that is not the custom of the navy, as to sea-going ships, even now, and still less was it so then; there was no clerical organization by which it could have been done, and as the men had no expectation of it, there was no hardship. After the battle, and during the fearful mortality at Dover—a mortality which even in the Ark and Triumph and Victory seems to have exceeded 35 per cent. of the ships' companies (vol. ii.—Hawkyns to Burghley, Sept. 4) —they demanded to be paid for the month ending on the 25th of August, and were greatly discontented that they had not received in full what was already due to them (vol. ii.—Howard to the Council, Aug. 22 ; Hawkyns to Burghley, Aug. 26). As the Treasurer of the Navy had been busy fighting and attending to the welfare of his own men, the delay does not necessarily imply any gross depravity or dishonesty on his part.

The system of pay in force throughout the century was peculiar. Many of the details are still obscure, but the broad principle was that—with the exception of the captain—every man on board, independent of his quality, should receive the same pay, the amount received by the officers being increased by allowances given under the name of 'dead-shares' or 'rewards.' Out of this had grown the custom to calculate the total amount payable to a ship's company at an average per head, which, in the earlier years of Elizabeth's reign, was 9s. 4d.[1] for the month of 28 days; but in 1586, consequent on a representation from Hawkyns (vol. ii. App. D), it was raised to 14s., and at this rate it remained in 1588. The uniform pay of every man was thus

[1] *S.P. Dom. Eliz.* xxv. 66.

raised from 6*s*. 8*d*. to 10*s*., the allowances being increased in the same proportion. As the nominal pay of the captain was thus brought up to 2*s*. 6*d*. *per diem*, it follows that previous to 1586 it was 1*s*. 8*d*. In addition to this, however, he had some allowance for his table; possibly also for lights, &c. ; the whole, lumped together, formed his diet,[1] or daily pay, the amount of which varied, according to the size of the ship, and the circumstances of his command.

With this one exception, every man on board received the same uniform pay of 10*s*. a month ; but an indeterminate number of non-existent men, known as 'dead-shares,' were also allotted 10*s*. a month ; and these dead-shares were divided amongst the officers and petty officers, according to some scale not yet known. The master and the master-gunner seem to have each received a whole dead-share ; so also probably did the boatswain ; quarter-masters had half a dead-share, some of the gunners—the modern gunner's-mates —one-third. In addition to these, further payments were made under the name of 'rewards,' concerning which there seems to have been no regulation ; the disbursement was probably determined partly by custom, partly by personal bargain, and partly at the discretion of the captain ; though, judging by the light of later experience, there must have been some machinery for preventing his assigning an exceedingly large reward to himself.

It would appear certain that, according to the class of ship, a large 'reward' was assigned to the master, who was, in most cases, a man of high

[1] Cf. Skeat's *Etymological Dictionary*, s.v. 'Diet.'

standing and great responsibility. In the larger
ships commanded by Howard's 'noblemen,' he was
virtually the captain ; in the Ark he must have been
actually so ; so also in the E. Bonaventure, which
was commanded by Raymond before the Earl of
Cumberland joined her off Portsmouth, and after he
left her at Harwich. Towards the end of the season
Thomas Gray, the master of the Ark, commanded
a small squadron with the pay of 6s. 8d. a day,
besides probable allowances, and the style of rear-
admiral (vol.ii.—Scale of pay). It is not to be supposed that these men served for the nominal 20s. a
month, pay and dead-share, or for anything like it,
when lieutenants had their pay made up to 3l., and
chaplains to 3l. 10s. (vol. ii.—Hawkyns to Burghley,
Estimate No. 5, Sept. 12). It is suggested (p. 173 n.)
that Polwhele was promoted from being captain of a
small vessel to be master of a large one, the understanding being that the master's pay and reward in
a large ship was really higher than the captain's diet
in a small one.

The Lord Admiral's pay is returned as 3l. 6s. 8d.,
or 5 marks, a day, besides unknown allowances.
Seymour's daily pay was 2l. ; that of Drake was
30s. In early times the pay of an admiral or
general largely depended on his social rank or title.
Howard's rank was of the highest, and to it he owed
the honourable position he occupied at this critical
period. He had indeed served at sea, and had more
experience than fell to the lot of most admirals, but it
must not be supposed that it was on that account that
he was made Lord High Admiral of England. It
was rather because his father and two of his father's

brothers had previously been Lord High Admirals ; it was because both he and his wife were nearly related to the Queen; it was because by birth or marriage he was related to or connected with almost every person of importance in the kingdom.

The Howards of the sixteenth century were remarkable by their high position, their political influence, their brilliant services, and in a scarcely less degree by their extreme fecundity. Most of them married twice ; most of them had large families, so that the number of people, men and women, who could claim near relationship with the Lord Admiral was enormous. Thomas, the second Duke of Norfolk, who commanded the English army at the battle of Flodden, had five sisters ; he was twice married, and had issue ten sons and six daughters. One of the sons, William, created Lord Howard of Effingham, was twice married, and had issue, besides six daughters, two sons, the elder of whom, Charles, born in 1536, succeeded as second Lord Howard of Effingham in 1573; was appointed Lord High Admiral in 1585; commanded the fleet against the armada of Spain in 1588, and at the taking of Cadiz in 1596, when he was created Earl of Nottingham. He retained the office of Lord High Admiral till 1619, and did not die till 1624, preserving his faculties to the last. Elizabeth Howard, one of the six sisters of the first Lord Howard of Effingham, married Sir Thomas Boleyn, and was the mother of Mary and Anne Boleyn. Anne married Henry VIII. and was the mother of Elizabeth. Mary married William Carey, and was the mother of Henry, created Lord Hunsdon, whose daughter,

Catherine, married Charles, Lord Howard of Effingham.

This relationship is more satisfactorily shown by a table, which—omitting the other members of the very numerous families—appears thus :—

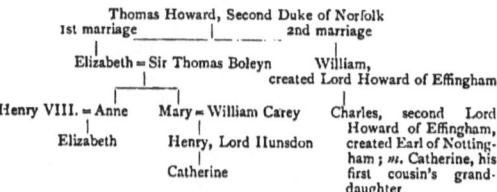

One of Lord Howard's sisters married Edward Seymour, Earl of Hertford, eldest son of the Protector, Duke of Somerset, whose second son, Henry Seymour, commanded the squadron in the Narrow Seas through the summer of 1588, and wrote many of the letters contained in these volumes. Of the other men who served in the fleet of 1588, Lord Thomas Howard, captain of the Golden Lion, was son of the fourth Duke of Norfolk and grandson of Lord Howard's first cousin, the Earl of Surrey, executed in 1545. Lord Sheffield, captain of the White Bear, was the son of Howard's sister Douglas, who, after her first husband's death, married Sir Edward Stafford, but retained the style of Lady Sheffield. Sir Robert Southwell, who commanded the Elizabeth Jonas, had married one of Howard's daughters ; another had married Richard Leveson, then serving as a volunteer in the Ark, but afterwards Vice-Admiral of England. Sir Edward

Hoby, who was also with Howard in the Ark, had married his youngest sister-in-law, daughter of Lord Hunsdon. The appointment of all these men, without any knowledge or experience of the sea, to posts of high command, would now-a-days be called nepotism. In Howard's days it was the rule for men in office to make the public service provide for their families; and Howard would certainly have defended his right to do so on the ground that he knew his kinsmen and could depend on them. It was the custom of the age for landsmen of high rank to command afloat, and under the conditions of the navy at that time they did very well.

But men like Drake, Wynter, Hawkyns, Palmer, Frobiser, Fenner, Fenton, Luke Ward and many others, come into a different category. They had followed the sea from their boyhood, and though all men of respectable or even good family, were, by the necessities of their education and calling, of a different social rank from the others. Drake belonged to the family of Drake of Ash in Devon, and was born at Tavistock about 1540. Hawkyns, some years older, and of a family rising to wealth by trade and maritime adventure, was a native of Plymouth. The relationship between them would seem to have been on the mother's side, for Drake had family arms, Hawkyns had not. After his loss at San Juan de Lua Hawkyns retired from the sea. He had married the daughter of Gonson, the Treasurer of the Navy, and in due time succeeded him in his office, in which—according to the statements of his enemies—he enriched himself by irregular, if

not by fraudulent methods.   Some of these charges,
which had been persistently made, are repeated here
(pp. 34–44; vol. ii. Oct. 8), but the evidence does not
seem to have been sifted ; and the fact that the ships
were found strong and seaworthy when they were
wanted for service (pp. 79, 81) goes far to show that
it was mainly the voice of spite or malice.   After the
defeat of the armada Hawkyns commanded an
expedition to the coast of Portugal in 1590, and
later, under Drake, in the West Indies, where—off
Porto Rico—he died on the 12th of November,
1595.

Drake's career was much more active and
brilliant than that of his older kinsman.   Hawkyns
laid the foundation of a large fortune by cheating
the Spaniards, and increased it, it was suspected, by
cheating his own countrymen.   Drake also founded
a handsome fortune at the cost of the Spaniards,
but it was by openly plundering them in what he
and the generality of Englishmen considered legitimate and honourable war.   After his return from
the celebrated voyage round the world in 1580, he
was not at sea except in the Queen's service.   In
1585–6 he commanded a strong squadron which
ravaged the West Indies, sacked Cartagena and
the Spanish settlements on the mainland of Florida;
and in April 1587, with another squadron, forced
his way into Cadiz, where he burnt the ships
which were preparing for the intended invasion of
England, and struck terror into the Spaniards and
Portuguese along the coast.   William Borough,
the second in command of the squadron—a man
distinguished as a navigator and hydrographer, but

of no experience in war—was aghast at what appeared the Admiral's recklessness, and remonstrated against his conduct in very strong terms. Drake answered by putting him under arrest on board his own ship. Borough believed, or pretended to believe, that his life was in danger, and not improbably worked on his men to run away with the ship and return to England. The quarrel was afterwards smoothed over by the influence of Burghley (pp. 74–5), and Borough commanded the galley Bonavolia through the summer of 1588, when his best service was sketching a chart of the Thames, which is here reproduced in facsimile, though smaller (p. 337). Borough's name still lives, not as that of a warrior, but of a navigator, hydrographer, and early investigator into the apparent vagaries of the compass.

In 1589 Drake, jointly with Sir John Norreys, commanded a powerful armament against Lisbon in support of the claims of Dom Antonio to the throne of Portugal. They met no enemy by sea; on shore they met the most terrible of all enemies—a wasting and deadly sickness—and, having lost many thousand men, returned helpless to England. In 1595 he was again afloat on an expedition to the West Indies. No secrecy had been preserved in fitting it out, and the Spaniards, forewarned, had everywhere prepared for it, either by removing their treasure or strengthening their defences. An attack on Porto Rico failed, and though Santa Marta, Nombre de Dios, and some other places were burnt, little harm was done and no advantage gained. The disappointment preyed on his spirits and aggravated an attack of dysentery, which proved fatal on the 28th of January, 1596.

Frobiser, of an old Yorkshire family, seems in early life to have been engaged in trading to the Mediterranean. He was afterwards suspected of piracy, though the charge was not brought home to him ; and in 1576-7-8 he made three successive voyages to the Arctic, where his name still lives in 'Frobiser's Strait,' now known to be only a deep inlet or gulf. In 1585-6 he was with Drake in the West Indies, in 1590 with Hawkyns on the coast of Portugal. In 1594 he commanded a squadron on the coast of Brittany, co-operating with Norreys, and in an attack on Crozon was mortally wounded. He died at Plymouth in the early days of January 1595. Though he played a foremost part in the campaign of 1588, both as a councillor and as captain of the Triumph, the largest ship in the fleet, and everywhere in the front of battle, there is not one letter from him among the papers here printed. The fact is that though a bold and skilful seaman, a good navigator, and a man of cultivated intelligence, he had neglected the more ordinary paths of book learning, and could do little more than write his name, which—after trying various other forms—he decided on spelling Frobiser.

Of the volunteers who joined the fleet after the Spaniards came into the Channel little can be said. According to Camden, they were :—The Earls of Oxford, Northumberland, and Cumberland ; Thomas and Robert Cecill ; H. Brook, Charles Blount, Walter Ralegh, William Hatton, Robert Carey, Ambrose Willoughby, Thomas Gerard, Arthur

Gorges, and others. Of these, only three are mentioned in these papers as having joined the fleet: —the Earl of Cumberland, Charles Blount, and Thomas Gerard. Robert Cecill was at Dover, writing to his father (p. 342), and, on the 30th of July, neither was nor had been on board any of the ships. That Oxford, Burghley's son-in-law, or Thomas Cecill, Burghley's son; that Northumberland, Seymour's first cousin; Robert Carey, Howard's brother-in-law, and Sir Walter Ralegh, a man of high repute and official rank, could be in the fleet and not be once mentioned by Howard, by Robert Cecill, by Seymour, or by any of the correspondents of Burghley and Walsyngham, or by these, would seem incredible if we had not Robert Carey's own statement to the effect that, at the battle of Gravelines, he was on board the E. Bonaventure.[1] It must therefore be admitted as possible that the others were also in the fleet, though—without corroborative testimony—it remains extremely improbable. That Ralegh had a command in the fleet and 'led a squadron as rear-admiral'[2] is virtually contradicted by the evidence now before us.

Another man who, though neither in nor belonging to the fleet, is often said to have rendered efficient service, is David Gwynn, actually a slave on board the Spanish galley Diana, but described as serving on board the Bazana. On the way from Lisbon, in heavy weather off Cape Finisterre, the Diana—it is said—went down with all hands. The other three galleys were in great danger, and the

---

[1] *Memoirs* (1759), p. 18.
[2] Edwards, *Life of Sir Walter Ralegh*, vol. i. p. xxxvii.

captain of the Bazana applied to Gwynn, whom he knew as an experienced seaman, to get them out of the mess. Gwynn consented, and as a first step desired that the soldiers should be sent below. Most of them were so sent; whereupon Gwynn, waving his cap as a signal, struck his dagger into the heart of the captain. His comrades, at the same moment and in the same manner, killed all the Spaniards who were on deck; then they killed all who were below; and having thus obtained possession of the Bazana, they attacked and won the Capitana, killing all the Spaniards on board. The fourth galley, the Princesa, made her escape, and succeeded in rejoining the fleet and getting into Corunna.

Such in brief is the story, absolutely unknown to early English and Spanish writers, which is told by the Dutch chroniclers, and has been repeated from them by later historians, notably by Motley,[1] who ought to have been warned by the many absurdities, such as the slaves being unchained and all having daggers. For, in point of fact, the story is a lie from beginning to end. Gwynn, as has been said, was serving in the Diana, not the Bazana. It was after the fleet left Corunna, not before it arrived there; it was in the Bay of Biscay, not off Cape Finisterre, that the galleys made such bad weather of it. The Diana did not go down in the open sea, but bore up for Bayonne, where in trying to run into the harbour she ran aground and became a total wreck, but without any serious loss of life. The officers and men were entertained by the

[1] *History of the United Netherlands* (cab. ed.), ii. 447.

governor of the town, and went 'home by land. The other three galleys, with better success, put into different French ports and in due time returned to Spain.[1] Gwynn and some other English slaves, in the confusion following the wreck, made their escape, got to Rochelle and thence to England ; whence, as speaking Spanish, Gwynn was sent over to Ireland to assist in the examination of the Spanish prisoners. His true story is told clearly enough by the Lord Deputy (vol. ii.—Fytzwylliam to the Council, October 18). It is, perhaps, not impossible that Gwynn, after being ignominiously sent out of Ireland as a liar, a thief, and a lewd person, sought service in the Low Countries, where he spun his 'galléy-yarns' to the credulous, from whom Bor received them. It is not often that a fable can be so completely exploded as this now is.

Of the many other myths which have been foisted on to the true history of the campaign, it is unnecessary to speak. The first test of their truth ought to be an examination of the evidence on which they are based. It will be found that many of them rest on no evidence at all, and others on that of the Dutch chroniclers, more especially Bor. It must be remembered that Dutch writers had no special facilities for knowing what happened ; that they were by no means crushed under a sense of gratitude to Elizabeth, and were bitterly hostile to the Spaniards. English and Spanish writers— Camden, for instance, and Herrera—might be as badly informed, but the spirit of hatred was not so

[1] Duro, i. 65 ; ii. 279.

dominant in them. They were willing to do their enemies justice.

The papers here printed are strictly what they are called on the title-page—State Papers; letters and memoranda written by or to the officers of the fleet and the high officers of State. A large proportion of the letters are written by Howard or Seymour to Lord Burghley, the Lord High Treasurer, or to Sir Francis Walsyngham, the Principal Secretary of State. Many, too, are written by Drake and by Hawkyns; others by men not so well known, but all of unquestionable authenticity. About one document alone is any doubt possible, the Relation on pp. 1–18. As stated in the note on p. 1, there are strong reasons to suppose that it emanated from Howard; but it is quite possible that it did not, and was only written from hearsay. If so, the writer was curiously well informed on points of detail which were not then public property.

Many of the letters are extremely difficult to read. Howard's writing is singularly perplexing; Seymour's is very bad; Drake's is a scrawl; Walsyngham's is atrocious. But the badness of the writing is not the worst part of them. Many of them, especially of the most interesting and important, have been very badly treated, carried about in pockets, opened and folded, read and re-read, till the edges and the folds were much frayed and torn. More than two centuries of damp afterwards tried to wash away what remained, and have too often very nearly succeeded. In 1798, John Bruce, the Keeper of State Papers, was directed by Mr. Pitt, in view of possibilities then threatening, to prepare a Report on the measures taken for the defence of the country in 1588. To his Report Bruce appended many of these documents, which he certified as examined. Since that time the papers have suffered still more from damp, sometimes also from bad mending, and no doubt many words now wanting were then still legible. The Report was thus a natural reference in cases of difficulty, but a very little experience of it showed that the transcripts were made by a very ignorant and careless man, and that, notwithstanding the official certificate, the value of them is extremely slight. With the present copies every practicable care has been taken to ensure verbal accuracy ; and though it is impossible to affirm that there are no errors, it is confidently believed that there are not many, and none of serious importance. Words which might be thought doubtful are in all cases enclosed in square brackets, and if supplied from Bruce's Report or from conjecture, the fact is duly noted.

In accordance with the resolution of the Council, the spelling has been modernised ; but wherever the original spelling seemed to have any interest, either from the social position of the writer or from its peculiar eccentricity, it is given in a note. Howard's spelling is sometimes very curious, but apparently phonetic, and is thus a guide to the Court pronunciation, as Cely's still more extraordinary spelling may be to that of middle-class society in Bristol. Obsolete or obscure words and phrases or allusions have been also noted, the Editor being instructed to act on the supposition that many members of the Society have little practice in

Elizabethan English, and have not ready access to the larger works of reference, such as the New English Dictionary (N.E.D.) or the Dictionary of National Biography (D.N.B.).

Names of men are spelt uniformly, and, wherever practicable, according to their own signatures. It is commonly supposed that the spelling of 16th and 17th century names is indeterminate : a mistake, due partly to the carelessness of other people, but still more to what seems now the curious custom of brothers, or members of the same family, differencing their names by the spelling, in much the same way that they differenced their armorial bearings by marks of cadency.   Humphrey Gylberte and John Gilberte, Thomas Cecill and—after his father's death—Robert Cecyll, Marmaduke Darell and his cousin William Darrell, are some amongst many belonging to this period.   The point is really one of some importance, for attention to the spelling of signatures is frequently the only way of avoiding great confusion ; as, for instance, between George Cary of Cockington, afterwards Lord Deputy of Ireland, George Carey of the Isle of Wight, afterwards Lord Hunsdon, and George Carew, Master of the Ordnance in Ireland, afterwards Earl of Totness.   Each of these men, and indeed every man who could write, had an established signature, which he no more thought of varying than does anyone at the present time ; whether his peculiar spelling was dictated by reason or fancy, it marks his name, and as such, the Council has directed it to be used.

With the exception of a very few in the British Museum, with the distinguishing reference B.M., and

of one at Hatfield, now abstracted from the Report
of the Historical MSS. Commission, all the papers
here given are in the Public Record Office, mostly
in the collection of Domestic State Papers. The
exact reference is in all cases given. They are
arranged in nearly strict chronological order, the
occasional slight deviations from it readily explaining themselves. The editorial dates at the
head of the papers, in the notes and in this Introduction, are, without exception, according to the
Old Style, then in use in England. The New Style,
already adopted in France, Spain, and the Low
Countries, which occasionally appears in the body of
a document, differed by ten days from the Old.
Thus the 20th of May O.S. was 30th of May N.S. ;
the 21st of July O.S. was 31st of July N.S. ; and
the 29th of July O.S. was the 8th of August N.S.,
which un-English date Sir Oswald Brierley has
affixed to the engraving of his delightful picture of
the battle of Gravelines. The legal and official year
in England began on the 25th of March ; but in
historical writing it was frequently supposed to begin
on the 1st of January, as it did on the Continent.
The date 1587 affixed to the letters written between
the 1st of January and the 25th of March, is his-
torically, and according to modern usage, 1588.

Most of the papers are, of course, in English.
Some, originally in other languages, have been
preserved in a contemporary translation, and are
referred to as ' Englished.' Others, which remain
only in the original language, are referred to as
' Latin,' ' French,' &c., and have been translated by
the Editor, who has endeavoured to avoid the in-

congruity of appearing to put new cloth to an old garment.

It only remains for the Editor to express his grateful sense of the kindness which he has received from the many friends and some strangers whom he has consulted on doubtful or obscure points. He would record his obligations to his colleague at King's College, Professor J. W. Hales; to Mr. M. Oppenheim; to the Hydrographer, Captain Wharton, R.N., F.R.S.; to Mr. C. H. Coote of the British Museum; to M. Alfred Spont; to Mr. Hubert Hall of the Record Office; to the Director of Naval Intelligence, Rear-Admiral Bridge, who has assisted him in revising the proof-sheets, and in a very special degree to Mr. Edward Salisbury of the Record Office, to whose tireless generosity and marvellous skill in piecing out words from the faintest conceivable indications the accuracy of the present transcripts is largely due.

Errata.

P. 13. Note 2, last line, delete *year*
,, 161. Note, for *July* read *April*

DEFEAT

OF THE

SPANISH ARMADA

ANNO 1588.

A RELATION OF PROCEEDINGS.[1]

[B.M. Cotton, Julius, F. x. ff. 111–117.—No date, title, signature, or endorsement. A neat, clerkly, contemporary writing.]

WHEREAS the Queen's most excellent Majesty had of late years sundry and most certain intelligences of the great warlike preparation both for sea and land which the King of Spain of late years made from all parts, not only of the mightiest and most puissant ships and vessels that he could prepare, as

---

[1] The MS. has nothing externally to indicate its origin ; internally, there is much in favour of the opinion that it is official ; and it does not seem improbable that it was drawn up under Howard's authority, as 'the more particular relation' with which he proposed 'at better leisure' to supplement 'the brief abstract of accidents' sent to Walsyngham on August 7. It must, however, be remembered that this is only a conjecture, and that the Relation has not the authority of an authenticated document. Still, none of the statements in it are contradicted by other papers of greater value ; and most of them are directly corroborated, often in the very words.

well from foreign places as in his own dominions,
and by arresting of the ships of other countries that
came into his dominions, but also of all kind of
munition and victuals, and of captains, soldiers and
mariners, and of all other provisions for a mighty
army by seas, to come out of Spain and Portugal;
for the more strength whereof it was notorious to
the world how he had drawn into Spain and Portugal
his principal and most experimented captains and
old soldiers out of Naples, Sicilia, Lombardy and
other parts of Italy, yea, and from sundry remote
places of the Indies; the preparation whereof,
with the numbers of ships, men, victuals, ordnance
and all kind of munition, was made patent to the
world by sundry books printed and published both
in Spain, Portugal, and in many other countries of
Christendom, carrying the titles of the ' Happy
Armada [1] of the King of Spain,' and in some specially
expressed to be against England: And in like
sort, where [2] her Majesty had the like knowledge of
the mighty and puissant forces of horses and footmen
sufficient to make many armies prepared in the Low
Countries under the conduct of the Duke of Parma,
the King's Lieutenant-General, and of multitude of
ships, bylanders, [3] boats and other vessels fit for the
transporting and landing of the said forces, armies
from the coast of Flanders, with a general publication
to the world that all these so mighty forces, both by
sea and land, were intended to the invasion of her
Majesty's realms, and as was pretended, to have

---

[1] *Felicísima Armada.* It is so called in the official Relation
published at Lisbon.
[2] Whereas.
[3] Bylander (Fr. *belandre*), from the Dutch *binnenlander*, was
originally a small vessel adapted to Dutch inland navigation. At
this time it seems to have been a one-masted craft carrying a
spritsail; later on, the name was more especially applied to a
kind of snow.

made therewith a full conquest: Yet for that, in this time of their preparation, the King of Spain, by his Lieutenant-General, the Duke of Parma, caused certain offers to be made to her Majesty for a communication of a peace betwixt their Majesties ; howsoever, by the common judgment of the world, the same was done but to abuse her Majesty and to win time whilst his preparations might be made complete ; her Majesty, nevertheless, like a most godly and christian prince, did not refuse to give ear to so christian an [1] offer, for which purpose she sent certain noblemen of her privy council into Flanders to treat with certain commissioners, who continued there without any good success by reason of the unreasonable delays of the King's commissioners ; yea, they continued there until the navy of Spain was overcome and forced to fly.

And yet, notwithstanding this her inclination to peace, and her princely offers of most reasonable conditions of peace, she, like a prince of wisdom and magnanimity, for defence of herself, her realm and people, was not negligent of her princely office to which God called her, and wherein He had stablished her and preserved her very many years, but providently did prepare a princely and strong army by sea, and put in readiness also sundry armies by land, to prevent and withstand the foresaid attempts so published to be made by such great armies, both by sea and land, as never were so great made in any part of Christendom, either by the said King or the Emperor, his father. For which, her preparations by seas, such diligence was used, as the same being begun to be made but about the 1st of November, yet the same was fully ready to take the seas by the 20th of December, a time very short for such an enterprise, having respect to the length

[1] MS. and.

of sundry years which the Spanish navy was in preparing.

But yet such it was as God specially favoured, and as the force thereof hath been proved to have overmatched the mightiness of the enemy's navy; the charge whereof was committed by her Majesty to Charles Lord Howard, of the ancient house of Norfolk, High Admiral of England, who was accompanied with a great number of noblemen and others, the most sufficient and best experimented men for the seas. And after that he had continued a good time with the army upon the Narrow Seas betwixt England and Flanders, the said High Admiral, by her Majesty's commandment, sent Sir Francis Drake into the west part of this realm towards Spain, with certain of her Majesty's ships, and other ships of the subjects of the realm, to the number of fifty sail great and small, there to continue until such time as the Lord Admiral, with a great and strong force, should repair thither, if occasion should so require. And in the meantime, the Lord Admiral, with the Lord Henry Seymour, vice-admiral of that army, and many noblemen and gentlemen having charge of sundry of her Majesty's ships, continued in the Narrow Seas, having to attend upon them 20 ships of the city of London, very well and in good sort sent out, and sundry other good ships for the war which the coast towns, from the River of Thames to Newcastle northward, did send out for this service in warlike manner.

And then, upon further intelligence of the readiness of the Armada of Spain to come to the seas, the 21st of May, 1588,[1] the Lord Admiral, leaving the Lord Henry Seymour in the Narrow Seas, with a convenient force both of her Majesty's ships and of her subjects', to withstand all enterprises that the Duke

[1] Cf. *post*, May 23, Howard to Burghley.

of Parma should make by sea, did depart from the
Downs towards the west with certain of her Majesty's
ships and twenty other ships and barks of London,
which arrived at Plymouth the 23rd of the same,
where Sir Francis Drake, with the number of 60
sails, until that time under his charge, met [1] with the
Lord Admiral in good order, whereupon his Lordship, commanding that fleet unto his own, made Sir
Francis Drake his vice-admiral.

His Lordship, upon his arrival at Plymouth, took
present order for the victualling and putting in a
readiness of the whole army, being then near about the
number of 90 sails of ships and barks ; which being
accomplished, his Lordship put out of harbour again
into the sea, and lay off and on in the Sleeve,[2] betwixt
Ushant and Scilly, abiding the coming of the Spanish
fleet; and afterwards his Lordship having spent long
time, sometimes near the coast of France, and sometimes near the coast of England, retired with the
fleet to Plymouth to refresh them.

In the meantime there were discovered betwixt
Ushant and Scilly certain ships of the Spanish fleet,
to the number of 14 sail, which afterward were known
to be separated from their fleet by force of foul
weather, and before they could be met with by any
of the English army, they had a northerly wind
which carried them back to the Groyne,[3] whither the
rest of the fleet returned and watered.   Hereupon
his Lordship had intelligences sundry ways that
the Spanish army was dispersed into sundry ports of
Spain, distressed, spoiled, in necessity of victuals and
great mortality grown amongst their people ; which

[1] Cf. *post, ib.* These details could then scarcely be known
outside the official circle.

[2] The Sleeve (Fr. *La Manche*) is more properly the Channel.
It will be seen, however, that Howard, like this unknown writer,
always applies it to the Chops of the Channel, the sea between
Ushant and Scilly.   [3] Corunna.

notwithstanding did not so fall out in truth ; whereupon his Lordship, seeing our own coast clear and
the coast of France also, which he had very narrowly
searched, thought it good, with liking and advice of
his council, to take the opportunity of the next north
wind that should happen, and to bear with the coast
of Spain, there to seek out the Spanish fleet in the
Groyne or other ports of Galicia, which course was
held from the 8th of July, 1588, until the 10th of the
same, with a north wind, at which time the same
changed to southerly, 40 leagues short of the coast
of Spain, or thereabouts.   His Lordship therefore,
doubting that which afterwards fell out in very deed,
and having his chief care and regard to the defence
of the realm of England, and finding that with that
wind the enemy might pass by the fleet of England
undescried, with that change of wind being prosperous for the fleet of Spain to come for the coast
of England, returned with his whole company and
arrived at Plymouth the 12th of the same, where,
with great expedition, his Lordship put divers things
in order, watered and refreshed his ships with
victuals.

The 19th of July, 1588, we had intelligence by
one of the barks that his Lordship had left in the
Sleeve for discovery, named the [Golden Hind],[1]
wherein was Captain Thomas Flemyng, that the
fleet of Spain was seen near the Lizard, the wind
being then southerly or south-west ; and although
the greater number of ships of the English army,
being then in Plymouth, with that wind were very

---

[1] Blank in MS. Flemyng is said by Sir William Monson to
nave been a 'pirate,' 'at sea a-pilfering,' an idea which Kingsley
elaborated in *Westward Ho !* It is, however, distinctly contradicted by the State Papers. He was, through the Gonsons, a near
connection of Hawkyns, and is frequently named during the
following ten years as commanding a ship of war, either in the
Queen's service or with the Earl of Cumberland.

hard to be gotten out of harbour, yet the same was done with such diligence and good will, that many of them got abroad as though it had been with a fair wind. Whereupon, the 20th of July, his Lordship, accompanied with 54 sail of his fleet, with that southwest wind plied out of the Sound ; and being gotten out scarce so far as Eddystone,[1] the Spanish army was discovered, and were apparently seen of the whole fleet to the westwards as far as Fowey.

The next morning, being Sunday, the 21st of July, 1588, all the English ships that were then come out of Plymouth had recovered the wind of the Spaniards two leagues to the westward of Eddystone,[1] and about 9 of the clock in the morning, the Lord Admiral sent his pinnace,[2] named the Disdain, to give the Duke of Medina defiance, and afterward in the Ark bare up with the admiral[3] of the Spaniards wherein the Duke was supposed to be, and fought with her until she was rescued by divers ships of the Spanish army. In the meantime, Sir Francis Drake, Sir John Hawkyns,[4] and Sir Martin Frobiser[4] fought with the galleon of Portugal, wherein John Martinez de Recalde, vice-admiral, was supposed to be. The fight was so well maintained for the time that the enemy was constrained to give way and to bear up room[5] to the eastward, in which bearing up, a great galleon, wherein Don Pedro de Valdes was captain, became

[1] MS. Idye Stone.

[2] This is not mentioned in any of the State Papers ; though the Lord Admiral's pinnace Disdain is.

[3] The flag-ship. The use of the word admiral in this sense, common in the Elizabethan period, continued till the end of the seventeenth century.

[4] So called by anticipation. They were not knighted till the 26th.

[5] Room=to leeward. It is only used adverbially, as ' to bear room,' ' to go room,' ' roomwards,' and seems to conceal the same idea as the still familar ' to sail large.'

foul of another ship which spoiled and bare overboard his foremast and bowsprit,[1] whereby he could
not keep company with their fleet, but being with
great dishonour left behind by the Duke, fell into
our hands. There was also at that instant a great
Biscayan, of 800 tons or thereabouts, that, by firing
of a barrel of gunpowder, had her decks blown up,
her stern blown out, and her steerage spoiled. This
ship was for this night carried amongst the fleet by
the galleasses.

This fight continued not above two hours ; for
the Lord Admiral, considering there were forty sail
of his fleet as yet to come from Plymouth, thought
good to stay [2] their coming before he would hazard
the rest too far,[3] and therefore set out a flag of
council, where his Lordship's considerate advice
was much liked of, and order delivered unto each
captain how to pursue the fleet of Spain ; and so,
dismissing each man to go aboard his own ship, his
Lordship appointed Sir Francis Drake to set the
watch that night.

This night the Spanish fleet bare alongst by the
Start, and the next day, in the morning, they were
as far to leeward as the Berry. Our own fleet,
being disappointed of their light, by reason that Sir
Francis Drake left the watch to pursue certain hulks
which were descried [4] very late in the evening,
lingered behind not knowing whom to follow ; only
his Lordship, with the Bear and the Mary Rose in
his company, somewhat in his stern, pursued the
enemy all night within culverin shot ; his own fleet
being as far behind as,[5] the next morning, the

---

[1] MS. bolspreete.   [2] Await.
[3] This sentence must surely have emanated from Howard.
[4] Cf. *post*, August 10, Starke's Deposition. Starke's word
is ' scryed.'
[5] As=that.

nearest might scarce be seen half mast high, and
very many out of sight, which with a good sail recovered not his Lordship the next day before it was
very late in the evening. This day, Sir Francis
Drake with the Revenge, the Roebuck and a small
bark or two in his company, took Don Pedro de
Valdes, which was spoiled of his mast the day before;
and having taken out Don Pedro and certain other
gentlemen, sent away the same ship and company
to Dartmouth, under the conduction of the Roebuck,
and himself bare with the Lord Admiral, and recovered his Lordship that night, being Monday.

This Monday, being the 22nd of July, 1588, the
Spaniards abandoned the ship that the day before
was spoiled by fire, to the which his Lordship sent
the Lord Thomas Howard and Sir John Hawkyns,
knight, who together, in a small skiff of the Victory's,
went aboard her, where they saw a very pitiful sight
—the deck of the ship fallen down, the steerage
broken, the stern blown out, and about 50 poor
creatures burnt with powder in most miserable sort.[1]
The stink in the ship was so unsavoury, and the sight
within board so ugly, that the Lord Thomas Howard
and Sir John Hawkyns shortly departed and came
unto the Lord Admiral to inform his Lordship in what
case she was found; whereupon his Lordship took
present order that a small bark named the Bark
Flemyng,[2] wherein was Captain Thomas Flemyng,
should conduct her to some port in England which
he could best recover, which was performed, and the
said ship brought into Weymouth the next day.

That night fell very calm, and the four galleasses
singled themselves out from their fleet, whereupon
some doubt was had lest in the night they might

[1] These details are not found in the State Papers.
[2] Many ships are similarly named after their owner. The true
name of the Bark Flemyng was Golden Hind.

have distressed some of our small ships which were
short of our fleet, but their courage failed them, for
they attempted nothing.

The next morning, being Tuesday, the 23rd of
July, 1588, the wind sprang up at north-east, and
then the Spaniards had the wind of the English
army, which stood in to the north-westward, towards
the shore. So did the Spaniards also. But that
course was not good for the English army to recover
the wind of the Spaniards, and therefore they cast
about to the eastwards ; whereupon the Spaniards
bare room, offering [to] board our ships. Upon which
coming room there grew a great fight. The
English ships stood fast and abode their coming,
and the enemy, seeing us to abide them, and divers
of our ships to stay for them, as the Ark, the
Nonpareil, the Elizabeth Jonas, the Victory, &c.,
and divers other ships, they were content to fall
astern of the Nonpareil, which was the sternmost
ship.

In the meantime, the Triumph, with five ships,
viz., the Merchant Royal, the Centurion, the Margaret and John, the Mary Rose and the Golden
Lion, were so far to leeward and separated from
our fleet, that the galleasses took courage and bare
room with them and assaulted them sharply. But
they were very well resisted by those ships for the
space of an hour and a half. At length certain of
her Majesty's ships bare with them, and then the
galleasses forsook them. The wind then shifted to
the south-eastwards and so to SSW, at what time a
troop of her Majesty's ships and sundry merchants'
assailed the Spanish fleet so sharply to the westward
that they were all forced to give way and to bear
room ; which his Lordship perceiving, together with
the distress that the Triumph and the five merchant
ships in her company were in, called unto certain of

her Majesty's ships then near at hand and charged
them straitly to follow him, and to set freshly upon
the Spaniards, and to go within musket-shot of the
enemy before they should discharge any one piece
of ordnance, thereby to succour the Triumph;
which was very well performed by the Ark, the
Elizabeth Jonas, the Galleon of Leicester, the
Golden Lion, the Victory, the Mary Rose, the
Dreadnought and the Swallow—for so they went in
order into the fight. Which the Duke of Medina
perceiving, came out with 16 of his best galleons,
to impeach his Lordship and to stop him from
assisting of the Triumph. At which assault, after
wonderful sharp conflict, the Spaniards were forced
to give way and to flock together like sheep. In
this conflict one William Coxe,[1] captain of a small
pinnace of Sir William Wynter's, named the Delight,
showed himself most valiant in the face of his
enemies at the hottest of the encounter, where [2]
afterwards lost his life in the service with a great
shot. Towards the evening, some four or five ships
of the Spanish fleet edged out of the south-west-
wards, where some other of our ships met them,
amongst which [the] Mayflower of London dis-

[1] Poor Coxe has had rather hard measure served out to him.
Lediard, unable to distinguish an *x* from a *p* in Elizabethan
writing, has changed his name into Cope ; Fuller, whom Southey
follows, calls him Cock ; and Motley speaks of him as ' one
Wilton, coxswain of the Delight.' Cf. *Don Juan*, viii. 18.

[2] 'Where' must be a clerical error for 'who.' Camden, referring probably to a copy of this Relation, says, 'Solus Cockus
Anglus, in sua inter medios hostes navicula, cum laude periit ;'
and this has been repeated over and over again by English, French,
and Spanish writers.   But it will be seen (*post*, August 1,
Wynter to Walsyngham) that he was alive on July 29, and that
the 'navicula' was Wynter's. Motley describes his 'Wilton' as
killed in boarding the great galleass. But Coxe was killed by a
great shot, and Wynter's expression ' who sithen that time is slain,'
clearly puts his death later. He was probably slain in the fight
off Gravelines

charged some pieces at them very valiantly, which ship and company at sundry other times behaved themselves stoutly.

This fight was very nobly continued from morning until evening, the Lord Admiral being always [in] the hottest of the encounter, and it may well be said that for the time there was never seen a more terrible value of great shot, nor more hot fight than this was ; for although the musketeers and harquebusiers of crock [1] were then infinite, yet could they not be discerned nor heard for that the great ordnance came so thick that a man would have judged it to have been a hot skirmish of small shot,[2] being all the fight long within half musket shot of the enemy.

This great fight being ended, the next day, being Wednesday, the 24th of July, 1588, there was little done, for that in the fight on Sunday and Tuesday much of our munition had been spent, and therefore the Lord Admiral sent divers barks and pinnaces unto the shore for a new supply of such provisions. This day the Lord Admiral divided his fleet into four squadrons, whereof he appointed the first to attend himself ; the second his Lordship committed to the charge of Sir Francis Drake ; the third to Sir John Hawkyns, and the fourth to Sir Martin Frobiser. This afternoon his Lordship gave order that, in the night, six merchant ships out of every squadron should set upon the Spanish fleet in sundry places, at one instant, in the night time, to keep the enemy

[1] The harquebus was a very heavy sort of musket, fired from a rest or crock. The word 'crock' is still in use, in the sense of 'a little stool.'

[2] 'The shot continued so thick together that it might rather have been judged a skirmish with small shot on land than a fight with great shot on sea.' This is Sir George Carey's account of this action, in his letter to the Earl of Sussex, of July 25.

waking; but all that night fell out tŏ be so calm that nothing could be done.

The next morning, being the 25th of July, 1588, there was a great galleon[1] of the Spaniards short of her company to the southwards. They of Sir John Hawkyns his squadron, being next, towed and recovered so near that the boats were beaten off with musket shot; whereupon three of the galleasses and an armado[2] issued out of the Spanish fleet, with whom the Lord Admiral in the Ark, and the Lord Thomas Howard in the Golden Lion, fought a long time and much damaged them, that one of them was fain to be carried away upon the careen; and another, by a shot from the Ark, lost her lantern, which came swimming by, and the third his nose. There was many good shots made by the Ark and Lion at the galleasses in the sight of both armies, which looked on and could not approach, it being calm, for the Ark and the Lion did tow to the galleasses with their long boats. At length it began to blow a little gale, and the Spanish fleet edged up to succour their galleasses, and so rescued them and the galleon, after which time the galleasses were never seen in fight any more, so bad was their entertainment in this encounter. Then the fleets drawing near one to another, there began some fight, but it continued

---

[1] This was the Santa Ana, Recalde's *capitana* or flag-ship. She had received much damage on the 21st, which now brought her into danger from Hawkyns' squadron, and after she had beaten off their attack was no longer able to keep the sea. She parted company unobserved during the night, and drifted over to Havre, where she became a total wreck.

[2] An English corruption of the Sp. *armada*, and in our literature is used in exactly the same sense—a fleet. Thus Shakespeare has (*King John*, iii. 4) 'A whole armado of convicted sail.' In these papers, however, it is distinctively used as meaning a galleon, a large ship out of the armada, or, in fact, 'a fleet ship,' a term suggested a few year years ago for what is now called 'a battle-ship.'

not long, saving that the Nonpareil and the Mary Rose struck their topsails and lay awhile by the whole fleet of Spain very bravely, during which time the Triumph, to the northward of the Spanish fleet, was so far to leeward as, doubting that some of the Spanish army might weather her, she towed off with the help of sundry boats, and so recovered the wind. The Bear and the Elizabeth Jonas, perceiving her distress, bare with her for her rescue, and put themselves, through their hardiness, into like perils, but made their parties good notwithstanding, until they had recovered the wind; and so that day's fight ended, which was a very sharp fight for the time.

Now, forasmuch as our powder and shot was well wasted,[1] the Lord Admiral thought it was not good in policy to assail them any more until their coming near unto Dover, where he should find the army which he had left under the conduction of the Lord Henry Seymour and Sir William Wynter, knight, ready to join with his Lordship, whereby our fleet should be much strengthened, and in the meantime, better store of munition might be provided from the shore. On Friday, being the 26th of July, 1588, his Lordship, as well in reward of their good services in these former fights, as also for the encouragement of the rest, called the Lord Thomas Howard, the Lord Sheffield, Sir Roger Townshend, Sir Martin Frobiser and Sir John Hawkyns,[2] and gave them all the order of knighthood aboard the Ark. All this day and Saturday, being the 27th of July, the Spaniards went always before the English army like sheep, during which time the justices of peace near the sea-coast, the Earl of Sussex, Sir George Carey, and the

---

[1] 'Wasted' frequently occurs in the sense of 'expended,' 'consumed.'

[2] Sir George Beeston was also knighted at this time, though his name is here omitted.

captains of the forts and castles alongst the coast, sent us men, powder, shot, victuals and ships to aid and assist us. On Saturday, in the evening the Spanish fleet came near unto Calais on the coast of Picardy, and there suddenly came to an anchor over against betwixt Calais and Calais Cliffs,[1] and our English fleet anchored short of them within culverin shot of the enemy.

The Spaniards sent notice of their arrival presently unto the Duke of Parma, but because[2] there should be no time detracted[3] to permit their forces to join, the Lord Admiral, the 28th of July, 1588, about midnight, caused eight ships to be fired and let drive amongst the Spanish fleet; whereupon they were forced to let slip or cut cables at half and to set sail. By reason of which fire the chief galleass came foul of another ship's cable and brake her rudder, by means whereof he was forced the next day to row ashore near the haven's mouth and town of Calais; whereupon the Lord Admiral sent his long boat, under the charge of Amyas Preston,[4] gentleman, his lieutenant, and with him Mr. Thomas Gerrard[5] and Mr. . . . .[6] Harvey, together with other gentlemen, his Lordship's followers and servants, who took her and had the spoil of her. There entered into her above 100 Englishmen. And

[1] MS. Scales Cleeves.   [2] MS. by cause.
[3] Drawn out, spun out.
[4] Was here severely wounded. He continued serving during the war; commanded an expedition to the Spanish Main in 1595; and in 1596 was captain of the Ark under Howard, in the expedition to Cadiz, when he was knighted.
[5] Not improbably the eldest son of Sir Gilbert Gerard, Master of the Rolls; created Baron Gerard of Gerard's Bromley in Staffordshire in 1603.
[6] Blank in MS. Bor and others give his name as William. Probably, therefore, the William Harvey who was knighted at Cadiz in 1596, and commanded the Bonaventure in the Islands voyage in 1597.

for that she was aground and sewed[1] two foot, and could not be gotten off, they left her to Monsr. Gourdan, Captain of Calais, where she lieth sunk.

Now that the Lord Henry Seymour and Sir William Wynter were joined with us, our fleet was near about 140 sail—of ships, barks and pinnaces &c. During the time that this galleass was in taking by the Lord Admiral, Sir Francis Drake in the Revenge, accompanied with Mr. Thomas Fenner in the Nonpareil and the rest of his squadron, set upon the fleet of Spain and gave them a sharp fight. And within short time, Sir John Hawkyns in the Victory, accompanied with Mr. Edward Fenton[2] in the Mary Rose, Sir George Beeston in the Dreadnought, Mr. Richard Hawkyns[3] in the Swallow, and the rest of the ships appointed to his squadron, bare with the midst of the Spanish army, and there continued an hot assault all that forenoon. Sir George Beeston behaved himself valiantly. This fight continued hotly; and then came the Lord Admiral, the Lord Thomas Howard, the Lord Sheffield, near the place where the Victory had been before, where these noblemen did very valiantly. Astern of these was a great galleon assailed by the Earl of Cumberland and Mr. George Raymond[4] in the Bonaventure most worthily, and being also beaten with the Lord Henry Seymour in the Rain-

---

[1] Dried : akin to the modern sewer = a drain, and Fr. *essuyer* = to wipe dry. 'A cow when her milk is gone is said *to go sew*; a ship is *sewed* when she comes to lie on the ground or to lie dry. To *sew* a pond is to empty or drain it' (Wedgwood). 'A ship resting upon the ground . . . is said to be sewed by as much as the difference between the surface of the water and the ship's floating mark. If not left quite dry, she sews to such a point' (Smyth).

[2] Hawkyns' brother-in-law.   [3] Hawkyns' son.

[4] MS. Ryman. He commanded the expedition which sailed for the East Indies in April 1591, and was lost, in the Penelope, off Cape Corrientes.

bow, and Sir William Wynter in the Vanguard, yet she recovered into the fleet. Notwithstanding, that night she departed from the army and was sunk. After this, Mr. Edward Fenton in the Mary Rose and a galleon encountered each other, the one standing to the eastward and the other to the westward, so close as they could conveniently one pass by another, wherein the captain and company did very well. Sir Robert Southwell that day did worthily behave himself, as he had done many times before ; so did Mr. Robert Crosse [1] in the Hope, and most of the rest of the captains and gentlemen. This day did the Lord Henry Seymour and Sir William Wynter so batter two of the greatest armados that they were constrained to seek the coast of Flanders, and were afterwards, being distressed and spoiled, taken by the Zealanders and carried into Flushing. In this fight it is known that there came to their end sundry of the Spanish ships, besides many other unknown to us.

After this Monday's fight, which was the 29th of July, 1588, the Lord Admiral on the 30th of July appointed the Lord Henry Seymour, Sir William Wynter and their fleet to return back again unto the Narrow Seas, to guard the coasts there, and himself, determining to follow the Spanish army with his fleet until they should come so far northward as the Frith in Scotland if they should bend themselves that way, thought good to forbear any more to assault them till he might see what they purposed to do, verily thinking that they would put into the Frith, where his Lordship had devised stratagems to make an end of them ; but the Spaniards kept a course for the Isles of Scotland,

---

[1] Was with Drake in the West Indies in 1585, and continued serving during the war. Was knighted at Cadiz in 1596.

and of purpose, to our seeming, to pass home that way, by the north of Scotland and west part of Ireland.

When we were come into 55 degrees and 13 minutes to the northward, 30 leagues east of Newcastle, the Lord Admiral determined [1] to fight with them again on the Friday, being the 2nd of August, but by some advice and counsel his Lordship stayed that determination, partly because we saw their course and meaning was only to get away that way to the northward to save themselves, and partly also for that many of our fleet were unprovided of victuals ; for our supply, which her Majesty had most carefully provided and caused to be in readiness, knew not where to seek for us. It was therefore concluded that we should leave the Spanish fleet and direct our course for the Frith in Scotland, as well for the refreshing of our victuals as also for the performing of some other business which the Lord Admiral thought convenient to be done ; but the wind coming contrary—viz. westerly—the next day the Lord Admiral altered his course and returned back again for England with his whole army, whereof some recovered the Downs, some Harwich and some Yarmouth, about the 7th of August, 1588.

---

[1] This is surely official optimism. It appears certain that he had little or no ammunition remaining.

STATE PAPERS.

Dec. 21, 1587.—*COMMISSION TO HOWARD.*

[Patent Roll, 30 Elizabethæ, part 17, m. 7 d ; S.P. Dom. Eliz. ccvi. 41.—Latin.[1]]

Elizabeth, by the grace of God, &c., to all to whom &c., greeting :

Know ye that we, reposing special trust and confidence in the fidelity, prudence, zeal, experience, circumspection, industry and diligence of our beloved Councillor, Charles, Lord Howard, Baron of Effingham, knight of our illustrious order of the Garter, High Admiral of England, Ireland, Wales, and of the dominions and islands thereof, of the town of Calais and the marches of the same, of Normandy, Gascony and Aquitaine, and Captain General of the Navy and mariners of our said kingdoms of England and Ireland—do, by these presents, assign, make, constitute, ordain, and depute the said Charles to be our lieutenant-general, commander-in-chief, and governor of our whole fleet and army at sea,

[1] An extraordinary conventional jargon, setting grammar and dictionary alike at defiance. The present translation has been made after a careful comparison with other commissions of the same or nearly the same date—including one to the Duke of Buckingham in 1625—drawn up in an English only less extraordinary than the Latin.

C 2

now fitted forth against the Spaniards and their
allies, adherents or abettors, attempting or compassing any design against our kingdoms, dominions
and subjects ; and also of all and singular our vice-
admirals, captains, sub-captains[1] and lieutenants, of
our barons,[2] lords and knights, of the masters of our
ships, our mariners and men at arms, employed or
to be employed,[3] of our gunners,[4] and of any others
whatsoever, retained or to be retained in our royal
fleet and army : Giving and granting to this same
Charles full power and authority to lead and command all and singular our lieges and subjects of
whatever estate, degree, or dignity they be in our
said fleet or army, and in whatsoever way they have
been or may be retained, or in whatever way they
have been engaged in this present service for resisting and destroying the Spaniards and others,
their allies, adherents, abettors or assistants, attempting or compassing any design against our kingdoms,
dominions and subjects ; as also—with our fleet and
army aforesaid, and our subjects assembled or arrayed for war[5]—according as there shall be occasion,
and wherever and whenever he shall deem it fitting,
to invade, enter, spoil and make himself master of
the kingdoms, dominions, lands, islands and all other

---

[1] Sub-capitaneorum. It is impossible to say what were meant,
in the days when post-captains were not ; but the distinction
seems to correspond to captains and commanders. It does not
occur anywhere else.

[2] Baroniorum, baronettorum, dominorum : greater and lesser
barons, and the sons of barons (lord by courtesy), or lords of
manors. What is perhaps the same phrase appears elsewhere as
' earls, viscounts, barons.'

[3] Delectorum sive destinatorum.

[4] Sagittariorum : bows and arrows are frequently mentioned
among the stores, but never ' archers ' as a distinct class of men.
The ships' companies are always divided into mariners, gunners,
and soldiers.

[5] Ad bellum congregatos sive arraiatos.

places whatever belonging to the said Spaniards and others, their allies, adherents or abettors, attempting or compassing any design against our kingdoms, dominions and subjects; and with force of arms to spoil, offend, repress, subdue and make war upon the Spaniards, their allies and adherents: And for the spoiling and utter subduing of these, whether by invasion, or in some other manner as heretofore set forth, to direct, rule, order and command our said fleet, army and subjects; and if need be, to go and to sail with our said fleet, army and subjects, to our said kingdom of Ireland, or to any other place, according to his own will and pleasure: Giving and granting to the same Charles full power and authority to muster, direct, lead, order and command all and singular our vice-admirals, captains, sub-captains, lieutenants, barons,[1] lords, knights, masters of ships, mariners and gunners,[2] and all others soever in our aforesaid fleet and army, which are armed in our service or appointed thereto: and also to hear, examine, discuss, order and determine all suits, causes, quarrels and other matters of all and each of them, so far as they pertain, either by right or by custom, to the office of our said lieutenant-general at sea: Also to make, constitute and ordain laws and ordinances for the effective good conduct of our said fleet and army; and furthermore, to make proclamations and enforce the due execution thereof;[3] and to punish, repress, reform and incarcerate any belonging to our said fleet and army who shall, in any manner, offend; and if it shall seem meet to him, to pardon, release, dismiss and deliver those

[1] As before—barones, baronettos, dominos.
[2] Sagittarios.
[3] Eademque debitum executionem : passing over the false concord, the ' eadem' would seem to be the translation of the Elizabethan ' which.'

incarcerated : further, to enquire into, examine, hear
and judge all capital or criminal charges relating to
loss of life or limb, and cases of murder in any
manner occurring in our said fleet and army, with all
matters connected therewith or rising out of the
same ; and also to determine, pass or publish
sentences or decrees of whatsoever nature, regarding the same ; and to command and order, and
cause such sentences or decrees [1] to be fully and
effectively executed ; and according to his own will
and pleasure, freely to do, ordain, forward, decree
and execute all other things needful for the good
conduct and government of our said fleet and army,
as in his wise discretion they shall from time to time
seem fitting, and with full power of coercion : And
also with power and authority, as often as it seemeth
to him fitting or necessary, to nominate, ordain, make,
constitute, assign, and appoint other deputy-lieu-
tenant or deputy-lieutenants to execute, perform,
forward or carry out, in our stead and in our name,
the aforesaid services or any of them ; and to recall
him or them if the case should require it, and to
order and appoint other or others in his or their
place, for the services aforesaid, or any part of
them.

Moreover, by these presents, we strictly command and enjoin all and each of the vice-admirals,
captains, sub-captains, lieutenants, barons, lords,
knights, masters of ships, mariners, gunners, and all
others soever in our said fleet and army, in whatever
manner they have been levied, retained or may be
retained, that as need shall be, from time to time,
they shall be attendant, counselling, helping and at
the commandment of the said Charles, our High
Admiral and Lieutenant General at sea, in the

[1] Easque sive ea executionem . . . demandandum . . .

execution of the aforesaid services, as they shall answer for it at their peril.[1]

In witness whereof &c. at Westminster, the 21st day of December. Per ipsam Reginam.

December 22.—*HOWARD TO BURGHLEY.*

[ccvi. 42.—Signed. Addressed.]

My very good Lord :—I now remain aboard the Bear ; and as yet the provisions for the ships could not be taken all in by reason of the weather, which hath been so tempestuous as that no boats could lie aboard them to put in the same ; yet I hope that within two or three days all things will be in a readiness.

Here is a very sufficient and able company of sailors[2] as ever were seen ; and because their long journeys out of all places of this realm, and this bad season, makes them unprovided of apparel and such necessaries, it were good for their relief to pay them one month's wages before hand.

Many great charges extraordinary hath grown this quarter, which I could hardly have believed unless with mine own eyes and good examination I had seen. Wherefore in respect of those causes, and for the furtherance of service, I am to entreat your good Lordship to give order that the rest of the warrant lately granted for the whole navy may be paid to Mr. Hawkyns, and 2,000*l*. more upon the old warrant of 29,000*l*. for the furnishing of those extra-ordinary charges, wherein your Lordship shall further a good service.

---

[1] Sub pœna gravissimi contemptus : *i.e.* under the penalty due to a most gross contempt of our authority ; *lèse-majesté*.

[2] MS. saylers. In these papers the word is rare, ' mariners ' being more commonly used.

We have entered into sea victuals this day, being the 22nd of this instant December, and not before, for the preserving of the six weeks' victuals. And Mr. Quarles [1] hath sent down divers supplies more than allowance—for the numbers were great before we entered into the six weeks' victuals.[2] Wherefore I pray your Lordship that he may be paid the rest of his allowed warrant, and that consideration for the rest which I spake to your Lordship for heretofore. And so I bid your good Lordship most heartily farewell. From aboard the Bear, the 22nd of December, 1587.

Your Lordship's most assured

loving friend to command,

C. HOWARD.

December 22.—*LIST OF CAPTAINS.*

[ccvi. **43**.—Endorsed :—The names of the captains that have charge of her Majesty's ships particularly sent to the seas.]

1. The Lord Admiral.
2. The Lord H. Seymour.
3. The Lord Thomas Howard.
4. The Lord Sheffield.
5. Sir Robert Southwell.
6. Sir W. Wynter.[3]
7. Mr. John Hawkyns.
8. Mr. Borough.
9. Mr. Beeston.[4]

[1] James Quarles, Surveyor of Victuals.

[2] 'For the numbers . . . victuals,' is interlined in Howard's own hand. 'Great numbers' as distinguished from 'small.' Cf. *post*, p. 31.

[3] Had been in the service of the navy for nearly fifty years ; was knighted in 1573, and was at this time Master General of the Ordnance.

[4] Had been serving as a naval captain since the beginning of the reign.

10. Mr. Frobiser.
11. Sir Henry Palmer.[1]
12. Mr. Roger Townshend.[2]
13. Captain Crosse.
14. Mr. Henry Ashley.[3]

December 24.—HOWARD TO BURGHLEY.

[B.M. Harl. MS. 6994, f. 102.—Holograph.   Addressed.]

My honourable good Lord :—I do understand by Mr. Cæsar[4] how much I am bound unto your Lordship for your honourable favour.   I have no ways to recompense it but with my love and service, which your Lordship shall be most assured ever of.

It may be there hath been some report made to your Lordship of some chance[5] that happened here, before my coming down, by fire in one of the ships ; and because I do understand that it is reported that it should be[6] done by Ascott, I do assure your Lord-

---

[1] Is first named as commanding a squadron of the Queen's ships in 1576.   In 1584 he was one of the commissioners for Dover Harbour, and in 1587 was knighted while commanding a squadron off Dunkirk.

[2] Though named in this list of captains, he had no experience of sea affairs, and did not command a ship either in 1588 or in any other year.   He was knighted on July 26 (*ante*, p. 14), and was probably then serving on the personal staff of the Lord Admiral, but his name does not appear elsewhere in these papers. He died in 1590.   His great-grandson, Horatio, was created a viscount after the Restoration.

[3] Probably the brother of Sir Anthony Ashley, Clerk of the Council, translator and editor of *The Mariners' Mirrour* (1588), knighted at Cadiz in 1596, and grandfather of the first Earl of Shaftesbury.

[4] Dr., afterwards Sir Julius Cæsar, Judge of the Admiralty Court.

[5] Mischance.

[6] This use of the conditional in oblique relation was very general.

ship it was after this manner.   There were two poor
knaves that came from Westchester [1] that strived for
a place to hang up their netting for to lie in, and the
one of them had a piece of a candle in his hand, and
in striving, the candle fell down where there lay
some oakum.   It might have bred some mischief,
but it was quickly put out.   It was in the Elizabeth
Bonaventure ; but I hope to make them a warning
to others to beware.

I am bold to send you by this bearer, my man,
the copy of a proclamation which I have drawn and
proclaimed in my own ship, and shall be this day and
to-morrow proclaimed in the rest.   I am but a bad
drawer of a proclamation, but it shall serve, I hope,
for to prevent some ill that might happen.

My good Lord, this bearer, my man, shall always
attend at the court, and shall attend on your Lordship always to know your pleasure, if you will command him anything unto me.   And so, resting
always most beholden unto your Lordship and most
ready to do your Lordship any service, I humbly
take my leave.   Aboard her Majesty's good ship the
White Bear, the 24th of December, 1587.

Your Lordship's most assured to command,

C. HOWARD.

[1] Chester.

January 5.—*DISPOSITION OF SHIPS.*

[ccviii. 6.   Rough list ; captains' names scribbled in
in Burghley's hand.]

5th of January, 1587.

Ships to remain at Queenborough with their
numbers diminished, in the charge of the Admiral :

[Men]			[Men]	
500	The Bear	. .	275	Lord Admiral
500	Triumph .	.	275	Lord Henry
500	Elizabeth Jonas		275	Sir Robt South-well
400	Victory .	.	225	Lord Sheffield
400	Ark Ralegh	.	225	Lord Thomas
250	Mary Rose	.	125	Edward Fenton
250	Lion	. .	125	Borough
250	Bonaventure	.	125	John Hawkyns
250	Vanguard	.	125	Sir Wm Wynter
200	Dreadnought	.	100	Beeston
250	Rainbow .	.	125	with Sir H. Palmer
160	Foresight	.	80	Cap. Frobiser
30	Merlin	. .	15	
24	Sun .	. .	12	
36	Brigandine	.	20	
20	George .	.	12	

4,020   A 2,139   rest in charge

1,881 abated

£3,208. 10s.

Ships for the Narrow Seas and Flushing, to serve
under Sir Henry Palmer :

[Men]

The Antelope	.	Ch. Baker	. 160
Swallow	.	Benjamin	. 160
Bull .	.	Turner	. 100
Tiger.	.	Bostocke[1]	. 100
Tramontana		Luke Ward[2]	70
Scout.	.	Henry Ashley	70
Achates	.	Capt. Riggs	60
Charles	.	.	. 40
Moon	.	.	. 40

B 800 rest in charge

At Portsmouth for Sir Francis Drake :

[Men]					[Men]
250	The Hope	.	.	.	. 140
250	Nonpareil.	.	.	.	140
35	Advice	.	.	.	20
535					300

At Queenborough for Sir Francis Drake :

[Men]

The Revenge	.	Rob. Crosse	.	140
Swiftsure	.	Fenner	.	100
Aid	.	. Fenner	.	80

[Men]
550 { whereof to be dis-
     { charged 230 } . 320

total 1,085 for Sir Fr. Drake   C 620 in charge

465 abated

---

[1] John Bostocke. A Thomas Bostocke was Sir George Bond's
agent at St. Jean de Luz.
[2] Had been employed against the pirates in the Channel in
1578, and commanded the Edward Bonaventure with Fenton in
the voyage of 1582.

In wafting of the Artillery   [Men]

The Spy .   .   .   .   . 35.

Upon the Coast of Spain

The Makeshift 35

D 70 rest in charge

A 2,139) 3,629 men.   Note when the 3 ships[1] sent
B   800 (westward shall have their numbers full,
C   620 [which are 1,085,[1] then the total monthly
D   70) charge will be 4,657*l.*

£
3,208
1,200
930
105
———
£5,443 [2]
add   637
———
£6,080

January 6.—THE CHARGE OF THE SHIPS.

[ccviii. 7.]

To continue in charge with the Lord Admiral:
16 ships, the number of 2,139.

To continue upon the Narrow Seas under the
charge of Sir Henry Palmer: the Antelope and 8
other ships, with the number of 800.

Total, 2,939 in men, 4,408*l.* 10*s.* in money.

[1] So written in Burghley's hand. He includes, however, not
only the three ships at Portsmouth with Drake, but also the three
ships at Queenborough, under orders to join him. And where
the 4,657*l.* comes from does not appear. The charge really
amounts to 6,141*l.*

[2] This is the monthly charge for the men under A, B, C and
D, at 30*s.* a month. The charge for the additional men (465) in
the western squadron, which should be 697*l.*, is added in as 637*l.*,
giving, of course, a false total.

To be sent to Sir Francis Drake: the Revenge, the Swiftsure and the Aid, with the numbers only of 320.

To be sent also from Portsmouth to Sir Francis Drake: the Hope, the Nonpareil and the Advice, with the number of 300.

Total, 620 in men, 930*l.* in money.

To continue in charge: the Spy with 35, and the Makeshift, on the coast of Spain, with 35.

Total, 70 in men, 105*l.* in money.

Total in charge presently   .   3,629

Her Majesty is to continue the charge hereof, being monthly   .   .   . £5,443 10*s.*
To be added the charge of Sir Francis Drake's ships to the number of   .   .   1
The charges of wages and victualling after the rate of 30*s.* a man is per month   1

January 8.—*ESTIMATE OF CHARGES.*

[ccviii. **8.**]

An estimate of the charge of the ships that serve under the charge of Sir Francis Drake westward, viz. :

Her Majesty's ships.

Men		Men
250	The Revenge	140
250	Hope . . .	140
250	Nonpareil. . .	140
180	Swiftsure	100
120	Aid	80
35	Advice . . .	20
35	Makeshift. . .	20
1 120		640

¹ Left blank.

Men	At London.	Men
120	The Edward Bonaventure	60
120	Roebuck . . .	60
100	Hopewell . . .	50
80	Galleon Fenner .	40
100	Golden Noble . .	50
520		260

Men	At Plymouth.	Men
180	The Merchant Royal . .	40
100	Griffin	20
80	Minion	20
80	Thomas	20
80	Bark Talbot . . .	20
80	Spark	20
70	Hope	16
70	Bark Bond [1] . . .	16
70	Bark Bonner [2] . . .	16
60	Elizabeth Founes [3] . .	12
40	Unity	12
30	Elizabeth Drake . .	8
70	Bark Hawkyns . .	15
250	(Five hulks or other ships to make up 30 sail, which have in charge in harbour	80
1,260		315

The great Numbers	The small Numbers
1,120	640
520	260
1,260	315
2,900	Soldiers 100
	1,315

[1] Belonging, probably, to Sir George Bond, the Lord Mayor.

[2] The Bonners were a family of shipowners at Leigh in Essex. Robert Bonner, the head of the family at this time, married Elizabeth, sister of Launcelot Andrewes, afterwards Bishop of Winchester, and one of the translators of the Bible.

[3] Humphrey Founes was Mayor of Plymouth the next year, 1588-9.

First, the great numbers are 2,900 men, which for charge of wages, after the rate of 14*s.* the man, diets,[1] dead shares and reward accounted, is monthly, after 28 days to the month, amounteth to . 2,030 0 0

For the tonnage of 23 merchant ships accounted in 4,000 ton may amount unto, by the month of like days 400 0 0
_____
2,430 0 0

For the sea victual of the said 2,900 men at 16*s.* 4*d.* every man, by the month of 28 days, amounteth to 2,368 6 8

For transportation monthly . . 50 0 0
_____
2,418 6 8

Wages 2,430 0 0
Victuals 2,418 6 8
_____ { The monthly charge of
4,848 6 8 { the great numbers

For the small numbers, which are 1,315 men, the month's wages, after the rate of 14*s.* the man, diets, dead shares and rewards accounted, is 920 10 0

For the tonnage of the merchant ships, being 23 ships accounted in 4,000 ton, amounteth to by the month 400 0 0
_____
1,320 10 0

[1] Roughly speaking, diets were equivalent to the modern table-money ; dead-shares seem to have been the pay of fictitious men, similar to the ' widows' men ' of the eighteenth century, with the essential difference that they were borne, not for any charitable purpose, but to increase the pay of warrant and petty officers, who

For the victual of the said 1,315 men   £   s.   d.
monthly, as aforesaid, at 16s. 4d.
the man, after 28 days per month,
is 1,073 18 4
For transportation monthly   .   .   20   0   0
$$\overline{}$$
                 1,093 18 4

    1,320 10 0
    1,093 18 4
   $\overline{}$ { The monthly charge of
   2,414   8   4 { the small numbers

January 18.—*HAWKYNS TO BURGHLEY*(?)

[ccviii. 14.—Holograph. No address nor endorsement.]

My bounden duty humbly remembered unto
your good Lordship :—This day with God's favour
I shall make an end of the pay to all such as be
discharged through the navy, and have reduced them
to the numbers your Lordship did appoint. The
Revenge, the Swiftsure and the Aid's company were
reduced to 320 men, as was appointed, and they
departed and were well over the Land's End [1] the
16th day of this month, God be thanked.

Yesterday my Lord Admiral accompanied with
the Lords went over the Land's End towards Dover,
with the Vanguard, the Rainbow, and sundry of our
small pinnaces ; and mindeth to see Dover, Harwich
and other places, before his Lordship return. His
abode, I think, will not be long ; for his Lordship

also received special allowances under the name of rewards. The
subject is more fully discussed in the Introduction.

[1] Writing from Queenborough, he probably meant the Land's
End in Sheppey, which is Shell-Ness ; but he may have meant
the Land's End by Margate, which would seem to be Fore-Ness,
or possibly the North Foreland.

told me he would return within four days, if weather
served.

The treasure went over the 16th day of this
present, accompanied with the Bull, the Tiger and
the Charles ; so as there remaineth there at Queenborough 11 great ships, as followeth :—

	Men		Men
The Bear	275	The Mary Rose .	125
Triumph .	275	Bonaventure .	125
Eliz. Jonas .	275	Lion . .	125
Victory . .	225	Dreadnought .	100
Ark Ralegh .	225	Antelope .	160
	1,275	which is to go into the Nar- row Seas.	
	715		
	1,990	Swallow. .	80
			715

As there shall be any occasion grow here worthy
the writing I will inform your Lordship, and so
humbly take my leave. From Queenborough
aboard the Bonaventure, the 18th of January, 1587.
Your Lordship's humbly to command,
JOHN HAWKYNS.

THE AGREEMENT WITH MR. HAWKYNS.

[ccviii. 17.—Endorsed : Mr. Hawkyns, the conditions for the
bargain for the Navy upon the dormant warrant for 5,714*l.* ;
1579.]

The bargain of John Hawkyns for the navy, viz. :

Conditions in the behalf of her Majesty.

1. First, all that which was ordinary in such
time as it was 5,714*l.* yearly John Hawkyns shall
perform :

2. As first.—To pay and continue the same number of ship-keepers that hath been since the said ordinary was reduced to the said sum of 5,714*l.* together with the same number of gunners in Upnor Castle, the clerks &c., the watchmen, and rent that now is paid in the ordinary.

3. Item.—To keep in repair all her Majesty's ships, so as, upon a grounding, they may be ready to serve at the seas, until some one of them come to be new made in a dry dock.[1]

4. Item.—To moor the navy sufficiently, so that the ships may ride without danger.

5. Item.—To repair all manner of storehouses and wharves at Chatham, Woolwich, Deptford and Portsmouth, until any of them shall fall into such decay as they must be new built.

6. Item.—To continue all her Majesty's navy in serviceable order, and every year to do such reparations as shall be needful, either in making of a new ship, repairing in dry dock, or any way otherwise that shall be needful, so that the full number be kept as they are now at this present. If any ship be decayed, another to be put new in her place, of like length and breadth, sufficiently builded.

[None at all were made new by him.][2]

7. Item.—To ground the ships upon all occasions of sea-service, leaks or other needful causes.

8. Item.—All the boats, cocks,[3] pinnaces and lighters shall be kept in serviceable order; and as the old do decay, new to be made in their places.

9. Item.—He shall find Norway masts for all the small ships under the Aid;[4] and the topmasts and topsail yards of all the ships.

10. Item.—That at All-Hallowtide every year

---

[1] MS. docque. [2] Marginal note in Burghley's hand.
[3] Cock-boats. [4] That is, of less than 250 tons.

there shall be presented unto the Lord Treasurer,
the Lord Chamberlain, Mr. Secretary and Sir
Walter Mildmay, the names of twenty skilful men —
as captains, owners, shipwrights, and masters—of
which number the foresaid commissioners shall
appoint such a number as they will to make report
of the estate of the navy, and to show their opinion
what shall be needful to be done to the navy the
year following, which shall be likewise performed.

Conditions in the behalf of John Hawkyns.

1. First.—The said John Hawkyns shall have
paid him for the service to be done of the other side,
the old ordinary warrant of 5,714*l.* 2*s.* 2*d.* monthly
as it was, in *Anno* 1578.

2. Item.—He shall be holpen with the commission, as in *Anno* 1578.

3. Item.—It shall be lawful for him to entertain
as many shipwrights as he will, and as few as he
will, and at all seasons and times as the service shall
require, and no more.

4. Item.—If any of the ships shall come to a
mischance—as God forbid—either by fire, wreck,
spoil in war, or such like ; or the boats, cocks, or
pinnaces ; then the said John Hawkyns shall have
allowance for the supply of such ships, boats and
pinnaces, as the charge shall require, and be judged
by the commissioners or officers of the navy.

5. Item.—That if the whole navy shall go to the
seas, or a great part of them, whatsoever provisions
of timber, board and plank, shall be taken into them
for sea service, the said John Hawkyns shall not be
charged with above the value of 40*s.* in such stuff
for every ship ; to say boards, planks, fishes [1] for
masts, spare masts for topmasts, and such like.

[1] MS. fyshers.

6. Item.—The said John Hawkyns shall have the assistance of the shipkeepers for the help of grounding of the ships, loading and unloading of provisions, and such like; the use of the hoy for carriage, launching-tackles and crane-ropes &c., as hath been in time past.

7. Item.—He shall also have the use of the wharves, storehouses, forges, and lodgings at Chatham, Deptford, Woolwich, and Portsmouth, for those ministers that shall be needful to attend this service, and for the laying of all manner of provisions readily for the said service.

8. Item.—That if the ships shall ride in any other place by her Majesty's order, then, by the discretion of the commissioners, it may be judged what shall be increased for the same mooring, calling unto them the officers and masters of the navy.

9. Item.—That when a new ship shall be made and ready to be launched, the said John Hawkyns shall make his commodity [1] of the old.

10. Item.—If any ambiguity or doubt shall happen of either part that ought to be considered in equity and conscience be omitted in this bargain, and that the same cannot be agreed [2] upon amongst the officers, that then the commissioners aforesaid shall, by their discretions, moderate the doubt and order the same.

[1] Advantage, profit.
[2] If on either part there shall happen any . . . doubt on some point omitted in this bargain, it ought to be considered &c. ; and if the same cannot be agreed &c.

January 22.—*REPORT BY PETT AND BAKER.*

[ccviii. 18.—Endorsed, in Burghley's hand : An opinion of Peter
Pett[1] and Matthew Baker[2] the shipwright upon certain articles
of Mr. J. Hawkyns. Torn and frayed away at the edges.]

The examination of the bargain of Mr. John
Hawkyns, how far it is performed and accomplished.

First, to the behalf of her Majesty ; the condition
divided into [ten several articles] in the first page.

1. First.—All that which was ordinary at such
time as it was 5,714*l.* yearly &c.

In this article is to be noted how this 5,714*l.*
yearly was employed ; as first the ordinary of the
carpentry was undertaken by the master shipwrights
for 1,000*l. per annum* ; the moorings by Mr. Hawkyns
for 1,200*l. per annum* ; the shipkeepers' wages, clerks
&c. for 1,814*l. per annum* ; so was spared and remained
to her Majesty's farther uses 1,700*l.* yearly ; which
whole warrant is continued in Mr. Hawkyns' hands
to this day.   It is said that he employed this 1,700*l.*
yearly during 6 years in provision of cordage,
canvas, anchors &c., to furnish the storehouse with a
double furniture, to be in readiness for all suddens.
How the same is performed there resteth a question.
And touching the 1,000*l.* a year undertaken by the
shipwrights, Mr. Hawkyns is to perform the conditions, for that he took from them the benefit
thereof from the first day they entered, and they are

---

[1] Master builder of the navy from the time of Queen Mary.
The office remained in his family for the next hundred years.
   [2] Son of James Baker, master shipwright under Henry VIII.,
and himself master shipwright early in the reign of Elizabeth. He
is described by John Davys in the dedication to his *Seaman's Secrets*
as one who, 'for his skill and surpassing grounded knowledge for
the building of ships advantageable to all purpose, hath not in any
nation his equal.'

to abide his reward.   After the tîme of 6 years to
this time, being two years and a half, Mr. Hawkyns
undertook for that 1,700*l.* [a year] to discharge her
Majesty of all extraordinary reparations, new building of ships, as shall come to be said more in place
following.

2. Item.—To pay and continue the number of
shipkeepers &c.

Touching this article, the condition may be
observed so long as the number of the ships are
continued and remain in harbour.   But being of late
often and long time at the seas, so are the number
decreased and the charge greatly eased.

3. Item.—To keep in repair all her Majesty's
ships so as upon a grounding &c.

This article was much better observed before
Mr. Hawkyns undertook the extraordinary than
now it is; for before, the master shipwrights did
direct, but now they are to be directed ; and being
but hirelings were glad to please their master,
feeding his humour so long as they doubted to
hazard all and reap both shame and dishonesty ; for
such ships as had been tried at the seas and their
weak state discovered, to remedy the same the shipwrights could not be suffered ; but that which was
done was drawn by force and reported to be more
than needed, and besides the shipwrights restrained
from grounding of divers ships, which notwithstanding was done [by] force, without order from Mr.
Hawkyns.   Nevertheless, five of the greater ships
are departed from Chatham very foul and not
grounded, which is both dangerous, and great
hindrance to their working and sailing.   How this
condition is performed may easily be judged.

4. Item.—To moor the navy sufficiently, so as
the ships may ride without danger &c.

Touching this article, as the ships hath not been

damaged one way by want [of] good moorings, so
hath they been in dangerous state by reason of ill
oakum,[1] [which] heretofore was had out of the old
moorings that now is made into ropes [again] to a
great gain, whereby no oakum is to be had but at
the hands of such as [make] it of rotten ropes so
that the good hemp oakum that was accustomed to
be used [is] banished.

[The best ocom is called pocket-ocom.][2]

5. Item.—To repair all manner storehouses,
wharves &c.

Concerning these reparations, they are easily
maintained, being lately new builded [at] her
Majesty's charge.

6. Item.—To continue all her Majesty's navy in
serviceable order &c.

Touching this article something is said in the
third ; but concerning any one new ship builded at
Mr. Hawkyns' charges, it is unknown ; though there
hath been a nomination of 3 or 4 to be new builded
ere this time ; and the Elizabeth Jonas[3] as this year ;
but divers were repaired in dry docks, as shall be
noted in the sequel hereof ; but the greatest part
was done at her Majesty's charge, so that Mr.
Hawkyns kept himself within the compass of his
1,700 a year.   And the greatest and [chargeable]
building now being at hand, good time it is to
revoke.   And for the continuing of [the number of]
ships, he hath put away one old ship and put
another in her place.   [Whether this be] answerable
to the condition or no, let it be judged.

7. Item.—To ground the ships upon all occasions &c.

[1] MS. ocome.
[2] Marginal note in Burghley's hand. ' Pocket ' perhaps means
' picked.'
[3] To be rebuilt must be meant. She was thirty years old.

Touching this article it hath relation to the third.

8. Item.—That all the boats, cocks, pinnaces and lighters, shall be kept &c.

Concerning boats, cocks, and pinnaces, there hath been a late supply of divers and many new ones to answer such as were decayed and wanting. At whose charge the same is, may easily be known.

9. Item.—He shall find Norway masts for all the small ships, &c.

What masts hath been found at his charge is uncertain; but well known it is that there hath been above 20 thrust in among the Queen's Majesty's masts at Chatham, of Norway trees, and an entry made of 200*l.* for the same, at her Majesty's charge.

10. Item.—At All-Hallowtide every year there shall be presented unto the Lord Treasurer &c.

Touching this article, the condition is not observed, unless it may have relation to the two master shipwrights' late survey, which is far more favourable than otherwise it would have been, being laid open to so many; which, if it had so come to pass, many do doubt that divers of the ships now upon the way to sea should have tarried behind.

The conditions tending to the behalf of Mr. John Hawkyns, divided into 10 several articles.

First.—The said John Hawkyns shall have paid him for the services &c.

Touching this article, if Mr. Hawkyns had performed his bargain and contented himself with a reasonable gain, then the warrant of 5,714*l.* 2*s.* had been well bestowed. But having a further allowance not less than a 1,000*l.* a year, as his fellows the officers affirm, and yet thinketh all too much that is done, saying the ships are in good state and

order for these 7 years, and their state known to the
contrary,—who can say in truth this money well
bestowed, the condition on the other side not performed ?

2. Item.—He shall be holpen with the com
mission as in *Anno* 1578 &c.

This commission hath been very beneficial unto
him, not only in furnishing her Majesty's yard with
planks, timber, boards &c. ; but also one other
yard in Deptford, which he reapeth benefit as a
partner ; which yard hath and doth consume more
than her Majesty's yard hath done within 2 years, in
serving the subject ; which breedeth ill speeches in
the country, and may hinder the service to come.
Besides let it be examined how he exacteth of her
Majesty in the prices of such stuff as is proper to
the service, either at Deptford or Chatham.   Let it
be at this instant viewed at Chatham, and truly
reported what stuff there is which is taken account
of for the charges of this quarter to come.   All
shells and imperfect timber is vented[1] there.   The
shipwrights must use it, but cannot remedy it ; so it
will continue in disorder still in making an officer a
purveyor.

3. Item.—It shall be lawful for him to entertain
as many shipwrights as he will &c.

In this condition he spared himself and charged
her Majesty.   For upon the late setting forth the
ships, when the Lord Admiral would have the
workmen augmented, he said there were too many,
and more than could be well occupied.   And such
other as he kept in ordinary, divers of them he
promised much and performed nothing.

4. Item.—If any of the ships come to mischance,
as God forbid &c.

This condition her Majesty hath accomplished

---

[1] Discharged, shot out.

to the uttermost. In the Revenge, which ship, by
beating upon the ground at Portsmouth, had some
decayed place in her keel, which was perfected for a
matter of 40, but he had a recompense of 70 ; the
rest was easily borne. As for boats, cocks, and
pinnaces, it is to be thought a sufficient allowance is
given for such as are lost.

5. Item.—If the whole navy should go to the
seas, or a great part of them &c.

In this article Mr. Hawkyns is not charged at
the setting forth of the ships for [all [1]] sea store
above 40s. The rest is borne by her Majesty.
But who hath the dividing [the sea [1]] store, the
examining of the quantity, the manner of the stuff,
and the rates of the [same [1]] ? Most times his
partner or his man. The master shipwrights may
look upon them and [open [1]] their eyes, but cannot
remedy it ; but it will be seen and easily perceived
when the d[ividing [1]] is made.

6. Item.—The said John Hawkyns shall have
the assistance of shipkeepers &c.

This condition is not denied him, though it be
with grief of poor men, which he at the first did
gratify, and giveth nothing now.

7. Item.—He shall have the use of the wharves,
storehouses &c.

Although the use of her Majesty's wharves, yards,
storehouses were proper and incident to his bargain,
so, that being void, they are at liberty for any service
to come, and no condition broken.

8. Item.—If the ships shall ride in any other
place &c.

If he shall require a recompense of a small matter
in his moorings, he may consider what hath been
spared by those ships that hath been abroad at the

---

[1] These words in brackets are conjectural. A piece of the
margin of the MS. is quite torn away.

seas and spent nothing; besides the yearly gain gotten by the moorings, not so little as 500*l.* a year, all pensions and charges paid.

9. Item.—When a new ship shall be made and ready to launch &c.

That new ship is yet to make at Mr. Hawkyns' charge; but he hath made the commodity of an old one aforehand, as it is noted in the first page, the 6 article.[1]

10. Item.—If any ambiguity or doubt shall happen of either part &c.

If the premises be well considered according to equity and conscience, her Majesty hath great cause to call the conditions in question and be resolved of the same; which the honourable [2] at their discretions are to consider of, as God shall move them.

Ships repaired in the time of Mr. Hawkyns' bargain for 2 or 3 y[ears] at the most, except the Revenge:

The Elizabeth Jonas ⎫
The Triumph ⎭
⎧The charge of these ships
⎪was borne by the venturers
⎨with Sir Francis [Drake] at
⎪the setting forth of the Bona-
⎪venture, Sea Dragon and the
⎩Aid, the last of July 1585.

The Antelope ⎫
The Hope   ⎪
The Victory ⎬
The Aid   ⎪
The Swallow⎭
⎧For those ships he had so large
⎨allowance by the officers, as a small
⎩charge besides was bestowed.

The Revenge.—For the Revenge he had allowed him 700*l.*, and the whole charge was under 1,000*l.* lately done at Woolwich.

The Merlin
a small pinnace.

[1] P. 40.   [2] 'Commissioners' seems to be omitted.

January 23.—*HOWARD TO BURGHLEY.*

[B.M. Harl. MS. 6994, f. 112.—Holograph. Addressed.]

My honourable and good Lord :—I have received your Lordship's favourable letter, and am much bound unto your Lordship for your Lordship's favours. I would to God your Lordship's health and strength were answerable to your mind ; then I am sure this company here with me should be happy to see your Lordship here.

My Lord, on Wednesday last I went to Harwich to see the town and the haven, which I had not seen this 27 years. My Lord, it is a place to be made much of, for the haven hath not his fellow in all respects not in this realm, and specially as long as we have such enemies so near us as they be in the Low Countries, and not more assured than we are of Scotland. My Lord, we can bring all the ships that her Majesty hath, aground there in 3 springs. I know not that we can do so in any place else but here at Chatham. That which is a-doing above the town will be to very good purpose for any sudden [attack [1]], and for my part I wish it were as strong as Flushing.

I received a letter from my Lord Cobham, of an enterprise that is sent down to burn all such ships of her Majesty's as shall ride before the Rammekens or thereabouts. I received this letter as I was half the way coming homewards from Harwich. I presently sent away a pinnace, with John Wynter in her, your Lordship's servant, and did send the advertisement unto Sir William Russell,[2] with a letter

[1] Word omitted.
[2] Fourth son of Francis, Earl of Bedford, the godfather of Sir Francis Drake. At this time Governor of Flushing ; Lord Deputy

of my own; and likewise I did write unto the captains of her Majesty's ships, with certain instructions, which, if the device be attempted, I believe you shall hear they shall smart for their device. There is two ships and a pinnace : their victuals cometh out about an eight days hence, so that then they will come away. In the meantime, if nothing be done already, I doubt not but they shall safely come away. My good Lord, God send you ever well to do : and so I bid your Lordship most heartily farewell. From aboard the Bear, the 23rd of January, 1587.

Your Lordship's most assured always to command,

C. Howard.

January 24.—HOWARD TO WALSYNGHAM.

[ccviii. 22.—Holograph. Addressed.]

Sir :—I most humbly thank you for your letters. I cannot tell what to think of my brother Stafford's [1] advertisement ; for if it be true that the King of Spain's forces be dissolved, I would not wish the Queen's Majesty to be at this charges that she is at ; but if it be but a device, knowing that a little thing maketh us too careless, then I know not what may come of it. But this I am sure of; if her Majesty would have spent but a 1,000 crowns to have had some intelligence, it would have saved her twenty times as much. Assure yourself he [2] knoweth what we do here; and if the army be or do dissolve, it is the preparation that her Majesty

of Ireland in 1594 ; raised to the peerage in 1603, as Baron Russell of Thornhaugh, in Northampton ; died in 1613.

[1] Sir Edward Stafford, the English ambassador in Paris, had married Howard's sister Douglas, the widow of Lord Sheffield.

[2] The King of Spain.

hath made that is the cause; for he cannot abide
this heat[1] that is provided for him. He did never
think that we would thus have provided for his
coming, but that the number of false alarums that
he hath given her Majesty would have made her to
have taken no alarum, and so to have had the
vantage; and the chopping[2] up of his friends here I
am sure he doth not like; and if they be up, I wish
they should continue so till there be a good peace,
which I pray to God to send us.

Sir, if your next advertisements do assure the
dissolving of the army in Spain, then it were good
we did so here; yet if the Duke of Parma continue
his, and that there be any doubt of anything
intended for Scotland, put but three or four more
ships to them in the Narrow Seas and I dare assure
you it shall beat any power he shall be able to make,
and impeach him of any attempt in Scotland; and
I will take upon me the service myself; for I assure
you it doth grieve me to see her Majesty at more
charges than is needful, and this charge will not be
great. I would fain keep the Narrow Seas three
or four months; I persuade myself I shall do some
service.

Upon your next advertisement, as the cause upon
that shall require, I will write to you, Sir, my good
friend, my opinion, and then you may use it as you
shall think best. And so I pray you to write me
frankly; for I do assure you I will take it kindly
and friendly at your hands, and think myself much
beholden unto you for it; for I may sometimes,
upon a good conceit in my opinion, make such a
journey as I did now to Harwich; and yet it may
not be so well taken there; but I know no cause

[1] MS. heet.
[2] MS. chappyng. The arrest of; to chop = to seize, to lay
hold of. We still speak of 'a fox chopped in cover.'

why it should be but well taken. I do assure you, on my honour, it cost not the Queen's Majesty one halfpenny, nor shall not, when I make any such journey. I will rather spend myself one hundred pounds than to spend her one penny. Thus, good Mr. Secretary I am bold with you, as my special good friend ; and so bid you most heartily farewell, and God send you health and strength. From the Bear, the 24th of January.

Your assured loving friend to use,

C. Howard.

January 27.—HOWARD TO WALSYNGHAM.

[ccviii. 30.—Signed. Addressed.]

Sir :—I most heartily thank you for your letter and for your advertisements. If it were not for you I should live in a dead place for hearing of anything.

Touching Sir Francis Drake, I have likewise received a letter from him with the like advertisement. There happened a mischance in one of his ships at Portsmouth, that a piece broke and killed a man, with some other hurt. If you would write a word or two unto him to spare his powder, it would do well.[1]

Sir, I send you herewith enclosed all the copies of the letters from my Lord Chamberlain again, which I most heartily thank you for, and I pray to God the Scottish King do deceive me, but I am afeared he will not. For my own part, I have made of the French King, the Scottish King, and the

---

[1] This scarcely seems to warrant Mr. Froude's inference of the Queen's parsimony. ' Drake,' he says, ' had offended her by consuming ammunition at target practice. She would not give him a second opportunity ' (*History of England*, xii. 369).

King of Spain, a Trinity that I mean never to trust to be saved by; and I would others were, in that, of my opinion.

Sir, there was never, since England was England, such a stratagem and mask made to deceive England withal as this is of the treaty of peace. I pray God we have not cause to remember one thing that was made of the Scots by the Englishmen; that we do not curse for this a long grey beard with a white head, witless, that will make all the world think us heartless. You know whom I mean.[1]

I have received a letter from Sir Henry Palmer, that there is at Dunkirk divers hoys and lighters, that be filled with ballast and great stones, surely [means [2]] for the stopping of some haven. I will have a watch on them.

I pray you, Sir, send me word when you think the Commissioners will be sent over, that I may have all things ready for them; and I pray you let me know if any go in Sir Amyas Poulet's[3] place; for if he be able to go himself, if I may know of it, I will have especial care of him, that he may go at ease.

[1] Motley thinks that Lord Burghley is here indicated. More probably it is Sir James Croft, comptroller of the household, and one of the commissioners for the treaty. He was suspected of holding traitorous correspondence with Parma, and on his return in August was sent to the Tower, where he remained till December 1589. He was very old, and perhaps dotard rather than traitor. He died in 1591.

[2] Torn away.

[3] Of Hinton St. George, Somerset, grandson of that Sir Amyas Poulet who is reputed to have set Wolsey in the stocks. He had himself earned the hatred of the Catholic party by the strictness of his conduct when charged with the custody of the Queen of Scots. At this time he was Chancellor of the Order of the Garter, Governor of Jersey and Guernsey, and one of the commissioners for the treaty. His failing health prevented his going to the Low Countries. He died September 26, 1588, and was buried in London, in the church of St. Martin's-in-the-Fields.

Sir, if there be at any time any matter of importance wherein I may do any service there with you, I can be quickly there and here again.

I pray you, Sir, let it be thought on, as you see cause upon your advertisements, it will ask a good time[1] to furnish our fleet again with men as they were. I do not look to see it ever bettered. I pray God it be as well when there shall be cause. And so giving you most hearty thanks for your most friendly dealing with me in all causes, and your friendly remembrance, I bid you most heartily farewell. From aboard her Majesty's good ship the White Bear, the 27th of January, 1587.

> Your assured loving friend,
> C. HOWARD.

January 28.—*HOWARD TO WALSYNGHAM.*

[ccviii. 31.—Holograph. Addressed.]

Sir :—I had forgotten in my last letter to answer the matter you did write in touching Captain Morgan, my man. If he had been here I would have sent him unto you ; but he is extreme sick at London, and, as I do understand, in some danger ; which I am very sorry for, for he is a tall gentleman. He hath the charge of all my soldiers in my ship, and hath done his duty very well. I hope he will answer all honestly and well.

Sir, if the Commissioners be once[2] gone over and that there be a surcease of arms, it shall be but folly and to no purpose for me to lie here. I think both I and the noblemen, leaving sufficient lieutenants in our ships, and the officers, as Sir W.

---

[1] Let it be borne in mind that it will need a good time &c.
[2] MS. wonse.

Wynter, Mr. Hawkyns and Mr. Borough,[1] remain here with the navy will be sufficient[2] ; for before these ships can have their full number of men again it will be a month to gather them, do what we can. And I pray to God we have them when we shall need ; for many are gone abroad, and specially the chiefest men ; God send me to see such a company together again when need is. I protest it before God I write not this to you because I am weary with being here ; for if it were not for her Majesty's presence I had rather live in the company of these noble ships than in any place. And yet would I be glad that there were something to do. I am more sorrier for the noblemen than any ways for myself ; for I would have them save, to spend when need shall be. I do assure you they live here bountifully, and it will be hard finding of such noblemen as these be, so well affected to this service and that will love the sea so well as they do.

Sir, if you think that my continuing here with the navy serve to good purpose, I shall like well of it ; but methinks if there be a surcease of arms, then my lying here will make a jest to many, and they have reason. I think it will be a most fittest time to ground our ships in, for now, at our coming out, it was you know on such a sudden as we could not ground but two or three of the middle sort, so as the great ships were not grounded. I have, with the advice of the officers and masters, thought good to begin with some the next spring, and so in a three springs dispatch them all, and have them all in most excellent order by the midst of March, all save the

[1] MS. Bowros.
[2] His meaning is—I and the noblemen (see *ante* p. 24) may come up to the court, leaving our ships in charge of the lieutenants, the principal officers of the navy remaining in command of the fleet, which will be sufficient.

men ; and I doubt not but the ships shall prove
some[1] notable liars, and if cause fall out, do a better
day of service for England than ever ships did for it
yet.   But this assure yourself, if the forces of Spain
do come before the midst of April, there will be as
much ado to have men to furnish us, as ever was ;
but men we must have, or else the ships will do no
good.   God knows it is but a bare sight to see us
now to that it was, and I would not wish any to take
the pains to come to see us till we are newly supplied, when cause shall be.   Sir, God send you well
to do and continuance of your health, and so I bid
you most heartily farewell.   From aboard her
Majesty's good ship the Bear, the 28th of January.

Your assured loving friend,
C. HOWARD.

Jan. 29.—CONDITIONS OF JAMES QUARLES.

[ccviii. **35.**]

XXIXmo die Januarii 1587.—The humble
petition and demand of James Quarles, surveyor of
the victuals for her Majesty's navy, if it be her
Highness' pleasure that he shall serve by rate :—
videlicet—

First, he desireth to be allowed from the first of
July last, 7*d.* the man at the seas, and 6½*d.* in
harbour, as Mr. Baeshe[2] then had by virtue of privy
seal, and so to continue unto it shall please God to

---

[1] Some persons to be &c.—*viz.* those who have spoken ill of
Hawkyns.   See *ante*, p. 38 *et seq.*

[2] Edward Baeshe, of an old Gloucestershire family, was Sur-
veyor-General of Victuals for the navy for upwards of forty years.
He was twice sheriff of Hertfordshire, and died in April 1587.
The fact that he left his widow but poorly provided for seems to
speak of an integrity then far from common.

send mitigation of the dearth of victuals that now be, to such reasonable prices as are here under-written ; where it doth appear what they were at such time as Mr. Baeshe did first serve by rate, and so did continue a long time, until late years, and what now they be ; whereby then he was able to serve for 5½*d.* in harbour and 6*d.* at the seas, and so will I do most willing her Majesty the like service.

Item, whereas Mr. Baeshe had two thousand pounds to continue with him to amplify his store for all sudden service, I do but desire to have 500*l.* to furnish two thousand men for one month upon 16 days warning.

Item, forasmuch as the store of clapboard [1] is for the most part wasted, and that it is most necessary that her Majesty should not be unfur-nished, to have in readiness to make three thousand tons of cask, I would pray for the speedy perfor-mance of the same, to have one thousand pounds delivered unto me, to make provision of the said cask ; which thousand pounds I will repay again into her Majesty's Exchequer at the end of 6 years next following.

Item, I desire that I may have all such her Majesty's brewhouses, bakehouses and storehouses, with the grounds thereunto belonging, in such manner and form as the said Mr. Baeshe had.

The charges of one man's victual at the seas for one flesh day :

$$
\left.\begin{array}{l}
\text{Biscuit, 1 lb.} \quad . \qquad . \qquad 1d. \\
\text{Beer, 1 gallon.} \quad . \qquad . \qquad 1\tfrac{3}{4}d. \\
\text{Beef, 2 lb.} \qquad . \qquad . \qquad 5\tfrac{1}{2}d.
\end{array}\right\} 8\tfrac{1}{4}d.
$$

[1] Small oak boards used for cask staves. The word still appears in Customs' schedules.

The charges of one man's victuals at the seas on the fish day :

Biscuit, 1 lb. . . . 1*d.* ⎞
Beer, 1 gallon. . . 1¾*d.* ⎟
Butter, ¼ lb. . . . ½*d.* ⎬ 4¾*d.*
Cheese, ¼ lb. . . . ½*d.* ⎟
Stockfish, ¼ fish . . 1*d.* ⎠

Mem : in these two days victuals there is nothing demanded for biscuit bags, necessary lading charges, clerks' wages, surveyors' wages and all other incidents pertaining to sea service, which maketh a further increase of money.

A declaration of the prices of sea victuals that was at such time as Mr. Baeshe first served at a rate and so continued a long time till these late years, and what prices be at this present.

	What they were	What they are
Wheat	16s. the qr.	20s.
Beer	18s. the tun	26s. 8d.
Beef, being good	12s. the cwt.	17s.
Butter	{40s. & 42s. the dearest	4l. 10s.
Stockfish	11l. the last	20l.
Casks	5s. 4d. the ton	8s.
Canvas for biscuit bags	3½d. the ell	8d.

When hereafter it shall appear unto your Honours that the high prices of victuals which now be are in any remarkable sort mitigated, and especially beef, I will serve her Majesty most willingly at such rates as hath been heretofore ; otherwise I am not able to serve without extreme loss and undoing, as by due proof I am able to make it appear unto your Honours.

MEMORANDA BY LORD BURGHLEY.

[ccviii. 43.—Autograph.   Not dated.]

That the whole navy be ready to go out of Thames by the 10th of March ; to be in Portsmouth by the end of March ; to pass with the 3 part of their charges.[1]

That the Swallow pass from Portsmouth westward with mariners and gunners.

That soldiers be in readiness upon the coasts to be shipped.

That two men be found out to pass to Lisbon for intelligence.

That all English ships of subjects meet for service be stayed and put in order to be in readiness against April, to serve as cause shall require.

To provide muskets out of Holland at 23s. 4d. a piece.

That Nicholas Gorges[2] and some such as Thomas Digges[3] may, by order of the Earl of Leicester, make a view through Holland and Zealand of all kind of ships, and of the number of mariners.

[1] To be paid an imprest, or advance.

[2] Great-grandson of Sir Edmund Gorges of Wraxall, in Somerset, by his wife Anne, eldest daughter of. John Howard, first Duke of Norfolk. He was thus third cousin of the Queen, second cousin once removed of the Lord Admiral, and first cousin of Edward Gorges of Wraxall, the father of Sir Ferdinando Gorges, who has been styled 'the father of English colonisation in America.' In July and August he commanded the ships fitted out by the city of London.

[3] A mathematician, surveyor and military engineer of high repute ; muster-master general of the English forces in the Netherlands, 1586-94 ; died 1595. He was the author of many works on mathematical and military subjects ; among others, of *A Treatise on the Art of Navigation ; A Treatise of Architecture Nautical ; A Treatise of Great Artillery and Pyrotechny ; A Treatise of Fortification.*

That the Earl of Leicester do solicit the States
to arm a power of ships to attend on the Queen's
navy.

A bargain for 2 great galleons and one meaner,
and 6 pinnaces.

MEMORANDUM OF SPANISH SHIPS.

[ccviii. **44.**—In Howard's hand.   Not dated.]

These in Guipuscoa.

In Santander .	16 new ships between 100 and 140.
In the Passage .	. 14 of the like burden.
In Laredo . .	. 8 pataches.
In San Sebastian.	. 6 ships of 300 and 4 of 200.
In Bilbao . .	. 6 pataches.
In Figuera . .	. 4 ships of 100.

Some built in the River of Fuenterrabia.

In the River of Seville,	8 ships of 300 and 200 apiece and 4 pataches.
In Saint Mary Port .	2 galleys made short and broad and 4 pataches.

February 1.—*HOWARD TO WALSYNGHAM*

[ccviii. **46.**—Signed.   Addressed.]

Sir :—I have received your letter, and by the same
messenger, a letter from my Lord Treasurer, and
my Lord Steward,[1] whereby I perceive the great
preparation in Dunkirk for Scotland.

I am advised by their Lordships to have care of
it, which I will do to the uttermost of my power.   It

---

[1] The Earl of Leicester.

doth appear no less by your letter but that we may assure ourselves that Scotland is the mark which they shoot at to offend[1] us, and therefore most necessary to provide for that. I have written mine opinion at large in mine answer to that their Lordships' letter, which I know you shall be acquainted with; and therefore, if you do think it reasonable that I have written for her Majesty's service, I pray you let it have your furtherance, knowing that you are so well bent to spend her Majesty's purse, rather than to hazard her honour; and for my own part, had rather be drawn in pieces with wild horses than that they should pass through for Scotland and I lie here.

Sir, thus her Majesty shall see what will come of this abusing peace in hand.

For your advertisements of Spain which should come in April, if we cut off this matter of Scotland, I hope we shall not need to fear the forces in Spain, neither in April nor in May.

Sir, I pray you bear with me that I remember you of this. It doth appear by mine instructions, as also as a matter determined in Council, that the setting forth of this fleet which we have here was for these two purposes:—the one for an invasion from the Duke of Parma upon this part of the realm; the other for going with forces into Scotland. Now what did move her Majesty, or upon what ground, I know not, to diminish our forces here; for if any of both those should happen upon the sudden, we shall be able to do even as much good for the service as the hoys[2] which lie at Lyon Quay[3]; for there is no master in England that will undertake, with those men that are now in them, to carry back again the ships to Chatham; and I do warrant you our state is well enough known to them in Flanders, and as

[1] Injure.   [2] MS. whoyse.   [3] Just below London Bridge.

we were a terror to them at first coming out, so do they now make but little reckoning of us ; for they know that we are like bears tied to stakes, and they may come as dogs to offend us, and we cannot go to hurt them. But as I would be loth to be any deviser of her Majesty's charge, so do I thank God I was no counsellor of this that is done ; and I hope that if things fall not out according to your expectation and the rest of my Lords, that I may be excused. Yet will I not fail with the uttermost of my power to be ready to impeach any mischief that may be intended.

I have a good company here with me, and so good willers to her Majesty's service, that if the Queen's Majesty will not spare her purse, they will not spare their lives and that which they have. And so I leave; looking every hour to hear from you of more mischief coming by this disputation of peace than any good that ever shall come of it, I bid you most heartily farewell. From off aboard her Majesty's ship the White Bear, this first of February, 1587.

Your most assured and
affectionate friend,
C. HOWARD.

February 1.—*HAWKYNS TO WALSYNGHAM.*

[ccviii. 47.—Signed. Addressed.]

My duty humbly remembered unto your Honour : Having of long time seen the malicious practices of the papists combined generally throughout Christendom to alter the government of this realm and to bring it to papistry, and consequently to servitude, poverty and slavery, I have a good will from time to time to do and set forward something as I could have credit to impeach their purpose. But it hath prevailed little, for that there was never any substantial ground laid to be followed effectually, and therefore it hath taken bad effect, and bred great charge, and we still in worse case and less assurance of quietness.

I do therefore now utter my mind particularly to your Honour how I do conceive some good to be done at last. I do see we are desirous to have peace, as it becometh good christians, which is best for all men ; and I wish it might any way be brought to that pass ; but in my poor judgment the right way is not taken.

If we stand at this point in a mammering [1] and at a stay, we consume, and our Commonwealth doth utterly decay. I shall not need to speak of our estate, for that your Honour knoweth it far better than I do : neither need I to rehearse how dead and uncertain our traffics be ; most men in poverty and discontented, and especially the poorer sort ; our navigation not set on work ; but the French and Scots eat us up, and grow in wealth and freights, and not assured to us in friendship. Our treasure doth consume infinitely with these uncertain wars, and nothing assured to us but new and continual charge. We have to choose either a dishonourable and uncertain peace, or to put on virtuous and valiant minds, to make a way through with such a settled war as may bring forth and command a quiet peace.

This peace which we have in hand hath little likelihood to be good for us, but to win a better time for them. They may easily see how glad we are to embrace peace, and might dissolve their forces without fear of any danger if they meant well. But they do rather increase their forces ; and

[1] Hesitating.

although they do nothing, yet in keeping us in charge both abroad and at home, they will both shake our store and impoverish the poor commons.

Therefore, in my mind, our profit and best assurance is to seek our peace by a determined and resolute war, which no doubt would be both less charge, more assurance of safety, and would best discern our friends from our foes both abroad and at home, and satisfy the people generally throughout the whole realm.

In the continuance of this war I wish it to be ordered in this sort, that first, we have as little to do in foreign countries as may be but of mere necessity, for that breedeth great charge and no profit at all.

Next, that there be always six principal good ships of her Majesty's upon the coast of Spain, victualled for four months and accompanied with some six small vessels, which shall haunt the coast of Spain and the Islands, and be a sufficient company to distress anything that goeth through the seas. And when these must return, there would be other six good ships, likewise accompanied, to keep the place. So should that seas be never unfurnished ; but as one company at the four months end doth return, the other company should be always in the place.

The charge of these companies would not be above 1,800 men in one fleet, which may be 2,700*l.* a month for wages and victuals. And it will be a very bad and an unlucky month that will not bring in treble that charge, for they can see nothing but it is presently their own.

If this may be done with so easy a charge, and recompensed double and treble, why should we stick at it ? Some will say, the King will always make a fleet to beat us from the coast. There is no doubt but, with an infinite charge, he may make an army. But it shall be sufficient that this small company shall live daily in their sight and weary them, and gain daily upon them. For an army, as he provideth, cannot continue any long time. His fleet from the Indies and all places can have hard escaping ; which if we might once strike, our peace were made with honour, safety and profit.

For these six ships, we shall not break the strength of the navy ; for we shall leave a sufficient company always at home to front any violence that can be any way offered unto us. I do herewith send a note how the ships may be fitted, and what they are, and what will be left at home. In open and lawful wars, God will help us, for we defend the chief cause, our religion, God's own cause ; for if we would leave our profession and turn to serve Baal (as God forbid, and rather to die a thousand deaths), we might have peace, but not with God. By open wars all the subjects of this realm should know what to do. They would not only be satisfied in conscience, but they would, every man that loveth God, the Queen and his country, contribute, set forward, fight, devise, and do somewhat for the liberty and freedom of this country. By open wars, all the Jesuits and ill affected persons would be discerned and cut off from the hope of their malicious practices. Many things more might be said to the preferring of open war before a dis-sembled peace, which God doth best allow, and the well affected people of the realm do desire, even to the spending of a great portion of their substance. And therefore I conclude that with God's blessing and a lawful open war, the Lord shall bring us a most honourable and quiet peace, to the glory of his church and to the honour of her

Majesty and this realm of England ; which God for
his mercy's sake grant. And so I leave to trouble
your Honour. From aboard the Bonaventure, the
first of February, 1587.

> Your Honour's humbly to command,
> JOHN HAWKYNS.

February 5.—*LIST OF SHIPS TO BE IN
ORDER OF SERVICE.*

[ooviii. 52.—Endorsed.]

Ships to be in order of service with their full
numbers at the seas, as followeth :
At Queenborough with my Lord Admiral.

	Men
The Ark Ralegh . . .	400
Bonaventure . . .	250
Mary Rose . . .	250
Lion	250
Vanguard	250
Dreadnought . . .	200
Swallow	160
Foresight	160
Spy	35
Merlin	35
Sun	30
Cygnet	20
Fancy	20
Two Ketches	20
The George	20
Men	2,100

With Sir Henry Palmer.

					Men
The Rainbow	.	.	.	.	250
Antelope	.	.	.	.	160
Bull	.	.	.	.	100
Tiger	.	.	.	.	100
Tramontana	.	.	.		70
Scout	.	.	.		70
Achates	.	.	.	.	60
Charles	.	.	.	.	40
Moon	.	.	.	.	40
			Sum	.	890
					2,100
			All the men at sea		2,990

The whole numbers of men serving at the seas, besides the ships with Sir Francis Drake, are 2,990 men, which makes in charge monthly, for wages and victuals [1] .   .   .   .   4,534*l.* 16*s.* 8*d.*

Ships to remain at Chatham with 200 men as followeth :

The Elizabeth Jonas	.		.	50
Triumph	.	.	.	50
Bear	.	.	.	50
Victory	.	.	.	50
				200 men

Which may be a charge monthly for wages and victuals.   .   .   .   .   .   303*l.* 6*s.* 8*d.*

The monthly charge of the whole is

4,785*l.* 1*s.* 8*d.*[2]

[1] At 30*s.* 4*d.* per man for the month.

[2] The Merlin, in the Queenborough list, was at first omitted and afterwards written in between the lines. In the other places affected, the totals of men and money were corrected ; but in this final result the error was allowed to remain. It should be 4,838*l.* 3*s.* 4*d.*

Feb. 5.—*ESTIMATE OF CHARGE OF SHIPS*

[ccviii. 53.]

The 5th of February, 1587.

The charge of the ships with Sir Francis Drake :

The Revenge	250	The Advice .	35
Hope .	250	Makeshift	35
Nonpareil	250	Twenty - three	
Swiftsure	180	other ships	
Aid . .	120	which have	
	——	in number	1,780
	1,050		——
	——		1,850
			1,050
			——

Total 2,900 men

The monthly charge of these 2,900 men is for wages and victuals . . . 4,398*l.* 8*s.* 8*d.*

By the last conclusion before my Lord Treasurer it was agreed that there should be continued in charge only 1,315 men, which is a charge for wages and victuals monthly . . . 1,994*l.* 8*s.* 4*d.*

There is already order given to Mr. Quarles for to victual all the ships under my Lord Admiral's charge and Sir Henry Palmer's to the 14th day of March next.

Now there is a new order to be given to the said Mr. Quarles to victual the ships which are to be wholly under my Lord Admiral's charge, which have in them 2,955 [1] men and shall be victualled to the 20th day of April next which is 37 days, to begin the 15th of March next and to end the 20th

[1] The Merlin being omitted.

of April following, both days included, which victualling is a charge of . . 3,188*l.* 14*s.* 9*d.*[1]

The 200 men left in the four great ships may be victualled from time to time upon the ordinary.

Feb. 11.—*HOWARD TO SIR F. WALSYNGHAM.*

[ccviii. 64.—Holograph. Addressed.]

Sir :—I was no sooner come down but I imparted unto my Lord Sheffield that which you had told me, who went presently aboard with no small care to find out his party ; and I assure you, with much grief that any such thing should happen in his ship. Himself was to depart to London that afternoon upon very earnest business, which I gave him leave for ; but he left such a strait commandment with Mr. Ha. Sheffield, his lieutenant, for the finding out of the truth of this, as he said to him, being his kinsman, if he had care of his honour or well doing, he would take pains in it. And yet my Lord himself, as great haste as he had, made the barber, and three or four more which he suspected, to be sworn ; and so they were ; and they utterly[2] renounced the Pope's authority.[3]

Mr. Sheffield, after my Lord's departure, took great pains and did examine the barber, and found that a two or three years agone, he was something inclined to papistry, but being matched by his wife with a honest race,[4] as it seems they converted him. I have talked with the man myself. He offers to receive,[5] and to do anything that a good Protestant should do.

This was the cause I think that bred the doubt

[1] At 7*d.* a day, or 16*s.* 4*d.* a month of 28 days, this should be 3,188*l.* 18*s.* 9*d.* No known rate can give the 14*s.*
[2] MS. outerly.   [3] MS. atoryte.
[4] His wife's relations.   [5] The Blessed Sacrament.

in him. He had a book that was done by an
English papist beyond the seas ; a bad book ; but
he brought it to the preacher, with dislike of the
book ; and the preacher is counted to be a most
zealous man and very honest. The barber had
many good books, as the New Testament, the Book
of Common Prayer, the Book of the Psalms which
he daily sang with the company. The man was prest
by the Company of Surgeons, for he is a barber-
surgeon, and not by my Lord ; and he hath sailed
often in her Majesty's ships, and accounted a very
honest man. I think my Lord Sheffield will send you
the party, and I believe you will not mislike him.

Mr. Ha. Sheffield, who is very earnest and zealous
in religion, sware unto me that it made him rejoice at
the heart to see how earnest my Lord Sheffield was
in it, and to hear him use those words he did, which
was most vehement [1] against papists, so be-traitoring
them, saying he that was in his ship that would not
be sworn against the Pope, he would take him for a
traitor, and so use him. And this I dare assure you :
no man whosoever is readier to communicate than
my Lord Sheffield is, which I thank God for.

Sir, Newton,[2] my man, who came from Dover
yesterday, telleth me that one that came from
Calais doth report for certainty that the Duke of
Guise hath sent down to St. Omers 20 ensigns [3] of
soldiers, and that they are to come to Dunkirk. If
it be true, I think my Lord Cobham [4] hath certified
you. I hope this next spring, which will be on
Friday next, if the wind suit us, to go into the
Narrow Seas ; but this wind, as it is, locks us in
fast enough. The Antelope and the Swallow,
which should have gone to Sir Ha. Palmer this day

---

[1] MS. vemente.

[2] This is probably the William Newton who appears in the
list as master of the admiral's pinnace Marygold.

[3] MS. ansynse.   [4] Lord Warden of the Cinque Ports.

sennight, could never since stir, if a realm had been on it. Therefore you may see, in time of service, it is better to be at sea, than locked up in harbour. This wind, a Dunkirker cannot stir out ; they are fast locked in as well as we are.

We have had much ado here in changing out of one ship into another[1] ; but now it is done, victual and all.

If it be true that I do hear there is 900 mariners come to Dunkirk, it may be, whilst the treaty is, they will attempt something to Walcheren ; or if it be true of these forces to be come down of the Guiseans,[2] they will make a short treaty for manners' sake, and presently, upon the breaking up, they will put into Scotland. I hope, with God's goodness, to have a eye to both. But this would I fain know of you, if there be a surcease of arms betwixt her Majesty and the Duke, and not with the States, if in the meantime they attempt anything to the isle of Walcheren, I hope it is not meant but that I should seek to relieve[3] it ; for I mean to do so, except I have contrary commandment. If there be no surcease of arms, if the Dunkirkers come out, I mean not[4] to follow them, and if they come out with any number, whereby I may perceive that they carry soldiers with them, although there be a surcease of arms, I mean if I can to stay them, till I know more. Sir, I pray let me have your good advice in this ; for whatsoever I shall do it will fall out as it doth continually all things as it is taken.[4]

Sir, I will trouble you no more at this time, but God have you in his keeping, and so I most heartily bid you farewell. The 11th of February.

Your most assured loving friend,

C. HOWARD.

[1] From the White Bear to the Ark.   [2] MS. Gwysans.
[3] MS. syke to relyve.   [4] So in MS.

F 2

Feb. 12.—*MR. HOLSTOK TO JAMES QUARLES.*

[ccviii. 65.—Copy.]

Mr. Quarles :—These are to pray you to deliver victuals for 3,035 men to serve the Queen's Majesty in the ships hereunder written, being now appointed to the seas under the charge of the Lord High Admiral of England, for 37 days, to begin the 15th day of March, and to end the 20th day of April then following ; which ships, some are at Queenborough, and some at the Narrow Seas. Thus, fare you well. Written the 12th day of February, 1587.

Queenborough.

	Men
The Ark	425
Elizabeth Bonaventure .	250
Lion	250
Vanguard	250
Mary Rose . . .	250
Dreadnought . . .	200
Antelope	160
Swallow	160
Foresight	160
Charles	40
Spy	35
Merlin	35
Sun	30
Cygnet	16
Fancy	16
Two Ketches	8
The George Hoy . . .	10
White Lion . . .	50
	2,345
	690
	3,035

Ships at the Seas.*

	Men
The Rainbow	250
Bull	100
Tiger	100
Tramontana . . .	70
Scout	70
Achates	60
Moon	40
	690

Total men in all . . . 3,035

For 37 days' victuals at 7*d.* the man per diem, 3,220*l.* 10*s.* 9*d.* Your loving friend,

WILLM. HOLSTOK.

Mem. 40*l.* of this sum above written is for transportations.[1]

Feb. 14.—*HOWARD TO SIR F. WALSYNGHAM.*

[ccviii. 67.—Holograph. Addressed.]

Sir :—I have received your letter with the advertisement from my Lord of Hunsdon,[2] which I thank you most heartily for, and I am very glad to hear that the King[3] doth run so good a course. I pray to God to continue it. And, Sir, if the Queen's Majesty should stick to relieve him[4] in this

---

[1] The charge of thirty-seven days' victuals for 3,035 men at 7*d.* amounts to 3,275*l.* 5*s.* 5*d.*, which, with 40*l.* added for transportation, gives a total of 3,315*l.* 5*s.* 5*d.*

[2] Henry Carey, born about 1524, created Lord Hunsdon in 1559, was, by his mother, Mary Boleyn, the Queen's first cousin. He had been since 1568 Governor of Berwick and Warden of the East Marches towards Scotland, and since 1583 Lord Chamberlain of the Household. He died in 1596. His eldest daughter, Catherine, was the wife of the Lord Admiral.

[3] Of Scotland. Lord Hunsdon's letter is missing.

[4] MS. styke to relyve.

small matters, she is no good housewife for herself;
for I do not see but this small matter, which my
Lord Chamberlain writeth of, if it be supplied, but
that it is like and most certain to save her 100
thousands of pounds, besides a great deal of blood
of her Majesty's subjects.   For I hold it certain
if the neck of that be broken in Scotland, it will
break all their intent in Spain.   But it must be
done in time, that it may be known in Spain before
they be ready to come out.   And this being done
by her Majesty, she shall be sure that the King of
Spain will never be at that charge he hath been at,
upon any Scottish promise.

Sir, where[1] you write to me that you wish I were
at the seas, I do assure you I long for it ; but the
weather hath been and is so extreme here, the wind
being at East, that we were not able to have our
victuals out of the hoys into the ships before yesterday ; and yet all is not in.   But as the wind is, it
is so in our teeth, as[2] if a realm lay on it we could not
get out.   But assure yourself I will not lose an hour.

I hear for certain that the Duke[3] hath now
gotten a great number of mariners together, and his
ships full rigged, and victuals and all in, so it is like
the next wind that[4] is fit for them they will attempt
something.   But if they do, I hope I shall meet
with them.   My Lord Ha. Seymour hath had an
extreme cold, but yet he will not forbear to do all
services and to be stirring abroad.   I brought him
and old Gray,[5] my master, who was very ill of the

---

[1] Whereas.   [2] That.   [3] Of Parma.   [4] MS. at.
[5] Thomas Gray, the master of the Ark. In 1585 he petitioned,
in the name of the masters of the navy and on behalf of the seamen
of Norfolk and Suffolk, for the maintenance of a watch-light on the
steeple of Winterton, in the town of Great Yarmouth.   He was a
man of some substance ; a shipowner in a small way.   Towards
the end of this year he was in command of the Rainbow. See *post*,
Howard to Burghley, and also Hawkyns' Note of Ships, August 28.

cold, to Rochester, whilst the ships received in their victuals ; and I thank God they are much amended. I think if I had not made them come to Rochester, they would not have been able to have gone to the seas with me; but I found by my Lord Harry that how sick[1] so ever he were, he would not tarry behind me.

Sir, I do hear by report that Campvere[2] and Arnemuiden hath sworn to the Queen's Majesty. If it be so, I am glad of it ; and if Middelburg do not the like, Flushing may easily make them weary. I pray to God to bless her Majesty, and send her to agree and to do that which is best. And so, Sir, with my most hearty thanks unto you for your favours, which I will requite in anything that shall be in my power, God send you health ; and so I bid you most heartily farewell. Chatham, the 14th of February.

Your ever assured and loving friend,
C. HOWARD.

February 15.—HOWARD TO BURGHLEY.

[ccviii. 70.—Copy.]

My very good Lord :—The late bitter time[3] hath sharply handled our men, for that many of them are but ill apparelled ; and the wind is now very bad for us and not likely to change hastily. We may also be forced to seek the coast of Scotland before our return. Therefore I think it fit, with your Lordship's good liking (which all of them earnestly desire), that before their going forth there may be paid unto every of them, for their further relief, six weeks' wages, which is ended since the 11th of this present month of February. The money that is

[1] MS. syk.
[2] Or Vere. Arnemuiden or Armuijen is here generally written Armew or Armu. [3] Time=weather. Cf. Fr. *temps.*

already received was employed for the making of a general pay through the whole navy, from the first of December to the first of January, and for the wages and conduct in discharge of 2,000 men out of the navy to the 18th of January, upon the last diminishing of our numbers.

The sum now required for 6 weeks pay is, for 3,015 men, as I have hereafter noted, at 21*s*. every man, the sum of 3,165*l*. 15*s*. ; which I pray your Lordship may be paid to the Treasurer of the navy, or such as he shall appoint. And so I bid your Lordship right heartily farewell. From Rochester the 15th of February, 1587.

At Queenborough.		The Narrow Seas.	
	Men		Men
The Ark Ralegh .	425	The Rainbow .	250
Bonaventure .	250	Antelope .	160
Lion . .	250	Bull . .	100
Mary Rose .	250	Tiger . .	100
Vanguard .	250	Tramontana .	70
Dreadnought	200	Scout . .	70
Swallow .	160	Achates .	60
Foresight .	160	Charles . .	40
Spy . .	35	Moon . .	40
Merlin . .	35		
Sun . .	30		Men 890
Cygnet . .	20		
Fancy . .	20		
Two Ketches .	20		
The George . .	20		

Men 2,125

Total : 3,015 men at 21*s*. per man is 3,165*l*. 15*s*.

Your Lordship's assured to command,
C. HOWARD.

Feb. 17.—*WM. HAWKYNS*[1] *TO J. HAWKYNS.*

[ccviii. 72.—The bill is signed ; the rest in autograph.]

I have received of Anthony Goddard of Plymouth, merchant, the sum of twenty and five pounds of current money of England—I say 25*l.*—which is to be paid him or to the bringer hereof in London, at sight of this bill, by the hands of the right worshipful John Hawkyns Esquire, Treasurer of her Majesty's navy. Dated in Plymouth, the 17th of February, 1587.

Your loving brother,
Wm. HAWKYNS.

The Hope and Nonpareil are both graved, tallowed and this tide into the road again ; and the Revenge, now aground, I hope she shall likewise go into the road also to-morrow. We have, and do trim one side of every ship by night and the other side by day, so that we end the 3 great ships 3 days this spring. The ships sit aground so strongly, and are so staunch as if they were made of a whole tree. The doing of it is very chargeable, for that it is done by torchlight and cressets, and in an extreme gale of wind, which consumes pitch, tallow and firs abundantly. I wrote you two days past by Clayton who is gone post. Yesterday I received your letter sent with Sir Francis Drake ; and so I take my

---

[1] William Hawkyns, elder brother of the more celebrated John, was at this time Mayor of Plymouth, an office he had held twice before. It was he, rather than John, who, as the owner of numerous privateers, rendered the name of Haquin, Achines, Acle, or de Canes, the terror of French and Spanish merchant ships. He died in October 1589, and was buried in the church of St. Nicholas at Deptford.

leave, this 17th of February, 1587, at 7 of the clock
at night.   Your loving brother,
                                                    WM. HAWKYNS.

Our barrel pitch is all spent 3 days gone, and
very scarce to be had here. If you send 4 or 5 last,
it will serve well for sea-store. These hulks here
have none. If they had, I would buy some.
                                                    W. H.

February 21.—*WM. BOROUGH TO BURGHLEY.*

[ccviii. 77.—Signed. Addressed.]

Right honourable and my very good Lord :—
Inasmuch as I am most deeply bound unto you,
well might I be reputed blameworthy if I should
not, by all good means that possibly I can, acknowledge the same in dutiful wise, and endeavour to
show myself thankful for so great favour and kindness extended towards me in my late distress,[1] even
in such sort as you did, both in time and place,
when and wheresoever great need required, which I
well understand to be far greater than I expected,
and even as much as I could in reason desire.
Wherefore, with faithful heart and loving mind, I
yield most humble and hearty thanks, confessing
myself as much beholden unto your Honour as I
am or may be to any man in the world; which I
cannot, nor will not be unmindful of, God willing,
while breath is in my body. Although I be unable
(I would I were not) to make such requital as I
earnestly desire, yet nevertheless, I am your Lordship's at command in whatsoever you please, and

[1] This refers to his quarrel with Drake in the expedition to
Cadiz, an account of which is given in the Introduction.

will be most ready to do you any service I am able or shall be while I live; yea assuredly, I shall not think my life too dear to do your Honour such good as I desire. Unfeignedly I protest it, humbly desiring your Lordship to accept my good will. As touching the great discontent I have received through Sir Francis Drake's injurious, ungodly, and extreme dealings, which are insupportable, though I have suppressed my grief in the respect of the commandment and charge given me, hoping upon redress for the restoring my credit; and that, inasmuch as I was openly defamed, and causelessly condemned in so vile and shameful sort, I should, likewise in public manner, upon due examination of my guiltless cause, have had the innocency thereof made manifest, so as it might have been apparently known how unjustly and injuriously I have been slandered and abused; but yet I find it is not, neither can I conjecture it is like to be; and therefore must be fain to ease my grief as I may, hoping in good time I shall; who desire not of God any longer to live than I shall show myself a faithful and true hearted subject to my sovereign prince and native country, whose welfare and happy maintenance I beseech the ever living Lord long to continue.

Herewith I send your Honour mine answer[1] touching an objection against me for the coming away of the Lion.

Now it may please your good [Lordship[2]] to be advertised that this day about noon, the Lord Admiral set sail from hence with his fleet, being 8 ships of her Majesty's, viz.—the Ark, the Bonaventure, the Golden Lion, the Vanguard, the Mary Rose, the Dreadnought, the Swallow, and the Foresight, besides the White Lion of my Lord's,

---

[1] This is missing.   [2] Omitted in MS.

and six pinnaces and a ketch. The four great ships remain here at Queenborough, and with them Mr. Hawkyns, myself, and Captain Beeston; which ships we are to bring up to Chatham as soon as we can, and then to ground them and make them ready, as we shall be appointed.

Furthermore, my very good Lord, concerning Mr. Hawkyns' bargain for the navy, Sir Wm. Wynter and I delivered a writing of late to my Lord Admiral, desiring to be resolved therein by his Lordship; who willed us to acquaint your Honour withal. Whereupon I do send you hereinclosed the copy[1] thereof, beseeching your Honour we may understand your Lordship's resolutions touching the same, so as we may be directed by some special warrant. And thus I cease from troubling you, my good Lord, any further, but shall not cease to pray unto Almighty God for your welfare, happiness and bliss; to whose most blessed tuition I commend your Honour, humbly taking my leave. Aboard the White Bear, at Queenborough, the 21st of February, 1587.

Your Lordship's most bounden,

W. Borough.

February 17.—SIR WM. WYNTER AND WM. BOROUGH TO THE LORD ADMIRAL.

[ccviii. 77, I.—Copy.   Signed by Borough.   The enclosure referred to in the foregoing.]

Whereas upon speeches had at Greenwich, before your Lordship and the rest of the Lords of her Majesty's Privy Council, touching a bargain which was offered to be taken by Mr. Hawkyns for the yearly charge of ordinary and extraordinary

[1] The next letter.

in harbour, for keeping and maintaining all her
Majesty's ships and vessels that she then had, there
passed an agreement by your Honours with Mr.
Hawkyns for the said bargain in form as he had set
it down, as himself did shortly after inform us; and
thereupon he proceeded in the execution thereof,
and hath ever since continued the same; till of late,
finding the charge far to surmount the demand
which by his said bargain he required, in such sort
as he was not able to continue it, did therefore (as
he hath informed us) signify the same to the
Queen's Majesty and your Honours, and became
humble suitor that he might leave it at Christmas
last, which he hath done, and maketh account from
that time forwards the office and charge for the navy
is to be ordered and borne as it was in former time,
before any bargain was undertaken.

The charge of the office of late hath grown
great and very intricate by means of the often
rigging, grounding &c., and the number of new
ships and vessels added to those that were there
when the bargain was spoken of; by which means
we are somewhat troubled in dividing the charge.
True it is, that of the said bargain we never saw
any warrant in writing from her Majesty, your
Lordship, nor from any her Majesty's Privy Council; neither have we received any such warrant for
his leaving the same at Christmas last as he accounteth he hath done. We know that it were
hard for him to continue it; nay, that he is not able
to continue it; yet notwithstanding, it must be
left by order; and therefore we desire your good
Lordship, to be directed by special warrant what to
do therein, which we will observe as becometh
faithful servants to her Majesty.

17th of February, *Anno* 1587.
W. WYNTER.   W. BOROUGH.

February 21.—*HOWARD TO BURGHLEY.*

[ccviii. 78.—Signed.   No address nor endorsement.]

My very good Lord :—My son-in-law, Dick
Leveson,[1] hath acquainted me how his father is
about to make sale of some portion of his living, for
the discharge of 2,300*l.* ordered by us presently to
be satisfied to a Dane, in respect of his suggested
losses ; whereunto we were drawn by an opinion
we had conceived of Sir Walter Leveson's victualling and furnishing of the ship, that he had taken
the goods disorderly.   But now, finding, by certain
examinations taken in the Admiralty Court, cause
to conceive far otherwise than was then determined,
and that he is not to be charged but in respect of
the discharge of the promise made by Mr. Dr.
Cæsar and her Majesty's pleasure; and finding himself unable to pay the same presently without such
sale so made before, I am earnestly to pray your
Lordship, both on the behalf of Sir Walter Leveson
and my son-in-law, whose successive inheritance it
doth in like sort concern, to take some such course,
as in your Lordship's wisdom shall seem best and
most convenient, that her Majesty may discharge the
present payment unto the Dane, and that he again,
in some reasonable time, may repay the same unto
her Majesty, whereby the inheritance may be
reserved unto my son-in-law, whose well doing I
must needs be careful of.   And so hoping of your

[1] Richard Leveson, of Lilleshall in Shropshire, born in 1570,
married Margaret, daughter of Howard, in December 1587.   At
this time he was serving as a volunteer in the Ark.   He was
knighted at Cadiz in 1596 ; served continuously through the war ;
was Admiral of the Narrow Seas in 1600, and Vice-Admiral of
England in 1604.   He died without issue in 1605, and was buried
in the old church at Wolverhampton, where there is a monument
to his memory.

Lordship's favourable furtherance to effect this my request, I bid your Lordship most heartily farewell. From aboard her Majesty's good ship the Ark Ralegh, the 21st of February, 1587.

Your Honour's most assured to command,

C. HOWARD.

February 21.—*HOWARD TO BURGHLEY.*

[ccviii. 79.—Holograph. Addressed.]

My honourable and good Lord :—I have received your letter even as I was weighing to go out ; and for the first part, I am most heartily to give your Lordship thanks for your honourable favour. I will acknowledge it with all my love, and ready to do you any service.

For Mr. Hawkyns' bargain : he is presently to repair to the Court, where he shall be best able to answer in his own defence ; but this much I will say to your Lordship : I have been aboard of every ship that goeth out with me, and in every place where any may creep,[1] and I do thank God that they be in the estate they be in ; and there is never a one of them that knows what a leak means. I have known when an Admiral of England hath gone out, and two ships in fleet could not say so. There is none that goeth out now but I durst go to the Rio de la Plata[2] in her ; and yet the Mary Rose and the Swallow be with me, who were ships in the King's Majesty's her father's time.[3] And therefore I dare presume

---

[1] MS. krype.   [2] MS. Ryall de Plato.

[3] Howard was certainly wrong in this. The Mary Rose of Henry VIII.'s time was sunk at Spithead in 1545, and this Mary Rose was not launched till after Elizabeth's accession. Cf. Derrick's *Memoirs of the Royal Navy*, pp. 16, 19, 20, 25. The Swallow seems to have been rebuilt once, if not twice, since the

greatly that those that have been made in her Majesty's time be very good and serviceable, and shall prove them arrant liars that have reported the contrary. And I thank God her Majesty, I hope, may be well assured of their goodness ; yet everything hath his time, and must be helped as need requireth.

My Lord, I had no meaning to carry away all the officers.[1]   I have none with me but Sir W. Wynter.   I leave Mr. Hawkyns and Mr. Borough behind to wait on your Lordship, and to put the four great ships in readiness, which we shall greatly need if the Spanish forces come out.   And so, my Lord, having no more leisure to write at large, being under sail, I bid your Lordship most heartily farewell.   The 21st of February, at 12 o'clock the afternoon.

Your Lordship's most assured to command,

C. HOWARD.

February 28.—*SIR WILLIAM WYNTER TO THE PRINCIPAL OFFICERS.*

[ccviii 85.—Signed.   Addressed :—To my loving fellows, John Hawkyns, Wm. Holstok and Wm. Borough, Esqrs., Officers of the Queen's Majesty's Admiralty.]

Since my last letters sent unto you there is nothing happened worthy the writing other than

death of Henry VIII. ; once in 1558, and again about 1580.   Cf. *Ha,field MSS.* No. 846, *Otho* E. ix ; and *S.P. Dom. Eliz.* cciv. 20.
  [2] The principal officers of the navy, viz. : the Treasurer (Hawkyns), Master of the Ordnance (Wynter), Comptroller (Borough), and Comptroller of Victualling (Wm. Holstok).   In the next century these officers, with some additions, *e.g.* the Surveyor and the Clerk of the Acts, formed the Navy Board, which, under the control of the Board of Admiralty, continued to administer much of the details of the affairs of the navy, until it was abolished by Act of Parliament in 1832.

that the Commissioners did pass away under the charge of Sir Henry Palmer upon Sunday night last past, and as we think, landed the next day following, having a most pleasant passage.

You shall do well to call upon the Lords that it would please their Honours to be mindful that provisions might be made in time to supply the wants which will grow amongst the navy if we make any long continuance abroad, for I dare assure you that which we have and was thought to be sufficient (as it was indeed) at our coming forth, will grow by reason of our too timely coming abroad not to be able without a great supply to serve us out this summer. This winter's weather, although we have been but a while abroad, hath so stretched our sails and tackle, torn many of our blocks, pullies, and sheevers, stretched our boats, and destroyed some of our pinnaces—as the Lion's for one, who is utterly lost and must be furnished of another—as [1] a man would never believe it unless he doth see it; these be the fruits that the seas bring forth, especially in this time of the year, as it is not unknown to you. If you be not careful to call for these things to the Lords, although they are unpleasant suits for her Majesty or them to hear of, you shall not do that that becometh you, nor avoid the peril and danger that may grow thereby; for learn this of me: Lords will be found in no fault if matters come in question.

I trust you do not forget to set forward the masts that should serve for the great ships, although I hope in God we shall not greatly need them.

Our ships doth show themselves like gallants here. I assure you it will do a man's heart good to behold them; and would to God the Prince of

[1] That.

Parma were upon the seas with all his forces, and we in the view of them ; then I doubt not but that you should hear that we would make his enterprise very unpleasant to him. But with sorrow I speak it, I am afraid that they will keep me from the baths of Bath by their long detraction,[1] where I meant to have been to seek health by the beginning of May next.

My Lord Admiral being accompanied with the lords[2] and other captains, and I also waiting upon his Lordship, not with much ease did land at Dover pier and viewed the same ; where I must tell you I saw nothing that pleased me but only the Pent.[3] I had well hoped that it should have been a harbour for good shipping, but now I see it is made a place for passage boats. I do not discommend the harbour for that there will want water ; but I do mislike it in respect that 'the coming into it is not laid in good soil, which time will discover.

Thanks be to God, my Lord Admiral with all his followers do keep themselves in good health, which I pray God to continue. And thus leaving for this time, I bid you farewell. Written aboard the Vanguard, being in the Downs, ready to cut sail,[4] the wind at East and by North, to bear over with the other coast, 28th of February, 1587.

Your loving fellow,
W. WYNTER.

[1] Delay.

[2] Lord Henry Seymour, Lord Sheffield, and others serving afloat. See *ante*, p. 24.

[3] The eastern basin of Dover harbour, still so called. It was first constructed in 1583 (cf. *S.P. Dom. Eliz.* clxi. 36, 39), as a sluiced basin or 'large pent to contain water enough to let out to scour the haven's mouth.'

[4] To loose and let fall. When a sail was farthelled or furled, it was bound to the yard with rope yarns, which were cut to loose the sail. See Manwayring's *Seaman's Dictionary.*

February 29.—*HOWARD TO BURGHLEY.*

[ccviii. 87.—Signed.   Addressed.]

My very good Lord :—Upon Tuesday, being in the Downs, the wind came to the east, that we were fain to put over to Blackness.[1]   This day, being the last of this present, being up alongst the coast towards Calais, I met Sir Henry Palmer, who had wafted over the Commissioners, and afterwards went to Flushing.   I have sent your Lordship a packet of letters that he brought from thence.   I perceive by a letter that I have received from my Lord Governor of Flushing that the Count Maurice is come to Middelburg ; his errand is, as it is thought, to persuade them of Campvere and Arnemuiden from her Majesty, but by my Lord Governor's letter it doth appear they will stand fast for her Majesty. I also perceive by his letter that Famars[2] and Villiers have besieged Colonel Sonoy,[3] and that

[1] Gris-nez.   [2] MS. Famus.

[3] MS. Coronall Snoye.   When the Earl of Leicester returned to England in December 1587, though without formally resigning the authority which the States General had conferred on him, Prince Maurice of Nassau was elected Stadtholder and Captain General of the States' army.   On this, Sonoy, who commanded in North Holland, declaring himself bound by his oath of obedience to Leicester, refused to acknowledge Maurice, and shut himself up in Medemblik, where he was promptly besieged by Maurice's troops, under Marshal Villiers : it does not appear that Famars was with him.   About the middle of March 1588 Sonoy received tardy orders from Queen Elizabeth to surrender the fortress and submit himself to the Prince, which he did.   He was deprived of his command, and shortly afterwards took refuge in England, where the Queen allotted him a congenial piece of fenland in Lincolnshire.   Owing to his ignorance of English, and perhaps also to his impracticable temper, his attempt to drain it proved a failure.   He returned to his own country and settled in East Friesland, on a small pension from the States.   Afterwards he.

G 2

if he have not some comfort, it will go hard with
him. I do wonder I have not heard some answer
touching my letter which I sent by Kirkman ; but
the case being as it is, I mean the first wind that
shall serve, to send two ships thither [1] ; for I had
rather adventure to send, than the gentleman that is
so well devoted to her Majesty should therefore
perish. I have his man aboard with me, and hath
been these four days ; and if the wind had served
anything these two days, I had sent him and two of
her Majesty's ships to his master.

The first wind that doth serve I do mean to put
with [2] Flushing, and I hope thereby to encourage her
Majesty's good friends of Campvere and Arnemuiden
and to discourage Count Maurice and his followers.
I perceive by Sir Henry Palmer that my coming
thither will do good many ways, and I think our
being here alongst the coast hath done much good.

There are two French ships that are come out
of Spain, that doth report wonders of the Spanish
army, and that upon pain of death every man must
be ready to cut sail the 25th of March, and that
their coming is for England, and that they bring
some galleys with them hauled [3] at ships' sterns. If
this be true, it is sure for the Isle of Wight or Sluys. [4]
If I may have the four great ships come to me in
time, and 20 good hoys, but with [5] 20 men apiece,
which is but a small charge, and each of them but
with two iron pieces, I doubt not but to make her
Majesty a good account of anything that shall be

became imbecile, and died in 1597, of the effects of falling into the
fire. The countenance which the Queen appeared to give Sonoy
and other rebels against the States, during the early months of
1588, naturally estranged Maurice from the English for the time.

[1] To Medemblik.

[2] With, following a verb of motion, means towards or to. To
put with = put over to.

[3] Towed.   [4] MS. Scluse.   [5] With but.

done by the Spanish forces, and I will make him wish his galleys at home again.

If the Commissioners bring peace it is the happiest thing that can be; but if they come without it, look for great matters to ensue presently upon it ; for the charge is so great that the King is at, both in Spain and here, in the Low Countries, that it cannot continue long, if he had five times the treasure he hath.

Rowland Yorke[1] is dead of the small-pox. I would Stanley[2] were with him.

The Dunkirkers dare not stir abroad. Sir Henry Palmer this day did rescue a man of Dort[3] from them, which they had taken, and one of the Dunkirkers ran into Dunkirk and the other two into Calais ; he that went into Dunkirk had his errand[4] with him to his smart. If we keep them in thus, they will starve.

I protest before God, and as my soul shall answer for it, that I think there were never in any place in the world worthier ships than these are, for so many. And as few as we are, if the King of Spain's forces be not hundreds, we will make good sport with them. And I pray you tell her Majesty from me that her money was well given for the Ark Ralegh,[5] for I think her the odd ship in the world for

---

[1] A soldier of fortune, distinguished alike by his impetuous courage and the impudence of his treachery. His last achievement in this line had been the betrayal of the Zutphen fort, of which he was governor, to the Spaniards, in January 1587.

[2] Sir William Stanley, a man of family and influence, had been employed in Ireland ; and afterwards, in the Low Countries, had been appointed by Leicester Governor of Deventer, which he betrayed to the Spaniards in January 1587. See Motley, *History of the United Netherlands*, vol. ii. chap. xiii.

[3] Or Dordrecht.   [4] MS. hat his arrant.

[5] She was bought from Sir Walter Ralegh for 5,000*l.*, which, however, was not paid in cash. The amount was struck off Ralegh's debt to the Crown in May 1592 (*S.P. Dom. Eliz.* ccxlii. 21).

all conditions ; and truly I think there can no great
ship make me change and go out of her. We can
see no sail, great nor small, but how far soever they
be off, we fetch them and speak with them. And so
I bid your Lordship most heartily farewell. From
aboard her Majesty's good ship the Ark, the last
of February 1587.

Your Lordship's most assured to command,

C. HOWARD.

February 29.—*RICHARD BARREY*[1] *TO LORD
BURGHLEY.*

[ccviii. 88.—Holograph.[2] Addressed.]

My most humble duty unto your Honour remembered :—This day there arrived from Ostend one
of the barks of this town that transported the Earl of
Derby's stuff. The master and owners of the bark is
William and Henry Tydyeman.[3] In their coming
from Dunkirk, a man of war of Dunkirk, of the burden
of three score tons, with 60 men in her, very well appointed, boarded them and have rifled[4] and spoiled
them of all the money they had; and that one Thomas
Baker of Folkestone and one Thomas Hurleston
of Sandwich, who went over for pilots.[5] That which
is taken from them in money and other furniture
and apparel is worth 30*l.* ; and they have carried
William Tydyeman unto Dunkirk, and the passport
of the Earl of Derby. A letter from the Earl of

---

[1] Lieutenant-Governor of Dover Castle.
[2] A very difficult scrawl.
[3] It may seem a fair presumption that these were of the same
family as the Sir Thomas Teddeman of Charles II.'s time.
[4] MS. ryfeled.
[5] The meaning is doubtful. Perhaps it is :—and that (rifling
and spoiling) they did also to one Thomas Baker &c.

Derby unto your Honour was nailed under the bytack,[1] so as they could not find it, the which was brought unto me by Baker of Folkestone, the which I send unto your Honour here enclosed. They have done divers other spoils unto these that came from Ostend, the which your Honour shall hear of. Most humbly ceasing [2] from troubling your Honour, praying for the continuance of your Honour's health with long life. Dover, the last of February.

Your Honour's most loving at commandment,

RICHARD BARREY.

March 3.—*HAWKYNS TO BURGHLEY.*

[ccix. 5.—Holograph. Addressed.]

My bounden duty humbly remembered unto your good Lordship :—I have been very ill since I was with your Lordship, but now better I thank God.

I do daily hear good report of the good estate of the ships abroad, as it may appear to your Lordship by the letters I send herewith enclosed ; so do I hear many of good judgment that have served now in them report, wondering how these lewd bruits [3] could have been cast abroad, and the ships in that sufficient and strong estate. But not to be troublesome to your Lordship, when the shipwrights saw I took a course to put the navy in such order as there should be no great cause to use any extraordinary reparations upon them, then they saw the multitude of their idle followers should lack their maintenance, and so began to bruit [4] out weakness in the state of

---

[1] So in MS. It is probably the Sp. *bitácula*, whence the Eng. bittacle, now binnacle.
[2] MS. sessyng.   [3] MS. brewtes.   [4] MS. brewt.

the ships; but they knew not where; and then
every man tare[1] up that which was sufficient, and
said this[2] we will weary Hawkyns of his bargain.
And as this shall be a thing most manifest to your
Lordship and the whole world, that the navy is in
good and strong estate, contrary to their hypo-
critical practice and vile reports, so your Lordship
shall find the rest of their informations much like
unto this.

I would to God her Majesty were so well provided
of all furniture that belongeth to the ships as her
Highness is of good carcasses of ships, which indeed
is the least matter I fear.   But the provisions[3] that
come from foreign countries, and such as require
long time to provide, do most trouble me—as great
cables, anchors, cordage, canvas, great masts, and
such like; waste and spoil of boats and pinnaces by
this winter weather, as Sir William Wynter doth
well note.

I am now about to gather together the great
issuing that hath been this year of *anno* 1587 of
cordage, canvas, and other provisions out of her
Majesty's store, which I think will be 12,000 or
13,000 pound, which must be cared for and supplied in time, without the which the ships cannot
serve.   There hath been great service abroad these
two years past, and the ships mightily supplied
from time to time with many provisions, and now call
daily in such sort as I am both afraid and sorry to
present it to your Lordship.   Howbeit, it must be
done and care had to do it in time.   The expenses
extraordinary have been great, and such as before
this time hath seldom come in use; for the navy is

---

[1] Tore : spoke evil of, disparaged, condemned.
[2] In this way : thus.
[3] Provisions means stores ; what we now understand as provisions were, in 1588, distinguished as victual.

great, and men more unruly and more chargeable than in time past, so as it doth not only amaze me to answer everything, but I do grieve at the charge as much as it were to proceed from myself.

I have been careful to replenish the store, for I found it not worth 5,000*l.*; and now I think with this year's issuing, it is worth 16,000 pound. So likewise the ships I found in weak estate, and now they are as your Lordship doth see; and this is done in effect upon the sparing out of the ordinary warrant of 5,719*l.*, yet I am daily backbited and slandered. But your Lordship doth know what a place this is to hold, that I am in. Many are to receive out of this office, and among a multitude, there are some bad and unreasonable; and although I endeavour myself to pay and satisfy all men with order and equity, yet some be displeased.

The matters in the office are great and infinite. My men are sick and dispersed. The trust I am forced to commit abroad and at home is very much; and with great difficulty I keep things in that order as [1] I can give reason for the things that are paid; and many losses I receive by negligence of servants, by such as I put in trust, and by prests [2] which be without number.

Therefore, my good Lord, consider in your wisdom the burden I bear. My service to her Majesty I grudge not, but all my ability and life is ready to be employed in her service. When it shall be your Lordship's pleasure, I will give mine attendance to inform your Lordship substantially what is to be done touching the provisions that are to be provided for the navy, and the debt that the office

---

[1] Such order that.
[2] A prest, or imprest, was an earnest, or advance paid on account. A prest-man was really a man who received the prest of 12*d.*, as a soldier when enlisted.

doth and will daily grow into ; and so, wishing
your Lordship health and prosperity, I humbly take
my leave. From London, the 3rd of March, 1587.
Your Lordship's humbly to command,
JOHN HAWKYNS.

March 3.—*FENNER TO WALSYNGHAM.*

[ccix. 6.—Holograph. Addressed.]

Here cometh advertisements daily from out of
Spain, most of them running upon one point.
Amongst others, by the way out of Brittany, as
from Nantes,[1] by reason of a Portingal there dwelling, who sent his son unto Lisbon, and by one his
special kinsman there, having to do for the King's
provision, gave understanding, as followeth :

At Lisbon and forthwith to be there and to serve
the enterprise :

		Ships
Of ships out of divers parts pro- vided to the number of	.	400
Of galleys	.	50

Footmen.

		Men
Out of Italy . .	.	5,000
the Indies .	.	3,000
Spain . .	.	17,000
Portugal . .	.	12,000
Flanders . .	.	25,000
More to be levied in Italy .	.	12,000
		74,000

Horses.

Light horse . .	.	1,200
Horses garnished .	.	1,400
		2,600

[1] MS. Naunce.

Men for the service of the artillery   1,200
Mariners and sailors   .   .   . 8,912

10,112

Biscuit.[1]

Quintals

From Andalusia. .   .   . 27,557
  Malaga 12,000
  Cartagena and Murcia . . 12,000
  Seville 25,000
  Burgos and Tierra de Campos 56,000
  Naples 40,000
From all the Islands .   .   . 12,000

184,557

Bacon and pork, from five
  several places   .   . 23,000 quintals.[2]
Wines, from four several
  places .   .   .   . 26,000 butts.
Cheeses, out of four several
  places .   .   . 43,000 quintals.
Fish, from three places . 19,000 hogsheads.
Beef, from three places . 11,000 quintals.
Roves[3] of oil, from two
  places .   .   . 23,000 roves.
Beans, from four places . 36,000 haniks.[4]
Barley, from two places . 35,000 haniks.
Rice, from Genoa[5] and Va-
  lencia .   .   . 24,000 roves.[3]
Great store of horseshoes, nails and girths.

[1] MS. bysquet. This list of stores may be compared with that given by Duro (i. 275), as suggested by Santa Cruz in March 1586.
  [2] MS. kintals. The quintal is 100 (five score) Spanish pounds, or 102 lbs. av. nearly.
  [3] Arrobas. The arroba is a measure of nearly four gallons, or a weight of 25 pounds.
  [4] Hanegas or fanegas. The hanega is about a bushel and a half.   [5] MS. Jenovaye ; from the Spanish Génova.

Captain Coxe[1] came from the coast of Spain within five days before the date hereof, in a pinnace of Sir William Wynter's. [He reporteth[2]] the like number of ships, or little different ; as also of a great number of flyboats that keepeth the coast of Spain, thereby their provisions coming in fleets together to Lisbon in safety. Their intents are known unto your Honour. I would to God we had been now upon that coast ; the impediments would have been great unto their army gathering together, more than I dare presume to write, in my poor opinion. We rest here, a great number of valiant men, and to great charge unto my gracious mistress, and a great grief of mind to spend her Majesty's treasure and do nothing upon the enemy.

I fear when we shall be hastened to go, our provision of victual needful will not be ready in a month ; in which time it will be no small matter, the waste in doing of nothing. If there were three months' provision ready for the proportion of 3,000 men, it would not amount unto above 9,000*l.* ; and if there should need no use of it, there would not be 1,000*l.* lost by it ; and the contrary, the time of stay before it be ready, if cause move the proceedings,

---

[1] Cf. *ante*, p. 11. In 1576 William Coxe of Limehouse commanded the Bear in a voyage to the Spanish Main under Captain Andrew Barker, who, after quarrelling with his master and other officers, was put on shore by Coxe in the Bay of Honduras, and there killed by the Spaniards. The Bear was afterwards lost, with the greater part of her men ; but Coxe and eight others escaped, and, after much suffering, arrived in England only to be accused of the murder of Barker, and condemned to a term of imprisonment. How long Coxe remained in prison does not appear ; but in 1583 he was master of the Golden Hind of 40 tons, Edward Hayes captain and owner, in the tragic voyage of Sir Humphrey Gylberte to Newfoundland (see Lediard, 163, 197). In 1588 he proved himself a good navigator and bold man, and was slain, probably — as has been said—in the great fight off Gravelines.

[2] Omitted in MS.

will cost half so much money and more in victuals and wages before victual can be provided, as also the opportunity of time to encounter the enemy lost.

I had rather have occasion to be at service, that your Honour might hear of some happy success in beating down the pride of the enemy, wherein we are assuredly strengthened in God of good and happy success. God grant it to his good pleasure, and send your Honour your heart's desire ; craving pardon of your Honour for my boldness herein, not doubting your taking in good part the rude lines that cometh from a soldier. Plymouth, from aboard her Majesty's good ship the Nonpareil, this 3rd of March, 1587.

Your Honour's in all duty,
THOMAS FENNER.

OPINION OF SIR FRANCIS DRAKE.

[ccix. 128.—Signed.]

Mine opinion touching those notes delivered by Captain Coxe.

1. First these flyboats are those which were reported to have the carrying of those pilots from Dunkirk which were provided by the Prince of Parma for this fleet now prepared at Lisbon and now employed by the Cardinal[1] and Marquis of Santa Cruz, as men of war upon that coast, until the fleet be ready, that thereby their passage for all manner of victuals and other provisions may be the safer, as also that there shall be no certain advertisements from thence, and in what readiness their fleet is for what their pretence[2] is.

[1] The Cardinal Archduke Albert, Governor of Portugal ; a younger son of the late Emperor Maximilian, King Philip's first cousin, and of the Empress Maria, Philip's sister.
[2] Design.

2. It is the likelier, for that the said Captain Coxe likewise affirmeth that both French and Dutch men have vowed unto him that they are sworn, before they depart Spain, that they shall not strike sail to any English man of war ; and if they be not able to make resistance, then to throw all their letters whatsoever overboard.

3. He also thinketh that there are by the least 30 sail of those flyboats, men of war, which he hath at sundry times seen ; and that the said flyboats have in every one of them some Spaniards, for that they are all full of small shot.[1]

4. He farther reporteth that the Rochellers told him at his first coming upon that coast that there were flyboats men of war, and that they durst not abide upon that coast for fear of them. And farther he himself confesseth that, upon consultation had with his company, they were contented to come away for their better safety, which otherwise they had not done, for that they had good store of victuals left.

5. In my poor opinion it were not amiss that the Lords did think of the continual going to the seas of the smaller sort of our shipping daily upon letters of reprisal, which can do little good ; for that all men of war which come home report that there is no shipping to be seen upon the coast of Spain but such as bring victuals and other provisions in great fleets for Lisbon, and they are wafted with [2] men of war ; but [3] those Flemish flyboats, which go in fleets, by the least five, seven and nine in company, which will not leave one English man of war untaken upon that coast, and I doubt lest some are taken already.

6. At this instant there arrived a bark of this town from Bordeaux, who reported that the King of

[1] Musketeers.   [2] Convoyed by.   [3] And also.

Navarre is with his army within five leagues of the town and stoppeth the passage of the river, so as little recourse is had thither, and that the inhabitants of the city are every night in arms, and divers alarms made among them.

FRA. DRAKE.

March 6.—JOHN HAWKYNS TO BURGHLEY.

[ccix. 7.—Holograph. Addressed.]

Right Honourable mine especial good Lord :— I have herewith brought unto your Lordship a brief note of the material things that hath issued this last year by warrant of the officers out of her Majesty's store ; and as I can overcome it, your Lordship shall see it more particularly, as we have been accustomed in all our demands yearly for the supplying of the same.

There is already taken into the storehouse and provided to the value of 5,000*l.*, which is unpaid for ; and order given for great cables to be made this winter in Muscovia, for the value of 3,000*l.*, which will be most needful. If your Lordship do give order for the one half[1] of this demand to be paid, the credit of the office may be satisfied ; and so, with some time and leisure the rest may be paid, as your Lordship shall from the office have information, as the necessity requireth, and not before.

For[2] the great masts is a matter of importance, and requireth some speedy order to be taken in it, your Lordship may speak with Mr. Allin[3] in it,

---

[1] MS. hallf.   [2] For=since, because.
[3] Thomas Allin, officially described as ' her Majesty's merchant for Danzig.' His name is frequently mentioned in connection with the supply of masts, cordage, &c.

which [1] doth know how they may best be had and
with the most speed; and for that purpose there
would be some prest delivered as the necessity shall
from time to time require. I will attend upon your
Lordship to know what order your Lordship shall
think meet to be taken herein, and to satisfy your
Lordship of any doubt that may be had in these
matters ; and so leave to trouble your good Lordship. The 6th day of March, 1587.

Your honourable Lordship's humbly to command,

JOHN HAWKYNS.

March 9.—HOWARD TO BURGHLEY.

[ccix. 9.—Signed.   Addressed.]

My very good Lord :—On Friday, being the
first of March, riding under Blackness [2] on the coast
of France, the wind came out of west, so as we did
put off to have borne over to the coast of England ;
and being half seas over, the wind came to the
West-South-West and a very hard gale, so as we
were driven to put over either for Yarmouth or
Flushing. And because Yarmouth was so much to
the northwards, we rather chose Flushing. So on
Sunday about 12 of the clock in the forenoon, we
came in with much wind and passed by the town to
the Rammekens. The Elizabeth Bonaventure in
coming in, by the fault of the pilot, came aground
on a sand where there had been a hulk cast away
but a month before, having in her one of the best
pilots in the town. I must commend my Lord H.
Seymour wonderfully for his honourable mind ; for
although many of the ship went out to save themselves for fear, he would by no means stir out of

---

[1] Which=who.   [2] Gris-nez.

her, but said he would abide her fortune, and so encouraged them all. I and Sir Wm. Wynter came presently aboard of her, where we found my Lord Harry sparing no labour for her help. Myself and Sir Wm. Wynter remained still in her and devised all helps that might be ; but that tide could do no good. The next tide, by the goodness of God and great labour, we brought her off, and in all this time there never came a spoonful of water into her well. My Lord, except a ship had been made of iron, it were to be thought unpossible to do as she hath done; and it may be well and truly said there never was nor is in the world a stronger ship than she is, and there is no more to be perceived or known any ways of her being aground than if she were new made. She is 27 years old ; she was with Sir Francis Drake two voyages [1] ; and there hath been no voyage which hath been, but she hath been one. Your Lordship shall find it so in your books. And this is one of the ships which they would have come into a dry dock, now before she came out. My Lord, I have no doubt but some ships which have been ill reported of will deceive them as this ship doth. And for that which Sir Wm. Wynter and I have seen now, we will take upon us that the good ship the Elizabeth Bonaventure shall serve her Majesty these 12 years ; and I do not know but that the Triumph, the Elizabeth Jonas, the Bear and the Victory should be in better case than this ship ; for they are no elder, nor as yet they never had journey to wring them as this ship hath had. Well, my Lord, they will be found good ships when they come to the seas.

Upon Tuesday my Lord Governor [2] intreated me and all our company to dinner with him, which

[1] To the West Indies in 1585-6, and to Cadiz in 1587.
[2] Sir William Russell.

we did.   There came to me thither all the States of
Zealand and Mons. de Valke, their Councillor, who
presented from all the islands and towns all service
to her Majesty, and by especial speech from the
town of Middelburg, that they were all her
Majesty's, and that none shall come into the town
but such as shall always please her Majesty, and
that Campvere nor Arnemuiden shall any ways show
their duties more than they will do.   I gave them
thanks on her Majesty's behalf ; and yet I spared
not to let them know how in some things they had
forgotten their duties.

The Count Maurice being there, as soon as ever
we came in went his way to Lillo, where some of
his fleet lay, and carried with him all that he had,
yet he did send a gentleman of his to me with the
most humblest message that ever he sent to any,
offering all his service to her Majesty, which way
soever I would appoint him.   I took. occasion upon
this offer of his, to write a letter unto him touching
Mo. Sonoy, and also sent my brother Hoby [1] with it,
with a message concerning it.   He wrote unto me
again.   His letter and also the copy of mine, I have
sent to Mr. Secretary, which your Lordship may
see.   He hath promised to do what he can in it,

---

[1] Sir Edward Hoby, born in 1560, was the eldest son of Sir
Thomas Hoby, ambassador in France in 1566.   His mother,
Elizabeth, daughter of Sir Anthony Cooke, was sister to Lady
Burghley and to Lady Bacon.   Hoby was thus first cousin of Sir
Francis Bacon (Lord Bacon), and of Sir Robert Cecill, afterwards
Earl of Salisbury.   After his father's death, his mother married
John Lord Russell, elder brother of Sir William Russell ; her
younger sister was the wife of Sir Henry Kyllygrew, the English
Resident at the Hague.   Hoby himself had married the youngest
daughter of Lord Hunsdon, and was thus Lord Howard's brother-
in-law.   He was serving at this time as Howard's secretary, and
seems to have had a position somewhat analogous to that of the
modern Captain of the Fleet.   He was the author of some
polemical pamphlets, and died in 1617.

and said if it were in his own power he would, but
he must deal with the States; and so went the next
morning into Holland to deal with them. I dealt
also with the States of Zealand in it; and privately,
with Mo. de Valke. I believe they will deal well in
it, for so they have promised him. My Lord
Governor and I thought it best to forbear four or
five days the sending of any ships thither,[1] to see
what they will do. I have the Tramontana and the
Charles ready, and shall go to Flushing and do as
my Lord Governor shall see cause. My Lord, it is
very hard to get a pilot in Flushing that will go
thither; for I desired Mo. Sonoy's agent to see
what he could do to get two pilots, but I could not
hear of any. Upon Wednesday, all the captains
and chiefest men of Campvere and Arnemuiden came
aboard to me to dinner. I did never see men show
more love than these do to her Majesty. The captains
give her Majesty most humble thanks for her boun-
tiful goodness to them. They of Campvere invited
me to dinner with them; and they of Arnemuiden, to
supper. I could not deny them, they were so
earnest; but the next morning, it was so foul
weather that I was driven to send my excuse. That
same day there came to me the two burgomasters
of Middelburg and five of the principal men of the
town, and invited me to dinner to them on the
Sunday, which I could not at that time deny them;
but with condition that if the wind should serve me
to go out, they would pardon me. My Lord, the
preparations which were made were very great;
such as, our merchants said, the like was never in
that town at any time.

On Friday, when the wind came to serve our
turns, I sent my son Leveson[2] and three or four
gentlemen to them, to make my excuse, and also to

---

[1] To Medemblik.   [2] MS. Lewson.

visit the Princess of Orange.[1] My Lord, all the
mariners and seamen of Campvere and Arnemuiden
came to the governors and captains and told them
that they would all serve under me, and be commanded by none but by me ; and said whensoever
I would send for them, they would come from
Count Maurice or any, to me.   They of Middelburg heard of it, and they did the like.   My Lord,
this I dare assure her Majesty, at this hour she is
no more assured of the isle of Sheppey to be at her
devotion any ways, than she is of the whole isle
of Walcheren and all the towns.   Our merchants
find, as they say, a great change ; for they were
never so kindly handled as they are now.   My
Lord, I think we have had aboard our ships, to
view and look on them, 5,000 people on a day.

My Lord, in my going to Flushing, I took a
vessel of Nieuport, and released him again with
money in his purse, and told him that I was not on
the seas to offend any of them if they would not
give occasion ; and that I hoped, ere it were long,
we should be all good friends.   I told them they
saw whether I was able to starve both them and
Dunkirk if I listed ; for I could impeach all victuals
coming to them, and not suffer any to stir to fish ;
but I had no such meaning, if they gave not first
cause.

The Charles, coming from the coast of England,
met with a Dunkirker, half seas over, chasing two
English barks.   The Charles rescued them, and
had a good fight together ; but the Charles at
length made him run on ground under the town of
Dunkirk, for he was surely sped.   We will not
meddle with them except they come out and seek it,
for I would be loth to do anything in this time of

[1] Louise de Colligny, widow of William the Silent, and step-
mother of Count Maurice.

treating, that might hinder it; but yet I must not suffer her Majesty's subjects to be spoiled. We had but one in the Charles which was ill hurt. He is hurt, even like Sir Philip Sidney,[1] above the knee, and the bone all broken; a very great hurt. I have him aboard mine own ship, and am in hope to recover him.

There came into Flushing on Monday a Dane that came from Lisbon, who doth affirm that the Marquis de Santa Cruz is dead[2]; but he saith the preparations go on very great.

My Lord, as I was in writing hereof entering into Margate Road, Sir Henry Palmer came aboard and told me for certainty that there are letters come into Middelburg and to Mo. Sonoy's agent that the siege of Medemblik[3] is raised; which I am persuaded upon the hearing of my coming they did. I [had] forgotten to write unto your Lordship that they of Campvere and of Arnemuiden offered to suffer me to bring into their towns what English companies I would, and what number I listed. In like sort I had forgotten Count Maurice, at his departure out of Middelburg, bade them of the town farewell, and told them that he went out of that town as his father did out of Antwerp. He left behind him neither bed-hanging nor anything else, but carried all away with him.

There is much more than I am able to write. This gentleman, Mr. Browne's relation, who will more at large impart the rest unto your Lordship. And this [4] I bid your Lordship most heartily well to

---

[1] The author of *Arcadia*; Leicester's nephew and Walsyngham's son-in-law; mortally wounded in the thigh at the battle of Zutphen.
[2] He died on Jan. 30–Feb. 9.
[3] MS. has Middlebecke.
[4] With this, thus.

fare.   From aboard the Ark, this 9th of March,
1587, at Margate road.

> Your Lordship's assured to command,
> C. HOWARD.

March 9 (?).—HOWARD TO BURGHLEY. (?)

[ccix. 10.—Holograph.]

My good Lord :—I thought good to advertise
your Lordship of a flyboat and a hoy.   The flyboat
is of Calais, the hoy of Dort.   The flyboat was
very lately in Spain.   They are laden with a 1,000
quarters of wheat of the best.   Their cocket is for
Rochelle or Middelburg, neither of both the places
any great friends to us.   This cocket passed from
Mr. Wauton.[1]   The Flemings report there is as
much to come away to-morrow by the like warrant.
If wheat go away in such plumps, the market will
rise quickly, and the poor in hard case, after such a
year as the last was.   I have stayed it till I hear
from your Lordship, and as you will let me know
your pleasure and it shall be done.   My good Lord,
it is much that the enemy is relieved withal after
this manner.   Their great army could not continue,
nor their ships be victualled, if it were not by these
means.   I pray your Lordship let me know your
pleasure by this bearer ; and so I bid your Lordship
most heartily farewell.   Aboard the Ark, thwart of
the Naze.[2]

> Your Lordship's assured friend to command,
> C. HOWARD.

[1] Probably Roger Walton, a merchant of Calais, and a Catholic, suspected of being in correspondence with the Duke of Parma.

[2] Orfordness.   The letter is not dated, but would seem to have been written on the passage from Flushing to Margate, and sent with the preceding letter of March 9.

March 9.—*HOWARD TO WALSYNGHAM.*

[ooix. 12.—Holograph.   Addressed.]

Sir :—As I had made up my other letter,[1] Captain Frobiser doth advertise me that he spake with two ships that came presently from Lisbon, who declared unto him that for certainty the King of Spain's fleet doth part from Lisbon unto the Groyne the 15th of this month, by their account. Sir, there is none that comes from Spain but brings this advertisement ; and if it be true, I am afraid it will not be helped when the time serveth.   Surely this charge that her Majesty is at is either too much or too little ; and the stay that is made of Sir Francis Drake going out I am afraid will breed grave peril.[2] And if the King of Spain do send forces either into this realm, Ireland or Scotland, the Queen's Majesty shall say the Duke of Parma is treating of a peace, and therefore it is not princely done of his master to do so in the time of treaty.   But what is that to the purpose, if we have by that a *casado*[3] ?   And if her Majesty cannot show the King's hand, his servant's hand will be but a bad warrant, if they have their wills.   Sir, for myself I am determined to end my life in it, and the matter is not great.   I protest my greatest care is for her Majesty's honour and surety.

I send you a letter that now as I write I received from a man of mine which affirmeth the like ; and so, Sir, I take my leave.   From aboard the Ark Ralegh, the 9th of March, at 12 a clock at night.

Your very loving friend,

C. HOWARD.

[1] A duplicate of that to Burghley of same date. [2] MS. parell.
[3] So in MS.   He probably thought he was writing *camisado*, a sudden, unexpected attack in the dark.

March 10.—*SEYMOUR TO WALSYNGHAM.*

[ocix. 13.—Holograph.   Addressed.]

Sir :—Being assaulted as well with grief as with joy, I stand doubtful whether of them both I should embrace; either to conceal or to open such accidents as befell unto the Lord Admiral and the rest of his navy ; but leaving the same unto your honourable judgment, do proceed accordingly.

The Lord Admiral, being earnestly laboured and solicited by letters from the Lord Governor of Flushing to provoke him to ride there with his navy, the wind being also contrary to all his other harbours, thought good to take the same as it served.

Sunday, being the third of March, his Lordship entered into the harbour of Flushing, where, by great misfortune, the Elizabeth Bonaventure came on ground betwixt 12 and one of the clock in the day time, and could not that tide get off. But by the goodness of God, with the presence of the Lord Admiral, and help of the rest of the captains and masters, the same was recovered at the next tide, which was twelve hours after, to the great admiring of the whole island.

The next day after, being the 5th of this month, his Lordship dined with the Lord Governor, where he was very honourably entertained and feasted. There repaired unto his Lordship during his harbour at Flushing, divers of the States and companies of Middelburg, Arnemuiden, and Campvere, who earnestly desired his Lordship's presence in every of their towns, making great protestation and offers of their sincere love and affection which the whole island bare unto her Majesty, so much the rather (as I gather and find) for that the Lord Admiral brought thither his navy to their great liking, and greater discouragement of the enemy, for presently Count Maurice being at Middelburg, departed suddenly with all his stuff and furniture to Lillo, and was assured by divers soldiers and mariners that if he enterprised anything against the Queen they would leave him and stick and serve her Majesty.

Whereupon the Lord Admiral, well advising himself before that he would attempt anything for the relieving of Monsieur Sonoy, wrote very honourably and wisely to the Count Maurice, desiring and wishing him to desist his action and enterprise ; which if he would conform himself thereunto her Majesty would be very thankful. Otherwise in not regarding the same, her Majesty should be enforced to relieve them whom she knew and took to be her good friends. Hereupon Count Maurice returned answer by letters with Sir Edward Hoby (who was the messenger) altogether excusing himself, and condemning Monsieur de Sonoy, who did very much forget himself towards him and the rest of the States, whereby he was enforced to proceed as he did ; yet meaning (as I think) to advise himself with the rest of the States to make good satisfaction to her Majesty.

Now the eight of this month the wind coming very aptly about at the North-North-East, my Lord Admiral omitted no time to make his return to our English coasts, and thanked be God is well arrived to Margate road.

To conclude : I wish that this honourable ship, being grounded 12 hours upon the sands, had been as long in fight and trial with the Spaniards in good sea-room, where with the help of the Lord Admiral and the rest of his fleet, every one of us (I hope) should have acquitted ourselves in duties both to God, her Majesty and country.

So meaning no further to trouble you, being glad to understand of your good health, desire that my humble commendations may be presented to the Lord Chancellor, the Lord Treasurer and the Lord Steward.

From aboard the Elizabeth Bonaventure, the fortunate ship where Sir Francis Drake received all his good haps, the 10th of March, 1587.

Your assured friend to command,
H. SEYMOUR.

March 10.—*HOWARD TO WALSYNGHAM.*

[ccix. 15. and I.—Holograph.   Addressed.]

Sir :—Mr. Frobiser is now come in to the road here in Margate, who hath passed up and down in the Narrow Seas to see who passed and whither. He met with 4 hulks that came from Rochelle, who told him for certain that the Prince of Condé is dead,[1] and that they saw the mourning for him, and great sorrow in the town for it. Within 5 days after word was brought to the town that the King of Navarre was also in great danger. They were both poisoned much about one time, yet they were not together. It is but 10 days since they parted from Rochelle. I pray God the King be not dead. It is too great a loss of the other, if it had pleased God. I pray God that her Majesty take good care

[1] The Prince of Condé died at St. Jean d'Angely on Feb. 24. It was believed then that he had been poisoned, and two servants were executed. The Princess was also suspected, and was kept in prison for seven years before she was declared innocent. It is now considered more probable that he died of fever (see the Duc d'Aumale's *Histoire des Princes de Condé*, ii. 179-182). The report of the poisoning of the King of Navarre seems to have been unfounded.

of herself, for these enemies are become devils,[1] and care not how to kill.

Yesternight there came one to me of purpose from Dunkirk, who doth assure me that on Wednesday last there came a Scottish gentleman out of Spain to the Duke of Parma, and brought a packet from the King and declared that the Spanish forces by sea are for certain to part[2] from Lisbon the 20th of this month with the light moon,[3] and that the number of the fleet when they all do meet, of great and small, will be 210 sails ; and the number of soldiers, besides the mariners, are 36,000. I am sorry Sir F. Drake is not in more readiness than he is. I know the fault is not in him. I pray to God her Majesty do not repent this slack dealings. It had been good he had been ready, though he had but lien[4] on our coast. I am afraid he will not be ready in time, do what can be done. All that cometh out of Spain must concur in one to lie, or else we shall be stirred very shortly with heave and ho.[5] I fear me ere it be long her Majesty will be sorry that she hath believed some as much as she hath done, but it will be very late. By all that I can gather it should be Hunter that is come out of Spain. The party saw the Scottish gentleman, and describeth him much like Hunter.

For her Majesty's four great ships, I am out of hope to see them abroad, what need soever shall be. If things fall out as it is most likeliest, they shall be to keep Chatham Church when they should serve the turn abroad. I protest before God, I speak not

---

[1] MS. dyvles.   [2] Depart.
[3] Mowne.   [4] MS. lyne.
[5] MS. hev and o. Howard seems to have rather affected the phrase. Cf. *Hist. MSS. Com.*, XI. Appendix iii. 124 : 'If you despatch not these things forthwith, I will send for you with heave and ho.'

for myself any ways, but for her Majesty's service and surety; for whensoever they should come, I mean not to change out of her I am in for any ship that ever was made.

Sir, I pray you let me hear from you how the peace is like to go on; for if I may hear in any time that it is not like to come to pass, I will make some provision for the choking of Dunkirk haven, although it serve but for a month; for from thence do I fear most. They look daily at Dunkirk for 1,200 mariners out of France; but if I have knowledge in any time, I hope to stop their coming out, and so the better able to look some other way.

Sir, if her Majesty think that her princely preparation of Sir F. Drake's fleet, and this that I have, should be a hindrance to a peace and that the King of Spain should take it ill, why should not the King of Spain think that her Majesty hath much more cause to think ill of his mighty preparations? It will peradventure be said he hath many ways to employ them, and not to England. That is easily answered, for it is soon known by the victualling; and he never prepares so many soldiers for the Indies. Sir, I will for this time bid you farewell. From Margate road, the 10th of March.

Your assured loving friend,
C. HOWARD.

Sir :—I pray you that there may be order taken for the staying of all shipping in England for a cause that I will write more at large hereafter.

March 13.—*MEMORANDUM AS TO VICTUALLING.*

[ccix. 16.—Rough note in the autograph of Lord Burghley.]

The proportion of victualling to the seas:

Nota 28 days to 1 month; whereof—
Fish days . 10 ┐ Whereof 4 Fridays that have but
Flesh days . 16 ┘ 4 meals; so there wants 2 days.[1]
Fish days . 20 meals.
Flesh days . 32 meals.

The fare of fish days for every man per diem:

Biscuit . 1 lb. Beer . . [1] gallon.
In fish . 1 qr. of stockfish, or the 8th part of a ling.
In cheese, per diem, 1 qr. of a pound.
In butter, half qr. per diem.

The flesh day:

Beer and biscuit, ut supra.

Flesh, 2 lbs. salt beef per diem, so as every man hath 1 lb. for a meal, and 4 men have 4 lbs. for a meal.

For one day in the week:

A device for bacon for 1 day in a week.
1 lb. of bacon for a man per diem.
A pint of pease for 1 man for a meal.
1 pottle of pease for 4 men.

4,000 cask will serve for 10,000 men for beer and beef for 3 months.

[1] This was ingenious. On Fridays only half allowance was to be issued, so that the saving on four Fridays amounted to whole rations for two days; and the victuals for twenty-six days served for twenty-eight.

So there will be 3 days in the week—viz. Sunday, Tuesday and Thursday—for beef; and 3 fish days—Wednesday, Friday and Saturday ; and Monday, for bacon and pease.

March 12.—*SUGGESTIONS FOR REDUCING EXPENDITURE.*[1]

[ccix. 17.—Noted, in Burghley's hand :—Saving by . . .[2] of beef.]

For the saving of her Majesty 2,666*l.* 13*s.* 4*d.* by altering the provision of beef into other victuals, the manner whereof ensueth.

Every man's victual of beef standeth her Majesty 4*d.* the day, at 2*d.* the pound, besides cask and salt. And so the mess, being 4 persons, amounteth to 16*d.* the day for their meat, besides bread and drink.

By altering that kind of victual as before, to fish, oil and pease, her Majesty's charge will be but 3*d.* for 3 fishes the day, at 10*s.* the hundred of newland-fish ; 2*d.* in oil for the mess the day, and 2*d.* in peasen at 2*s.* the bushel, with one penny upon every mess the day for cask and other charges; which amounteth to in all but unto 8*d.* the day. So do you save the other 8*d.* on every mess the day, which is half the charge that the beef did stand. Which for the 20,000 men aforesaid, according to her Majesty's allowance, did amount unto 5,333*l.* 6*s.* 8*d.* The moiety wherof saved is, as before,

2,666*l.* 13*s.* 4*d.*

---

[1] This is an early instance of the sort of suggestions that all officials are probably familiar with, as well as newspaper readers during the silly season. It is certainly unjust to attach the discredit of them to either Burghley or the Queen. Mr. Froude has called the writer a 'miserable scoundrel' (*History*, xii. 369) ; 'ignorant blockhead' would perhaps be more appropriate ; he could not even work his arithmetic correctly.   [2] Torn away.

March 12.—*JOHN HAWKYNS TO BURGHLEY.* (?)

[ccix. 18.—Holograph.]

My most honourable and very good Lord :—
Although I doubt not but your Lordship is advertised of the coming over of the navy with my
Lord Admiral to Margate, yet I thought good your
Lordship should see what my Lord doth write, for
that daily they consume and call for that which I
did always fear.

The Bonaventure, which was condemned before
your Lordship for a decayed ship, doth prove far
contrary ; yet I desire not they should come to such
trials.

I will take order to send my Lord 200 men with
speed, if they be to be had in Thames.

I have already made a new shift of sails for the
Rainbow, for they have not been renewed since she
was made ; and were at the first single, but now
double.

If I had known the purpose that is meant for
the two hoys, I could have fitted them thereafter ;
but it is like they are to sink in some place, or to
beat in shoal water with great ordnance. This will
be a matter of some charge, therefore I do acquaint
your Lordship with it ; for it may be your Lordship
is advertised of the purpose.

I do prepare and am doing for 20 great anchors,
which is a very great work and costly. So do we
take up canvas and other provisions upon credit,
which is not the best way. If the service continue,
we shall not be able to supply the want without
your Lordship's help.

My Lord doth specially commend the Ark
Ralegh, which indeed is the best ordered ship that

I have seen for all conditions and purposes, although there be many others most excellent ships.

I would be glad to follow your Lordship's opinion for the hastening of the four great ships, and so in all the rest ; for your Lordship can best discern what is of necessity ; and so praying God long to preserve your Lordship in health, I humbly take my leave.   From my house in Mincing Lane, the 12th of March, 1587.

Your honourable Lordship's humbly to command,
JOHN HAWKYNS.

March 20.—*REPORT OF CHARGES.*

[**ccix. 25.**—Signed.]

For John Hawkyns :

The charge of the four great ships for one month sea wages, harbour wages, prest and conduct, sea-store, with a supplying of sea-store to the ships serving now at the seas under the charge of the Lord Admiral, and conduct in discharging, is   .   .   . 3,092 10 0

£ *s. d.*

For James Quarles :

The charge of the victual for one month for these 4 ships for 1,900 men is 1,551 13 4
The charge of the victuals for 2,990 men serving under the charge of the Lord Admiral now in the Narrow Seas for one month, is 2,441 16 8
For transportation of these victuals   200 0 0
_____
4,193 10 0

For these parcels we humbly pray your Lordship to give order to Mr. Peter to make an order for payment of money,—

	£	s.	d.
To John Hawkyns . £3,092 10 0 } 7,285	0	0	
To James Quarles . 4,193 10 0 }			

So the business may proceed according to her Majesty's pleasure and your Lordship's order.

We also humbly pray your Lordship to be a mean that the supply of cordage, canvas, masts, anchors and such like, may be supplied, whereof your Lordship hath a note; without the which we cannot furnish the navy but for small time.

> JOHN HAWKYNS.
> WILLM. HOLSTOK.
> JAMES QUARLES.

March 20.—VICTUALLING ESTIMATE.

[ccix. 26.—Endorsed.]

Sir Francis Drake, two months' victuals:

The victual for two months for 2,900 men to serve in the ships under the charge of Sir Francis Drake, after 32s. 8d. the man, amounteth to the sum of 4,736 13 4

And for transportation &c. . . 150 0 0

Sum total 4,886 13 4

Ships with my Lord Admiral, one month's victuals:

For the victualling of one month for all her Majesty's ships now in the Narrow Seas under the charge of the Lord Admiral, and for the four great ships now at Chatham, being in all

4,890 men, to begin the 21st of April   £   *s.*   *d.*
next and to end the 19th of May ; after
the rate of 16*s.* 4*d.* the man per month,
amounteth to the sum of   .   .   .   3,993   10   0
    And for transportation &c.   .   .   200   0   0

Sum total   4,193   10   0

Sum total of both the victuallings, £9,080   3   4

March 20.—*ESTIMATE OF CHARGES FOR THE
FOUR GREAT SHIPS.*

[ccix. 27.—Holograph of John Hawkyns.]

An estimate of the charge to prepare four of her
Majesty's great ships to the seas, and the furnishing
of the navy serving under the charge of the Lord
Admiral.

                     Men

The Elizabeth Jonas   .   500 ⎫
   Triumph   .   .   500 ⎬ in all 1,900 men.
   Bear   .   .   .   500 ⎪
   Victory   .   .   400 ⎭

                              £   *s.*   *d.*

For prest and conduct of 1,200
sailors to be had out of sundry shires,
at 8*s.* every man, with the prester's
charges   480   0   0
For the prest and conduct of 500
gunners and soldiers at 2*s.* 6*d.* the man,
with the prester's charges   .   .   .   62   10   0
For harbour wages of 200 men for
20 days   75   0   0
For sea-store for the said ships at
50*l.* the ship   200   0   0
For sea-store to renew the ships'
provision serving with the Lord Ad-
miral in the Narrow Seas   .   .   .   500   0   0

	£	s.	d.
For conduct in discharge of the 1,200 men at 7s. the man . . .	420	0	0
For conduct in discharge of the 500 men at 12d. the man	25	0	0
	1,762	10	0

For the sea wages of the 1,900 men abovesaid serving in the said ships, at 14s. the man per month . . . 1,330 0 0

Total 3,092 10 0

JOHN HAWKYNS.

£ s. d.

The victual for one month of these 1,900 men serving in the 4 ships above-said is, at 16s. 4d. a man per month . 1,551 13 4

March 22.—ESTIMATE OF CHARGES.

[ccix. 29.—Signed.]

22nd of March, 1587.

An estimate of the charge of the augmenting of 2 months' charge, to be increased for the ships that are now westward under the charge of Sir Francis Drake, Knight; together with other charges for the furnishing of our four great ships, and our navy abroad under the charge of the Lord Admiral.

Sea wages.

£ s. d.

First, for the sea wages of 2,900 men by the space of two months, at 18s.[1] the man; diets, dead shares, and rewards in the same accounted . . 4,060 0 0

---

[1] So in MS. It should be 14s. for one month, or 28s. for the two months, and is so calculated in the total.

Tonnage.

For the tonnage of the merchant ships taken to serve with her Majesty's ships, being 23 ships for 4 months being esteemed at 400 ton, which is 400*l.* a month 1,600 0 0

Sea-store and Grounding.

For an increase of sea-store for all the ships there, and for the trimming aground with tallow, being all 30 ships with her Majesty, at 10*l.* every ship with one another 300 0 0

Prest and Conduct.

For the prest and conduct of 1,200 sailors which are to serve in her Majesty's four great ships at 8*s.* every man. with the prester's charges . . 480 0 0

For prest and conduct of 500 gunners and sailors at 2*s.* 6*d.* a man, with the prester's charges . . . 62 10 0

Sea-store.

For the sea-store of the said four great ships at 50*l.* every ship . . 200 0 0

For sea-store for to renew the provision in the 24 ships and pinnaces serving in the Narrow Seas under the charge of the Lord Admiral . . 500 0 0

Conduct in discharging.

For conduct in the discharging of the 1,200 men, at 7*s.* every man . . 420 0 0

For conduct in the discharging the 500 men abovesaid, at 12*d.* every man 25 0 0

7,647 10 0

Victuals.

For the victuals of the abovesaid £   *s.*   *d.*
2,990[1] men for two months serving in
the ships westward under the charge of
Sir F. Drake, at 32*s.* 8*d.* every man   . 4,736 13   4
For transportation of the said victual   150   0   0

	£	*s.*	*d.*
	4,886	13	4

John Hawkyns 7,647 10   0
James Quarles 4,886 13   4

The whole sum 12,534   3   4

JOHN HAWKYNS.
JA. QUARLES.

March 23.—*FENNER TO WALSYNGHAM.*

[ccix. 30, 31.—Holograph.   Addressed.]

Right Honourable :—I have sent you the names
noted on the other side of such captains as are here
and have had places heretofore ; as also lieutenants
and ancients.[2]   And as there are of them that are
now, if the service go forward, to proceed as
captains, their experience and deserts deserving the
same, so there are a great number of serviceable
gentlemen and soldiers that are to step up into
place ; which is left undone, until perfect directions
from your Honour of the proceedings be known ;
which I pray God be not pretermitted, but to take
the opportunity of time.   And thus, as one in all
duties wishing most happily unto your Honour, I

---

[1] The number should be 2,900 ; 2,990 agrees neither with
the statement p. 64, nor with the arithmetic here.
[2] MS. auntients.

commit your Honour unto the Almighty. From aboard her Majesty's good ship the Nonpareil, Plymouth, this 23rd of March, 1587.

Your Honour's always to command,

THOMAS FENNER.

Captains in her Majesty's ships :

Sir Francis Drake, Knight, General in the Revenge

Thomas Fenner, Vice-Admiral in the Nonpareil
Robert Crosse, Rear-Admiral in the Hope
Edward Fenner   ,,   in the Swiftsure
William Fenner   ,,   in the Aid

Captains:

Platt	Erisey [1]	Hawes [1]
Marchant [1]	Hawkyns [1]	Baker [1]
Whyte [1]	Sydenham [1]	Pepper
Poole [1]	Rivers [1]	Wilson [1]
Spindelow [1]	Yonge [1]	Seager [1]
Acton [1]	Whiddon [1]	Harris [1]
Polwhele	Roche	Flicke [1] } both being
	Manington[1]	Lancaster [1] } in London

Lieutenants :

Scudamore	Jugge	Frost
Williams	Rottenbury	Nichols
Martin	Vernothrey	

Ensigns :

Strowde	Tether	Nicholson
Snicklowe	Tomson	

[1] Commanded a ship during the summer. The others, as well as the lieutenants &c., presumably served in some capacity, but it has not been recorded. A few of the names, which there is no way of checking, seem impossible in the spelling here given.

Sergeants :

Moon	Fenner	Judson
Deckham	Jones	Gowen
Austin		

March 29.—EARL OF SUSSEX TO SIR F. WALSYNGHAM.

[ccix. 39.—Signed. Addressed.]

It may please your Honour :—Whereas I sent forth a boat for discovery, and that the weather grew so stormy and tempestuous that they were not able to continue and abide the seas, but to return with small advertisements, nevertheless I have thought good to send unto your Honour herein enclosed the note of the captain's declaration. I have also sent unto you herein the declaration of the master of a hoy, who came into this harbour yesterday from Newhaven.[1]

I have also thought good to advertise your Honour that this morning I have sent a bark, and therein one in whom I repose some trust, to learn news and also to discover what he may. And for that I perceive these actions will not well be brought to pass, without some action by other matters to colour the same, I have put into her fifty quarters of wheat, and have willed him to make two ports, whereof St. Malo, or some port near to the same, to be one, the other as he may, and both to be as wind and weather will serve.

[The rest of the letter refers to other matters, especially the examination of Mr. Richard Cotton of Warblington, described as 'an obstinate recusant.' The letter is signed at ' Portsmouth, the 29th of March, 1588.']

[1] Havre.

[ccix. 39, I.—Copy.   First enclosure in Lord Sussex's
letter of March 29.]

Captain Story his note of the voyage made in a
small boat for discovery the 10th of March, 1588.

Imprimis, upon Sunday, being the 10th of
March, the boat was brought on ground to be
trimmed and made ready for the voyage.

Item, on Tuesday at night, she being made
ready, we hauled her out into the channel, pretend-
ing to have gone the same night to sea ; but the
wind was easterly.

On Wednesday morning we rowed out of the
haven, the wind being easterly ; with sail and oars,
we gat St. Helen's Road, were we rid with the
wind at South-East and could not get out until it
was Thursday morning.

On Thursday, we rowed to sea as far as Dunnose,
where we descried a fleet of ships to the windward,
the wind being easterly, and bare towards them
with sail and oars till we fetched up one of them,
which was a ship of London come from Rochelle,
whom we asked what the other were, and he said
they were hulks bound home from Brouage.

News from Rochelle he could tell none, but that
the Prince of Condé was dead.   Then the wind
came to the North-East, and we went over with the
coast of France, so near the East as we could lie,
thinking we could have fetched to Seine Head,
but we could but fetch to the Bay of Hogges,[1] for
that wind blew so and that sea went so high, that
we could maintain no sail save our main course[2]
very low set.

On Friday morning we saw the land, which was
between Barfet-nes[3] and the Bay of Hogges, and
sailed alongst the shore till we came to Cherbourg,[4]

[1] La Hogue.   [3] MS. mayne crosse.
[2] Cape Barfleur.   [4] MS. Sherbrooke.

where we met with two tall ships of Cherbourg bound for Spain, as we think; but we could not speak with them ·by reason of the foul weather. And from thence we went to Alderney, thinking to have gotten some harbour; but the weather was so extreme foul that we could not. Yet the same night we got to Herm,[1] where we rid Saturday, Sunday and Monday, with very foul weather, not able to look out. Yet I sent over to that castle to know if there were any news, and the soldiers came aboard and told us that there were many great fleet passed by, both of Frenchmen and Flemings, both to the eastward and to the west. Then the weather being fair, we came to sea and met a southerly wind, that blew so sore that we were able to maintain no sail but our main course.[2]

On Wednesday morning we met with a great fleet of ships betwixt Portland and the Isle of Wight, fifty sail or thereabouts. Five of them gave us chase, and the headmost man of them we bare with him and spake with him and asked of him whence the rest were. He said they were all Dutch ships bound for Brouage. Other news they could tell none. And from them, we came in at Needles and went to speak with the men of war at St. Helen's, and so came in.

[ccix. 39, II.—Copy.   Second enclosure.]

The declaration of Robert Keble, master of a hoy, part of Ipswich and part of Harwich, called the William, 28th of March 1588, who came from Newhaven upon Tuesday last.

He saith he arrived at Newhaven upon Saturday next shall be a fortnight, being the 16th of March, laden with coals; and the next day after his arrival

---

[1] MS. Arme   [2] It is here written 'course.'

a Frenchman told him that the French King was
marching towards Normandy and the sea coast ; and
other told him that it was against the King of
Navarre.   And that there was a flyboat of Danske,[1]
which came from Cadiz in Spain, who arrived at
Newhaven this day sennight, and had been at sea
about 18 days, who saith that all the French shipping
is stayed in Spain and Portugal, for the service of
the King of Spain; and thinketh that all other ships
be stayed, for he himself had been stayed, if he had
not stolen away.   Also he saith that a Frenchman
did swear to him by God that the King of Spain
would come, and that they would be ready the 24th
of this month ; and the man answered ' Tush, he
will not come yet.'   ' Yes,' saith he.

2. He also saith that he spake with a man of
Marseilles, who did also affirm the same and said
that there was in that fleet 24 great galleasses ; and
they both affirmed that the whole fleet was between
4 and 500 sail.

3. He also saith that he heard both the Scots
and French say that they looked for them of Spain
daily ; and that when they came, they would join
with them.

There were now, at his being at Newhaven, 56
or 57 sail of Scots there, who were there before his
coming, and, as they said, bound for Brouage ; but
whether, he could not justly learn ; but they might
have gone out at his coming away, if they would ;
and therefore, why they tarry, he knoweth not.

He saith the Scots fell out with him and caused
him to pay 30 crowns to the church there and other
places, by order of the Governor's officers ; and that
the Governor would not hear him speak for his
answer and trial.

He saith that the Scots said unto him that if

[1] Danzig.

they might catch him at sea, they would heave him and his overboard, and all other Englishmen, and would pull their hearts out of their bodies ; calling them ' English dogs,' saying they would be revenged of the blood of their queen.

The Governor of Newhaven doth not trust the townsmen there, and is now building of a fort to command the town, and is a very hard man against Englishmen.

He saith that he heard him that came from Marseilles say that Andrew Doria, Prince of Mellita,[1] was come unto Lisbon with a great sort of galleys, and should be admiral of the King of Spain his fleet, and that, as he remembereth, the number of the Spanish army should be 50 thousand.

March 30.—DRAKE TO THE COUNCIL.

[ccix. 40.—Signed. Addressed.]

. Right honourable and my very good Lords :— Understanding by your good Lordships' letters her Majesty's good inclination for the speedy sending of these forces here unto the seas for the defence [2] of the enemy ; and that, of her Majesty's great favour and your Lordships' good opinion, you have made choice of me (although the least of many) to be as an actor in so great a cause, I am most humbly to beseech my most gracious Sovereign and your good Lordships to hear my poor opinion with favour, and so to judge of it according to your great wisdoms.

[1] Presumably Melfi ; but none of the family served in the Armada. It will be noticed, too, that the numbers given in this report are grossly exaggerated.
[2] The fending off.

If her Majesty and your Lordships think that
the King of Spain meaneth any invasion in England,
then doubtless his force is and will be great in
Spain; and thereon he will make his groundwork
or foundation, whereby the Prince of Parma may
have the better entrance, which, in mine own
judgment, is most to be feared.   But if there may
be such a stay or stop made by any means of this
fleet in Spain, that they may not come through the
seas as conquerors—which, I assure myself, they
think to do—then shall the Prince of Parma have
such a check thereby as were meet.

To prevent this I think it good that these forces
here should be made as strong as to your Honours'
wisdoms shall be thought convenient, and that for
two special causes :—First, for that they are like to
strike the first blow; and secondly, it will put great
and good hearts into her Majesty's loving subjects
both abroad and at home; for that they will be
persuaded in conscience that the Lord of all strength
will put into her Majesty and her people courage
and boldness not to fear any invasion in her own
country, but to seek God's enemies and her
Majesty's where they may be found; for the Lord
is on our side, whereby we may assure ourselves
our numbers are greater than theirs.   I must crave
pardon of your good Lordships again and again,
for my conscience hath caused me to put my pen
to the paper; and as God in his goodness hath put
my hand to the plough, so in his mercy it will never
suffer me to turn back from the truth.

My very good Lords, next under God's mighty
protection, the advantage and gain of time and
place will be the only and chief means for our good;
wherein I most humbly beseech your good Lordships
to persevere as you have began, for that with fifty
sail of shipping we shall do more good upon their

own coast, than a great many more will do here at home ; and the sooner we are gone, the better we shall be able to impeach them.

There is come home, since the sending away of my last messenger, one bark whom I sent out as an espial, who confirmeth those intelligences whereof I have advertised your Lordships by him ; and that divers of those Biscayans are abroad upon that coast wearing English flags, whereof there are made in Lisbon three hundred with the red cross, which is a great presumption, proceeding of the haughtiness and pride of the Spaniard, and not to be tolerated by any true natural English heart.

I have herein enclosed sent this note unto your Lordships, to consider of our proportions in powder, shot and other munitions, under the hand of the surveyor's clerk of the ordnance ; the which proportion in powder and shot for our great ordnance in her Majesty's ships is but for one day and half's service, if it be begun and continued as the service may require ; and but five lasts[1] of powder for 24 sail of the merchant ships, which will scant be sufficient for one day's service as divers occasions may be offered. Good my Lords, I beseech you to consider deeply of this ; for it importeth but the loss of all.

I have stayed this messenger somewhat the longer for the hearing of this Dutchman who came lately out of Lisbon, and hath delivered these advertisements herein enclosed, under his hand the 28th of this March, before myself and divers justices.

I have sent unto your good Lordships the note of such powder and munition as are delivered unto us for this great service ; which, in truth, I judge to be just a third part of that which is needful ; for if we should want it when we shall have most

---

[1] The last was twenty-four barrels of one cwt. each.

need thereof, it will be too late to send to the Tower for it. I assure your Honours it neither is or shall be spent in vain. And thus resting at your Honours' further directions, I humbly take my leave of your good Lordships. From Plymouth, the 30th of March, 1588.

Your good Lordships' very
ready to be commanded,

Fra. Drake.

March 26.—*NOTE OF POWDER.*

[ccix. 40, I.—Enclosed in Drake's letter of March 30 ;
with autograph postscript.]

Powder remaining aboard her Majesty's ships appointed to the seas in her Majesty's service under the charge of Sir Francis Drake, Knight, viz.:—

Powder : Aboard

The Revenge	.	1½ lasts 2 cwt.	
Nonpareil	.	1¼ lasts 5 cwt.	
Hope	. .	1⅓ lasts 1 cwt.	
Swiftsure	.	1 last	
Aid	. .	½ last	6¼ lasts

Remaining in the castle of Plymouth for the furnishing of the merchant ships likewise appointed to the seas under the charge of the said Sir Francis . . . . . 5 lasts

11½ lasts

Jo. Davey.

Forget not 500 muskets and at least one thousand arrows for them ; with such other munition, as by the particulars you shall find most wanting and best to be procured.   Fra. Drake.

MEMORANDA

[ccix. 41.—Rough notes in Burghley's autograph. Not dated nor endorsed.]

One thousand mariners to be brought to the ships, 1,075*l.*
That musters be made of all the watermen upon the Thames.

That letters be written to $\begin{cases} \text{Essex} \\ \text{Kent} \\ \text{Suffolk} \\ \text{Cambridge} \end{cases}$

That all ships be stayed in every port of the realm.

Essex	1,000
Kent	1,000
Sussex	500
Hampshire . . .	500

April 2.—WM. COURTENEY[1] *TO WALSYNGHAM.*

[ccix. 59.—Engrossed.]

To the Right Honourable Sir Francis Walsyngham, Knight, Principal Secretary to her Majesty.

May it please your Honour to take into her Majesty's service certain hoys of the burden of 120 tons and upward apiece, to the number of 15 or 20; which hoys will carry, to their burden, cannon,

---

[1] A master mariner of Dover, whose ship, the Katharine, had been taken by a privateer of St. Malo in or about 1580. His name frequently occurs in reference to proceedings, about this capture, in the Admiralty Court.

demi-cannon, culverin, demi-culverin and saker ; for
that the number of mariners will be few ; for the same
hoys will not ask above 20 or 25 mariners apiece,
and 50 or 60 soldiers in every hoy with the small
shot. And these 20 sail of hoys shall not stand
her Majesty in so much charges as the setting out
of 6 sail of ships ; and 500 mariners will serve
the 20 sail of hoys, and 800 will not serve 5 sail
of ships ; and these 20 sail of hoys shall do as
good and rather better service than 40 sail of ships
shall.

Imprimis, 15 or 20 sail of hoys to be set forth
with their spar-deck or netting to be made musket
free by the sides, from the mast afterward, and with
light spardeck or netting overhead for the safeguard
of the men.

Item, these 15 or 20 sail of hoys, to be set in
order five and five in a rank, and to be half shot
one from another, will make as good service for
the enemy as 40 sail of ships ; for that if they may
have any wind to turn them, they will shoot twice
to a ship's once, and the more wind the better they
are.

Item, they are good to be set foremost of a fight,
that shall happen if the enemy come ; and for the
Narrow Seas, your Honour cannot desire better
ships than these hoys.

Item, I will not have above 4 or 6 guns in a hoy ;
for that 5 or 6 men will serve to stand by her sails,
and the rest of her mariners to help the gunners
to traverse the ordnance ; and to have the soldiers
stand by their small shot.

Item, your Honour cannot have a ship of 100
or 120, but they must have 10, 15 or 20 gunners,
and 150 or 200 men in a ship, besides others to help
to tackle her about ; which in every hoy 20 mariners
will serve for all turns.

Wherefore if any service in her Majesty's affairs be required, if it shall please your Honour to accept of my poor service in these hoys, I will rest at her Majesty's or your Honour's commandment.

Your Honour's most humble at commandment,
WILLM. COURTENEY.

April 5.—THE MAYOR AND ALDERMEN OF POOLE TO THE COUNCIL.

[ccix. 70.—Signed.   Addressed.]

Our obedient duties unto your Honours in most humble wise remembered :—Your Honours' letters of the first of this present month of April to us directed, we have received the third of the same ; the contents whereof is that her Majesty doth understand that there are a good number of very apt and serviceable ships and vessels appertaining to this town, and that we should make choice of one serviceable ship of the burden of 60 tons, and one pinnace, to be furnished for two months, to be in a readiness by the 25th day of this present month ; and further importing that some merchants of this town have set forth certain ships in warlike sort, by way of reprisal, whereby they have received no small profit.   May it therefore please your Honours to be advertised that there is but one ship in this harbour at this present above the burden of threescore tons ; which ship is called the Primrose of Poole, and is of the burden of 120 tons or thereabouts, being ready rigged and victualled to depart for the New-found-land, having in her two sakers, four minions, one falcon, and two falconets, with shot for the same and 500 pound weight of powder, and eight calivers.   And for a pinnace, there is one small bark of this town, of the burden of 30 tons or thereabouts, called the Elephant, able to serve for that purpose, if she had munition and other furniture to set her forth.   Both the which we have made stay of until we shall receive further order from your Honours.   And for the merchants of this town there is not one that hath set forth any ship by way of reprisal, or otherwise gotten anything that way.   Our humble suit and petition unto your good Lordships now is, that it may please the same to consider of the great decay and disability of this poor town, by reason of embargoes, want of traffic, loss at sea, and by pirates, which have and do continually lie at Studland Bay, being the mouth of this harbour, robbing both our poor neighbours and others resorting to this town.   And lately having been at great charge in making of necessary provision for the defence of the enemy, whereby we are utterly unable to perform your Lordships' commandment for setting forth of a ship and pinnace, most humbly beseeching your Honours to discharge us of the same, being compelled to set down the truth of our poor estate to our great grief.   Wishing that we were as able as willing in all dutiful and obedient services as becometh good and faithful subjects, we most humbly pray for the preservation of your Honours in prosperous estate, long to continue.   From Poole, the 5th of April, 1588.

Your Honours' most dutiful at commandment,

JOHN BERGMAN, Mayor.

WILLM. NEWMAN.	JOHN BRAMBLE.
WILLM. DICKER.	EDWARD MAN.
ROGER MUNDLEY.	WM. REDE.
	THOMAS TUPPER.

April 6.—SIR G. CAREY[1] *TO WALSYNGHAM.*

[ccix. 71.—Signed. Addressed.]

My duty to your Honour humbly remembered :—
Having received letters from the Lords of her
Majesty's Council the fifth of this present, by the
which it appeareth that the preparation of the
Spanish forces are continued, and thereupon their
resistance intended in their honourable wisdoms, by
arming a competent number of ships out of the
maritime cities and places of good shipping within
this realm ; and that it seemeth an advertisement
hath been exhibited to her Majesty that there are a
good number of very able and serviceable ships
appertaining to the merchants and inhabitants of
this island ; whereupon their Lordships have thought
good to require of the inhabitants of this island the
furnishing of a warlike ship and pinnace, fit and able
for service, furnished for two months with victuals,
mariners, munition and other necessary provisions,
by the 25th of this present, to be in readiness to
attend the Lord Admiral :

It may please your Honour to understand that
—albeit I shall, for mine own part, be most ready,
by any service, to testify my dutiful and zealous
affection towards her Majesty and my native
country, as also the inhabitants of this place are
most desirous, by all possible means, to maintain
her Majesty's good opinion so graciously conceived
of them ; yet for that the island is utterly unprovided
of any warlike ships or vessels fit for employment in
such services, the greatest thereunto belonging not
exceeding the burden of seventy tons, and that the

[1] The eldest son of Lord Hunsdon, whom he succeeded in
1596. At this time he was Captain of the Isle of Wight.

K 2

insufficiency and great poverty of the merchants of Newport is such (being rather a poor market than a merchant-like town) as may hardly extend to the furnishing of one quarter of a ship fit in so warlike manner to be set forth—I have thought it fit first to advertise your Honour of the error of that information by the which I conceive the direction of your letters grew of this place,[1] before I would terrify the minds of this country with so great a charge, neither usual nor accustomed, which might breed discontentment and work no effect, seeing they continue the burden of continual charge in their daily preparations for defence of this place.

Wherefore I shall humbly beseech your Honour to acquaint the Lords with the poor state of this country, [and[2]] the difficulty of effecting their commandment; and if they shall [will that[2]] we proceed with this preparation, to send me your further direction, whether by way of subsidy, or in what sort this charge intended should be levied; being of opinion that my authority will neither stretch to charge them with a matter of so great innovation, nor that it may be done without the general taxation of the island, which I conceive is not meant, in respect the like is not done by the inland men of the mainland. Besides, out of this place no shipping hath been sent by way of reprisal at any time, saving only by myself; and having sustained more loss than gain thereby, I hope it be not their Honours' pleasure to charge me with what I shall be so hardly able to bear.

And so presuming to crave from your Honour farther direction, in a matter so strange and unapt to be offered to this place, before I shall proceed, I

[1] Information concerning this place, which I conceive has caused the directions given in your letters.
[2] Words omitted in MS.

shall rest most ready to perform what may be in my power to accomplish in this and in all other matters, upon your farther honourable directions ; and so humbly commit you to the tuition of the only · Almighty. From Carisbrooke Castle, this 6th of April. Your Honour's most humbly
and assured to command,
GEORGE CAREY.

April 7.—HOWARD TO WALSYNGHAM.

[ccix. 74.—Holograph. Addressed.]

Sir :—By your other letter I find her Majesty cannot be brought to have for her surety, to lie near unto her, the 4,000 footmen and the 1,000 horse. I am sorry her Majesty is so careless of this most dangerous time. I fear me much, and with grief I think it, that her Majesty relieth upon a hope that will deceive her and greatly endanger her ; and then will it not be her money nor her jewels that will help ; for as they will do good in time, so will they help nothing for the redeeming of time being lost.

For the setting out of the galley,[1] I think there is no man of judgment but doth think it most meet for her to be abroad now, being summer ; and when should she sail if not at such a time as this is ? Either she is fit now to sail, or fit for the fire, and I will never hereafter wish her Majesty to be at the charge of the keeping of her, for I hope never in my time to see so great cause for her to be used. I dare say her Majesty will look that men should

---

[1] The galley Bonavolia. It will be seen (*post*, Borough to Walsyngham, July 28) that she proved utterly useless, and at the critical moment of the campaign had to be sent into the river as unable to keep the sea.

fight for her, and I know they will. At this time
the King of Spain doth not keep any ship at home
either of his own, or any other, that he can by any
means get for money. Well, I pray heartily for a
peace, for I see that which should be the ground of
an [1] honourable war will never appear ; for sparing
and war have no affinity together.

Sir, touching the releasing of the Scottish ships
and the French,[2] in my opinion it were not amiss to
have them stayed a while ; and better to have them
stay there, than for me to stay them when they are
come out ; for I know for certain, there is none of
the Scots nor French but they carry in their ships
Englishmen and colour them for Scots ; but for the
Scots that are to go into Scotland, they may be
suffered to depart ; but for the French, I pray let
us stay as well as the King of Spain. He hath
stayed all, but with their will ; for I am sure a great
number of them went of purpose. I am afraid we
shall find them all false in France, from the highest.

Sir,[3] the great Swede [4] that is stayed, and hath
goodly masts in her, and most fittest for her
Majesty, otherwise her Majesty should have been
fain this next year to have sent a ship of her own
for masts into the East Countries,[5] which would
have been a great charge, I mean as soon as I can,
to send her up to Chatham or to Blackwall ; but I
do assure you the chiefest matter of all is that we
keep them from serving the King of Spain's turn.
There be many things else in her that will serve
well the turn now ; but it must be considered how
they shall be contented ; for I mean not in this time
to let any such ship to pass into Spain. She is a
very great ship, and well appointed with ordnance ;

---

[1] MS. a honourable.   [2] Cf. *ante*, p. 127.
[3] As to the great Swede &c. It is a common Elizabethan idiom.
[4] MS. Swethen.   [5] Danzig and the neighbourhood.

she hath many things in her, and I believe for
certain, much belonging to Spaniards. I would
wish when she cometh up, that some order might
be taken for her unlading, and then to return to
me to serve ; and so, for this time, I leave you to
the Almighty to bless you with health.   Margate,
Easter day.   Your loving friend to use,
                                          C. HOWARD.

*April 7.—THE MAYOR AND ALDERMEN OF
KINGSTON-UPON-HULL TO THE COUNCIL.*

[ccix. 75.—Signed.   Addressed.]

Most Honourable, our most humble duties
remembered :—We have received your Lordships'
letters by David Jenkyns, her Majesty's pursuivant,
dated at Greenwich the first of this instant month,
wherein your Honours do require us to make
choice of two serviceable and good ships, not to
be under the burden of three score tons, and of
one pinnace ; and to cause the same presently to be
put in a readiness and furnished for two months, with
victuals, mariners, munition, and other necessary
provision and furniture, by the 25th of this present
month of April, to join with her Majesty's navy in
the seas, or to be otherwise employed as we shall
receive further directions from your Honours or
from the Lord Admiral of England.

May it therefore please your good Lordships to
be advertised that, before the receipt of your Lordships' said letter, all the mariners now in the town
any way able to serve, to the number of ninety
and four, were and are pressed the sixth of this
present month, to serve in her Majesty's navy, by
Christopher Chapman, by virtue of a commission
under the Great Seal of England, directed to John
Hawkyns, dated at Westminster the 2nd of February

in the two and twenty year of her Majesty's reign ;
and of a deputation from the said John Hawkyns to
the said Christopher Chapman, bearing date the first
of April, *Anno Domini* 1588 ; which said mariners
were appointed by him to be at Chatham the 20th
day of this instant month.   And forasmuch as all
the best ships meet for service belonging to this port
be abroad in the parts beyond the seas and at
London, and the town destitute of mariners at this
present (as appeareth by a note hereinclosed [1]), we
are no way able, as most willingly we would, to
accomplish your Lordships' appointment in so short
time, until God send the ships and mariners (now
being abroad) to be comen home.   Whereof we
have thought it our duties (in most humble manner)
to certify your Honours.   Nevertheless when it
shall please God to send some better store of shipping
and men home, we shall, to the uttermost of our
powers, show all readiness and willing disposition
to the performance thereof, as becometh good and
dutiful subjects, upon further direction from your
Lordships, and warrant for taking of such ships and
men as shall be thought meet, with all other furniture
meet for that service.   And thus most humbly we
take our leaves.   Kingston upon Hull, the 7th day
April, 1588.

Your Lordships' humbly at commandment,

WILLAM BRAYE, Mayor.

WILLM. WILSON.	JOHN THORNETON.
EDWARD WAKEFIELDE.	WILLM. GEE.
LEONARD WYLLAN.	JOHN SMYTHE.
LUKE THORSCROS.	ROBT. GAYTON.
ROBART DALTON.	

[1] This enclosed note (75, I.) is a statement of the names of the
ships and number of mariners belonging to the town of Kingston-
on-Hull, which are at present on distant voyages ; with the
number of mariners pressed into the navy.

April 8.—HOWARD TO BURGHLEY.

[ccix. 78.—Holograph. Addressed.]

My honourable and very good Lord :—I thought good to put your Lordship in remembrance how necessary it is to have a better proportion of victual than for one month, considering the time and the service that is likely to fall out ; and what danger it might breed if our want of victual should be at the time of service.[1] We shall be now victualled, beginning the 20th of this April, unto the 18th of May, at which time the last month's victual doth end ; and by the advertisements that giveth the largest time for the coming out of the Spanish forces, is the midst of May, being the 15th. Then have we three days' victual. If it be fit to be so, it passeth my reason. I think there is none that will venture to carry these ships to Portsmouth[2] under a month's victual. My Lord, this would[3] be cared for in time ; for whensoever our victual shall come, it will ask 4 or 5 days, the taking in of it ; and the weather may so fall out as in 10 days we shall scantly take it in. I think since ever there were ships in this realm it was never heard of that but a month's victual was prepared for to victual withal. King Harry, her Majesty's father, never made a lesser proportion of supply than 6 weeks[4] ; and yet there was a marvellous help upon any extremity ; for there was ever provisions at Portsmouth, and also at Dover ; and his baking and brewing there ; so as, for the service then, which

[1] This is exactly what did happen. See *post*, Darell to Burghley, July 22.
[2] MS. Porchmouth.   [3] Should.
[4] Howard's information as to the practice in King Harry's time was strangely at fault. See Introduction.

was only for France, it was ever at hand upon any necessity.

My good Lord, let me be borne withal for the writing this plainly. It is my duty; and your Honour knoweth what danger want in such a time may do, and how people are disposed upon want to be mutinous; yet have I great cause to think they would suffer much hardness before they would do so. My Lord, I think there was never a more willing company to venture their lives in her Majesty's service than be here. Therefore it were pity they should lack at the time of service. If it be thought fit for us to be victualled for a longer time, it would [1] be gone in hand withal.

The Ark is arrived this morning here at Margate, wonderfully well trimmed and mended of her leak, which was a bolt forgotten to be driven in, and the outside covered with pitch, so it could not be seen; and when the sea had washed it off, then brake in the leak; and she was not well caulked in any place, but now most perfect. So I end to trouble your Lordship any further, praying God to send you health with your little strength. Margate Road, the 8th of April.

Your Lordship's most assured at command,

C. HOWARD.

April 9.—*THE MAYOR OF LYME REGIS TO THE COUNCIL.*

[ccix. 81.—Signed. Addressed.]

Right honourable Lords, our duties in most humble manner remembered :—It may please your Honours to understand that your honourable letters

[1] Should.

of the first of this April concerning making choice, putting in a readiness, and furnishing of certain shipping to serve under the conduct of Sir Francis Drake, Knight, were received the third of this said April, at 8 of the clock at night; upon receipt whereof— for that there was not at the present, nor as yet, any ship here at home of the burden of 60 tons, but three small vessels far under that burden—we have made choice of one of the best and fittest of the same vessels for a pinnace, being handsome for the purpose and of the burden of 40 tons or thereabouts, called the Revenge of Lyme, whereof is owner and captain Richard Bedford. The which bark we have caused and appointed to be manned with thirty good mariners, and furnished for two months of victuals, munition, and other furniture, as with minions, falcons, fowlers, muskets, calivers, and with all other necessary provision for the wars. And so being furnished in a readiness, shall (by God's grace), with wind and weather convenient, be sent unto her Majesty's navy at Plymouth, by the time limited by the said letters accordingly.

And as concerning order for the levying of this charge—The said three towns of Lyme, Axminster and Chard, upon conference had together of the matter, have agreed that the whole charge thereof should only rise upon those persons amongst us that are set in subsidy to her Majesty, proportionably; all which persons so set in subsidy do yield hereunto, saving certain persons of Axminster aforesaid, of sufficient ability, which refuse. Whereupon our humble request unto your Honours is that your Lordships would take further direction concerning those persons of Axminster so refusing, that they might likewise be contributory with us in the premises accordingly. And furthermore, we finding amongst us, of the said three towns, none that have received any benefit by reprisals, except one stranger very lately come in amongst us; as also, divers of our merchants having received of late great losses in foreign countries, and chiefly in France, do humbly request your Honours that if hereafter we shall be further charged in like sort as afore, that we might by your honourable direction (to be taken in that behalf) have aid therein by others sufficient, dwelling in the towns near adjoining and trading amongst us. Thus leaving further to trouble your Lordships, do commit the same to the protection of the most Highest. From Lyme Regis, this 9th of April, *Anno Domini* 1588.

Your Lordships' at commandment,
with all obedience,
JOHN JONES, Mayor.

April 10.—*A NOTE OF CHARGES.*

[ccix. 82.—Copy.]

A note of the charge of one month's wages and victuals for all her Majesty's ships and other vessels that serve under the charge of the Lord Admiral.

	£	s.	d.
Ships at sea with the Lord Admiral: First, for the sea wages of 2,990 men for one month of 28 days, serving under the charge of the Lord Admiral; to begin the 11th day of March last, and to end the 7th of April following, both days included, at 14s. the man, *per mensem*	2,093	0	0

Elizabeth Jonas, Triumph, Bear, Victory:
For the sea wages of 1,900 to serve for one month of 28 days in her

Majesty's said four great ships ;   £   *s.*   *d.*
to begin the 19th of May, 1588,
and to end the 15th of June, both
days included, after the said rate
of 14*s.* the man, *per mensem,* is .   1,330   0   0

Sum 3,423*l.*, which was paid unto Mr. Hawkyns
the 8th of May, 1588.

Ships with the Lord Admiral :   £   *s.*   *d.*
For the sea victuals for one month
of 28 days, for 2,990 men ; to
begin the 19th of May, and to
end the 25th of June, 1588, both
days included, at 16*s.* 4*d.* the
man, *per mensem*   .   .   . 2,441   16   8

The 4 great ships :
For the sea victual of one month
of 28 days, for 1,900 men serving
in the four great ships ; to begin
the 19th of May, and to end the
15th of June, both days included,
at 16*s.* 4*d.* the man, *per mensem* . 1,551   13   4

For transportation of the said
victuals   200   0   0

Sum 4,193*l.* 10*s.*, which was paid to him [1] the
13th of April, 1588.

C. HOWARD.   JOHN HAWKYNS.
                JAS. QUARLES.

April 10.—*BURGHLEY TO WALSYNGHAM.*

[ccix. 83.—Holograph. Addressed.]

Sir :—I cannot express my pain newly increased
in all my left arm. My spirits are even now so

[1] Quarles.

extenuated, as I have no mind towards anything but to groan with my pain. Therefore pardon me for not answering to you.

I am sorry to see more respect had to accidents than to the substance. Surely, Sir, as God will be best pleased with peace, so in nothing can her Majesty content her realm better than in procuring of peace; which if it cannot be had, yet is she excused afore God and the world. I have received many letters from the Lord Cobham urging my furtherance for resolution[1] of things; but I can only answer his expectation with my prayers. I am bold to send you two letters from Robert Cecill. When you have leisure to read them, I refer the longest to your consideration; only I would not that thereby we should be made slower in our preparations.

If you have an alphabet in cipher which I sent to her Majesty by Windebank,[2] to decipher Sir Edward Stafford's letters to her, I pray you let me have the use of it but for a day or two, and I will return it again.

And so, even forced with pain, even from my arm to my heart, I end.   10th of April, 1588.

Yours most assured,

W. BURGHLEY.

[1] Settlement.

[2] Thomas Windebank was in 1560 travelling tutor and governor to Burghley's elder son Thomas, afterwards first Earl of Exeter. In 1568 he was appointed Clerk of the Signet, and so continued till the death of the Queen. On his retirement, he was knighted by James I. Sir Francis Windebank, Secretary of State under Charles I, was his son.

April 11.—*THE MAYOR AND CITIZENS OF
EXETER TO THE COUNCIL.*

[ccix. 84.—Signed. Addressed.]

Our most humble and bounden duties remembered :—Having received your Honours' letters for
the setting forth of three ships and a pinnace, to
attend on Sir Francis Drake, we caused a present
view to be taken of all our shipping, but found none
left fit for that service, saving two only bound for
Newfoundland, which were gotten out of the haven,
and being still upon the coast are now stayed for
this purpose ; which ships being of good burden, Sir
Francis Drake, whom we have made it known unto,
accepteth, rather than three others of lesser portage.
But by reason your Honours' letters are directed
only to Exeter and Topsham, all the rest of the
places and creeks belonging to the Port of Exeter,
whereunto the most number and best ships of the
whole harbour doth belong, do allege that because
they are not specially named in your Honours'
letters, this service concerneth them not ; whereas
in truth, there is but one serviceable ship of the
said harbour in all, belonging in part to some of
the inhabitants of this city, namely the Rose of
Exeter, of the burden of one hundred tons or more ;
which, being one of the two ships aforesaid, together
with a fine pinnace, we mind, according to your
Honours' direction, to cause to be thoroughly furnished and prepared by the appointed time, although
the same will be to our very great charge ; most
humbly beseeching your Honours to direct your
honourable letters unto Topsham, Kenton, Exmouth,
Lympstone, Sidmouth, Seaton, Colyton, Dawlish,
Teignmouth, Tiverton and Collumpton, for the
preparing of that other ship so stayed, or some

other like, for the better furtherance of this her
Majesty's service, which God prosper.   To whose
most gracious protection we most humbly recom-
mend your Honours, with all humble dutifulness.
Exon, the 11th of April, 1588.
  Your Lordships' most dutiful and
              humble at commandment,
      The Mayor and Citizens of Exeter,
                       Jo. PERYAM, Mayor.
  G. PERYAM.   NICHOLAS MARTIN.
  GEOFFREY THOMAS.   RICHARD PROUZ.[1]

April 12.—*THE MAYOR AND ALDERMEN OF
    KING'S LYNN TO THE COUNCIL.*

[ccix. 87.—Signed.   Addressed.]

  Right Honourable :—After we, the Mayor,
Aldermen, and Company of the borough of King's
Lynn, had received your honourable letters which were
directed to this town of King's Lynn and the town
of Blakeney, concerning the furnishing of two ships
of war, either of them of the burden of 60 tons at
the least, and one pinnace fit for that service, we
had conference with some of the chiefest of the said
town of Blakeney, and with some of the towns of
Cley and Wiveton, which be members of the same
town of Blakeney, and we find that they are unwilling to be at any charge near the furnishing of
a ship.   We sent also to the town of Wells, which
is a member of our port, a town very well furnished
with shipping, within which there be many rich men
inhabiting ; but they have denied altogether to contribute to our charge ; and we made diligent enquiry
if any of our port had sent forth any ship of war or

[1] The modern name is Prowse ; this citizen of Exeter wrote
it Prouz. Cf. *Visitation of Devon*, 1620 (Harl. Soc.), p. 223.

taken any goods by way of reprisal, but we cannot find that there is any such. And we received your Honours' said letters the 7th of this month, before which time there were gone out from hence, for Iceland, six of the best ships of our town, and divers others into Holland and other places, so that we were left destitute of all ships fit for that service except one, called the Mayflower of Lynn, being of the burden of one hundred and fifty tons, of which we have made choice ; and we have chosen also one pinnace, of the burden of forty tons, and we intend, God so permitting, to furnish the said ship and pinnace with 100 men and all other things fit and necessary for her Majesty's wars. Howbeit, the truth is that our town is very unable to bear the charge thereof without assistance. Wherefore we humbly crave your Honours' letters to be directed to the towns of Cley, Wiveton, Blakeney, Wells, and other the coast towns towards Lynn, and to the dealers with corn, merchandise, and marine causes, in the towns near adjacent, commending them to join herein in the charge with us; and we shall, according to our bounden duty, pray to God for your Honours' preservation. King's Lynn, this 12th of April, 1588.

Your Honours', in all humbleness,

THOMAS SANDYLL, Mayor.

RICHARD CLARCK. ROBART HULLVOR.
THOMAS BOSTON. THOMAS OVEREND.

April 12.—*THE BAILIFFS OF IPSWICH TO SIR F. WALSYNGHAM.*

[ccix. 88.—Signed. Addressed.]

After our bounden duties to your Honour humbly remembered :—Where[1] we lately received letters

[1] Whereas.

from your Honour, and other of her Majesty's most
honourable Privy Council, for the furnishing of two
ships and one pinnace presently to be put in readiness and furnished by the towns of Ipswich and
Harwich for two months with victuals, mariners,
munition, and other necessary provision and furniture, to join with her Majesty's navy on the seas, or
to be otherwise employed as we should be directed
from their Honours or from the Lord High Admiral
of England, mentioning therein that such merchants
of those towns who had set forth ships in warlike
sort by way of reprisal, supposed to have received
great profit thereby, should bear the greater part of
that burden :

And where [1] sythens it hath pleased the said Lord
Admiral, by his letters to us and the inhabitants of
the said town of Harwich directed, to require us to
make choice of three sufficient and serviceable hoys
instead of the said ships and pinnace, and to furnish
them with six or eight of the meetest great serviceable ordnance for each of the same hoys, besides
forty men in every such hoy, whereof most to be
musketeers, as by the said letters this bearer hath
ready to show to your Honour may appear :

We thereupon, according to our bound duties,
have endeavoured ourselves to the uttermost of
our power and abilities about the accomplishment
of the premises, and cannot find or get sufficient
great ordnance serviceable for the same. It would
therefore please your Honour, for our better service
of her Majesty, whereof we have a care, to be a
mean for the obtaining of that kind of munition out
of her Majesty's store in London or elsewhere.

And as touching the charge meant by the said
letters to be imposed upon the said merchants who
set forth ships by way of reprisal, we have imparted

[1] Whereas.

the contents of the said letters to the said merchants, who, for answer thereof, affirm that they have thereby rather sustained loss than gain ; so as there is no hope of obtaining any greater help of them towards that contribution than of the other inhabitants of the said town of Ipswich, rate for rate, unless we have further direction in that behalf from your Honour. And forasmuch as heretofore, in like cases of charge, we have found some very unwilling to contribute, and fear to find some such at this time, we humbly beseech your Honour's direction in that matter, what order we shall take with such as we shall find obstinate therein. And thus being willing in every behalf to the uttermost of our power to accomplish your Honour's former commandment, we humbly take our leaves of your Honour ; praying to Almighty God for your Honour, in health and goodly felicity, long to endure. Ipswich, this 12th of April, 1588.

Your Honour's most humble to command,

JOHN BARKAR
EDWARD GOODDINGE } Bailiffs of Ipswich.

April 13.—SIR F. DRAKE TO THE QUEEN.

[ccix. 89.—Signed. Addressed.]

Most gracious Sovereign :—I have received from Mr. Secretary some particular notes, and withal a commandment to answer them unto your Majesty.

The first is that your Majesty would willingly be satisfied from me how the forces now in Lisbon might best be distressed.

Truly this point is hardly to be answered as yet, for two special causes : the first for that our intelligences are as yet uncertain ; the second is, the

L 2

resolution of our own people, which I shall better understand when I have them at sea. The last insample at Cadiz is not of divers yet forgotten ; for one such flying now, as Borough did then, will put the whole in peril, for that the enemy's strength is now so great gathered together and ready to invade.

But if your Majesty will give present order for our proceeding to the sea, and send to the strengthening of this fleet here four more of your Majesty's good ships, and those 16 sail of ships with their pinnaces which are preparing in London, then shall your Majesty stand assured, with God's assistance, that if the fleet come out of Lisbon, as long as we have victual to live withal upon that coast, they shall be fought with, and I hope, through the goodness of our merciful God, in such sort as shall hinder his quiet passage into England ; for I assure your Majesty, I have not in my lifetime known better men, and possessed with gallanter minds, than your Majesty's people are for the most part, which are here gathered together, voluntarily to put their hands and hearts to the finishing of this great piece of work ; wherein we are all persuaded that God, the giver of all victories, will in mercy look upon your most excellent Majesty, and us your poor subjects, who for the defence of your Majesty, our religion, and native country, have resolutely vowed the hazard of our lives.

The advantage of time and place in all martial actions is half a victory[1] ; which being lost is irrecoverable. Wherefore, if your Majesty will command me away with those ships which are here already, and the rest to follow with all possible expedition, I hold it in my poor opinion the surest

---

[1] Compare Nelson's ' Time is everything; five minutes makes the difference between a victory and a defeat.'—Nicolas, iv. 290.

and best course ; and that they bring with them
victuals sufficient for themselves and us, to the
intent the service be not utterly lost for want
thereof ; whereof I most humbly beseech your most
excellent Majesty to have such consideration as the
weightiness of the cause requireth ; for an Englishman, being far from his country, and seeing a present want of victuals to ensue, and perceiving no
benefit to be looked for, but only blows, will hardly
be brought to stay.

I have order but for two months' victuals,
beginning the 24th of April, whereof one whole
month may be spent before we come there ; the
other month's victual will be thought with the least
to bring us back again. Here may the whole
service and honour be lost for the sparing of a few
crowns.

Touching my poor opinion how strong your
Majesty's fleet should be to encounter this great
force of the enemy, God increase your most excellent
Majesty's forces both by sea and land daily ; for
this I surely think : there was never any force so
strong as there is now ready or making ready
against your Majesty and true religion ; but that
the Lord of all strengths is stronger, and will
[defend] the truth of his word for his own name's
sake ; unto the which God be all glory given.
Thus, in all humble duty, I continually will pray to
the Almighty to bless and give you victory over all
his and your enemies. From Plymouth, this 13th
of April, 1588.

Your Majesty's most loyal,

Fra. Drake.

April 13.—*HOWARD TO BURGHLEY.*

[B.M. Harl. MS. 6994, f. 120.—Holograph.   Addressed.]

My honourable good Lord :—I received even
now a letter from Captain Frobiser ; the effect was
that there is come from the river of Seine, in France,
six English ships, who declared unto him that there
was great forces of soldiers come down to the sea
coast, and that it is spoken there that word is
brought by one that came out of Spain that the
Spanish fleet is at the sea, and that, upon the news,
the Frenchmen made great jollity and bravery, and
came down to the English ships and cut their cables,
and used them so badly as that they were driven to
come away with all speed and leave all their business.   And also Mr. Frobiser hath written that on
Friday last, being the 5th of this present, there
passed by Calais a hundred pilots, whereof two
were Englishmen : they came in a flyboat from
Dunkirk, and are gone to meet the Spanish fleet.
Her Majesty's pleasure was that this letter should
be sent to Sir Fr. Drake, for the wind being as it
hath been ever since, it is like they should not be
past the islands of Guernsey and Jersey, and therefore that he should send two or three nimble barks
to intercept them, if it be possible, and also if
they meet with any that cometh out of Spain, to
learn what they can of the readiness of the army
there, which in my opinion is readier than we
do think they be.   I would have been very glad
to have seen your Lordship myself, but I could
not obtain leave of her Majesty ; and yet it were
fit that I should make your Lordship acquainted
with her Majesty's resolution touching the service
on the seas, which, God willing, I will do before

I depart, if no sudden alarm[1] come, which I fear hourly.

My good friend Mr. Robert Cecill[2] did write me a letter, which I thank her Majesty she did read it over to me twice, with words of him that I was not sorry to hear. I am bold to send the letter unto your Lordship, praying your Lordship that after you have read it, that you will send it me again, for after her Majesty had read it twice unto me, she called for it again and read it to my Lord Steward.[3] I pray to God to send your Lordship strength and health, and so I take my leave of your Lordship. From Hackney, the 13th of April.

Your Lordship's most assured to command,

C. Howard.

April 16.—THE MAYOR AND CORPORATION OF WEYMOUTH TO THE COUNCIL.

[ccix. 94.—Signed. Addressed. Endorsed.]

Right Honourable, our humble duties remembered :—Whereas we have received direction from you—for that it is supposed that divers merchants of this place have had great benefit by setting forth their ships in warlike sort by way of reprisal—that this port should furnish her Majesty with two ships and one pinnace, men, munition and victuals, for two months, and forthwith to join with her forces in the fleet under the conduct of Sir Francis Drake, Knight, admiral thereof: And[4] before received order from the Lord Admiral for the like furnishing of two ships and one pinnace to join with her

---

[1] MS. alaroume.
[2] Burghley's younger son, the future Earl of Salisbury.
[3] The Earl of Leicester.   [4] And whereas we had.

Highness's navy royal in the east parts. And whereas the 13th of this present, a general press of mariners hath been in this port, by means whereof this place, at this instant, is much destitute :

May it please your good Lordships to be advertised that the benefit of those reprisals hath not been in this place of that great estimation, although some quantity of such merchandise hath been here landed ; for that the proper owners thereof, in the greatest part, are of other places and not inhabitants in this port, being a town of small ability and in part decayed. And it may further please your Lordships, of our own industry, to our very great charge, we have builded a platform for some defence of this town and country, at this instant not thoroughly furnished with needful ordnance, by reason of our poverty not able thereunto. Yet notwithstanding, our very good Lords, tendering in all duty her Majesty's service, with desire to satisfy as near as we can your honourable commands in this behalf, [we] have at our own charge provided one ship of the burden of 80 tons, furnished with fifty men and victualled for two months, to join with Sir Francis Drake, and one pinnace of 30 tons, furnished with thirty men and victualled for two months, to attend the Lord Admiral, and now ready to depart this harbour according to their direction ; besides two other ships providing likewise for the Lord Admiral, by order from his Lordship. In consideration whereof, we beseech your Lordships to accept our willingness in any service we shall be commanded ; and for that the charge is very great to us only and the benefit general to inhabitants out of this place, it may please you in your grave consideration, partly to disburse us, by adding some townships near adjoining to be contributory towards the same, being so general service, and as well their goods as others; wherein we shall as heretofore most humbly acknowledge ourselves bounden unto your Lordships for your great care in relief of us. And so most humbly do take our leaves. Weymouth and Melcombe Regis, this 16th of April, 1588.

Your Lordships' most ready to command,

RYCHARD PITT, Mayor.

WILLIAM PIT.   JOHN MOKET, Bailiff.
BARNARD MAJOR.   JOHN ALLEN.

April 17.—SIR ROBERT WYNGFELD[1] *TO THE COUNCIL.*

[ccix. 95.—Signed. Addressed.]

Pleaseth it your Honours to understand that where it pleased you to direct your honourable letters to the towns of Aldborough, Orford and others, for the furnishing and setting out of a ship and a pinnace to the sea, meaning thereby, as it is supposed, that only those people that use the trade to sea should be chargeable to that service, and not those that are charged to find any furniture to land service: yet notwithstanding, the inhabitants of Orford have, for their own ease and to levy a far more sum than will suffice to that service, charged one Reuben Collye, and one Gilbert, and their servants, who are otherwise charged by land, to be contributories to their charge, and have threatened to compel them to appear before your Honours to answer such complaints as they will exhibit against them. And for that I know the men of small ability and charged otherwise, as abovesaid, I have

---

[1] Justice of the Peace and Commissioner of Musters for the county of Suffolk, knighted in 1553.

thought good to signify so much unto your Lordships, most humbly entreating you that you will
receive no information against them to their prejudice, for that I know them as ready any way
to serve her Majesty as duty requireth. And so
humbly take my leave, this 17th of April, 1588.

Your Honours' to command,

ROBERT WYNGFELD.

PETITION OF ORFORD AND DUNWICH TO THE COUNCIL.

[ccix. 96.—Not dated nor endorsed.]

To the Right Honourable the Lords and others
of her Majesty's most honourable Privy Council.

In most humble wise beseeching your Honours,
your poor and daily orators,[1] the chief officers
and commonalties of the towns of Orford and
Dunwich &c., in the county of Suffolk, that where [2]
among themselves they cannot agree in the dissever-
ing [3] of the contribution and charge towards such
shipping for her Majesty's service as on them and
the town of Aldborough, in the said county, by your
Honours' late letters was imposed ; and only through
Aldborough, as your Honours' said orators hope
shall be adjudged ; which notwithstanding, there
is such order taken that the preparation in effect is
ready which at all their hands was required : it [4]
would therefore please your Honours to address
your letters to such knights and worshipful gentlemen as are next adjoining to those coast towns, who
best know their several estates, for the imposing of
every several town's charges for this service, ac-

[1] Suppliants.
[2] Whereas.
[3] Apportioning.
[4] We pray that it.

cording to the validity of their several estates. And that it would please your Honours that the town of Woodbridge, their next neighbour, which was omitted, and which your Honours upon former humble petition granted, may contribute unto the charge of the said towns, and not to Ipswich, which is not so charged as your said orators be ; neither is Woodbridge—as they account themselves—a limb of that port of Ipswich, as Ipswich hath alleged. And your said orators, according to their bounden duty, shall and will daily pray for the continuance of your Honours in all health and honour.

April 17. THE MAYOR AND ALDERMEN OF SOUTHAMPTON TO THE COUNCIL

[ccix. 97.—Signed. Addressed.]

May it please your good Lordships :—Immediately after the receipt of your letters of the first of this present,[1] which came to our hands the 6th of the same, whereby is signified her Majesty's pleasure that this town should prepare, furnish, man and set forth, at the proper charge of us and the rest of the inhabitants here, two ships and one pinnace to be employed in her Majesty's service, and for the defence of the realm, by the space of two months, we did, according to our duties and the abundance of our zeal and desire to do her Majesty faithful service, assemble ourselves together, as we have often done sithence the receipt of your Lordships' letters, to consider as well of the charge, as how the same might be levied among so poor and insufficient a number of inhabitants any way able to contribute

[1] See *Hist. MSS. Com.*, Report XI., App. pt. iii. 123.

towards the same ; and finding the charge to amount
to five hundred pounds or thereabouts, we see it
not possible how the same (no not the fourth part
thereof) can be levied among us, in respect of the
disability and poverty of the town, which ever
sithence the embargue[1] in Spain, being about 16
years, hath grown from time to time so to decay, as
within the half of that time there hath been almost
no trade or traffic within this town ; whereby not
only those among us that were of any reasonable
estate of wealth or stock to exercise trade of merchandise are so low drawn and impoverished as[2]
they have been constrained in effect to give up and
forsake their traffic, but even the handicrafts men,
which, by the common trade to this town, were in
some competent sort maintained, are wonderfully
decayed, and so the town dispeopled of many of her
Majesty's natural subjects ; in whose places some
few strangers of foreign countries are come to
inhabit here, and they (God knoweth) but very poor,
living with the labour of their hands.

Your Lordships will best consider the insufficiency of this place to furnish to so great a
charge as five hundred pounds, when the whole
subsidy within the same doth not amount to about a
hundred and twenty pounds, and that gathered with
much difficulty[3] and murmurs of the people ; who,
besides the said subsidy, have been of late charged
by direction from your Lordships with the provision
of certain powder and other munition to the sum of
250*l.*, which remaineth dead and without profit to
the town ; and now lately charged with reparations
about the town upon the sea banks, to defend[4] the
violence of the waters, with some little fortifications
to strengthen the town against the enemy.   And

---

[1] Embargo   [2] That.   [3] Difficilitie.
[4] Fend off, guard against.

whereas your Lordships are of opinion that benefit hath grown to some of the inhabitants in this place by way of reprisals against the Spaniard, we dare assure your Lordships, upon our poor fidelity and credit, that the town hath thereby been impoverished at the least four thousand pounds.

Thus, our very good Lords, after we had often assembled ourselves, considered, and propounded the effect of your Lordships' letters to the principal and best able of the inhabitants,[1] and finding the state of this town so weak and unable to be strained to the charge of the preparation required, and that the motion[2] thereof made to the people doth cause them greatly to murmur and grieve thereat, having nevertheless travailed therein hitherto to our utmost, we have thought it necessary, under your Lordships' humble correction, as well in discharge of our duties towards her Majesty, as finding the necessity and poverty of the town so great, with all humility to entreat your good Lordships to be a means to her Majesty, that it will please her, of her princely bounty and clemency, to discharge this town wholly of that burden and charge, because if the same should be laid upon us, it must grow out of the purse of a very few of us so utterly unable to bear the same, as that it would tend greatly to our impoverishment and beggary.

And whereas your Lordships have happily been informed that there should[3] be divers gentlemen inhabiting within this town of good ability whom you would have to contribute towards this charge, it may please your Lordships to be advertised that there is not above one gentleman that is inhabiting or remaining within the town that is not of the

---

[1] MS. inhabitauncie. [2] Proposal.
[3] This use of the conditional as denoting hearsay is very common.

bourgeoisie of the same ; and the rest are very few, who have only hired some lodgings and houses in the town for some part of this winter past, and are either now gone or shortly do depart to their houses and charge in the country ; so as if for our better ease they should be taxed towards the furnishing of the charge aforesaid, it would be but a small relief that would thereby grow unto us.

Furthermore, if the town were able to reach to so great a contentment, whereof we should be right glad, as well for that her Majesty's service might be furthered and advanced thereby, as that our town were in case of ability thereunto, yet we must let your Lordships understand that sithence the receipt of your letters before mentioned there have been prested and taken up within this town by John Thomas and John Younge, having her Majesty's commission under the Great Seal of England, above a hundred and ten mariners ; whereby, if we were able to levy the charge among us, it were not possible for us to find so many fit mariners in those parts as might serve to man the meanest of the three ships required.

These lacks and impediments therefore considered, we do most humbly pray and hope that her Majesty and your Lordships will have compassion of the poverty and inability of this poor town in remitting and discharging the same of the shipping, charge and furniture required, assuring your Lordships that it will be an act of great charity towards us, and we shall be bound to pray for her Majesty and your Lordships (as we do daily), and to be ready to expose our lives and slender substance to do her Majesty service when and where it shall please her Majesty to employ and command us, as knoweth God ; to whose holy protection we do most humbly leave your good

Lordships. From Southampton, the 17th of April, 1588.

Yo^r Honours' most bounden at commandment,
ANDREW STUDLEY, Mayor.

JOHN CROOKE.	JOHN BOLLACKAR.[1]
ROBT. KNAPLOCKE.	JOHN FAVOR.
JOHN JACKSON.	ALEXANDR. PENTE.
RICHARD BESUN.	WYLLM. EDMONDS.
WILLIAM BARWYKE.	

April 17.—HOWARD TO BURGHLEY.

[ccix. 99.—Signed. Addressed.]

My very good Lord :—It is now determined that I shall go westward with the greatest part of her Majesty's ships, whereof I have thought good to advertise your Lordship. The purpose and conclusion of her Majesty's intent, Sir William Wynter or Mr. Hawkyns will advertise your Lordship at large.

I wrote to your Lordship before this long since of sundry extraordinary charges that were then grown in furnishing of the navy, which doth daily increase many ways ; therefore I heartily pray your Lordship that there may be paid 2,000*l.* out of the warrant of 29,000, bearing date the second of February, 1586 ; whereby her Majesty's navy may be the better furnished, and thereby more able to do her and this realm service. And so I bid your good Lordship most heartily farewell. From my house at Deptford, the 17th of April, 1588.

Your Lordship's most assured to command,
C. HOWARD.

[1] Mayor the next year. *Hist. MSS. Com.*, XI. iii. 124.

April 19.—*THE BAILIFFS OF IPSWICH TO
SIR F. WALSYNGHAM.*

[ccix. 100.—Signed.   Addressed.]

After our bounden duties to your Honour humbly
remembered :—Where we lastly received your
Honour's most favourable letters on the behalf of
the town of Ipswich, for the obtaining of great
ordnance for our better furnishing of three serviceable hoys for her Majesty against her Highness's
enemies, by your Honour's means, of[1] the Right
Honourable the Lord High Admiral of England ;
for which we render to your Honour our most
humble and dutiful thanks.   And therefore we have
hereby made so bold, eftsoons[2] to commend the
same to your Honour for further remembrance
towards my said Lord Admiral in that behalf, by
your Honour's letters to his Lordship, or otherwise
as shall seem best for the accomplishment thereof,
at the time and place by his Honour appointed ;
for that otherwise, we cannot furnish the same as
we most willingly would, according to our duties.
And therefore have sent this bearer to attend your
Honour's direction therein, for that the time
appointed for that service approacheth so nigh at
hand.

And further, if it shall like your Honour, we
having considered of the great charge of the said
hoys, do perceive that the charge thereof will amount
to four whole subsidies, to be borne by the said
inhabitants ; and thereupon, having sithence proportionably rated ourselves and the other inhabitants of the said town of Ipswich able to contribute,
according to their abilities, for the setting forth of

---

[1] From.   [2] Forthwith, at once.

the said hoys in warlike manner, one Ralph Morrys, gent and inhabitant of the said town, and a man of sufficient ability to bear the burden and charge set upon him, hath most obstinately refused to pay his said rate cessed upon him, to the evil example of others, if he shall so pass away. Whereupon we, according to your Honour's direction, have bound him by obligation herewith sent, to her Majesty's use in the sum of one hundred marks to make his personal appearance before the Lords and others of her Majesty's most honourable Privy Council on Saint Mark's day[1] next coming, to abide their Honours' order, whereunto as duty bindeth us we submit ourselves. And thus humbly taking our leaves of your Honour, we cease; praying to Almighty God to preserve your Honour long in health and goodly felicity. Ipswich, this 19th of April, 1588.

Your Honour's most humbly to command,

JOHN BARKAR
EDWARDE GOODDINGE } Bailiffs of Ipswich.

April 20.—THE MAYOR AND BURGESSES OF KINGSTON-UPON-HULL TO SIR F. WAL-SYNGHAM.

[ccix. 101.—Signed. Addressed.]

Right Honourable, our duties humbly remembered:—Understanding to our great grief your Honour's misliking of our late certificate, made to the Lords and others of her Majesty's most honourable Privy Council, of the lack of sufficient ships and mariners here to furnish from hence two ships and one pinnace, according to their Lordships' direction, by

[1] July 25.

means of their absence upon their traffic, and the late press made by one Christopher Chapman :— We therefore, encouraged by your Honour's accustomed good affection to this town and the inhabitants thereof, and the good liking you have had of our readiness and willingness in her Majesty's service, and being very sorry to minister any cause whereby the same, your Honour's good affection and liking should be any way withdrawn, are emboldened to trouble your Honour with these few lines, and thereby to advertise you that in truth the lack was no less than was at that time certified, which we shall be ready evidently to prove, if it shall so please your Honour, and that we could not by any means have furnished the said ships and pinnace ; but that sithence that time, there be both ships and mariners returned from London and Newcastle ; whereupon, in part discharge of our bounden duties, and in accomplishment of the contents of their Lordships' letter in that behalf to us written, we have appointed for that service two ships and one pinnace, as most willingly we would have done at the first if by any means possible we could ; which, with as much expedition as possible may be, shall be furnished and set forth, which we trust will be the 25th of April instant ; for we, for the more speedier dispatch therein, have hired and set to work of them all the ship-carpenters in this town or in any place within twenty miles thereof. The names of the ships and pinnace and their burdens and in what sort they are furnished is set down in a particular note enclosed in our letter[1] to the Lords and others of her Majesty's most honourable Privy

---

[1] Their letter to the Council (ccix. 104), dated April 22, contains the same assurance as to the two ships and one pinnace, and the efforts making to set them forth ; but the enclosure here referred to is missing.

Council, which the bringer hereof hath to deliver to your Honour. And thus, humbly beseeching your Honour to accept this our boldness, to continue your accustomed good affection to us and this town, and to impute our slackness in this service to the lack of serviceable ships and mariners, the true and only cause thereof, we humbly take our leaves ; beseeching the Almighty to preserve your Honour in long health, with much increase of honour. Kingston-upon-Hull, the 20th of April, 1588.

Your Honour's humbly at commandment,

WILLAM BRAYE, Mayor.

JOHN THORNTON.	WILLM. WILSON.
WM. GEE.	WYLLYM SMYTH.
JOHN SMYTHE.	EDWARDE WAKEFIELD.
ROBT. GAYTON.	LEONARD WYLLAN.

April 20.—THE JUSTICES OF EAST BERGHOLT TO THE COUNCIL.

[ccix. 102.—Signed. Addressed.]

Right Honourable :—May it please you to vouchsafe the reading of a most humble petition which the township of East Bergholt, in Suffolk, have instantly required us to present unto your Honours in answer of your letter of the tenth of April, wherein they are required to make some reasonable contribution towards the furnishing of a ship and pinnace to be sent out of Colchester, in Essex ; and we the justices of these limits, at whose hands all due vigilancy for her Majesty's service may be required, have thought it our parts and bounden duties, under your favourable correction, to lay open some particularities that may move your honourable com-

M 2

passions towards the said township and decayed
state of this poor corner, growing chiefly (if we be
rightly informed) by restraint made by a statute
prohibiting that no Suffolk cloth should be transported, and not here dressed before they were
embarked, thereby changing the accustomed gainful
trade, and traded with such cloths making [1] as were
best saleable in Spain ; and now through long want
of vent into those parts, we find not only the stocks
and wealth of the said inhabitants greatly decayed,
but withal they, being very charitable and godly
bent, are driven, out of their own purses, to see all
the poor and needy artificers pertaining to the trade
provided for sufficiently with meat, drink and clothes,
without trouble of any other parts ; which amounts
to so great a charge, the number of the poor being
very many, as [2] we hope according to your accustomed
wisdoms you will take favourable regard of them.
Their readiness and forwardness otherwise, in all the
good services of God and her most excellent Majesty,
are and hath been always such as deserveth the
testimony of our hands, in hope thereby to purchase
your Honours' good and gracious favour towards
both them and ourselves, who in all humility will
become humble suitors to your honourable good
Lordships as far as we may without offence, that we
may not weaken our country to strengthen another,
and our coasts and coast men already so weakened
as we hold it fit for us rather with all due care and
circumspection to foresee how to strengthen the
services of her Majesty in these parts for such
shipping as is in like manner allotted hither, in the
furtherance whereof there had been ere this used
the help of the said town of Bergholt and others if
their estate would so have borne it. And so, our
most humble duties recommended, with our hearty

[1] Which was in the making of such cloths.   [2] That.

prayers to the Almighty for your long preservation, we humbly take our leave, this present 20th of April, 1588.   Your Honours' at command,

CHARLES FRAMLYNGHAM.   PHILL. PARKER.
PHILIPP TYLNEY.   EDMUND POLEY.
JOHN LANG.   JOHN MUNDEN.[1]

April 28.—DRAKE TO THE QUEEN.

[ccix. 112.—Signed.   Addressed.]

Most gracious Sovereign :—Sithence my last dispatch of Mr. Stallenge to the Court, I have three sundry ways received advertisements that the enemy continueth his preparations very mightily.   The first report cometh by a man of Dartmouth who very lately came from St. Malos, and saith that he heard it reported there by divers Frenchmen returned home from Spain over land, that fifteen ships of that town and as many (at least) of Rosco,[2] besides many more of divers nations, are stayed there ; affirming that their fleet is in number between four and five hundred sail, ready furnished with seventy or eighty thousand soldiers and mariners[3] ; and that for their better encouragement the wages of all the companies is advanced.

The second was delivered by one coming lately from Bayonne, who upon conference there had with another Englishman that dwelt at Bilbao doth con-

[1] This name is blotted, and quite uncertain.

[2] Roscoff.   It seems at this time to have had a considerable trade (cf. *post*, Seymour to Walsingham, July 18), which afterwards died out, leaving the town to dwindle to 'an insignificant hamlet,' till, in 1769, it suddenly started to life again as the depôt of smugglers.   See Shore's *Smuggling Days and Smuggling Ways*, p. 87.

[3] It is perhaps unnecessary to call attention to the gross exaggerations in this and other similar reports.   They were, however, the best intelligence that either the Queen's ministers or the officers of the fleet could get.

firm in effect the substance of the former reports ; adding also that there went to Lisbon out of Biscay between forty or fifty sail of tall ships to increase their fleet.

The last report is certainly declared [1] in France, and brought over by a merchant of Lyme, named Hasserde, that a Frenchman lately coming out of the Straits meant to put in at Cadiz ; and sending in his boat in the night, to discover such doubts as might annoy his entry there, had intelligence by one of his countrymen that they and their shipping were generally stayed in all ports of the coast, and their sails and yards landed ; and that if he came also in, he might not pass thence. Farther he reported that there were within that harbour twelve great argosies, the least of a thousand tons, and so upwards to the burden of fifteen hundred ; taking into them (for the most part) straw, barley, and other forage for those horses and asses which were ordained for their necessary carriage.

Most renowned Prince, I beseech you to pardon my boldness in the discharge of my conscience, being burdened to signify unto your Highness the imminent dangers that in my simple opinion do hang over us : that if a good peace for your Majesty be not forthwith concluded—which I as much as any man desireth—then these great preparations of the Spaniard may be speedily prevented as much as in your Majesty lieth, by sending your forces to encounter them somewhat far off, and more near their own coasts, which will be the better cheap [2] for your Majesty and people, and much the dearer for the enemy.

Thus much (as duty bindeth me) I have thought good to signify unto your Majesty, for that it im-

[1] Publicly spoken of as certain.
[2] The more advantageous.

porteth but the hazard or loss of all. The promise of peace from the Prince of Parma and these mighty preparations in Spain agree not well together. Undoubtedly I think these advertisements true, for that I cannot hear, by any man of war or otherwise, that any ship is permitted to depart Spain, which is a vehement presumption that they hold their purposed pretences.[1] And for farther testimony of these reports, I have sent this bearer, a captain of one of your Majesty's ships, who (if it shall please your Highness to permit him) can deliver some things touching the same.

Thus resting always most bounden unto your Majesty for your gracious and favourable speeches used of me both to Mr. Secretary and others (which I desire God no longer to let me live than I will be ready to do your Majesty all the dutiful service I possibly may), I will continually pray to God to bless your Majesty with all happy victories. From Plymouth, this 28th of April, 1588.

Your Majesty's most loyal,

FRA. DRAKE.

April 29.—LIST OF SHIPS.

[ccix. 113, 114.—In Howard's hand.]

The ships that shall go with the Lord Admiral towards the west country :—

1.	The Triumph.	The 20 ships of London.
2.	E. Bonaventure.[2]	Chichester . 1
3.	Bear.	Southampton 1
4.	Ark Ralegh.	Lyme . . . 1
5.	Victory.	Exmouth . . 2 and
6.	Mary Rose.	a pinnace.

[1] Designs. [2] In error for the E. Jonas.

7. The E. Bonaventure.
8.   Lion.
9.   Vanguard.
10.   Dreadnought.
11.   Foresight.
12.   Charles.
13.   Moon.
14.   Fancy.[1]
15.   White Lion.
16.   Disdain.
17.   Younker.[1]
18.   Duffield.[1]
19.   Monk.[1]
20.   Trumpet.[1]

The ships remaining in the Narrow Seas under the charge of Lord Henry Seymour:

1. The Rainbow.
2.   Antelope.
3.   Swallow.
4.   Bull.
5.   Tiger.
6.   Tramontana.
7.   Scout.
8.   Achates.
9.   Galley Bonavolia.
10.   Merlin.
11.   Spy.
12.   George.
13.   Sun.
14.   Cygnet.

The 5 ports   .   . 5 ships and one pinnace.
Newcastle   .   . 3 ships and one pinnace.
Hull   .   .   . 2 ships and one pinnace.

[1] Are not mentioned in any list as having served.

Lynn   .   .   .   2 ships and one pinnace.
Aldborough   .   .   1 ship and one pinnace.
Ipswich and Harwich 3 hoys of 60 tons apiece.

And all such as shall come out of the Low Countries.

April.—ADVERTISEMENTS FROM ROUEN.

[ccix. 127.—Endorsed.]

First, these are to certify you that yesterday there arrived here a Breton called Roderigues Haimond, who 13 days past departed from Cadiz in Spain, at which time all the ships, as well French as Flemish, were stayed until such time as the Spanish fleet should be departed, so that if a ship of Marseille had not touched at Cadiz in passing that way, neither this party nor none else could have come out of Spain by sea, until after the departure of the army. Which time, stay was made, for that no news should be carried for England. Touching the news he hath brought, what the army is and when they purpose to depart, and whither the talk went that they meant to shape their course,—First, he saith that in all there may be 200 sail of ships, whereof the more part is almost all arrayed at Lisbon, if, since he be come away, they be not departed ; and that 14 of the greatest galleons are at St. Lucar. Also that to man these ships, as the talk goeth in Spain, there are 30,000 men ready to go aboard when time serveth. Secondly, for the time of their departure, he saith that the common voices was that the galleons should depart from St. Lucar, and all the rest of the fleet, about the end of this month ; and he thinketh it to be the more certain, for that the news was there that the Duke of Medina, Admiral of Spain, had already received the King's packet, which

was not to be opened till he should be at sea with all
the fleet, so that no man could certainly tell to what
place they should go after the departure from Spain ;
but the place whither, according to the common bruit,
it was by most men in Spain said that they meant
to go for Scotland there to land, but of this there
is no certainty that the party now arrived could
tell.   I demanded him if corn was cheap and victuals
in Spain.   He said that it was very reasonable
for price, and plenty sufficient; and that this year
there is like to be great plenty by reason of the
moist spring.   Finally I prayed him to tell me what
news he heard of Sir Francis Drake ; and he said
that whilst he was at Cadiz the Spaniards made two
alarms, and put themselves all in arms, because they
saw certain great ships making in towards the bay,
which they thought had been Sir Francis Drake ;
and for his own opinion, being one who loveth
Englishmen, he thinketh that the Spaniards will
never be able to accomplish their determination, for
he thinketh they are too weak at sea, and I do not
doubt, God willing, they shall be overthrown.

May 10.—*RESOLUTIONS OF THE COUNCIL.*

[ccx. 11.—Endorsed.]

1. To appoint a proportion of money to be
delivered unto the Treasurer to provide victual in
case of necessity.

2. The ships furnished by the port towns, so
many as have two months' victual, to remain in
the Narrow Seas; and the other, furnished with
three months' victual, to attend upon the Lord
Admiral.

3. The instructions to refer the employment of

the navy that is to repair to the west parts of this realm, to the Lord Admiral's consideration; to be employed as by his Lordship shall be thought meet, upon such intelligence as he shall receive from time to time; having care, so much as lie in him, to impeach any attempt in Ireland, in Scotland, and England.

May 12.—*FENNER AND CROSSE TO DRAKE.*[1]

[ccx. 17.—Signed.   Addressed :—For her Majesty's service.]

Sir :—There arrived this 12th May in the morning Captain Polwhele[2] and the rest of the ships in company, all saving the caravel.   He was at Cape Finisterre and encountered with certain French ships, the ladings of many of them supposed to be Spaniards' goods; as also one flyboat; which ships came from several places out of the kingdoms of Spain and Portugal.   So as therefore he thought meet to return with them, for the better advertisement of the estate of the King's forts and fleet, and of their readiness, as by the examinations of divers of the masters and merchants by this bearer sent unto you at large appeareth.   And in that they generally, coming out of many several places, confirm in effect all one matter, we thought it very meet to despatch away a messenger with all haste, and therefore have taken their examinations briefly for the speedier despatch.

Most of them marvelleth that the fleet is not upon this coast.   There are six French ships and one flyboat brought in by Captain Polwhele; he hath great care to keep everything in good order,

---

[1] It does not appear where Drake was at this time ; nor yet how this letter addressed to him came among the State Papers.

[2] MS. Powlewheele.

without spoil. Presently after this messenger's despatch we mean to take special order for the safety of everything, and to take as due examination of the parties unto whom the goods doth appertain as our knowledge can bring to pass.

Here are arrived all the ships from Bristol and all the west parts with Sir Richard Greynvile [1] and Mr. St. Leger, for which two we pray your consideration in moneys they demand for victual. We take order upon this news that the fleet shall be maintained until Saturday next with petty warrants, so as the two months' store shall be kept whole.

We have observed the order of your letter sent by my cousin William Fenner, and we despatch of the worst men with as much speed as we may, notwithstanding there will be above the numbers. All the ships here are wonderfully well manned with mariners.

We will take a special care as may be to our charge in your absence; foreseeing, as much as may lie in us, that all be kept in good order and with as much readiness as the place will yield. We ride in a hole [2] where we cannot get out if the enemy should come. Divers of the best ships shall remove out of that place with as much speed as we may under the island, [3] to be the readier for their coming, or to follow them as occasion shall move. The mariners shall be kept aboard, and the soldiers in as great readiness as may be. We will order some powder and weapons aboard such ships as have not already.

Captain Polwhele had performed this message himself, but that we thought it meet, such his great care [4] in good order for the safety of the goods as

[1] MS. Greenfeild.   [2] Sc. Catwater.
[3] Sc. St. Nicholas, or Drake's Island.
[4] Notwithstanding this high testimony to Polwhele's merits, or perhaps in consequence of it, he had no command during the

will be to your good liking, and therefore to continue the same, that no fault may be found in him.

We do most humbly commend ourselves unto you, wishing honour and happiness in all your actions. All in generality do greatly desire your return; and in great love, many of the captains and gentlemen commend them to your good favour. And so we commit you to the Lord of Lords, who preserve and keep you in his favour for ever. Plymouth, this 12th of May, 1588, at 7 of the clock in the evening.

Your faithful and loving friends,
to be commanded by you for ever,
THOMAS FENNER.
ROBART CROSSE.

May 16.—SEYMOUR TO WALSYNGHAM.

[ccx. 19.—Holograph. Addressed.]

Sir:—Where news be daily current, be they good or bad, true or false, such I receive them, such I deliver them. This evening there came a pinnace into the Road which came from Cadiz in Spain this day fortnight. He delivereth unto me for certain there be in Lisbon 300 sail, half of them victuallers and the other half men of war; besides which they are greatly infected with sickness and mortality, and that they stand greatly upon their guard, hearing but of the name of Drake to approach them; further, that they be marvellously beset both with Moors and Turks, insomuch as

operations of the summer. He was probably promoted to be master of one of the large ships, but there is no further mention of him this season. He is named by Hakluyt (*Principal Navigations*, iii. 840) as being lost with Chidley in the expedition to the Straits of Magellan in 1589.

the Moors have within these six weeks overthrown
20,000 Spaniards, obtaining three notable towns
besides in that country.[1] He addeth further that
the Great Turk doth presently make a great army
ready to set the same forward to some great purpose, whereof the Spaniards stand in some fear.
So as truly, Sir, in my poor opinion, if these news
be true, her Majesty cannot but in manner make
what peace she list; so much the rather, when her
forces shall be seen ready upon the coasts everywhere, which me thinketh is too long deferred.
The author of these news is a Frenchman
dwelling at Cadiz, laden with good Spanish wines
and sacks,[2] and so cometh to London with some
leisure as the wind will give him leave.   This
leaving any further to trouble you, do recommend
me always to your honourable good favour.   From
aboard the Bonaventure, this 16th of May, 1588.
Your assured loving friend to command,
H. SEYMOUR.

Post.—If it please you to have any further conference with this Frenchman, you shall hear of him
at one Gerald Malines, a Fleming, who is resident
always at London, and doth receive these wines at
his hands.   The names of the towns that are conquered by the Moors he knoweth not, but surely,[3]
Sir, all things be not current with the Duke of
Parma, if her Majesty had a honourable peace.

[1] This comes under the head of 'false'; it had no foundation
in fact.
[2] The wine, the familiar drink of Sir John Falstaff.
[3] MS. saerely.

EXTRACTS OF LETTERS WRITTEN FROM LISBON.

[cor. 20.—Englished.]

Antonio de Taso Aquereis,[1] Alferez of two hundred soldiers, writing three letters out of Lisbon into Andalusia, saith as followeth :—

In the first letter :

Do you pray to God that in England he doth give me a house of some very rich merchant where I may place my ensigne, which the owner thereof do ransom of me in thirty thousand ducats. But I do fear that seeing us they will presently yield and agree unto all that the King will demand of them, for that the King's force is marvellous great as well by sea as by land.

In the second letter :

Do you incommend[2] me in your prayers to God that he give me a good voyage and fortune that I may get wherewithal to repair to my house to live at ease. I am embarked in the admiral of the hulks, a very good and new ship; only I do fear we shall not join battle, for that the great force the King hath is such; and again that the Prince of Parma hath, who stayeth for us with thirty thousand men in the field, and hath sent unto the King craving leave that he only may give the onset, and the King will not grant it him until the Duke do join with him. All things are embarked even to the mules[3] that must draw the artillery; and commanded here, upon pain of death, no man to go

[1] The name seems to be hopelessly corrupt; Duro has nothing even remotely resembling it.
[2] Incommend = recommend.　　　　[3] MS. Moyles.

ashore ; only we do tarry for a fair wind to go to sea. There is given every day two and twenty thousand rations of victual unto the people for sea and land, all Spaniards.

The third letter :

As touching the voyage, it is impossible to signify unto you the people that are therein, as well soldiers, gentlemen, as of noblemen ; only I can say that every day is given twenty two thousand rations of meat, and this only to Spaniards, besides strangers. All things are embarked, only tarrying for a wind ; and is commanded upon pain of death no man to disembark himself. I pray you to write me when our supply doth come, which now is making ready.

May 20.—*THE STRENGTH OF THE ARMADA.*

[ccx. 25.]

Relation of the Spanish Armada which departed from Lisbon the 30th of May, 1588, *stilo novo*, even as it is certified from Lisbon :

First, great hulks	40
Item, galleons	60
Item, great ships	30
Item, galleasses	4
Item, galleys	8
Item, pataches	24
In all	166
Item, Castilians, soldiers	16,000
Item, Portingals, „	3,000
Item, mariners	6,128
Item, pioneers	2,000
In all of men	27,128

In the same armada their cometh
friars 180
In all the said armada there is of
artillery pieces 1,493

General of the armada, the Duke de Medina
Sidonia. There cometh in the same as commanders, the Prince de Ascoli, the Conde de
Fuentes, the Conde de Paredes,[1] and 25 knights
of the second order, being sons and brothers of
marquises and earls.

May 22.—SEYMOUR TO BURGHLEY.

[**ccx. 27.**—Holograph. Addressed.]

My very good Lord :—The Lord Admiral and I
parted our companies on the Narrow Seas the 21st
of this month, his Lordship taking his course to
Plymouth, having a very good wind for the purpose,
and myself to Blackness, where I anchored the
same day. Presently Monsieur d'Aumale[2] sent a
messenger unto me, desiring me to command anything what I lacked, either for victuals, munition,
powder or shot. I heartily thanked him, and told
the messenger that her Majesty was well stored of

[1] Antonio Luis de Leyva, Príncipe de Ascoli, an illegitimate
son of the King : he served as a volunteer on the staff of the
Duke of Medina Sidonia, on board the San Martin, but was sent
from Calais to join the Duke of Parma (Duro, ii. 282, 372). Pedro
Enriquez de Acevedo, Conde de Fuentes, took an active part in
fitting out the fleet, but it does not appear that he sailed in it ; he
was certainly still at Lisbon on June 29 (*ib.* ii. 179). The Conde
de Paredes served, apparently, with Alonso de Leyva, and
perished with him on the coast of Ireland (*ib.* ii. 364).
[2] The Duke of Aumale, cousin of the Duke of Guise, and at
this time besieging Boulogne, which surrendered to the forces of
the League a couple of months later.

all necessaries to offend her enemies ; adding further
that her Highness could not but take his message
in better part, considering the league between her
and the French King; yet marvelling not a little
that so honourable a house as the Guise, being
advanced by French kings heretofore, could forget
themselves so far as to put themselves in arms,
thereby to rob him of one of his principal towns,
which was most like to be done without warrant
or commission from his sovereign.   To this was
answered that the French King and the Duke of
Guise were both at Paris, within these four days,
and become great friends ; assuring me further that
he would not fail to bring me letters from Monsieur
d'Aumale that should witness the same ; as also
farther authority from the French King to wish[1]
him to expel the Duke of Parma his lieutenant out
of Boulogne; all which I have expected all this
morning until noon, at which time the wind changed
at North and by West, and thereby enforced [us] to
sail over to our own coasts again.

I am further advertised that they of the higher
town of Boulogne are able to hold out a twelve
months, being furnished of all necessaries to withstand the siege.   Besides they made a sally forth
upon the Duke d'Aumale the same day he came
first to Boulogne in person, which was on Friday
last was sennight, and slew 16 persons outright,
hurting many, besides taking a prisoner of some
account, with his ensign.

Now, my Lord, touching our fleet, I would
gladly understand your pleasure for the revictualling
our navy, as also what order shall be taken for our
coast men ; whether her Majesty or the towns shall
continue the charge.   It is time to consider hereof,
for our victuals and days wear away apace.   I have

[1] To desire, order.

nothing else to trouble your Lordship, but leave you to the merciful protection of the Almighty. From aboard the Rainbow,[1] this 22nd of May, 1588.

Your Lordship's assured friend to command,

H. SEYMOUR.

May 23.—*HOWARD TO BURGHLEY.*

[ccx. 28.—Signed, and autograph postscript. Addressed.]

My honourable good Lord :—Although I have not much matter worthy the writing unto your Lordship at this present, yet I thought good to let your Lordship understand how that upon Tuesday last, being the 21st of this instant, the wind serving exceedingly well, I cut [2] sail at the Downs, assigning unto my Lord Henry Seymour those ships appointed to stay with him on the Narrow Seas ; and so parting companies the same morning athwart of Dover, and with a pleasant gale all the way long, came and arrived this day, being the 23rd, about 8 of the clock in the morning, at this port of Plymouth, whence Sir Francis Drake came forth with 60 sail very well appointed to meet with me ; and so casting about, he put with me into the haven again, where I mean to stay these two days to water our fleet, and afterwards, God willing, to take the opportunity of the first wind serving for the coast of Spain, with intention to lie on and off betwixt England and that coast, to watch the coming of the Spanish forces ; which I doubt not, if God send us the good hap to meet them, but that in like sort he will send us a good success to conquer and overcome them. Unto

[1] Between May 16 and 21 he moved from the Bonaventure to the Rainbow, in which he remained. The Bonaventure had gone to Plymouth, with Howard.

[2] Loosed (see *ante*, p. 82, *note*).

N 2

whom I commend your good Lordship, and so bid
you most heartily well to fare. From Plymouth, the
23rd of May, 1588.

Your Lordship's most assured to command,

C. HOWARD.

My good Lord, I pray you bear with me that
I have not written[1] with my own hand. I am so
busied as[2] I have no leisure, for now there is no
losing of time.

May 27.—WYNTER TO BURGHLEY.

[ccx. 32.—Signed.   Addressed.]

My singular good Lord :—It doth appear to me
by a letter which I received of late written by your
Lordship and Mr. Secretary Walsyngham as from
her Majesty, how greatly I am bound to her Highness, which I know is increased by the honourable
favour that doth always continue in you towards me.
I do and will pray for her Majesty to Almighty
God, and ever live, by his goodness, as her most
bounden, humble and dutiful servant, and always
honour and love you.

Since my Lord Admiral's departure, I have been
a-land at Dover pier to behold the works, as one
that wisheth well to it ; and I do find that the works
which is done are great, and the same which doth
want will be overcomed with a reasonable charge
being now followed. There is a place in the entering
of the harbour, which lieth on the north side, to the
eastward, that is fallen into decay, which would[3] be
taken in hand forthwith and mended ; for otherwise
it would put the harbour in danger in short time,
and that I would be very sorry to hear.

[1] MS. wryghten.   [2] As=that.   [3] Should.

The sending of victuals from London or Chatham to such of her Majesty's ships as serveth in the Narrow Seas is a great charge to her Highness ; beside the uncertain coming of it, and the danger the vessel doth run in, which transporteth the same ; and besides, the hurt the victual receiveth or [1] it can be laid aboard. Which matter, in my opinion, would be easily holpen, as by taking order that the victuals, to serve the ships which should be here, be made in Dover, from which it will be very easy for the ships to fetch it, or else for the victualler to send the same to them.

And as for other matters belonging to our Admiral's charge, I know his Lordship doth acquaint your Lordship and the rest of my good Lords with that which is needful, and therefore I leave to trouble your Lordship therein ; and so most humbly taking my leave, I desire God to make you ever happy. Written from aboard the Vanguard, the 27th of May, 1588.

Your honourable Lordship's most bounden,

W. WYNTER.

May 28.—THE DECLARATION OF GILES NAPPER.

[COX. 33.]

The declaration of Giles Napper, come out of Spain the sixth of May,[2] by their computation, and arrived here at Portsmouth the 28th day of May, after our computation.

He saith he was first taken by the Turks, in a ship of Sir Thomas Leighton's ; and afterwards, rowing in the Turks' galleys, taken by the Spaniards and put in the Spanish galleys, and

---

[1] Ere.   [2] April 26.

remained there a year and a half; and afterwards, he procured a Fleming to write to the King in his behalf, that for so much as he had been in captivity in Barbary two years and a half, to know his pleasure whether he should be released or kept still in the galley.   And the King answered that he should serve in the galleys as a mariner, and not as a captive; but he being unwilling thereunto, desired to be released out of the galleys, which the general did grant, paying his duties.   And so he was put to serve in the country, and served a Venetian a month, and afterwards agreed with a Frenchman to bring him to St. Malo.   And there were there 30 sail of Flemings, Frenchmen, and Scots, that were there imbarred[1] under the Castle of Puntales, which was lately made[2] for fear of Captain Drake; and they came all away together; and the Castle shot at them and smote never a man; but a piece broke in the Castle and smote many of the soldiers.

Upon the last of March,[3] after the Spanish computation, there came a Scot from Lisbon to Cadiz, and he asked him what store of shipping there was at Lisbon; who told him that there was a hundred great ships and some galleasses, so that they were 200 sail of great and small; and they looked to come away, by report of the common people, the 16th of May,[4] by their computation; and they looked for more ships out of Italy to be ready at that time.

Also he saith that he spake with one Mr. Fletcher, at that time, being an Englishman at Cadiz, in April last, who hath a factor in Lisbon who desired his master to send for him from thence. The sickness increased, so that there died in a day,

[1] Stayed, arrested.
[2] To command the anchorage at Cadiz.
[3] March 21.   [4] May 6.

in the fleet and in the town, four score or a hundred. And then there was such hate between the Portingals and the Spaniards that they were almost at open wars.

Also he saith that the report amongst the common people is that they think the Englishmen will be hard for them at sea; but if they set their foot on land, they hope to find some friends; and they say they look for help of the Scots. And the King of Spain himself commended Sir Francis Drake very much, to be a valiant man of war, saying that if he had him there he would use him well enough.

Also he saith that they make great account of the Dunkirk fleet, which is thought to be about 30 or 40 thousand men; and that they make as great account of that company as that which they bring from Spain.

Also they talked closely[1] that there was a fleet preparing to go to Guinea and the Indies; and he saw ten ships lading wines for that voyage; they appointed to go about midsummer. The wine they carry is called . . . .[2] a strong wine, and is bound with iron hoops.

Also he saith that Antonio Olivarez and Pedro Castillo be the principal officers for the King at Cadiz and St. Mary Port, and that they demanded of those French ships and others that came away a hundred of oldernes,[3] which was worth there 900 ducats, and then they should depart; which when they had provided and delivered, they answered they could by no means suffer them to pass.

---

[1] In secret, privately.   [2] Blank in MS.
[3] No such coin is known. It was perhaps a trade name for a money of account. In these papers a ducat is always taken as another name for a pistole; that is the golden ducat, worth about 9s. The intrinsic value of the olderne would thus be about 4l., or 100 pesetas.

Whereupon the French and others found themselves grieved ; which they perceiving, commanded presently their sails to be taken from them ; nevertheless, they conveyed some of their sails into casks, with the which they came now away.

Also he saith that the 25th of this present he came from St. Malo in Brittany, where the report was that the Parisians demand of the King whether they should accept of the Duke of Guise. And the . King answering nothing, nodded his head ; whereupon some of them afterwards pronounced *Vive le roi Guise !* [1]

Also he saith that many of the better sort there do judge that all this is but a policy and device between the King and the Guise for some greater matter. And although the Guise be favoured of some, yet is he disliked of many.

May 28.—SEYMOUR TO WALSYNGHAM.

[cox. 34.—Holograph.   Addressed.]

Sir :—According to your direction, I send you here enclosed a perfect particular of our coast men, both of shipping, numbers of men, as also the proportion of victuals, as well the beginning as the ending thereof. So as all that I am to desire you is that, hereafter, we be supplied of victuals at the least for six weeks, if so be that her Majesty make any account of service to be done ; for truly, Sir, without care and regard had of us, what with taking our months' victuals in, there are so many days spent in vain, that no manner of service can be attempted, by reason they consume so fast. And

---

[1] This refers to the events of May 2–12, *la journée des barricades.*

great reason is there to consider hereof; specially when any exploits are to be tendered either for the Low Countries, Scotland, or the west parts. Thus, having nothing else to trouble you, do take my leave. From aboard the Rainbow, this 28th of May, 1588.

> Your assured friend to command,
> H. SEYMOUR.

Post.—Sir William Wynter doth humbly desire you to put his letter within your packet, when you have any occasion to send unto my Lord Admiral.

May 27.—THE PERFECT PARTICULAR OF COAST MEN.

[ocx. **34,** I.—Enclosure in Seymour's letter of May 28.]

27th of May, 1588.—The names of the ships, hoys &c. set forth by the several towns underwritten, with the captains' names,[1] number of men,[1] their several tonnage,[1] and the quantity of victuals in them remaining the day of the date hereof; which ships, hoys &c. do serve under me, the Lord Henry Seymour, admiral of her Majesty's navy serving in the Narrow Seas, viz. :—

Newcastle.—Daniel (24) ; Galleon Hutchins (24); Bark Lamb (24); Fancy (24).

Hull.—Griffin (25); Little Hare (25); Handmaid (25).

Ipswich.—Hoys : William (30) ; Katharine (30); Primrose (30).

Lynn.—Mayflower (35) ; Susan (35).

---

[1] These particulars are given in the list of the fleet, and are here omitted. The figures following each ship's name denote the number of days' victuals she had.

Yarmouth.—Grace (35).
Lowestoft.—Matthew (21).
Alborough.—Marigold (21).
Colchester.—William of Brightlingsea.[1]
Dover.—Elizabeth [2] (50).
Sandwich.—Reuben (50).
Feversham.—Hazard (30).
Hythe.—Grace of God (34).
Romney.—John ([8]).
Rye.—William (31).
Hastings.—Anne Bonaventure (24).

May 28.—*HOWARD TO BURGHLEY.*

[ccx. 35.—Signed, and autograph postscript.   Addressed.]

My very good Lord :—I have received a letter
from my man Burnell,[4] whom I left to come after us
with the ten ships with victuals.   I perceive by his
letter that the ships, and also the victuals, be nothing
in that readiness that I looked they should be in,

[1] MS. Brickelsey.   The number of days' victuals is not given.
[2] Here, and in some other lists, this ship appears as Elinathan,
or Ellen Nathan.   Elizabeth, as in ccxv. 76 and elsewhere, is no
doubt correct.
[8] Not stated.
[4] Francis Burnell is in the list of the fleet, as captain of the
Mary Rose, the largest of the fifteen ships that transported victuals
westward.   From Seymour's letter to Howard of August 19, it
would seem that he afterwards rejoined the Ark.   The family of
Burnell belonged to Acton-Burnell in Shropshire, the manorial
rights of which were granted to the second Duke of Norfolk on
the restoration of the title after the battle of Flodden.   From
one branch of this family, which took the name of Acton, were
descended the Acton, prime minister of Naples, who was so
closely connected with Lord Nelson in 1798-9, and also the
present Lord Acton.   Another branch, keeping the name of
Burnell, is now represented in the navy by Captain John Coke
Burnell.

nor as Mr. Quarles did promise me; for he did ensure me that within seven or eight days at the farthest, they should be dispatched after my departure from the Court, which was the 14th of this month. Burnell's letter unto me beareth date of the 20th, and signifieth unto me that Mr. Quarles and Mr. Peter told him that it would not be ready to depart in 12 or 14 days after; and besides, that the ships were in no readiness that should bring it, and that there would be no mariners gotten for them. My Lord, I judged it would be so; for when there is more care had of the merchants' traffic than there is of such matter of importance as this is, it is like it will be no better.

My Lord, we have here now but 18 days' victual, and there is none to be gotten in all this country; and what that is to go withal to sea, your Lordship may judge; and to tarry, that we must not. For even this morning, Mr. Cary,[1] the sheriff of Devonshire, and Sir Richard Greynvile have brought me word of a bark that is come newly from the South Cape,[2] and was there within these seven days, and did take two or three fishermen off that place, who told them that the Spanish fleet was to come out with the first wind. And therefore very likely that, now the wind being so good for them, they are coming out. And therefore, God willing, the first wind that will serve to put us out, we will be gone towards them; for we have done watering and only are watching here for a wind, all things else being in a readiness. God send us a wind to put us out; for go we will, though we starve. The fault is not mine. We must do as God will provide for us. But, my Lord, it would have done well that they

[1] George Cary of Cockington, Lord Deputy of Ireland in 1603; died in 1617.
[2] Cape St. Vincent.

that are gone or going to Stade or Russia[1] had staid until these ships with our victuals had come to us. Your Lordship doth know what want of victuals did breed once in Ireland, when there were but four of her Majesty's ships with George Wynter[2]; and in like sort, when Sir William Wynter was there. God knoweth what this may do; and our ships that should have come with victual, if they had come hither, we might have taken it well in; but it will be now hard for them to find us, for God knoweth which way the Spanish fleet will bend, either to England, Ireland, or Scotland. But I mean to leave a bark here to bring them after us, for we will lie in the Sleeve[3] as long as we may, except there be cause to the contrary.

There is another bark come from the coast of Spain, belonging to Sir George Carey,[4] and past by this way towards the Isle of Wight; who doth report that the Spanish forces, for certainty, do set out as yesterday. We have the like advertisements out of France, by divers several barks that are come thence. God send the wind to serve to put us out; for I believe surely, if the wind hold here

[1] The Russian trade at this time was to St. Nicholas in the White Sea.

[2] George Wynter, brother or cousin of Sir William, commanded a squadron of *three* of the Queen's ships on the coast of Ireland in 1577. He was ordered to cruise between the Cape of Cornwall and the River Shannon, looking out for a Frenchman named La Roche, who was reported to be preparing some private expedition against Ireland; and to stay out as long as his victuals lasted. The squadron went to the seas on July 20, and returned on October 18; but there does not seem to be any record of the trouble to which Howard refers. *S.P. Dom. Elis.* cxiv. 60; cxvii. 1.

[3] See *ante*, p. 5, *note*.

[4] Afterwards second Lord Hunsdon, Howard's brother-in-law and Governor of the Isle of Wight; not to be confused with George Cary of Cockington. Both names frequently recur in these papers.

but six days, they will knock at our door. If they do so, the fault is not ours ; for I hope [1] we have lost no one hour nor minute of time, nor will suffer any hereafter to be lost. Therefore I pray you, good my Lord, to cause our victuals to be hastened after us with all speed ; and to speak to Mr. Quarles that there may some supply be made again against anything that may happen. And so I bid your good Lordship heartily farewell. From Plymouth, the 28th of May, 1588.

Your Lordship's very loving friend to command,
C. HOWARD.

I pray you let this messenger be returned with some speed ; for although the wind do come to suit us and that we be gone, I will leave a pinnace to bring him after me.

May 28.—*HOWARD TO BURGHLEY.*

[ccx. 36.—Signed, and autograph postscript. Addressed.]

My very good Lord :—I have received your Lordship's letter of the 22nd of this instant, wherein you desire that a certain ship, called the Mary of Hamburg, stayed at Plymouth, may be suffered to pass with her lading of rice, almonds, and other goods, to London, whither she is bound.

Your Lordship shall understand that we have scarcely three weeks' victuals left in our fleet, being bound in by the wind, and watching the first opportunity of the same to go forth unto the seas ; and that therefore, for our better provision and prolonging of our victuals, I have caused the said rice to be stayed and taken for her Majesty's use, paying

---

[1] Feel sure, dare affirm. The word is still used in this sense in Cumberland.

for the same as it is valued at. And for the ship,
and the rest of her lading, I will give order that she
may pass hence to London, according to your
Lordship's request. And so I bid your Lordship
most heartily well to fare. From Plymouth, the
28th of May, 1588.

Your Lordship's very loving friend to command,

C. HOWARD.

My good Lord, there is here the gallantest[1]
company of captains, soldiers,[2] and mariners that I
think ever was seen in England. It were pity they
should lack meat,[3] when they are so desirous to spend
their lives in her Majesty's service.[4]

I would to God I did know how the world went
with our Commissioners; for if I know nothing I
must do thereafter, and think of the worst. I pray
God all things be in best readiness, if the worst do
fall out. And God send us the happiness to meet
with them before our men on the land discover
them, for I fear me a little sight of the enemy will
fear the land men much.

REASONS WHY THE SPANIARDS SHOULD ATTEMPT THE ISLE OF WIGHT.

[**cox. 47.**—Endorsed. Not dated.]

Reasons why the Spaniards should rather land
in the Isle of Wight than any other place of
England.

If by this preparation of the ships and the
galleys, an invasion be intended to any part of
England—then, entering into consideration what
ports are fittest for his advantage, and most dan-

[1] MS. gallants.   [2] MS. sogers.
[3] MS. lake meet.   [4] MS. sarvis.

gerous to work our annoyance, let us look into these ensuing circumstances, and we shall the better judge where he will make his first descent.

Three things he will principally respect.

First, where he may find least resistance, and most quiet landing.

Secondly, where he may have best harbour for his galleys, and speediest supplies out of Spain, France and Flanders.

Thirdly, where he may most offend the realm by incursions, and force her Majesty, by keeping many garrisons, to stand upon a defensive war.

To the first, It carrieth no appearance in reason that he will land in any part of the realm where he shall not be able so soon to put himself on shore, and to intrench himself in strength, but [1] that the whole body and force of that shire, with their neighbouring aids, may and will so disturb him, or prevent him with a battle, that he must either retire to his ships, or hazard his greatest forces and the overthrow of his wearied army ; we being daily to be reinforced with fresh men and greater supplies ; small strength being sufficient to keep them awaking and busied, until a strong head may be made against them.

To the second point, What place can be assigned that may stand indifferent for Spain, Flanders and France, but that they are too remote from the one and too near the other, except the Isle of Wight, Hampton or Portsmouth ? To the latter two places, the precedent reason may give cause of security, which holdeth not in the first; but by all winds may be supplied out of one of the three countries before specified.

To the third, There is no doubt to be made, but landing in the Wight—which with an army of 8,000

[1] Without.

men, divided into four parts, he may easily do, the
force of the Island being unable to resist them with
that force—in very short time they may so fortify
themselves and possess those parts and places that
lie convenient for passing over our supplies, and are
by nature more than three parts fortified, that he
may keep in safe harbour his galleys to make daily
invasions into the firm [1] lands, where they shall perceive the standing of the wind will impeach her
Majesty's ships to come to their rescue.   So that all
the castles and sea towns of Hampshire, Sussex
and Dorsetshire will be subject to be burnt, unless
her Majesty will keep garrisons in those places, the
number and charge whereof will be no less exceeding [2] than how long they shall be forced to continue [will be] uncertain.

June 9.[3]—WALSYNGHAM TO HOWARD.

[ccxi. 8.—Copy.   Endorsed.   Nearly obliterated by damp.]

My very good Lord:—Her Majesty, perceiving
by your Lordship's late letters to me that you were
minded to repair to the Isles of Bayona, if the
wind serve, there to abide the Spanish fleet or to
discover what course they meant to take, doubting
that in case your Lordship should put over so far
the said fleet may take some other way, whereby
they may escape your Lordship, as by bending their
course westward to the altitude [4] of 50 degrees, and
then to shoot over to this realm, hath therefore
willed me to let your Lordship understand that she
thinketh it not convenient that your Lordship should

---

[1] *Terra firma*, the mainland.   [2] Very great.
[3] The endorsement has a smudged 7 ; but Howard in his
letter of the 15th (*post*, p. 202) refers to this as of the 9th.
[4] Latitude.

ro so far to the south as the said Isles of Bayona,
)ut to ply up and down in some indifferent place
)etween the coast of Spain and this realm, so as you
nay be able to answer any attempt that the said
]eet shall make either against this realm, Ireland or
5cotland. And so &c.

June 9.—THOMAS BOSTOCKE TO SIR GEORGE BOND.[1]

ccxi. 11.—Endorsed :—The copy of a letter written to Sir George
Bond from St. John de Luz, the 19th of June, 1588.]

Jesus in St. John de Luz, the 19th of June, 1588.
Right Honourable, my duty considered &c. : —
[t may please your Honour, my last I wrote per
/our son, William Bond, in the Black Dog, of
whose arrival at Falmouth, in company with the
Jane Bonaventure, we have understood by your
son ; as also in my other letters I have wrote your
Honour at large as concerning your affairs here ;
and according to my request, I doubt not but that
your Honour and my friend Mr. Howe will furnish
ne with a ship and commodities, as to your said son
and to my letters I refer me[2] ; provided for the
copper you send[3] let it be all in squares and rounds,
and to send me as little in bricks as possible you
can.

I doubt not but that my friend here will accomplish[4] with me for the wools according to our
concert,[5] so that all my doubt is that any good
shipping may not be suffered to come out of

[1] Sheriff of London, 1578; Lord Mayor and knighted
1587-8.
[2] As to which, I refer you to your said son &c.
[3] MS. sent.   [4] Conclude the business.
[5] MS. consorte. The meaning is clearly agreement, or bargain.

England ; for we hold it here for most certain that the Spanish army departed out of Lisbon of the 29th and 30th of the last ; and the report goeth that they be bound for our country of England, or else for some other place whereby to annoy her Majesty ; and they are 150 sails with men.   I pray God of his mercy to prevent them of their purpose, and that we may have the victory of them ; which I doubt not, through the help of Almighty God, if her Majesty have intelligence of their coming.

Now if the Spanish army be arrived in her Majesty's dominions or other ways, to her Majesty's disliking, I pray your Honour to inform some of her Majesty's Council that here, in these parts, betwixt Fuenterrabia and the Groyne, there is preparing 50 or 60 sails of ships, small and great, and do lade only victuals for a new supply to refresh their foresaid army, as biscuit, cider, bacon and wines.   If they could be met withal, but with six or eight good ships with their pinnaces, no doubt they would take them, although they come together [1] ; for they be most of them very small shipping.   But I do think rather they will go in three or four fleets, because some of them will be assured to pass, as they report, to the north parts of Scotland, where they say their army is.   And thus your Honour may partly guess in what order we remain, until it please God we hear of her Majesty's good proceeding against our enemy ; which God grant according to our heart's desire.   And thus, doubting the conveyance will not be very speedy, I rest— praying God to prosper your Honour in all your proceedings with continuation of health.

Your Honour's servant,
THOMAS BOSTOCKE.

---

[1] Even if they sail all together.

June 13.—*HOWARD TO WALSYNGHAM.*

[ccxi. 17.—Signed. Addressed. In bad condition.]

Sir :—I have received your letter by this bearer, of the 8th of this present, with two advertisements therein ; the one, out of France, of the demands that the Duke of Guise doth make and require of the King ; the other, of Scotland from my brother Carey,[1] which I most heartily thank you for ; but for the abstract that you write of, of the news sent you from Lisbon from the man that I know, that came not with your letter. Notwithstanding, I perceived by your letter that by all likelihood the King's fleet is come out ; that you doubt, by the number of Irishmen that [they have with] them, that they are like to come for Ireland.

Sir, if they [should do] so, or for Scotland, if all the world lay on it, we can do [no] good as this wind is ; for it holdeth here at West and South-West, and bloweth up so as that no ship here but her Majesty's great ships dare ride in this Sound, but are fain to go into the haven. If it begin to show any likelihood to be northerly or easterly, I do go out straight and all my company ; but we are not able by any means to get the weather[2] of this harbour, but fain to come in again, or else we should be driven to the

[1] His brother-in-law, Robert Carey, born 1560, youngest son of Lord Hunsdon, was at this time ambassador to the Scottish King. He was created Earl of Monmouth in 1626, and died 1639. He is said, by Camden, to have served as a volunteer against the armada, but the statement seems very doubtful. These papers give it no support, and it appears (B.M. Calig. D. 1, f. 156) that he started for Scotland on July 16.

[2] To get to windward of &c. The expression was still in use a century later, as :—'The enemy had a great squadron to weather of the Prince's and Sir John Harman's divisions' (*Relation of the Engagement . . . on August* 11, 1673).

O 2

leewards, either to Portland or to the Isle of Wight.
I know not what weather you have there with you,
but here is such weather as never was seen at this
time of the year.

Sir, I protest before God I would I had not a
foot of land in England, that the wind would serve
us to be abroad ; and yet it is a hard matter and a
thing unpossible [for] us to lie in any place or to be
anywhere to guard England, Ireland and Scotland ;
and I would to God her Majesty had [thought] well
for it that she had understood their plot, which
w[ould] have been done easily for money. And
then it would have been [an] easy matter to have
made him [1] not able to have troubled [her] Majesty
again in one seven years. And if the wind had been
favourable unto us, we had been long since before
their doors, [that] they should not have stirred but
we would have been upon their jacks.[2] The wind
hath continued so bad these 15 days, [that] we could
by no means send any pinnace into the Trade.[3]
[God] will alter it when it shall please him.

Sir, if they h[ave] been at the sea so long as you
are advertised, and as I [think] it most true [4]—for
there were three hulks that stole out of Spain, and
as they came along the coast, they saw the fleet off
the Rock,[5] a 12 or 15 [leagues distant]. That was
on the 20th of May. It did confirm that which

---

[1] The King of Spain.

[2] Jack is a coat of mail. 'To be on one's jack' is explained
by Latham as 'to be down on one,' in the colloquial sense. 'To
dust his jacket' would seem an almost exact equivalent.

[3] The name, down to the beginning of the seventeenth century,
of that part of the sea between Ushant and Brest afterwards
known as the Broad Sound, and now the Passage de l'Iroise.
See vol. ii. App. B.

[4] He breaks off to tell why he thinks it true : the conclusion
of the sentence is nine lines lower down—'And if they mean to
go for Scotland or Ireland' &c.

[5] Lisbon.

another ship did advertise before, and therefore very likely [to] be true. The fleet did bear, and ran off West and by North, which they did to get the westerly winds, and the best course that they could keep either for Ireland, Scotland, or England. And if they mean to go for Scotland [or] Ireland, they are there before this ; and if I do hear of [it] I will not be long after them, if God will send us wind to do it.

But, Sir, I pray you see in what case we are. Our victuals are not yet come to us; and if this wind continue, God knoweth when it will come. The time of our victualling that we have doth come out[1] on Saturday next ; but by the good means and wise and well doings of Mr. Darell,[2] we have been refreshed here with some 12 or 14 days' victual at times, or else it would have been hard to have put to the seas any time these ten days, with 15 or 16 days' victuals. But yet we were and are resolved to go whensoever the wind shall serve, and to be as near as we can where we may meet with the King's fleet, which I pray God to send us to do ; for, Sir, since the world began, I think there was never a willinger company to do their prince service than these be.

---

[1] Come to an end

[2] Marmaduke Darell, knighted in 1603, was at this time victualling agent for the navy, or Assistant-Surveyor, apparently subordinate to Quarles. He was formerly a clerk in the Queen's avery, or stables, and in 1585 was appointed by the Council to attend upon Sir Amyas Poulet, 'and to have the defraying of all such sums of money as should concern the diet, charges and expenses of the Scottish Queen'—*Accounts relating to Mary, Queen of Scots* (Camden Soc.), p. 1. In February 1587 he was still at Fotheringay, where he witnessed the execution of the Queen of Scots, as he wrote to his cousin, William Darrell of Littlecote—a very different man in sober history from the Wild Darrell of poetry and tradition. Cf. *Rokeby*, v. 36, and Hall's *Elizabethan Society, passim.*

Sir, if you can by any means learn, or if we can, that they be in the Groyne, I doubt not but by God's grace we will make sport with them. If you hear that they be landed in Ireland or Scotland, I pray you let me have word with all possible speed. If the wind hold here you must send hither; if it change we are gone. Sir, I will never go again to such a place of service but I will carry my victuals with me, and not trust to careless men behind me. We came away scarce with a month's victuals; it had been little enough but to have gone to Flushing. We think it should be marvelled at how we keep our men from running away, for the worst men in the fleet knoweth for how long they are victualled; but I thank God as yet we are not troubled with any mutinies, nor I hope shall not; for I see men kindly handled will bear want and run through the fire and water; and I doubt not but if this month's victual come unto us from London before we depart, we will make it to serve us to continue very near three months. And if it does not come, yet assure yourself we will not lose any opportunity, nor we will not lack; there is good fishing in the seas. And if we be driven upon any occasion upon the coast of Spain, I durst meet with the King of Spain's 18,000 men on the land in any reasonable place; and therefore, fear not, we will not want. God send us wind. And if the wind had favoured us when we went out from hence, which was on the 29th of May, they should not have needed to have come thus far to have sought us.

Sir, I forbear to write unto my Lord Treasurer, because I am sure he is a very heavy man[1] for my Lady his daughter,[2] which I am most heartily sorry

---

[1] Heavy of heart.

[2] His eldest daughter, Anne, wife of Edward, 17th Earl of Oxford, died June 5, 1588.

for. And so I bid you most heartily farewell. From aboard her Majesty's good ship the Ark, the 13th of June, 1588.

Your loving friend,
C. HOWARD.

[ccxiii. 88.—Signed. A small slip of paper, without date, address, or endorsement. Probably a postscript to the preceding. It is in the same writing, on the same paper, and has suffered from the same bad usage.]

Sir :—Most of the ships do presently come out of their victuals, which Mr. Darell will presently supply, and the rest he cannot possibly victual as yet ; which, because they be better provided,[1] shall stay until he can provide for them, which will be within these 30 days at the farthest.

Sir, I pray you send to the committee of London for to send down hither some money for the relief of their soldiers and mariners, who have done their duties hitherunto very well.

Sir, You would not believe what a wonderful thing it is to victual such an army as this is in such a narrow corner of the realm, where a man would think that neither victuals were to be had, nor cask to put it in, which I believe is little thought on there.

C. HOWARD.

June 14.—HOWARD TO WALSYNGHAM.

[ccxi. 18.—Signed. Addressed. In bad condition.]

Sir :—The extremity of the weather in this place where it hath [held], hath caused me to continue here longer than I had meant. I have not marvelled

---

[1] Sc. than the others which ' do presently come out ' &c.

a little, continuing here so long, that I have not heard how the proceedings in the Low Countries have gone; for in my opinion it had been very necessary, that I might have carried myself thereafter in the actions.[1] For if the weather had served me to have gone out, or whensoever it shall serve, I will do my best endeavour to learn where the fleet is, and afterwards to find them out; and according as either I shall hear from you or find by them, thereafter to deal with them.

The opinion of Sir Francis Drake, Mr. Hawkyns, Mr. Frobiser, and others that be men of greatest judgment [and] experience, as also my own concurring with them in the same, is that [the] surest way to meet with the Spanish fleet is upon their own [coast], or in any harbour of their own, and there to defeat them; for if [they have] been so long at the sea as the advertisements do declare, they must [now] be landed either in Ireland or Scotland ere this, or else somewhere [on] the coast of France. But I [am] verily persuaded they mean [nothing] else but to linger it out upon their own coast, until they understand [that] we have spent our victuals here; and therefore we must be busy [with] them before we suffer ourselves to be brought to that extremity.

Sir, it is very strange that, in this time, the Commissioners cannot perceive whether they mean a peace without fraud, or use the same [2] to detract a time for a further device. And if our Commissioners do discover any detraction in them, only to serve their own turns, methinks her Majesty should use the like policy, and devise to beat them with their own rod. Then could I wish with all my heart

---

[1] In my actions; have guided my conduct thereby.
[2] The negotiation; detract = to draw out, to spin out the time. So also detraction = a spinning out of the time.

that King Anthony [1] were with us, that he might set
foot in his own country, and find the King occupied [2]
there, which we might easily do. Thus I do adventure to [offer] my mind privately unto you, as unto
my especial good friend, pray[ing you that] I may
hear from you speedily again of such proceedings
as the Commissioners have, of such advertisements
as you hear, and privately, of your own advice and
judgment herein.

Sir, we have endured these three days, Wednesday, Thursday and Friday, an extreme continual
storm. Myself, and four or five of the greatest
ships, have ridden it out in the Sound, because we
had no room in Catwater, for the lesser ships that
were there ; nor, betwixt the shore and the Island,[3]
because Sir Francis Drake, with four or five other
ships, did ride there. Myself and my company in
these ships do continually tarry and lie aboard in all
the storm, where we may compare that we have
danced as lustily as the gallantest dancers in the
Court. And if it may please God to continue her
Majesty's ships as strong to the end of the journey
as they have done hitherunto, her Majesty may [be
su]re (what false and villainous reports soever have
been made of them) [she hath] the strongest ships
that any prince [in] Christendom hath. A[nd all
the] masters and skilful men here say that it had
been better to have [been of] late in any of the
Spanish seas, than to have ridden out these storms
here, wherein we do not find that any one ship
complains.

Sir, our victuals be not come yet unto us ; and
if this weather hold, I know not when they will
come.

<hr>

[1] Dom Antonio, the popular claimant to the throne of
Portugal.
[2] Occupation.   [3] St. Nicholas or Drake's Island.

Sir, I must not omit to let you know how lovingly and kindly Sir Francis Drake beareth himself; and also how dutifully to her Majesty's service and unto me, being in the place I am in; which I pray you he may receive thanks for, by some private letter from you.

And so, praying you to present my most bounden and humble duty unto her Majesty, and that I will not trouble her with my letters before some matter of greater moment do fall out, I bid you heartily farewell. From off aboard her Majesty's good ship the Ark, in Plymouth Sound, the 14th of June, 1588.

Your assured loving friend,

C. HOWARD.

June 15.—HOWARD TO WALSYNGHAM.

[ccxi. 26.—Signed. Addressed.]

Sir:—Within three hours after I had written my letter, which herewith I send you, [I] received your letter of the 9th of this present[1] by a pursuivant. Which letter I do not a little marvel at; for thereby you signify that her Majesty, perceiving by a letter I sent you heretofore, that I was minded to go on the coast of Spain, to the Isles of Bayona, her pleasure is that I should not go so far, but only off and on, betwixt the coast of Spain and England; lest the Spanish fleet should come into the height[2] of 50, and then should bend their course directly to this realm.

Sir, for the meaning we had to go on the coast of Spain, it was deeply debated by those which I think [the] world doth judge to be men of greatest experience that this realm hath; which are these:

[1] See *ante*, p. 192.   [2] Latitude.

Sir Francis Drake, Mr. Hawkyns, Mr. Frobiser, and Mr. Thomas Fenner ; and I hope her Majesty will not think that we went so rashly to work, or without a principal and choice care and respect of the safety of this realm. We would go on the coast of Spain ; and therefore our ground was first, to look to that principal[1] ; and if we found they did but linger on their own coast, or that they were put into the Isles of Bayona or the Groyne, then we thought in all men's judgments that be of experience here, it had been most fit to have sought some good way, and the surest we could devise, by the good protection of God, to have defeated them.

[For] this, we considered that the Spanish forces, being for so long [time] victualled as they are, might in very good policy detract [time, to] drive us to consume our victuals, which, for anything we [can see], is not to be supplied again to serve the turn, by all the means that her Majesty and all you can do. And if her Majesty do think that she is able to detract time with the King of Spain, she is greatly deceived ; which may breed her great peril. For this abusing [of] the treaty of peace doth plainly show how the King of Spain will have all things perfect, [as] his plot is laid, before he will proceed to execute. I am persuaded he will see the Duke of Guise bring the French [King] to his purpose before he will [act]. If his intention be so, I pray you, when our victuals be consumed in gazing for them, what shall become of us ? Whether this [may] not breed most great danger and dishonour, I leave it to her Majesty's wisdom ; but if it should fall out so, I would I had never been born ; and so I am sure many here would wish no less, [on] their own behalf.

And if [we] were to-morrow next on the coast

[1] Principally.

of Spain, I would not land in any place to offend
any; but they should well perceive that we came
not to spoil, but to seek out the great force to fight
with them; and so should they have known by
message; which should have been the surest [way]
and most honourable to her Majesty. But now, as
by your directions to lie off and on betwixt England and Spain, the South-West wind, that shall
bring them to Scotland or Ireland, shall put us to
the leeward. The seas are broad; but if we had
been [on] their coast, they durst not have put off,
to have left us [on] their backs; and when they
shall come with the south-westerly wind, which
must serve them if they go for Ireland or Scotland,
though we be as high as Cape Clear, yet shall we
not be able to go to them as long as the wind shall
be westerly. And if we lie so high, then may the
Spanish fleet bear with the coast of France, to
come for the Isle of Wight; which for my part,
I think, if they come to England, they will attempt.
Then are we clean out of the way of any service
against them.

But I must and will obey; and am glad there
be such there, as are able to judge what is fitter for
us to do, than we have here[1]; but by my instructions
which I had, I did think it otherwise. But I will
put them up in a bag, and I shall most humbly
pray her Majesty to think that that which we meant
to do was not rashly determined, and that which
shall be done shall be most carefully used by us;
and we will follow and obey her Majesty's commandment. But if we had been now betwixt Spain
and England, we had been but in hard case, the
storm being so strong and continuing so long as it
hath done; but upon the coast of Spain, we had
had a land wind and places of succour. We meant

[1] He means, of course : what is fit for us to do, better than &c.

not to have spoiled any town or village ; only we must of necessity water ; and when we lie betwixt both coasts, we must come to this coast to water, for so we are enjoined ; and if the wind do not serve us to come on our own coast, then in what case shall [we be, now] that we must not go on the coast of Spain ? We lay seven days in the Sleeve, which was as long as we could continue there without danger, as the wind was ; and if some had been with us, they should have seen what a place of danger it is to lie on and off in.

Sir, you know it [hath] been the opinion both of her Majesty and others, that it was [the sur]est course to lie on the coast of Spain. I confess my error at that time, which[1] was otherwise ; but I did and will yield ever unto them of greater experience. Yet you know it was thought by her Majesty that we might go into Lisbon to defeat them, which was the strongest place. Therefore I thought that if we had heard that they had been at the Isles of Bayona, or the Groyne, which be ten times more easy to defeat them in, I think it would have been good service.

But, Sir, I will persuade no [more], but do as I am directed ; and God send the wind do not force us thither ; otherwise, upon my duty, we will not go thither, now we know her Majesty's pleasure. And so I bid you most heartily farewell. From aboard her Majesty's good ship the Ark, in Plymouth Sound, the 15th of June, 1588.

Your assured loving friend,

C. HOWARD.

[1] When my opinion.

June 17.—*SEYMOUR TO WALSYNGHAM.*

[ccxi. 33.—Holograph. Addressed.]

Sir :—So long as I am in this action of service, [at] such times as will give me leave to consider advisedly thereof, [I] do bethink myself thereafter, by delivering my opinion touching the effect of your letter to Sir William Wynter, wherewith you wished me to be acquainted ; and so much the rather I busy my head, because yesterday hasty news flew from Calais to Dover of the Spanish fleet[1] being at Ushant.

But touching the Duke of Parma his intent for the annoyance of England, I am fully resolved[2] his enterprises will never go forward, but where beforehand he doth assure himself of a strong party of the contrary side ; which for England, God himself (I hope) doth prevent, as otherwise assisteth your Honours all with his Spirit, by restraining the papists' governments through every several shire,[3] whereby the same is avoided by that course.

And were it so that he might have a faction in England, surely those places remembered by Sir William Wynter are very likely to be attempted ; but yet I have bethought myself of a far more convenient hold, most fit above any yet set down, the Isle of Wight by name, aptest for a rendezvous.

And where Sir William Wynter doubteth the main chance for London by the Thames mouth,

[1] The ships that were reported by Godolphin on the 21st as having been met with off Scilly. See *post*, p. 221.
[2] Persuaded.
[3] Referring generally to the repressive policy of the Government, but more especially, perhaps, to the resolution of the Council on the previous day, to commit a dozen of the principal recusants to the Tower.—*S.P. Dom. Eliz.* ccxi. 28.

adding his opinion for sconces and bulwarks, thereby to front the enemies, the charge growing thereof
can not be but great; besides, the weakness of those
places shall be thoroughly discovered, where now,
for the most part, the same are concealed. For
remedying whereof with a far less charge, twenty
such hoys as Harwich and Ipswich do set forth,
lying in the Thames mouth in several places, being
nimble of sail and quick in turning to and fro, will
prevent and greatly withstand any sudden attempt ;
and I am sure these twenty sails will be defrayed
under the rate of four such ships as the Rainbow.

But to proceed with the Duke of Parma. We
suspect, and I fear we shall find his great faction
with the Duke of Guise, by reason of the Holy
League. And where most commonly he giveth
forth his determinations, the same for the most part
doth fall out contrary ; as by the last year's experience, he made show for Ostend, and yet went to
Sluys. So likewise now, he would busy our heads
sometimes for Scotland, at other times for Ireland,
otherwise for Norfolk or Suffolk, the more to blind
our eyes by bending our forces those ways, and
taking his further advantages, for his inward conceits ; the same, no doubt, being resolutely determined for Holland and Zealand, or for Picardy ; in
which both places he presumeth to have strong
factions.

To prevent all which, in time, is [1] to call home
our Commissioners, if you stand doubtful of your
expectations for their proceedings. With all, her
Majesty shall ease her purse, by giving general
liberty to make open wars. Otherwise, in prolonging these actions with such charges, gaining a peace
fit for heretics, her Majesty, whom I beseech God
long preserve, will be in danger both of the foreign

---

[1] The way is &c.

enemies, as otherwise stand in great contempt among
her subjects, who do now manifest their duties and
good wills apparently.

Thus referring my opinion to better judgments,
and desiring to be excused for intermeddling so far,
with my most loving commendations, I betake[1] you
to God. From aboard the Rainbow, the 17th of
June, 1588.

Your assured friend to command,
H. Seymour.

Post.—Sir, I would be glad you would procure
her Majesty or my Lords to send the letters for
these hoys ; but rather I wish you would send me
word to take order to send them to Greenwich,
where they may be seen before her Majesty remove
from thence ; and I am sure my opinion will be confirmed among you. They may be better spared
now. Their victuals do expire within eight days.

June 19.—*HOWARD TO WALSYNGHAM.*

[ccxi. 37.—Holograph.   Addressed.]

Good Mr. Secretary :—You see it is very likely
to come to pass, my opinion that I always had of
the French King ; as also of the treacherous treaty
of peace, which was never to any other end but that
the King of Spain might have time, and not be
troubled in gathering his forces together, and her
Majesty's noble and princely nature most greatly
abused. And therefore, good Mr. Secretary, let
every one of you persuade her Majesty that she
lose no more time in taking care enough of herself,
and to make herself, every way that is possible, as
strong as she can ; for there is no question but the

---

[1] Commit.

King of Spain hath engaged his honour to the uttermost in this, for the overthrow of her Majesty and this realm, and doth employ all the forces, not only of his own, but also all that he can get of his friends, for this exploit ; and if he be put back from this this year, her Majesty may have a good and honourable peace. If not, yet she shall be sure he shall not be able to trouble her Majesty in many years after.

You see it is made in the world greatly for his honour that he is able to make such a power as that he will enterprise to invade England. Thanks be to God, the world shall also see that her Majesty hath provided sufficient forces to beat him by sea ; so would I wish that in time[1] her Majesty should gather some great force together for her defence on the land. It would be a great surety, and to the world most honourable. For if it come that her [Majesty] should draw the forces together on the sudden, it will breed a marvellous confusion[2] ; and all sudden causes breeds many doubts in multitudes. I hope in God the manifest discovery of their determination, as it may well happen by the arch-traitor Allen's book,[3] will awaken all men. If there be

[1] In good time.

[2] The sense is : But if her Majesty should neglect to do so, and afterwards have to gather her forces together in a hurry, on a sudden emergency, it will cause much confusion.

[3] William Allen, born at Rossall in 1532, was in Queen Mary's time Principal of St. Mary's Hall, Oxford. He resigned this office in 1560, and quitted England in 1561. He became a priest in 1565, and in 1568 founded the English college at Douay, where, in 1570, he was appointed Professor of Divinity. In 1582 he threw himself warmly into the polemical politics of the day, and was mixed up in the schemes of the Guises and in the plots in favour of the Queen of Scots. After her death he publicly asserted the title of the King of Spain to the throne of England, and—having been made a cardinal in 1587—published, in 1588, a violent and offensive pamphlet, entitled, 'An Admonition to the Nobility and People of England and Ireland concerning the

that will not awake with this, I would to God when they are asleep they might never awake.

Sir, because in service of so great moment as this is, it were not requisite that many should be privy of our counsels, I made choice of these whose names I here write, to be councillors of this service; made them all to be sworn to be secret:—Sir F. Drake, Lord Thomas Howard, the Lord Sheffield, Sir Roger Williams,[1] Mr. Hawkyns, Mr. Frobiser, Mr. Thomas Fenner. I chose Sir Roger Williams for his experience by land, what occasion soever might fall out to land in Ireland, or Scotland, or in England; for God willing, if it please God to send us wind to serve us, we mean to land some with them wheresoever they land in any of her Majesty's dominions. I do assure you, Sir, these two noble-men[2] be most gallant gentlemen, and not only for-

present wars, made for the execution of his Holiness' sentence by the high and mighty King Catholic of Spain.' It is to this that Howard here refers. It has been suggested that the violence of the style and the brutality of the matter are altogether alien to Allen's nature, and that he could not have been the real author. This is possible; but he acknowledged it, gave it the weight of his reputation as a man of piety, learning and rank, and must bear the odium which attaches to its publication. He died at Rome in 1594.

[1] A native of Monmouthshire; educated at Oxford. A soldier of fortune, he served for some time with the Duke of Alva. In 1585 he was with the Earl of Leicester in the Low Countries; was knighted in 1586; died in 1595. According to Camden, 'He was perhaps no way inferior to the best soldiers of that age, could he have put bounds to his courage, which ran away with his conduct and discretion.' He wrote *Actions of the Low Coun-tries* and other military works (see Somers' *Tracts*, i. 329). He did not now remain long with the fleet, but joined Leicester in the camp at Tilbury: see *post*, Leicester to Walsyngham, July 25.

[2] Lord Thomas Howard, born in 1561, second son of the 4th Duke of Norfolk, was at this time captain of the Golden Lion, and was knighted on July 25. In 1591 he commanded the fleet at the Azores, when Sir Richard Greynvile was slain and the

wards, but very discreet in all their doings. I would to God I could say for her Majesty's service, that there were four such young noblemen behind to serve her. God bless them with life, and they will be able to do her Majesty and the realm good service.

Sir, I am glad that the ships sent out by the towns are victualled for a month more. I would it were two. And for the love of God, let not her Majesty care now for charges, so as it be well used. And strengthen my Lord Harry in the Narrow Seas with as much force as you can, sike[1] by force of the sea to keep any from landing ; for landing will breed, I am afraid, great danger.

Sir, I pray send to us with all speed. But I hope to be gone before I hear from you, for I will not tarry one hour after our victuals do come to us, and if the wind will serve us ; for there must be no time lost now, and we must seek to cut off their time, which I hope in God to do.

Sir, as I have ever found you to be my most especial good friend, and the man that, for your honourable and faithful doings ever with me, hath made me to think myself ever greatly beholden unto you, I therefore now do most earnestly pray you to stand my good friend, as to move her Majesty this my humble suit and request : that if it please God

Revenge captured ; and in 1596 took part in the expedition against Cadiz. He was created Earl of Suffolk in 1603 ; was Lord High Treasurer 1614–19 ; and died in 1626. Edmund Sheffield, born in 1563, succeeded as 3rd Baron Sheffield in 1568. His mother was Howard's sister, at this time the wife of Sir Edward Stafford. He was now in command of the White Bear, and was also knighted by Howard on July 25. He was created Earl of Mulgrave in 1626, and died in 1646. Portraits of both are given in Doyle's Baronage.

[1] Such=such as, so as. The omission of the 'as' is not uncommon in Elizabethan English. Cf. *Richard III.* III. ii. 26 : 'I wonder he is so fond to trust the mockery' &c.

to call me to him in this service of her Majesty, which I am most willing to spend my life in, that her Majesty of her goodness will bestow my boy upon my poor wife.[1] And if it please her Majesty to let my poor wife have the keeping either of Hampton Court or Oatlands,[2] I shall think myself more bound to her Majesty. For I do assure you, Sir, I shall not leave her so well as so good a wife doth deserve.

Thus, Sir, I have been bold to trouble you, and can yield you no other requital but my love and good will as long as I live ; and so I recommend me most heartily unto you, and bid you farewell. [From] aboard the Ark, the 19th of June.

Your most assured loving friend to use,

C. HOWARD.

June 20.—*WYNTER TO WALSYNGHAM.*

[ccxi. **38.**—Signed.   Addressed.]

I do most humbly thank your Honour for your letters I received yesterday in the evening, bearing date the 18th of this present, whereby it appeareth that my letters lately written to your Honour, in answer of yours, had favourable construction, both by her Majesty, yourself, and all my very good Lords of the Council, which doth glad me greatly, and I, as becometh me in duty, by God's favour, will ever acknowledge your honourable kindness used therein towards me, as also for many other your favours.

---

[1] As ward : to assign the boy as ward of his own mother, who would thus receive the revenue of the estate.

[2] In Surrey. The park is now broken up and built over, and a big hotel stands on the site of the old palace.

It seemeth by your Honour's letters that the Prince of Parma his intention is towards Sheppey, Harwich, or Yarmouth ; two of the which I know perfectly, as Sheppey and Harwich ; the other not so well. And yet, if I do not mistake the situation of the said places, they are such as a small charge (in manner of speaking) will make a sufficient strength to withstand any sudden attempt. And whereas it is said the Prince's strength is 30,000 soldiers, then I assure your Honour it is no mean quantity of shipping that must serve for the transporting of that number and that which doth appertain to them, without the which I do not think they will put forth ; 300 sail must be the least ; and, one with another, to be counted 60 ton. For I well remember that in the journey made to Scotland, in the Queen's Majesty's father's time, when we burned Leith and Edinburgh,[1] and there was in that expedition 260 sail of ships ; and yet we were not able to land above 11,000 men, and we then in fear of none that could impeach us by sea. It may be said the cut[2] between Flanders and the places named is shorter than out of England to the Frith in Scotland, which is true ; but, Sir, men that do come for such a purpose, being so huge an army as 30,000 men, must have a mighty deal of all sorts of provisions to serve them, as your honourable wisdom can well consider.

But, Sir, I take the Prince's case to be far otherwise. For I suppose, if the countries of Holland and Zealand did arm[3] forth but only the shipping which the Lord Admiral at his departing delivered unto our admiral in writing that they would send from those parts to join with us here, and that was 36 sail of ships of war, and that it

---

[1] May, 1544.   See Froude, iv. 32.   [2] Cut=division, distance.
[3] Arm=equip ; so in French, *armer*.

were known to the Prince those did nothing but
remain in readiness to go to the seas for the
impeaching of his fleet whensoever they did come
forth, I should live until I were young again or [1] the
Prince would venture to set his ships forth.

And again, if her Majesty's ships, and such
others as doth but now remain under our admiral's
charge, may be continued in the state we are in,
and not to be separated, the Prince's forces, being
no other than that which he hath in Flanders at this
time (upon whom we mean to keep as good watch
for their coming forth as possible we can), dare not
come to the seas. But the sorrow we have is that
we think these dealings of his to be rather a scare-
crow, to hasten or bring to pass such an end of the
treaty as may be most for his master's advantage,
than that he meaneth to set forward the thing he
giveth out in show.

Your honourable opinion that 1,000 footmen
and 200 horsemen might [2] be assigned to each of the
three several places before rehearsed, to make head
upon any attempt, and to remain until it be seen
what the Prince's designs may be, is in my poor
conceit very good. For in these princely actions, a
man cannot be too provident ; and no wisdom were
it to put things to an even [3] balance, when more
weight may be added.

There was news sent over from Calais of late
to Dover, by one Skofield, [4] an English merchant
lying there (as it is said), that there arrived at Dunkirk lately certain Brittany ships, whose mariners
should [5] give out that they came in company from
Cape Finisterre with 150 ships of war of the King

---

[1] Or=ere.   [2] MS. moughte.   [3] MS. ayeven.
[4] The name is so written, and it cannot be verified. It was
probably Scholefield.
[5] Should=did, as we are told.

of Spain's ; and how that they parted from them
upon the coast of Brittany near the Trade.[1] Since
which time we have had perfect intelligence that the
Queen's Majesty's ship, the Elizabeth Bonaventure,
hath been within the Trade and thereabouts. Likewise we have spoken with the masters and company
of three flyboats of Hoorn and Enkhuysen,[2] that
were in Rochelle five days past, and came along all
the coast of Brittany, and through the Trade ; and
they said there was none upon that coast. Further,
they declared to us that there was a report at
Rochelle, seven days before their departing, that part
of the Spanish army, to the number of 150 sail,
were come to the Groyne, and stayed there for the
rest which should come from Lisbon to them. But
afterwards there was certain news brought thither
by ships of Rochelle, men of war that came home
and brought very good prizes of Spaniards with
them, that the army remained still in Lisbon,
and the infection continued very great among them.
It is a bad season of the year for any ships that
are in Lisbon, and to the southwards of it upon
the coast of Spain, to come to the northwards, by
reason of the north and north-westerly wind that
bloweth commonly from the middle of May until
the latter end of August upon that coast; after
which time it will not be wholesome for a Spanish
army to seek to the north part.

The men of the foresaid three flyboats informed
us that the King of Navarre was in Rochelle ; and
that they were in hand with a great fortification
without the town, whereupon daily, men, women,
and children did work, and the King himself. They
spake it as witness of sight.

We are informed that my Lord Admiral is at
Plymouth with his whole army, which is but a bad

---

[1] The Passage de l'Iroise.   [2] MS. Yackewson.

place for my Lord to be in, if the King of Spain's
navy should come.   For that wind which would
serve to bring them for England, Ireland, or Scotland, will not suffer my Lord to get out; and the
country is not very good to yield them that relief of
victual that they may need of.   The ships that
lately went with their provision of victuals from
London are with them, or else very near by this.

If we cannot have a good peace by the treaty
now in hand, and that shortly, which I wish for my
part might be, then if her Majesty, with the Low
Countries, as Holland and Zealand, did make a
sharp war out of hand (entertaining Scotland as our
friend), and to spare the pride of our backs and
some of our gluttons' fare, I do not doubt (by God's
grace) we should then make her Majesty's enemies
to come to reason shortly ; and if this be not done,
I fear me it cannot do well ; for that we shall be
wearied out with charges.   And that I take to be
their only policy they have ; into the which I know
your wisdom can sound deep, and therefore I leave
it to your honourable discretion, and humbly pray
your Honour to bear with my boldness.

If Mr. Hawkyns hath not left your Honour, or
my very good Lord, the Lord Treasurer, the book
of the issuing out of the store[1] of the storehouses,
to the end your Honours may know what the same
is, as[2] a supply may be made, he hath not well
remembered himself ; for it is needful there were a
care had of it in time ; for the year will now slide
away apace.

If it will please your Honour to cause some one
of your good friends hereabouts near the seaside to
bestow a buck upon me and Sir Henry Palmer,[3]
your poor well-willers, we should think ourselves

---

[1] Issuing of the store out of &c.   [2] So that.
[3] The buck was duly bestowed.   See *post*, July 27.

greatly beholden to your Honour, whom I beseech God to prosper and increase with much honour and good health.   Written from aboard the Vanguard, in the Downs, the 20th of June, 1588.

Your Honour's most assured to command,

W. WYNTER.

June 22.—*HOWARD TO THE COUNCIL.*

[ccxi. 45.—Signed.   Addressed.   In bad condition.]

May it please your Lordships, I have received your Lordships' letters of the 17th this morning, being the 22nd of this instant, whereby I do perceive her Majesty's gracious goodness that she thinketh us to be so careful of her s[ervice] as that she hath referred it unto me and such other my assistants here to do that which I and they shall think fittest and most convenient to be done for the more surety and service of her Majesty and [the] state.   And her Majesty shall be well assured, and your Lordships also, as it shall please God that wind and weather shall serve us, we will [take such] course that we may learn by all intelligence to find the [enemy], yet not so rashly to deal with them if we meet with the[m but that] her Majesty shall well perceive that it is done with judgment.   And yet [ho]wsoever we shall do it by the wisdom and [discretion] of man, yet God is he which disposeth all, who I doubt not [will favour] her Majesty and his people, and send her a most honourable victory.

I pray your Lordships to pardon me that I may put you in remembrance [to] move her Majesty that she may have an especial care to draw [ten or] twelve thousand men about her own person, that may not be men [un]practised.   For this she may well assure herself, that 10,000 men that be practised and trained together under a good governor [and] expert leaders, shall do her Majesty more service than any 40,000 which shall come from any other parts of the realm. For, my Lords, we have here 6,000 men in the fleet, which we shall be able, out of our company, to land upon any great occasion, which being as they [have] been trained here under captains and men of experience, and each man knowing his charge, and they their captains, I had rather have them to do any exploit than any 16,000 out of any part of the realm.

My Lords, our victuals are not yet come, but we hope shortly to hear of them if this wind continue 40 hours, or else we cannot tell what to think of them, or what should become of them ; and yet we have sent three or four pinnaces to seek them out. If they come not, our extremity will be very great, for our victuals ended the 15th of this month ; and if that Mr. Darell had not very carefully provided us of 14 days' victuals, and again with four or five days' more, which now he hath provided, we had been in some great extremity. Mr. Hawkyns hath disbursed money for all that, and for many other charges more, wherein Sir Francis Drake hath likewise disbursed some ; and therefore to avoid that danger and inconvenience that may fall out the thereby, it would do very well that her Majesty would send five or six thousand pounds hither, for it is likely we shall stand in great need of it.

[Several] men have fallen sick, and by thousands fain to be discharged, [and] other pressed in their stead, which hath been an infinite charge [with] great trouble unto us, the army being so great as it is, the ships so many in number, and the weather so ext[reme] foul as it hath been ; whereby great charges have risen and daily do. And yet I protest before God we have been more careful of her Majesty's charges than of our own lives, as may well appear by the scantyings [1] which we have made. And thus leaving to trouble your Lordships any further, I take my leave. From off aboard her Majesty's good ship the Ark, the 22nd of June, 1588.

Your Lordships' loving friend to command,

C. HOWARD.

June 22.—*HOWARD TO WALSYNGHAM.*

[ccxi. 46.—Holograph. Addressed.]

Sir :—I am very sorry that her Majesty will not thoroughly awake in this perilous and most dangerous time ; and surely it will touch her Majesty greatly in honour if the noblemen and the rest of the Commissioners should not safely come back again. It is to me a strange treaty of peace, but the end is like unto the beginning. There is not anything that ever cometh to a good end that hath not a good and sure foundation, which I could never discern in this work of Mr. Comptroller's.[2] A good will I think he had, but surely no good workman.

For the advertisement of the Bretons that came to Calais,[3] I think it cannot be true, for we have had pinnaces off and on, so as we should by some means have heard of it, but I will send presently some small pinnaces thither.

[1] It seems to be a stronger term than 'savings,' and includes putting the men on short allowance, or six men to a mess instead of four—that is, in familiar language, 'six upon four.'

[2] Sir James Croft, Comptroller of the Household, and one of the commissioners for the treaty.

[3] Cf. *ante*, p. 206. It appears to have been his first news of the Spanish ships reported by Godolphin, as detailed in the next paper.

I put out on Wednesday to the sea in hopes to have met with our victuallers, but on Friday we were put in again with a southerly wind. I hope now shortly we shall hear of our victuals, for the wind doth now serve them. I pray God all be well with them, for if any chance should come to [them], we should be in most miserable case. For the love of God, let the Narrow Seas be well strengthened, and the ships victualled [1] for some good time. This one month's victual is very ill, and may breed danger and no saving to her [Majesty]; for they spend lightly seven or eight days in coming to meet their victual and in taking of it in; and if the enemy do know of that time, judge you what they may attempt. Great hurt may come by it, but no good.

Sir, I pray let her Majesty be earnestly persuaded withal to have some forces of ten or twelve thousand soldiers near to her, that may know one another and their leaders. I had rather have ten thousand such, well trained and kept together, than forty thousand that shall be brought on the sudden, half amazed, as her Majesty shall be sure to find them. Her Majesty must assure herself she is not now in peace; and therefore most priceless service, and most to her honour, to provide as in war.

Sir, I pray you to present my most bound and humble duty to her Majesty; so, God willing, I will not trouble her Majesty with my rude writing till the matter be something worth. God, of his mercy, bless her Majesty with health and to have honour over her enemies. Fare you well, good Mr. Secretary, and God send you health. From aboard the Ark, the 22nd of this June.

Your assured loving friend,
C. HOWARD.

[1] MS. vytcled.

June 23.—*ADVERTISEMENT OF THE*
SPANISH FLEET.

[ccxi. **47, 48.**—In duplicate, with some verbal differences.
Endorsed :—From the Lord Admiral.]

On Friday last, the 20th[1] of this instant, Sir
Francis Godolphin[2] wrote unto my Lord Admiral,
that the Thursday before, a bark of Mousehole[3] in
Cornwall, being bound for France to lade salt, encountered with nine sail of great ships between
Scilly and Ushant, bearing in North-East with the
coast of England. Coming near unto them, he,
doubting they were Spaniards, kept the wind of
them. They perceiving it, began to give him
chase. So in the end, three of them followed him
so near that the Englishman doubted hardly to
escape them.

At his first sight of them there were two flags
spread which were suddenly taken in again, and
being far off could not well discern the same.
They were all great ships, and, as he might judge,
the least of them from 200 tons to 5 and 800 tons.
Their sails were all crossed over with a red cross.
Each of the greater ships towed astern them either
a great boat or pinnace without mast.

The same morning, or the evening before, the
Englishman had speech with a flyboat, who de-
manding of the Englishman whither he was bound,
told him for France to lade salt. He willed him in
any wise, as he loved his life, not to proceed ; for,
said he, the Spanish fleet is on the coast. He

[1] So in MS., but Friday was the 21st.
[2] Member of Parliament for Cornwall ; great-grandfather of
the Lord High Treasurer in the reign of Queen Anne.
[3] Probably St. Mawes.

further told him that he had spoken with some of his countrymen that had been two years with their ships imbarged[1] in Spain, and were there come in the fleet. The Englishman, little regarding his speeches, or at least to see the farther truth thereof, proceeded, and found some more likelihood of the same, as is before said.

On Saturday, there came another Englishman from the west part of Cornwall, who likewise had been chased with[2] a fleet of ships, being shot at by them, but recovered the shore with little hurt.

On Sunday, one Simons of Exeter gave advertisement to my Lord Admiral that on Friday last he was chased with a fleet of great ships, having some of his men hurt with shot from them ; escaping their hands, landed in Cornwall, and came post to Plymouth unto my Lord Admiral.

Each of their ships have red crosses on their sails. The two latter fleets which were discovered were, in the one, six sail, and in the other, fifteen sail.

June 23.—SEYMOUR TO WALSYNGHAM.

[ccxi. 49.—Signed.   Addressed.]

Sir :—I can advertise you but little since my last writing more than I have been at Gravelines some thirty hours, during which time issued forth from Dunkirk two small vessels, bending their course to Gravelines haven. Two of our pinnaces chased them, with the discharging of some saker shot, and yet would [they] not strike, till at the last one of our shot strake down the mainmast of one of their vessels, being a French bottom belonging to Calais, and had Monsieur Gourdan's[3] hand for his pass.

---

[1] Embargoed.   [2] By.   [3] Governor of Calais.

I demanded what he meant not to strike his sails and to come to the Queen's ships, knowing us so well. He answered that he took us for the King of Navarre's fleet, making himself ignorant what to do. I replied that if the Duke of Parma, or the Duke of Guise, should do the like, I would sink them, or they should distress me; adding further that my Sovereign Lady was able to defend her country against the Holy League, besides able to master any civil discord; and so dismissed them, with some little choler.[1]

The other ran himself hard aground right over against Gravelines, and voided themselves out of their vessel, wading through the water, and cut their sails from the masts, taking them also away. My boat, which I manned with some shot,[2] came upon their skirts, but a little too late; yet came there very near a hundred men, horse and foot, but durst not approach our shot[2]; by which time our men had some little leisure to cut down their masts, and would have fired her, but that suddenly the wind arose at North and by East, enforcing us to weigh for Blackness, where we anchored, with marvellous foul weather, some thirty hours.

These actions befell yesterday, the 22nd of this month, so as now the wind is come three points more, being North-North-East,[3] and thereby enforced to take our best harbours upon our own coasts; yet in the passage, far from us, we did descry 30 sail, to our judgment Hollanders, taking their courses westwards, which I would gladly have pursued, but that I feared they would have brought us too far west, being[4] not able to recover those coasts which we are to look unto.

This, having gathered out advertisements by

[1] MS. collor.   [2] Musketeers.   [3] So in MS.
[4] Sc. so that we should not be able.

private examinations a-seaboard within my own cabin, which also I send you here enclosed,[1] do take my leave. From aboard the Rainbow, this 23rd of June, 1588.

Your assured loving friend to command,

H. SEYMOUR.

Sir :—I have strained my hand with hauling of a rope, whereby as yet I cannot write so much as I would, and therefore am enforced to use the manner to *dictare*.

There are ten days expired of this last victuals, and when ten days more are spent, eight days will be little enough to come home and take in our victuals ; and the service that is to be done is most likely at the time of our revictualling, which I have often desired should be at the least for six weeks.

Sir, it is more than time our coast men were victualled, which was promised by your last letters should be forthwith supplied.

June 23.—HOWARD TO THE QUEEN.

[ccxi. 50.—Holograph.]

To the Queen's most excellent Majesty.

May it please your most excellent Majesty :—I have forborne this long time to write unto your Majesty, hoping that the wind would have served that on this I might have certified your Majesty of something worth the writing. We have often put to the sea, and have been fain to run off and on the Sleeve[2] with contrary winds ; and in the end, not being able to continue out for fear of being driven to the leeward as far as the Wight, were forced in again,

---

[1] Missing.   [2] MS. Slyve : cf. *ante*, p. 5, *note.*

into Plymouth.˙ Our victuals were spent, and the wind not serving our victuals to come to us, we expected the goodness of God to change the wind, which did happily change on Friday morning, so that on Saturday, late at night, they came to us. They were no sooner come, although it were night, but we went all to work to get in our victuals,[1] which I hope shall be done in 24 hours, for no man shall sleep[2] nor eat till it be dispatched ; so that, God willing, we will be under sail to-morrow morning, being Monday, and the 24th of this present. I humbly beseech your Majesty to think that there was never men more unwilling to lose any time than we are.

Even as I had written this much of my letter to your Majesty, I received this letter[3] from a man of mine, which I did send to lie with a pinnace betwixt the Land's End and Ushant.[4] The party himself[5] that was chased did bring the letter, who is a wise man and of good credit. There was also another ship in this man's company that was also chased with him. The ships they met withal, seven of them, were ships of eight and nine hundred.[6] The others were Biscayans of 300. It is very likely that this stormy weather hath parted the fleet.[7] I hope in God we shall meet with some of them ; we will not stay for anything. I trust we shall meet with them on the coast of France, for I have some intelligence that for certain they mean to come thither, and there to receive many Frenchmen into their ships.

For the love of Jesus Christ, Madam, awake thoroughly, and see the villainous[8] treasons round about you, against your Majesty and your realm, and

[1] MS. geet in our vyttelse.   [2] MS. slype.
[3] Probably Godolphin's letter referred to *ante*, p. 221.
[4] MS. Youshant.
[5] It would seem that this was Simons of Exeter (cf. p. 222), though he is nowhere else mentioned as a man of Howard's.
[6] Sc. tons.   [7] MS. flyte.   [8] MS. velynous.

draw your forces round about you, like a mighty
prince, to defend you.   Truly, Madam, if you do so,
there is no cause to fear.   If you do not, there will
be danger.   I would to God nobody had been more
deceived in this than I ; it would have been never a
whit the worse for your Majesty's service.

I humbly beg your Majesty to pardon me that I
do cut off my letter in this sort.   I am now in haste,
and long to set sail.   I beseech the Almighty God
to bless and defend your Majesty from all your
enemies, and so I do most humbly take my leave.
From aboard the Ark, ready to weigh, this Sunday
night at 12 of the clock.

Your Majesty's most humble
and obedient servant,
C. HOWARD.

June 23.—*HOWARD TO WALSYNGHAM.*

[ccxi. 51.—Holograph.   Addressed.]

Sir :—This Sunday, about 7 of the clock at night,
I received your letter of the 22nd of this present,
and the advertisements with them, which I do most
heartily thank you for ; but I perceive by your letter
there should another letter come from my Lords to
Mr. Darell, and also a warrant that the pursuivant
should bring, which should be open for me, but
he neither brought the Lords' letter nor any such
warrant.

Sir, I pray you pardon me that I do not send
you the names of the towns divided, such as be
willing, and such as be not.   Sir F. Drake hath the
names of them.   Now at this hour [he] is full
occupied, as I am also.   Our victuals came to us
this last night about 12 of the clock, and we will not
eat nor sleep till it be aboard us.   We must not lose

one hour of time. You shall see by a letter that I
have sent her Majesty what advertisement I have.
I mean to weigh presently and set sail. This foul
weather that was on Thursday, that forced us in,
surely dispersed the Spanish fleet. It shall go hard
but I will find them out. Let her Majesty trust no
more to Judas' kisses ; for let her assure herself there
is no trust to French King nor Duke of Parma.
Let her defend herself like a noble and mighty
prince, and trust to her sword and not to their word,
and then she need not fear, for her good God will
defend her.

Sir, I have a privy intelligence by a sure fellow
that this fleet of Spain doth mean to come to the
coast of France, and there to receive in the Duke of
Guise and great forces ; and it is very likely to be
true. I mean, God willing, to visit the coast of
France, and to send in small pinnaces to discover all
the coast along. If I hear of them, I hope ere it be
long after you shall hear news. Good Mr. Secretary,
let the Narrow Seas be well strengthened. What
charge is ill spent now for surety ? Let the hoys of
Harwich go with all speed again to my Lord Henry
Seymour, for they be of great service.

Sir, for these things here, I pray take order with
Mr. Darell, for I have no leisure to think of them.
I pray you, Sir, deliver my letter unto her Majesty
with my humble duty, and so in haste I bid you farewell. Aboard the Ark, this Sunday, at 12 of the
clock at night.

Your assured loving friend,
C. HOWARD.

Sir, God willing, I will cut [1] sail within this three
hours.

[1] Loose sail. See *ante*, p. 82 *note*.

June 23.—*LORD HOWARD TO THE COUNCIL.*

[ccxi. 52.—Signed. Addressed.]

May it please your Lordships :—Even as I had
made up a packet of letters unto Mr. Secretary, one
Richard Swansey, a pursuivant, came unto me.
Two hours after, another pursuivant, with your
Lordships' letters. I will take what order I can, as
the shortness of the time will permit me, for I mean,
God willing, to set sail within these two hours,
having received some advertisements which make me
to make all the haste I can out unto the sea. My
victual came but this last morning about two of the
clock ; and since, we have laboured very hard for
the taking of them in, for we were very bare left
before they came. And yet we meant, if they did
not come this day, to have gone out to the sea,
although we had but three days' victual. I pray your
Lordships that some money may be speedily sent
down unto Mr. Darell, for the avoiding of all danger
if the towns do not prove so ready to revictual their
ships as your Lordships do expect. And so most
heartily praying your Lordships to bear with my
hasty and short writing, being overcharged with
business now at our setting forth, I take my leave,
the 23rd of June, 1588.

Your Lordships' loving friend to command,

C. HOWARD.

June 24.—*DRAKE TO WALSYNGHAM.*

[ccxi. 53.—Signed, and autograph postscript. Addressed.]

Right Honourable :—Although I do very well
know that your Honour shall be at large advertised
by my very good Lord, the Lord Admiral, that the
Spanish forces are descried to be near at hand in

several companies on our coast, as it is reported for certain by three barks unto whom they gave chase and made shot, yet have I thought it good also to write these few lines unto your Honour; nothing doubting but that, with God's assistance, they shall be so sought out and encountered withal in such sort as (I hope) shall qualify their malicious and long pretended[1] practices. And therefore, I beseech your Honour to pray continually for our good success in this action, to the performance whereof we have all resolutely vowed the adventure of our lives, as well for the advancement of the glory of God, as the honour and safety of her Majesty, her realms and dominions. And thus, resting always ready to perform what shall lie in my power, either in duty or service to my prince and country, I humbly take my leave. From aboard her Majesty's ship the Revenge, this 24th of June, 1588.

Your Honour's very ready to be commanded,

FRA. DRAKE.

I leave the bearer, my servant Jonas Bodenham,[2] to solicit your Honour as occasion shall be offered.

Your Honour's faithfully,

FRA. DRAKE.

[1] Intended, designed. Cf. Shakespeare, 1 *Henry VI.* iv. 1: 'Such as shall pretend malicious practices against his state.'

[2] He continued a close follower of Drake, was with him, in the Defiance, in his last voyage, and witnessed the codicil to his will, by which Drake left him the manor of Samford Spiney, near Tavistock (*Wills from Doctors' Commons*, Camden Soc.). It is very probable that he was the nephew of Mary Newton, Drake's first wife, married in 1569, at St. Budeaux, where in 1560 Margaret Newton married John Bodenham. On the father's side he would seem to have belonged to Hereford, of which county Roger Bodenham was sheriff in 1585 and again in 1593. A Roger Bodenham commanded the Anchor in a Mediterranean voyage in 1551 (Hakluyt, ii. 99), settled in Seville, married there, made a voyage to Mexico in 1564 (*ib.* iii. 447), and was still living at San Lucar in 1580 (*S P. Spain*, xvi.).

[ccxi. 54.—Endorsed.]

24th of June, 1588.

A memorial for the Lord Admiral of the names[2] of all the ships, with their men and tonnage.

Flushing:

Cornelis Lonck,[3] Admiral . . .	75	130
Adrianson Cornisen Conoper . .	75	140
Legier Jacobson	85	160
Legier Pieterson . . .	52	120
Lucas Dano	45	120
Adrian de Doe	45	120
Marten Francis	45	120
St. Pieterson Skoyen . . .	45	120
Hans Cornelis Mortman . . .	45	65

Campvere:

Cornelis Harmonson Calis, Vice-Admiral	85	150
Evarte Pieterson	45	80

Middelburg:

Walter Longuevale	45	130
Pieter Jonson	45	110
	732	1,565

[1] These are the ships ordered to join Seymour for the guard of the Narrow Seas. They were prevented crossing over by the strong westerly wind, and seem to have afterwards formed part of the squadron under Count Justin.

[2] It will be noticed that the names are not of the ships, but of their commanders.

[3] Cornelis Lonck van Roozendaal. With this one exception, none of these names can be identified here, and the wild spelling of the original remains. About half of them reappear in similar lists of the ships with Justin in the Scheldt and off Dunkirk, in August (*S.P. Holland,* lvi.).

Hollanders.

Rotterdam :

Ewke Denbowte	.	.	.	. 76	120
Jacob Jonson Bacanela	.	.	. 75		130
Pieter Marten .	.	.	.	. 60	115

Enkhuysen :

Symond Jacobson	.	.	.	. 76	140
Jacob Jeretson .	.	.	.	. 45	60
Frederick Adrianson .		.	.	. 45	100

Amsterdam :

Arnold Rovere .	.	.	.	. 65	130
				442	795
Totalis	.	.	.	. 1,174	2,360

June 26.—*SEYMOUR TO WALSYNGHAM.*

[ccxi. 58.—Holograph. Addressed.]

Sir :—To iterate my opinion, with confirmation of better judgment, I fear no attempt for England this year more than still I doubt the continuance of private practising, policies wherewith these Italians have continually been trained.

To urge pro and contra this.

The Duke of Parma hath ready 30,000 expert soldiers, to transport either for England or Scotland. His own private strength (without the assistance of Spain or France) doth not exceed 40 sails of fly-boats and 220 bylanders. A time must be to land them and a time to back them.

Answer.

England, I least doubt, because he is cut off from faction within our own country ; besides, one of our men upon defence is worth two of an enemy for offence, being not supported through civil discord. Also our strength of shipping, being not severed, with some longer continuance of victuals, must cross and thwart the foresaid attempts, if wind and weather assist us to attend them.

All I fear is they will never offer themselves, specially on the seas, in place where service may be tried. And to that end, we have twice showed ourselves at Gravelines, desiring nothing more than to suffer them come out, rather than to stop them in by sinking vessels with stones or timber, which will be recovered again upon every ebb, and will serve them for their strength and better fortification.

Concerning Scotland, if the news be true which a Scot this day informed me from Dundee, it seemeth that the King doth take a course to keep friendship with us, by some acts lately performed four days past, videlicet, the executing the Lord Maxwell[1] his brother, and imprisoning the Lord Maxwell himself; which if the same be current and sure, I doubt not but your honourable wisdom will back the continu-

---

[1] Lord Maxwell, born in 1553, who had for many years been intriguing with Spain in the interests of the Queen of Scots, and had repeatedly suffered imprisonment or fine for offences against the King's government, had left Scotland in April 1587, on an undertaking not to return without the King's license. Notwithstanding this, he did return in April 1588, and began to assemble his followers, to be in readiness to assist the Spaniards, either in Scotland or England. He was declared a public enemy, was arrested (June 5), and kept a close prisoner till September, when he was released on giving caution to do 'nothing tending to the trouble or alteration of the state of religion presently professed and by law established.' He was killed in an affray with the Johnstones in 1593. Robert Maxwell, his bastard brother, escaped, and on June 23 a reward was offered for him alive or dead. David Maxwell, captain of Lochmaben Castle, with five of his dependents, was hanged, and a great many of the clan were bound over under heavy caution, or security (*Register of the Privy Council of Scotland*, iv. 275–292 ; Sir Wm. Fraser's *Book of Carlaverock*, i. 278–9).

ance of such good actions. Where otherwise they should join and take part with Spain, I hope their attempts shall cost more than one battle or two, before they should approach London.

Thus having answered your letter by delivering my private opinion, do wish that Zealand be circumspectly looked into ; for I understand that companies of Arnemuiden and Campvere are dismissed lately, which may give the enemy great advantages to lie in wait for the same. So expecting some seasonable weather and more favourable winds, do take my leave. Aboard the Rainbow, this 26th of June, 1588.

Your assured loving friend to command,
H. SEYMOUR.

The two brothers Musgrave, the one captain for Yarmouth the other for Lynn, as well by their own accord as the general consent, voluntarily yield another month's victuals, desiring in no sort to have her Majesty charged ; and truly, Sir, if you knew them as well [as ¹] I, they deserve special thanks.

Tomson,² a great agent for Archibald Douglas, is much resident in Dover ; to what end I know not.

June 26.—SEYMOUR TO WALSYNGHAM.

[ooxi. 59.—Holograph.³ Addressed :—To the Right Honourable Sir Francis Walsyngham, Knight, Principal Secretary to her Majesty. H. Seymour.]

I do what I can to lay in wait for the vessel that should go out of Dunkirk to Spain, but it is a hundred to one she may escape me ; yet I think

---

¹ As : omitted in MS.
² Not to be confused with Richard Tomson, the lieutenant of the Margaret and John.   ³ An almost illegible scrawl.

she may sooner fall into the hands of the Lord
Admiral; and as yet the wind being so contrary
hath retained all the shipping in Dunkirk; likewise
the Spaniards, if they have intention to set forward.
Thus much I return with speed, because my servant
Floyd[1] brought me letters from you to have care
thereof. So having unfolded my packet which was
ready to go, do leave you better satisfied herewith.
Haste.

June 30.—*A DECLARATION AS TO THE VICTUALLING.*

[ccxi. **70.**—Endorsed: 'For my Lord Treasurer'; and in
Burghley's hand: 'Ulto. Junii, 1588. Mr. Quarles' book of
the victualling of the Lord Admiral [and] Lord Henry.']

30ᵐᵒ die Junii 1588.

A declaration unto your Lordship how and
unto what time her Majesty's ships be victualled, as
well those that be with my Lord Admiral south-
ward as also those ships that be with my Lord
Henry Seymour on the Narrow Seas, videlicet:—

Ships 16 of her Majesty's which went with my
[Lord] Admiral.
Men in the said 16 ships, 3,736.

First, my Lord Admiral had one month's victual
which he took with him for all her Majesty's ships,
which victuals began the 19th day of May and
ended the 15th day of June, his Lordship being at
Plymouth, where Mr. Darell did presently victual
the said fleet for 6 days longer, which ended the
21st of June. The 22nd of June arrived at Plymouth

---

[1] The MS. here has Flud: in other places Seymour wrote
Fludd, or Floyd; the true name was probably the more familiar
Flood or Lloyd.

15 ships sent from London with one month's victual more, which doth serve the said fleet until the 20th day of July ; and then, as it appeareth by Mr. Darell's letter dated the 2nd day of June, he had both order and money by my Lord Admiral and Sir Francis Drake to provide one month's victual more, which beginneth the 21st of July, and doth end the 18th of August.

Besides this, his Lordship hath sent him by the said 15 ships a proportion for 14 days for biscuit and beer ; and more, as it do appear by Mr. Darell's letters dated as aforesaid, his Lordship hath, for a convenient time, biscuit, newland fish, wine, cider, rice, oil and pease, to serve the whole fleet.

Ships of her Majesty with my Lord Henry Seymour, 15.

Men with my Lord Henry Seymour on the Narrow Seas in the [15] ships, 1,471.

My Lord Henry Seymour had one month's victual sent him to the Narrow Seas, which began the 16th day of June and is to end the 14th day of July.

Likewise, by your Lordship's order, there was a supply of victual sent to my Lord Henry Seymour for 18 days more, which beginneth the 15th day of July and is to end the last of the said month, and so is to begin a new proportion the 1st of August.

Ships of sundry ports with my Lord Henry Seymour, and victualled for one month, 18.

Men in the ships from the ports, 800.

More, there is victualled by your Lordship's order divers ships, which serve under my Lord Henry Seymour, for one month, which doth begin their victuals the 25th of June and is to end the 23rd of July.

Money sent into the West Country, to Mr. Darell:

	£	*s.*	*d.*
Received and sent into the West Country out of the Exchequer, by three privy seals, for service down there	11,161	13	4

ADVERTISEMENT[1] *TO WALSYNGHAM.*

[ccxi. 95.—Endorsed.]

It is reported that all those ships that are seen for Spain, and from Spain hither, have aboard the English flag, the French flag, and the Bourgogne[2] flag ; and when they are hailed by her Majesty's navy, they say that they are French, and so speak French, by which means they go and come. It were very necessary that my Lord Seymour had word to command all his fleet that what boat soever they meet, that [they[3]] should bring him to him to be examined ; and my Lord should have aboard of himself some one discreet person, that had of late haunted these ports, thereby to discover their men and ships, and such as could speak Flemish. By these means, it is assured me you shall meet with many.

The three ships that I wrote unto you that were going out of Dunkirk, are manned with pilots to be distributed among the navy. My hope is that [they[3]] shall be met withal. They lads[4] be shipped ;

---

[1] The writing and spelling are singularly bad.

[2] The Burgundian flag—white, with a red saltire raguled—was adopted as the Spanish flag, on the accession of the Emperor Charles V., and so continued till the accession of the Bourbons.

[3] Omitted in MS.

[4] Those pilots are shipped, which seems an indication that presently &c.

and truly by that it may be thought presently they
will do somewhat.

It is here said that the Spanish navy shall be
reinforced with a number of French ships; and that
they shall have all the favour that may be in all the
French havens; and I do sooner believe it, for that
I hear that all the captains of these haven-towns are
sworn to the League.

July 4—MEMORANDUM BY DRAKE.

[ccxii. 9.—Copy.   Endorsed :—Sir Francis Drake's opinion
touching our going to the coast of Spain.]

To maintain my opinion that I have thought it
meeter to go for the coast of Spain, or at least more
nearer than we are now, are these reasons following :
written aboard her Majesty's good ship the Revenge,
this fourth of July, 1588.

The first, that hearing of some part of the
Spanish fleet upon our coast, and that in several
fleets, the one of eleven sail, the other of six sail,
and the last of eighteen, all these being seen the
20th and 21st of June ; since which time, we being
upon the coast of France, could have no intelligence
of their being there, or passing through our Channel ;
neither hearing, upon our own coast, of their arrival
in any place, and speaking with a bark which came
lately out of Ireland, who can advertise nobody of
their being in those parts, I am utterly of opinion
that they are returned, considering what ways[1] they
have had since that time ; otherwise they could have
been here without our knowledge.

[1] MS. wayes : possibly a mistake of the clerk who copied it,
for weather. In Elizabethan writing *th* is very apt to be mis-
taken for *y* ; and Drake's writing, at the best, is a very difficult
scrawl.

I say further, that if they be returned, our staying here in this place shall but spend our victual,
whereby our whole action is in peril, no service
being done. For the lengthening of our victual by
setting a straiter order for our company, I find them
much discontented if we stay there ; whereas, if we
proceed, they all promise to live with as little
portion as we shall appoint unto them.

Our being upon the coast of Spain will yield us
true intelligence of all their purposes.

The taking of some of their army shall much
daunt them, and put a great fear amongst them.

My opinion is altogether that we shall fight with
them much better cheap [1] upon their own coast than
here ; for that I think this one of the unmeetest
places to stay for them.

To conclude, I verily believe that if we undertake no present service, but detract time some few
days, we shall hardly be able to perform any matter
of importance.   FRANCIS DRAKE.

July 14.—*CONSIDERATIONS BY FENNER.*

[ccxii. 10.—Holograph.[2]   Endorsed.]

Considerations to move the proceedings of her
Majesty's fleet to go for the coast of Spain, to take
there opportunity of the accident fallen out by the
return of the Spanish fleet, the rather thereby utterly
to dissolve them.

First, I set down to your Lordship the reasons
we have of their return.   They were seen the 19th
of June, thirty of their fleet, in their general com-

---

[1] Cheap=market : much better cheap means, on better terms,
more advantageously.

[2] Fenner's language is always curiously involved and careless ;
in this instance, more than usually so.

panies, with crosses painted red on their foresails ;
they chased some of Falmouth, and near thereabout,
not many leagues South-West of Lizard, the parties
chased witnessing the same in their own persons.

The 21st of June, a bark of Dublin taken by
them some 15 leagues South-West of Lizard ;
which bark, being by them towed in foul weather,
the cable breaking, escaped with three persons, and
six of their company being into the Spaniards, and
so bare unto the sea South-West ; being 18 sail in
number, great hulks and very full of Spaniards, not
less than ten thousand by composition.[1]

From the 21st of June until the sixth of July we
could not intercept any news of their arrival in
England, France, Ireland, or Scotland, which argueth
plainly their companies dispersed. As also one
Mr. Hawes of London (if I mistake not his name)
met with several companies of them dispersed at
sea ; so as that they cannot be but returned, in that
they have had sundry times large[2] winds to enter
Sleeve again.

Which causes considered, it was thought meet
the 5th of July to bear out into the sea, until Ushant
bare of us East-South-East, and Scilly North-West
and by North, some 15 leagues of either, with
pinnaces placed between the body of the fleet and
Ushant, as also Scilly, thereby none to enter the
Sleeve but that we must have sight of them. Otherwise, lying in the middle of the Channel, as we did
before, with the body of the fleet, and Ushant as
also Scilly thereby, if the wind came southerly,
they might haul[3] the coast of France, if the North-

---

[1] Estimation.   [2] Fair ; we still say 'to sail large.'
[3] MS. hale. The expression was still in use 150 years later.
Burchett, writing in 1720, has 'which ship hauling the shore on
board more than the rest of the fleet did, she lay becalmed'
(*Transactions at Sea*, p. 484), and Lediard repeated it in 1735
(*Naval History*, p. 676). We still say ' to haul the wind.'

West, they might haul the coast of England, and not by us for the present to be impeached.

In the mean season, some of our fleet had been at Plymouth, as also at Conquet in France, and no news but that they were dispersed and returned in great misery, as by sickness and foul weather much beaten and spoiled. Also we understood of their return by a pilot of Conquet; the like in effect from the Mayor of Rochelle, in that he certified many of their fleet to be seen about Cape Finisterre some days after the sight of them upon the coast; withal [by] three English mariners now in our company, which came from Rochelle in a bark of Millbrooke. Upon their coming from thence, [they] were aboard a pinnace of Rochelle then coming from the sea,[1] and had taken two Spale[2] Spaniards of 30 tons apiece, laden with wine and oil, who did deliver the certainty of the dispersion of the fleet into many harbours of the coast of Biscay and other places.

Which several advertisements considered, and lying in the place aforesaid as between Scilly and Ushant, the wind coming up northerly, it was thought meet by my Lord Admiral and the rest of us of council to take the benefit of time, and not to lose the opportunity of so happy an accident, but to persecute[3] their waste and dissolving, by our going upon the coast of Spain to seek the place of their dispersed companies, and to seek by all possible means their waste.

It is to be considered so mighty an army of three years' preparation, and with so many estates and provisions of horsemen, being gathered together by so great a prince and so great colleagues out of so many and so far countries, wherein there are in

---

[1] From a cruise.
[2] Seville. The Latin forms are Hispalis, Spalis.
[3] Thoroughly to follow up ; to complete.

number above twenty thousand that have not tasted
the seas before. And now, by the providence of
God, the burdens aforesaid laid upon them have so
abated the pride of their minds, so as no doubt it
hath stirred a deadly grief in the secrets of their
hearts against all those that have been the procures
of their enterprise, wherein they have wasted themselves, touching their reputation, spent the colleagues' treasury, and abated (by their return) the
pride of the Prince of Parma his forces, in that the
thread of both their hopes by this accident is cut
asunder. Therefore more meeter to be followed
with effect.

Now were utterly to be beaten down the hope of
any good success to them, by visiting their coast and
following their ruin ; my most gracious Majesty
thereby delivered of their malicious determinations
and practices against her royal person and country.
We should now have to do with amazed and discontented companies, so as they cannot (in 'my poor
opinion) proceed against [1] this summer season, in that
their provisions are wasted, their companies wearied,
their fleet not to be relieved in the several places
where they are of their distresses. Their great
companies considered, not in season to be refreshed
with water for such a journey ; in that they must use
at least six thousand butts of water, wherein no
doubt they shall have great want of cask, considering
the use at sea in such journeys to save [2] their casks,
for keeping of their ships unpestered.

Withal their mariners, being of sundry nations,
and by all the advertisements we can gather very

---

[1] Again. This use of the word is noted in the *N.E.D.* as
very rare ; not improbably it is here a slip of the pen.

[2] To save their casks would seem equivalent to the modern
'to shake ' them ; that is, to knock the hoops off and let them
fall to pieces, for convenience of stowage.

unwilling to meet with our forces at sea, have been,
since their first proceedings, by severe punishment
and political orders kept together, otherwise their
minds have been to run away, both Spaniards and
Flemings, Portingals and French, by all which
nations they are but means [1] suited with mariners.

Many of the causes aforesaid have moved the
most part of us earnestly to give counsel to lose no
time in the proceeding to their coast, to the effect
aforesaid, so as no man to make estimate of their
lives, or burdens in want of victual, respecting [2] the
weightiness of the cause, and to relieve ourselves
upon the enemy, the greater to our reputation. To
have stayed and gone for the coast of England to
have relieved the wants of victual in some, by that
means the rest had been in the same predicament ;
and therefore, the wind being northerly, the 7th of
July at three of the clock in the afternoon [it was]
concluded to go for Spain, Ushant bearing of us
East-North-East, next hand [3] some 15 leagues off.

The 9th of July being shot [4] some ten leagues off
South and by West of Ushant, the wind came up at
South-West, blowing much wind. Thereby bear [5]
up for England again, in that divers of the small
shipping were but meanly victualled, so as to refresh
them and the rest, and so, at the first wind, to seek
them out on the coast of Spain, and as [6] her Majesty
may hear no news of them again. For this their
army at sea being thoroughly dissolved, he shall
never be able to gather together the like again, which
easily satisfy her Majesty and ease a mighty charge,
which may hereafter lie upon [her] Majesty and

[1] In a middling way ; moderately.
[2] Having regard to ; considering.   [3] So in MS.
[4] Pushed forward, advanced. Cf. *Psalms*, xxii. 7, 'They shoot
out the lip' ; and Spenser, *Faërie Queene*, V. vi. 19, 'Well shot
in yeares he seemed.'
[5] It was resolved to bear up.   [6] In such sort that.

[the] realm, if they be not now thoroughly dissolved. And therefore, since God hath made manifest the means, I pray unto the Lord to continue your willingness in mind to the execution thereof, which now is to be done (the fleet being together) with a far more easier charge and adventure than at another time.   THOMAS FENNER.

July 5.—DARELL TO THE COUNCIL.

[ccxii. 16.—Signed. Endorsed.]

Right Honourable :—According to your Lordships' commandment signified to me by Mr. Quarles, I have sent herewith a note of the ships now at sea under the charge of the Lord Admiral, with their numbers of men and time of victualling, so near as of myself I know or can learn. Wherein what shall remain doubtful unto your Lordships touching the determination[1] of the victuals for that fleet which came down with my Lord, it may please you to be more fully informed thereof by those that have had the charge of their former proportions, who, understanding by this note what hath been delivered here, will soon set down what ought to remain. As for the ships set forth by the port towns, forasmuch as the charge thereof did nothing concern me, I have not acquainted myself much with it ; only now, understanding your Lordships' pleasures, I have set down as much thereof as of late by credible report I have learned ; and also have required Richard Swanson, a messenger of the Chamber sent hither by your Lordships about those causes, in his return by the towns to bring unto your Lordships a certain note of the rest.[2]

It may please your Lordships also to understand

---

[1] Ending.   [2] See *post*, p. 259.

R 2

that by reason the ships which are at her Majesty's charge have been all supplied with fresh victual here, in this long time of their stay in harbour, I am grown indebted in the country near to the sum of 900*l*., as hath appeared particularly unto my Lord Admiral, and thereof I think he hath already informed your Lordships. I humbly therefore beseech you to give your speedy order for the discharge thereof, whereby your Lordships shall much help my poor credit amongst them. And so, with remembrance of my duty, I most humbly take my leave. At Plymouth, the 5th of July, 1588.

Your Lordships' most humble,

MAR. DARELL.

July 6.—DARELL TO WALSYNGHAM.

[ccxii. 17.—Signed.   Addressed.]

Right Honourable:—Having received commandment from the Council to certify what number of ships and men are now at sea under the charge of the Lord Admiral, and for what time they are severally victualled, I have performed the same as directly as I could, and do send your Honour herewithal a copy thereof, wherein if anything may [yet] seem doubtful unto their Lordships touching the victualling of the ships at her Majesty's charge, Mr. Quarles may inform their Lordships of it more particularly. Only I have omitted to set down in that note the number of men in the coast ships, the certainty whereof I could not learn ; and therefore have presumed to refer the same unto this bearer [1] (one of the messengers sent down by your Honour about those causes), who is to bring their

---

[1] Richard Swanson : see *post*, p. 259.

Lordships a true report thereof from the towns that have set them forth. And so leaving to trouble your Honour further at this time, most humbly take my leave. At Plymouth, the 5th of July, 1588.

Your Honour's most bounden,
[Mar.] Darell.

July 6.—HOWARD TO WALSYNGHAM.

[ccxii. 18.—Signed. Addressed. In very bad condition.]

Sir :—Being here in the midst of the Channel of the Sleeve, on Friday, being the 5th of this month, I received your letter of the 28th of June, and another of the same date which was written after you had made up your packet. The cause of the long time that these letters were in coming unto me was because the pursuivant, embarking himself upon Monday at Plymouth, was fain to beat up and down the [sea] with a contrary wind until Friday [before] he could [find me].

By your first letter I find how greatly you stand assured that neither the French King, nor the havens and port towns that stand for the King, will give any help or assistance unto the Spanish army. As for Newhaven, it is not a place to serve their turns.

By your other letter you perceive from an advertisement you have from my brother Stafford,[1] that there is money sent down to Brest and Conquet for the relief and assistance of the Spanish fleet if they arrive there. I [wish with all] my heart that they were there with the [best welcome they could] give them. [It should not be long] after but that I would give them another welcome ; for if it be they mean to touch there, then assuredly they have a

---

[1] Sir Edward Stafford, the ambassador at Paris.

meaning to join forces with the Duke of Parma. I
have no doubt but that my Lord Henry Seymour,
being [so] strong as he is, will have a care that he
shall not start any whither to meet them. And it
shall be very well that you have some trusty espial[1]
there to give certain intelligence when the Duke's
forces shall be ready, [that then, my Lord] Henry
Seymour may lie in the [mouth of] their haven to
interrupt their coming forth.

I am sorry to perceive by your letter that [her
Majesty hath] no more care to have forces about
her, considering the great peril that may come by
neglecting that which should be done in time. I
have written again unto her Majesty very earnestly
about it, and I hope that God will put into her
mind to do that which may tend most to her safety.

I am sure you have seen the letter which I sent
unto her Majesty of the discovery of certain of the
Spanish fleet not far off of Scilly, which made me to
make as much haste out to sea as I could ; for upon
Sunday our victuals came to us, and having the
wind at North-East, I would not stay the taking in
of them all ; but taking in some part of them, I
appointed the rest to follow with me, and so bare to
Scilly, thinking to have cut off those Spanish ships
[seen] there from the rest of their fleet ; but the
wind continued not 16 hours there, but turned
South-South-West, that we were fain to lay it off
and on in the Sleeve, and could get no further.
Then did I send Sir Francis Drake with half a score
ships and three or four pinnaces into the Trade, to
discover it. In his way, hard aboard Ushant, he
met with a man of mine, whom I had sent out in a
bark ten days before to lie off and on there for discovery, who had met with an Irish [bark and] stayed
her, which had been with the [18] great ships of the

[1] Spy.

Spanish fleet 16 [leagues South-South[1]]-West of Scilly. They had taken out of the said [bark] five of her most principal men, and left in her but three men and a boy. One of the greatest Spanish ships towed her at her stern by a cable, which in the night time, the wind blowing somewhat stiff, brake, and so she escaped in the storm. This did assure us greatly that the Spanish fleet was broken in the storms which had been afore ; and by all likelihood, we conjectured, if the wind had continued northerly that they [would have] returned back again [to the] Groyne ; but [as the wind] hath served [these] six or seven days, [we] must look for them every hour if they mean to come hither.

Sir, I sent a fine Spanish caravel an eight days agone to the Groyne to learn intelligence, such a one as would not have been mistrusted ; but when she was fifty leagues on her way, this southerly wind forced her back again unto us. Therefore I pray you, if you hear or understand of any news [or] advertisements by land, that I may hear of them from you with expedition.

I have divided myself here into three parts, and yet we lie within sight one of another, so as, if any of us do discover the Spanish fleet, we give notice thereof presently the one to the other, and there-upon repair and assemble together. I myself do lie in the middle of the Channel, with the greatest force. Sir Francis Drake hath 20 ships and four or five pinnaces, which lie towards Ushant ; and Mr. Hawkyns, with as many more, lieth towards Scilly. Thus are we fain to do, else with this wind they might pass by and we [never] the wiser.

Whatsoever hath been made of the S[leeve, it] is another manner of thing than it was taken for ; we find it by experience and daily observation to be

[1] So Bruce ; there is now nothing to guide conjecture.

an hundred miles over ; a large room for men to look unto. And whereas it is thought that we should have regard [unto the] forces of the [said] fleet, if [they] should bend for Scotland, they would in their [way] thither keep so far away westward off Cape Cl[ear] as they would be farther from us at any time than [it] is betwixt England and Spain ; so that the best advertisement that we must hope for must be from you by the knowledge that you shall have over land out of Scotland, if they be discovered there. And then our best and nearest course will be unto them through the Narrow Seas, where I have no doubt but we shall defeat them of their fleet, whatsoever they do with [their land] men. But for my own part I can not [persuade myself but tha]t their inte[nt is for Ireland]. Where there are so many doubts, we [must proceed] by the likelier ways, and leave unto God [to] direct for the best. And so I bid you most heartily farewell. From off aboard her Majesty's good ship the Ark, the 6th of July, 1588.

Your assured loving friend,
C. HOWARD.

July 8.—*THE COUNCIL TO DARELL.*

[ccxii. 23.—Endorsed.   A rough draft with many interlinear corrections.]

After our hearty commendations :—We find by a late note you have sent us, bearing date the 4th of July, of such ships as serve in those parts under our very good Lord the Lord Admiral, that for such of the said ships as were brought into those parts by his Lordship, you cannot set down a true estimate for what time they are victualled, unless you were made acquainted with their former victualling ; but for the rest of the ships that serve under Sir Francis Drake, and others that are entertained in her Majesty's pay there, as also the coast ships, it appeareth by your said note that they are victualled but until the 14th of July, saving that Sir Francis Drake hath a supply of seven days' victual more for the number of ships appointed to serve under him. Which being true, we do not see but the most part of the ships shall be forced to give over the service, a matter we do very greatly mislike of ; and therefore we think it very convenient that you should provide a month's victual for all the whole navy serving there under his Lordship, wherein there would[1] be all diligence possible used, especially if they be furnished for no longer time than the 14th of this month, as is contained in your said note.

And for such money as doth appear by your letters to be due there, amounting to the sum of 900*l.*, as also such further sums as shall be necessarily employed in the provision of the said month's victual, we will take order that the same shall be sent down with all speed by our loving friend Richard Quarles, Esq., whom we think very meet to repair to those parts for the better advancement of the service. In the meantime, we would have you take up, upon your credit, such provisions and other necessaries as the said service shall require. And for your better assistance therein, we send you certain commissions directed unto the Lieutenants[2] and other principal officers in the counties where the said provisions are to be made.

And so requiring [you] to advertise us by what time the said month's victuals will be ready, and whether in the meantime the provisions in the said ships will be able to hold out, whereby the service may not be given over. . . .

[1] Should.   [2] The Deputy-Lieutenants.

July 8.—*THE COUNCIL TO THE DEPUTY-LIEUTENANTS AND OTHERS.*

[ccxii. 23, I.—Rough draft.]

Whereas Marmaduke Darell, gentleman, a servant of her Majesty in household, is appointed to make certain provisions within the county, as well of grain as of flesh and other necessaries, for the victualling of her Majesty's navy serving in the western seas under our very good Lord the Lord Admiral, and is also to use divers necessary ministers [for] the said service :—

These are to will and require you, as also, in her Majesty's name, straitly to charge and command you, to afford the said Darell and his deputies bearing this placart under our hands, your uttermost aid and assistance—for such service requireth expedition—as well in taking up the said provisions as also for the transporting of them to Plymouth or other place upon the sea coast, where he shall appoint.

And such sums of money as shall be due to any of her Majesty's subjects, either for provisions taken of them or for their labour and pains employed in the carriage of the same or otherwise, we will take order the same shall be repaid unto them out of hand, to their contentment.

And therefore we are to require both you and them not to fail in the furtherance of this service, as you will answer to contrary at your perils.

To the Deputy-Lieutenants in the County of . . , and to all Justices of Peace, Mayors, Sheriffs, Bailiffs, Constables, or any other her Majesty's Officers, Ministers, and loving subjects, to whom it may appertain, and to every of them.

July 10.—*CHARGES OF THE LONDON SHIPS.*

[ccxii. 30.—Endorsed.]

There are in the sixteen ships and four pinnaces set forth by the City of London, 1,340 men.

	£	s.	d.
The wages of which men per month, after 14s. per man, one with another, amounteth to . .	938	0	0
The like we account for each man's victuals per month, after 14s. the man	938	0	0
The tonnage of the said ships and pinnaces amounteth to 4,150 tons, which, after 2s. the ton per month, amounteth to the sum of . .	415	0	0
Sum per month . .	2,291	0	0

	£	s.	d.
Besides powder, muskets, calivers, pikes, shot, and divers other furnitures put into the same ships and pinnaces, which at the least hath cost the City . . .	2,000	0	0
There was paid in wages to men, and for victualling of them, from the time they were prest to serve her Majesty until the first day of May last past	1,000	0	0

The Lord Mayor of London and the Common Council are contented, and do yield to victual the said ships for one month longer.

THOMAS CORDELL.

July 11.—*DARELL TO THE COUNCIL.*

[ccxii. 32.—Holograph.   Addressed.]

My duty unto your most honourable Lordships
humbly remembered :—Understanding by your letter of the 8th of this month (which came to my
hands yesternight) that it is your Lordships' pleasure
to have a month's victual more provided for the
whole navy now in service under my Lord Admiral
with all speed, and to be advertised from me in
what time the same may be ready ; as also whether
in the meantime, without it, the ships will be able
to continue at sea :—

It may please your Lordships there shall be
all diligence possible used in the performance of
it, according to your commandment. The commissions from your Lordships I do send away this
morning ; and will also despatch away such other
purveyors as shall be meet, with all the expedition
I can.

Yet, forasmuch as I do judge the whole number
of men that do serve in this fleet to be about 9,500,
which, to be furnished for a month, will require a
great mass of victual, I think it cannot be well performed in less space than a month ; and very true it
is that, according to the note I sent your Lordships,
the time of their former victualling will end in them
all long before. But so it is, Right Honourable,
that my Lord Admiral and Sir Francis Drake, to
prevent this want and inconvenience, which else
must of necessity now have been, did long since—
as I do certainly understand—take order for the
placing of six men to a mess at sea ; which no doubt
hath been observed, and thereby their victual much
lengthened. By means whereof, as also because

myself, expecting of late some further service, have already provided many things here beforehand, I hope to furnish them with this month's victual in due time, and without the inconvenience which your Lordships do doubt of. Only I will presume in the meantime, until I may understand your Lordships' further pleasure, to write forthwith unto my Lord Admiral that it may please him to send those ships hither for their victual first that have most need ; who no doubt—the fleet lying so near unto this coast—may return unto him again in short space, almost howsoever the wind be, and carry with them some store also for the rest. His Lordship may send, as he pleaseth, eight or ten sail at once, upon whose return others may come ; and to want so many for a short time, I trust will be no great weakening unto the whole fleet. Otherwise I do not know how I shall be able to send it from hence to them, the shipping that is left here is so small and unfit for such a purpose. And so leaving the rest unto your honourable considerations, I do most humbly take my leave. From Plymouth, this 11th of July in the morning, 1588.

It may please your Lordships, the Mayors of Bristol and Lyme have written unto me to furnish their ships with two months' victual more, according to your Lordships' last letters to them in that behalf.

Your Lordships' most humble,
Mar. Darell.

July 12.—SEYMOUR TO WALSYNGHAM.

[ccxii. 34.—Holograph. Addressed.]

Sir :—Such summer season saw I never the like ; for what for storms and variable unsettled

winds, the same unsettleth and altereth our determinations for lying on the other coast, having of
late sundry times put over, with southerly winds,
so far as Calais ; and suddenly enforced, still with
westerly great gales, to return to our English coasts,
where, so long as this unstable weather holdeth,
and that [1] the same serveth well many times for the
Spaniards to come (*vix credo*), yet shall they be
as greatly dangered by the raging seas as with their
enemies.

And to heap on braveries for conquering little
England, that hath always been renowned, and now
most famous by the great discovered strength, as
well by sea as by land, the same also united with
thousands resolute civil minds, how can the same
enter into my conceit they should any ways prevail ? when heretofore, our country, being divided
with many kings, the people barbarous and un-
civil, resisted mightily long before they could be
conquered.

But to digress from my own singular opinion,
and to give place to your honourable further authori-
ties, I received letters from Sir William Russell,
which I send here-inclosed, hoping that all your
Honours will be most careful to regard those
quarters, the same being of so great weight and importance for the enemy's advantages.

This, also returning a note of all our coast ships
discharged and that are absent, do leave any further
to trouble you.   From aboard the Rainbow, the 12th
of July, 1588, in the small Downs, where I have much
ado to send my letters ashore.

Your assured friend to command,

H. SEYMOUR.

The Duke levelleth at many marks, yet shooteth

[1] And that=even though.

but at one, I mean Zealand ; which, once obtained, his attempts for England will be far easier.

Sir, I pray you return me all my original letters both of Justinus Nassau[1] and of Sir William Russell.

July 10.—*NOTE OF THE COAST SHIPS.*

[ccxii. 34, I.—Enclosed in Lord H. Seymour's letter of July 12.]

10th July, 1588.—Ships of the coast that served in this fleet amongst others, which were discharged upon the considerations hereinunder written :—

Newcastle	The Daniel . . Galleon Hutchin Bark Lamb . Fancy . .	Sent away by the Lords of the Council's letters, for wafting the cloth fleet to Stade.
Hull . .	Griffin . . Little Hare . Handmaid .	These ships were discharged for want of victuals, 17th June.
Aldborough .	Marigold .	This ship was discharged for want of victuals, 13th June.
Lowestoft . This pinnace is not worth the charge.[2]	Matthew .	Discharged for want of victuals, 13th June.
Lynn . . Nor this of Lynn.[2]	Susan . .	Do., 3rd July.

[1] The Admiral of Zealand, illegitimate brother of Prince Maurice.

[2] Autograph notes by Seymour.

July 13.—*HOWARD TO WALSYNGHAM.*

[ccxii. 42.—Holograph. Addressed. In deplorable condition.[1]]

Sir :—I have received your letter of the 3rd of the present [this day[2]], being the 13th of the same, within two hours after I [had despatched[2]] Sir E. Hoby. The messenger had been at the sea to [seek me ever[2]] since Friday. I am very sorry to perceive by your [letter that[3]] her Majesty [doth think[3]] that we have not [sufficiently sought[3]] to understand some certainty of the Spanish fleet. Sir, we are here to small purpose for this great service, if that hath not been thought of. Both before my coming, by Sir Francis Drake, and since my coming, there hath been no day but there hath been pinnaces, Spanish caravels, flyboats, and of all sorts, sent out to discover there. The winds hath been so southerly, and such foul weather as that they could not [recover[3]] the coast of Spain so near as to take any of their fisher boats ; and to send some of our fisher boats to discover there, they would do as [much good[2]] as to send oysterboat of Billingsgate ; for neither can they bear sail [at all, nor able to[3]] brook the seas ; [and if any had[2]] been at the seas when the pinnaces were abroad, [they would not[3]] have seen home again ; and if the weather had [been such that[2]] some fisherman might have gone, yet as soon as ever they had been seen, they would have been taken up, with their boats, which [be the worst[3]] of the world.

[1] Much torn, and badly mended with opaque paper. Some of the missing words are supplied from Bruce ; others by conjecture.
[2] Bruce.   [3] Conjecture.

Sir, I did send a caravel of Sir F. Drake's [fourteen days [1]] agone, which was of any other least to be mistrusted ; but [before he [2]] could come to their coast, he met with a contrary wind [that turned [1]] him back and brake [his] mast and yard, and much [to do to rec[1]]over home again. I [sent] within three days after, a flyboat which is an excellent sailer. A man of Sir Walter Ralegh's went in her, one Hawes,[3] a very proper man. He met off Ushant 16 leagues with certain of their ships, as it shall appear by his letter which I send you. My own pinnace hath been well beaten [and] hath had 18 [grea]t sh[ot, which hath torn her hull and [1]] sails ; and by all likelihood, a Frenchman that served in their fleet ; for she was double manned and came from Spain, and a good tall ship. We have at this time four pinnaces on the coast of Spain ; but, Sir, you may see what [may co[2]]me of the sending me out with so little victuals, and the [evil of the same [2]]. For had I [not then [2]] been driven in for [lack] of victuals, we had met just with some of them not far [off Ushant [4]] ; for we came in with the storm at South the 22nd, and they fell with Scilly the next day after, an 18 sail of them. But, Sir, by all likelihood they be returned with very great harms.

Sir, I am now sending out two pinnaces more, and I trust her Majesty will think that shall be done

[1] Bruce.   [2] Conjecture.
[3] Possibly Ralph Hawes, who appears in the list of ships as captain of the Unicorn of Dartmouth.
[4] Conjecture. Bruce has 'off Scilly,' which seems inadmissible. Howard here says he came in to Plymouth on the 22nd and the Spanish ships were off Scilly on the 23rd. From his letter and advertisement of the 22nd (*ante*, pp. 220-1), it appears that he came in on the 21st and that the Spaniards were seen near Scilly the same day. Had he not been driven back on the 20th by a storm at South, he must have met them off Ushant rather than near Scilly.

that may be possible. I send you an advertisement that came to me even now, and I look every hour for more.

Sir F. Drake and all here do think no [gain] in sending any fishermen ; for as many as shall be sent, we [can] never look for any again. I know not what weather you have had there, but there was never any such summer seen here on the sea. God of his mercy [1] keep us from sickness, for we fear that more than any hurt that the Spaniards will do [this fleet], if the advertisements be true. Well, Sir, I would her Majesty did know of the care and pains that is taken here of all men for her service. We must now man ourselves again, for we have cast many overboard, and a number in great extremity which we discharged. I [have] sent with all expedition a prest for more men. And so I bid [you most] heartily farewell.

Your assured loving friend,

C. HOWARD.

It [2] hath pleased my Lord Admiral to command me to write my knowledge touching our espials. I assure your Honour there could not have been more care taken than his Lordship hath from time to time given order for ; and it is now certainly known that they are all returned back, much distressed ; and as for fisherboats, they are neither meet and can [not [3]] endure the seas.

Your Honour's faithfully to be commanded,

FRA. DRAKE.

---

[1] MS. marsy.   [2] In Drake's autograph.
          [3] Omitted in MS.

July 14.—*ABSTRACT OF THE ANSWERS OF THE MAYORS.*

[ccxii. 43.]

The Answer of the Mayors of the Coast Towns on the West parts to the letters of the Lords of her Majesty's most honourable Privy Council, touching the re-victualling of the shipping set forth by them. Taken by me, Richard Swanson, one of her Majesty's messengers :—

Robert Brockinge, deputy to the Mayor of Bridgwater, answereth, that upon receipt of letters from the Right Honourable the Lord High Admiral of England, the contents of your Honours' letters were accomplished before the receipt thereof ; and further answers, that if need require so, they will strain themselves for two months' more re-victualling.

Sir John Barron's answer, Mayor of Bristol, was that, after conference had with the rest of his brethren, both your Honours and Mr. Darell should be certified of their determination ; and upon my return thither, he said that one was sent to take order for re-victualling.

John Jones, Mayor of Lyme, sent one forthwith to take order for re-victualling ; but most humbly craveth at your Honours that the towns of Axminster and Chard, refusing to yield both to the first and this last victualling, may by your good Lordships be brought thereunto ; being towns appointed to be contributories thereunto. Answering further, that if need so require, the merchants of the town of Lyme are contented to disburse in whole two subsidies, so that the towns of Axminster and Chard may be brought to disburse but one subsidy ; which, as they judge, will be sufficient to discharge this past, and two months more to come.

s 2

John Peryam, Mayor of Exeter, answereth that order is taken, according to your Honours' letters, for the re-victualling of two months longer.

John Wyse, Mayor of Totness, answereth that order is taken, according to your Honours' letters, for the re-victualling of two months longer.

William Hawkyns, Mayor of Plymouth, answereth that order is taken, according to your Honours' letters, for the re-victualling of two months longer.

John Porter, Mayor of Saltash, answereth that order was taken with Sir Francis Drake, Knight, for the sum of 150*l*, to discharge them of all manner of charges of victualling; which money is already paid. But this composition, I learned, was taken at the first setting forth of their ship.

The names of the Ships set forth by the Coast Towns on the West parts, with the number of men [1] belonging to every of them :—

Bristol :—The Minion ; Unicorn ; Handmaid ; Aid.

Bridgwater :—The William.

Lyme, Axminster and Chard :—The Revenge ; Jacob.

Weymouth and Melcombe :—The Galleon ; Katharine.

Exeter and Apsam [2]:—The Bartholomew; Rose ; Gift.

Dartmouth and Totness :—The Crescent ; Flying Hart.

Plymouth :—The Charity, 80 men ; Little John.

Saltash :—The John Trelawney.

Fowey and Looe :—The Frances.

---

[1] For the number of men, see the list of ships.
[2] Topsham.

July 15.—*ORDER FOR VICTUALLING.*

[ccxii. 50.—Signed.]

An estimate of the money for the victualling 1,471 men at the Narrow Seas, her Majesty in her own ships,[1] under the charge of my Lord Henry Seymour, as also 850 men being there in sundry ships from divers ports, viz. :—

For the Narrow Seas, *mensis Augusti* :

	£	s.
First.—The victualling of 1,471 men, in 16 of her Majesty's own ships at the Narrow Seas, for one month of 28 days, beginning the first of August and ending the 28th of the same, at 14s. the man per month . . .	1,029	14
For the transportation thereof . .	150	0
For the victualling of 850 men, serving in sundry ships out of divers ports at the Narrow Seas, at the like rate ; beginning the 26th of June and doth end the 24th of July . . .	595	0
For transportation thereof . . .	80	0
Sum total . . .	1,854	14

Men, 2,321.
Money, 1,854*l*. 14*s*.

15th July, 1588.[2]

Mr. Peter, I pray you make an order for the payment of these sums to Mr. Quarles, for the victualling of her Majesty's ships under the charge of the Lord Henry Seymour ; and to return unto me this note again, or a copy thereof.

W. BURGHLEY.

[1] So in MS. [2] Note in Burghley's autograph.

July 16.—*MEMORANDUM BY SIR E. HOBY.*

[ccxii. 51.—Endorsed.]

The occasion of my Lord Admiral his sending
me up hath been only to signify unto her Majesty
what hath passed in all this season, and to resolve
her Highness of the present estate of her army ; as
also to bring down with me her Majesty's resolution
and free liberty how she would have him to lie, or
attempt aught on the enemy's coast.

July 17.—*THOMAS CELY*[1] *TO BURGHLEY.*

[ccxii. 57.—Holograph.   Addressed.]

Right Honourable, my duty remembered :—My
very good Lord,—I would write unto your Honour
more oftener than I do, but I am not in place where
I may do it.   My Lord Admiral and Sir Francis
Drake doth employ me to sea, for to see if I can
meet with any shipping[2] coming out of Spain, which
I have done divers times, and the intelligence[3] that
I have gotten from time to time I have done[4] my
Lord to understand of them.   I am bound unto my
Lord and to Sir Francis, for that they have such
trust in me to do those things which standeth a
trusty subject to do.   I pray God I may deserve
unto her Majesty, and to my Lord and to Sir
Francis, the credit and trust that they suppose in
me.

Your Honour hath had letters of late that their

[1] Some account of this man is given in the Introduction.   At
this time he was captain of the Elizabeth Drake.
[2] MS. to see for to sye yf I can myte wt eny shyppynge.
[3] MS. entelyjenes.   [4] Done=made.

fleet is dispersed. Truth is, I have been four times in France, and have brought[1] intelligence from time to time unto my Lord, and brought the ships with me sometimes, for that my Lord should get out some more matter than I could do. Captain Fenner[2] hath done the like, and Captain Crosse. I learn by these three hulks that Fenner and Crosse hath brought in, that the news which I had before is all one, and that there is two of their four galleys left, and two of their galleasses hath rolled their masts overboard, and many of their fleet hath broken their yards and other their tackling; notwithstanding, I learn by these men that they have a new supply of victual from Lisbon,[3] and that they arm[4] themselves as fast as they can to proceed in their wicked and malicious attempt. Therefore I think it good for us to arm ourselves to sea with all speed,[5] and to meet with them at sea, if God will give us leave.

My Lord was in a good way, if God had not sent a contrary wind. Our fleet was 80 leagues South and by West off Ushant. If the wind had holden[6] two days and two nights longer, we had had them in the Groyne, and within three leagues of the Groyne, all their whole[7] fleet in three sundry harbours, saving 30 hulks which we hear not of.

My Lord doth make what speed he may do to get out again to sea with the most part of the fleet. Truth[8] is, victual did fall out very short with many of our fleet, and very many contrary winds; and so they continue; God send better. If your Honour do write unto my Lord before we go to sea, haste us away. Good my Lord, I fear me we shall have

---

[1] MS. browethe. [2] MS. Venard. Cf. p. 171.
[3] MS. Lysheborne. [4] Arm=equip.
[5] MS. spide. [6] MS. howelden.
[7] MS. hoell. [8] MS. Trothe ys vytell dyd faull owet.

contrary winds and foul weather until we have a full moon.

My good Lord, a sharp war and a short, although it be chargeable, and that is fit for England. The Queen's subjects doth desire it. If I might a[1] been heard, it had been done ere this day, with a great deal less charges.[2] Our action hath not gone so forward as it might a done, if things had been furnished[3] to my desire. There is none that knoweth what I mean but her Majesty and myself; but this I will say unto your Honour and to all the rest of the Privy Council: that the King of Spain will make our mistress wise within few years, if it be not prevented. It might a been done ere this day if it had pleased her Majesty; and yet it may be done if the Duke of Parma[4] and the Guise and their friends be foreseen for doing us hurt upon the coast of England, or to enter our country: I say, if they may have the repulse for the year, and my Lord Admiral to defend[5] their fleet, as I trust in my God he shall do, for this year likewise, her Majesty shall have made for them the next year that they shall have desire to keep their own country.

Do not think to have any quietness with the King of Spain as long as his moneys comes out of the Indies. It is easily to be redressed. I have been desirous to have it known, and yet have I been afraid to move it; for that I have moved unto some of the Council, or at the least way was very willing; and when I have begun to enter into any matter of any importance, one of them told me and said this unto me: Cely, it is told me that you mell[6] with Councillors' matters. A rebuke I had, and so went my way. Another told me that if I could do

---

[1] Have.
[2] MS. gredell les charjes.
[3] MS. foorneshed.
[4] MS. Pallma & the Guics.
[5] Defend=fend off, repel.
[6] Meddle.

her Majesty any service, so that it did cost[1] money,
or that if charges should rise[2] upon it, never speak
of it, for she will never consent unto it. So I went
my way with a flea in mine ear.[3]

Another told me that if I did not make this and
this of my counsel, and not to go unto the Queen, I
should lose all the Council's good will. Why, my
good Lord, if I have or had commandment that I
should not open some matter which her Majesty
would not have known, should I utter it? No,
truly, if I should lose my life for my labour; and
peradventure it may be so. My good Lord, I am a
poor man, and one that hath been brought up
without learning, and one that hath but a patched
carcase[4]; for I had thirty-two sundry torments in
the Inquisition with the apretados[5]—you term them
in English rackings; and eight[6] years in prison
lacking but two months. I take it, it was for her
Majesty's sake and her subjects.

I have been towards her father and her brother
and herself this sixty and two years. I have been
no great craver, for I cannot spend one groat by the
year by her; and yet her Majesty hath promised
me good things; but I have been desirous to do her
good, and not always begging, as some be. And
yet have I lost above two thousand pounds since I
served her Majesty, besides the great and cruel
imprisonments in the Inquisition, and in the King
of Spain's most filthy galleys, and seven other
prisons; and God I take to witness without desert,
more than that they approved that I was her

---

[1] If it were to cost.
[2] MS. ryes : arise.
[3] MS. a flee yn my neer.
[4] MS. karkes.
[5] *Apretado*, past part. of *apretar*, is rather one who is pressed
or racked. A pressing or racking is *apretura*.
[6] It is doubtful whether the MS. has viii or xiii ; one seems
to have been written over the other. But cf. Cely to the Queen,
Dec. 12, 1579 (*post*, App. A).

sworn man. Truth is, I did strike their secretary
as I was before the Inquisidores, they sitting in
judgment. I had great reason to do it.

Let these things pass. I am now to crave your
Honour that you will be a mean to help to abate
the malicious intention of the Spaniard. If her
Majesty will, she shall have him brought to pass [1]
that he shall be glad to entreat her Majesty to have
a peace. And if it do cost her a hundred thousand
sovereigns, [2] she shall have two hundred thousand
again, and all of them of the action [3] well contented.
God is the only giver of victory. My trust is only
in him. I will not say but God may have put the
same secret [4] into another man's head as he hath
done into mine; but I believe that there is no
creature can do it but myself. I once [5] moved her
Majesty that she might have such a thing done.
Her Majesty looked very sadly upon me; so I
think, in my conscience, she thought it impossible
to be done. For in very truth there was a piece of
paper which her Majesty did read, and she answered
me and said, It cannot be done in time. I asked
her if I should show it to two persons in the world
living at this present. She said, No. I think in
my conscience it was more for that [she] stood in
doubt that I could not accomplish [it], and that her
Majesty would not have me to come to any foil [6];
for that I am assured her Majesty doth love me. I
take it, it was for this, more than for any other
thing. He that looks a man in the face knoweth
not what is in his purse. [7] I am of that opinion, that

---

[1] To such a pass.   [2] MS. soferanes.
[3] Those concerned, or who take part in the action.
[4] It nowhere appears what the secret was.   Probably, to look
out for the treasure fleet, but if so, it got into other men's heads.
See *post*, Seymour to Walsyngham, July 20.
[5] MS. woucnes.   [6] MS. foyell.   [7] MS. pores.

no man can do it but myself. Within one year
after it is done, it will bring her Majesty to more
quietness, and her countries, than all her Council in
seven years.

Good my Lord, bear with my rude and bold[1]
manner in writing this word so boldly. I have the
very same paper that her Majesty did read ; but I
do not send it to your Honour. Good my Lord,
tell her Majesty from me that I have not yet told
the Spaniards what we be doing in England, but
when God sends me to meet with them, I will tell
them. But I promise your Honour when I have
told them, I will bring them home with me into
England.

My Lord, there is three barks taken of late by
the Frenchmen, and one of the three is a son's of
mine, taken in the road of Lamoster,[2] near unto
Nantes.[3] Good my Lord, send my Lord Admiral
word whether I may not take a Frenchman for him.
Desire her Majesty to request my Lord Admiral
and Sir Francis Drake to continue the goodness
towards me ; and your Honour's words will be a
great credit unto me, favourably written. In haste,
this present 17th of July, 1588, by
Yours to command,
THOMAS CELY.

I doubt your Honour will have much ado to
read this letter. Desire her Majesty to help your
Honour ; her Majesty will. My[4]—but few words.

---

[1] MS. roed & boweld.
[2] Les Moutiers in the Baie de Bourgneuf.
[3] MS. Nans.
[4] It would seem as if he was going to break out again—My
good Lord &c. ; but as he began, it struck him that he had
perhaps written enough.

July 17.—*BURGHLEY TO WALSYNGHAM.*

[ccxii. 58.—Signed, and holograph postscript. Addressed.]

Sir :—I have at good length, as you may perceive, written to Darell, that hath the dealing for Mr. Quarles at Plymouth for the victualling of the navy. When you have read the letter, I pray you to cause it to be sealed and sent unto him by such means as you have. And so I commend me most heartily to you. From my house near the Savoy, this 17th of July, 1588.

Your assured loving friend,

W. BURGHLEY.

I am very sorry that our counsel for sending one expressly from her Majesty to the Duke of Parma doth not like her. It will be hard for our Commissioners to be informed[1] with such certainty as largely instructed both by speech and writing from hence ; but *fiat voluntas sua.*

I am at this present, by this last night's torment, weakened in spirits, as I am not able to rise out of my bed ; which is my grief the more because I cannot come thither where both my mind and duty do require.

July 17.—*BURGHLEY TO DARELL.*

[ccxii. 58, I.—Draft, with corrections in Burghley's hand. Endorsed :—Memorandum of my Lord's letter to Mr. Darell at Plymouth.]

I commend me unto you :—Since [2] such time as, this other day, you have been directed to make a new provision for the victualling of her Majesty's

[1] Sc. in any other way . . . as if they were fully instructed &c.
[2] Sc. since the other day, when you were directed &c.

fleet there under the charge of the Lord Admiral
and Sir Francis Drake, and money sent down to
you for that purpose, the merchants here, of the
city, have been dealt withal for a new victualling of
their ships for one month more, which they have
assented unto ; and are well contented to make the
same allowance, after the rate of 14s. the man, as
her Majesty giveth ; the numbers whereof, as the
same is delivered unto me by a note from them,
amounteth unto 1,340 men, who were victualled by
them, as they say, until the 10th of the month of
August, after the rate of four men to a mess ; which
being reduced to five to a mess, as they understand
my Lord Admiral brought them and the rest, for the
drawing out of the victuals, they have good reason
to think, together[1] considering the death of many of
their men, that the same should reach at the least to
a fortnight more.

But howsoever that falleth out, they are content
to allow for one month more after the rate aforesaid ;
wherein I pray you to use your best means and
credit for the speedy victualling of them ; and for
the money due for the same, I will undertake either
to have it to be sent down thither unto you, or paid
here, or made over by exchange to you, as you shall
appoint. And in like sort, I pray you to help, in the
best sort you can, the ships of the ports to be
victualled, who have also assented to re-victual their
own ships for one month more ; and therefore, what
furtherance you can give them, by your commissioners or otherwise, I pray you let them find it.

I do not doubt but, considering the order that
my Lord Admiral took for the putting of four first
to a mess, and afterwards increasing them to six to
a mess ; and withal the mortality of a great many,
whereof I was sorry to understand, that those

[1] As also.

numbers, both in my Lord Admiral's fleet and Sir
Francis Drake's, will be victualled for some good
time with this new supply for one month more; and
that the money sent down to you will be more than
sufficient for your purpose; but how to judge hereof,
I know not; for that there was some fault in you, in
that you made not your last certificate, which you
sent up hither, so perfect as had been requisite; for
that you neither particularly mentioned the numbers
of men, nor the vessels wherein they serve; which
I pray you by your next certificate to reform, so that
it may be understood what numbers serve in every
of the ships that were there with Sir Francis Drake,
before my Lord Admiral's coming to Plymouth; as
also of those numbers brought by my Lord Admiral
in every of the ships with him, and of any new
numbers supplied by his Lordship after his coming
thither.   And, as near as you can, what the number
at this present are in every of the said ships chargeable to the Queen [for] victualling, with all things
otherwise needful for the better understanding and
explaining of your doings.

For[1] surely, by your diversity of your certificates,
as Mr. Quarles showed them here to me, by your
first, we made account that the ships were victualled
to the 1st of August or farther, until, by your last,
you certified that the ships under Sir Francis Drake,
containing 2,821 men, and eight other ships, containing 299 men, being retained into her Majesty's
charge by the Lord Admiral, were victualled but to
the 14th of July; a matter so strange to us, as Mr.
Quarles, considering your former letters, imagined
that you had written July for August; but to our
grief here, we find it as you did write, which I am
right sorry for.

You write also that my Lord Admiral took with

[1] This paragraph is inserted in Burghley's own hand.

him 10 sail of the victuallers; but what men or
victuals they have, you know not; a matter also not
well ordered ; for I am sure my Lord Admiral, if
you had demanded of him the knowledge thereof,
he would have certified you.

Though you write that the Mayors of Bristol
and Lyme have written to you to furnish their ships
with two months' victuals more, according to certain
letters of the Council's written to them, yet it was
not meant that the charge thereof in money should
be upon the Queen ; but the provision [1] of the victuals to be made by you for more surety, and the
money to be afterwards paid by those two towns.
And so have the officers of those towns, and of the
rest of the ports, sent word to the Council that they
do mean to be at the charges.   And therefore you
shall do well, if you do make the provision for them
yourself, to acquaint them with the charge thereof.
If otherwise, they will not [2] make their own provisions

July 17.—HOWARD TO BURGHLEY.

[ccxii. 59.—Signed.   Endorsed.]

My very good Lord :—I have caused Sir Francis
Drake and Mr. Hawkyns to consider of your
charges, for that our companies grow into great
need, and many occasions in such an army doth
breed sundry great and extraordinary charges.   I
have sent herein enclosed an estimate thereof,
praying your Lordship that there may be some care
had that we may be furnished with money, without
the which we are not able to continue our forces

[1] That the provision . . . should be made &c.
[2] This 'not' would appear to have slipped in, in error.   The
meaning is evidently the exact opposite of what is written.

together. And when it shall please her Majesty that this army shall be dissolved, it shall be most beneficial to her Majesty that money be had here in a readiness to discharge such as be of this country; whereby a great sum of money may be saved in lessening of the companies, which will ease very much the charges of victuals, wages and conduct; which, without money, we shall not be able to do.

If your Lordship do give order to pay the money to Mr. Dr. Hussey, Mr. Hawkyns hath written to him that so much as shall discharge her Majesty's ships serving on the Narrow Seas until the 28th of July, shall be sent to Sir William Wynter, to Dover; for in this estimate those ships are included until that day. And so I bid your good Lordship heartily farewell. From Plymouth, the 17th of July, 1588.

Your Lordship's assured loving
friend to command,
C. HOWARD.

July 17.—HOWARD TO WALSYNGHAM.

[ccxii. 60.—Signed. Addressed. In bad condition.]

Sir:—I must write as I have occasion by advertisements. I had brought in to me two flyboats of Enkhuysen, which came from Aveiro, and in their coming they did put into the town of Bayona. This was within these twelve days, long since the return of the fleet from our coast. There were none of the fleet there. There was one galley that had been there all this year [to] keep and discover on that [coast[1]]. He reported that the whole fleet [were] in the [Groyne, saving a few that be[2]] in some other places. He also [said] that they do make ready to

---

[1] Conjecture.   [2] Bruce: conjecture.

put out again; and that [the K]ing doth send to them daily to put out. And, in my opinion, it is very like that they are [not [1]] divided into sundry places, as it was reported; for if they had, some would have been at Bayona.

Sir, I make all the haste I can possible out; and I, and all my company that came from London, will [not [1]] stay for anything. Sir Francis Drake and some of those ships will be ready; and the rest within three or four days after. And seeing the advertisements be no surer, I mean to keep the three great ships with me yet awhile, to see what will come of it. Some four or five ships have discharged [their men; for the [2]] sickness in s[ome] is very great, so that we are fain to discharge some ships, to have their men to furnish the others.

If it had not been to water, and that all the ships set out by the coast towns wanted victuals, I would not have seen this town, for it is hot, being here. Extreme business, which doth belong to such an army, enforceth me to be here more than I would; but there shall be neither sickness nor death which shall make you [3] yield until this service be ended. I never saw nobler minds than be here [in our] forces; but I cannot stir out but I have an inf[inite number] hanging on my shoulders for money. We do all we [can to re]lieve them. There was a fault, which I will not write of; but how, I will tell you when I come up; and if I had not in time looked into it, we should have had much more misery amongst some than we have.

Sir, I have heard that there is in London some hard speeches against Mr. Hawkyns because the Hope came in [to] mend a leak which she had. Sir, I think there were never so many of the prince's

---

[1] Not : omitted in MS.   [2] Conjecture.
[3] So in MS., but the sense seems to require ' me ' or ' us.'

ships so long abroad, and in such seas, with such
weather as these have had, with so few leaks; and
the greatest fault of the Hope came with ill grounding before our coming hither; and yet it is nothing
to be spoken of. It was such a leak that I durst
have gone with it to Venice. But may they not be
greatly ashamed that sundry times have [so] disabled
her Majesty's ships, which are the only ships of the
world? [Sir,] if you did know the leaks and weakness of other [ships that] be in this fleet, in respect
of them it would be said the Queen's Majesty's
ships were and are strong. For when the weather
hath been bad and rough, the most part of all the
navy have besought me that I, and the rest of her
Majesty's ships, would bear less sail, for they could
not endure it, when we made no reckoning of it.
And so I bid you most heartily farewell. From
Plymouth, the 17th of July, 1588.

Your very loving and assured friend,
C. HOWARD.

July 17.—*HAWKYNS TO BURGHLEY.*

[ocxii. 61.—Holograph.   Addressed:—For her Majesty's service.]

My bounden duty remembered unto your good
Lordship:—By the letter and estimate enclosed, your
Lordship may see how charges doth grow here daily.
My Lord Admiral doth endeavour by all means to
shorten it, and yet to keep the navy in strength.

In this demand is the ships serving under the
Lord Henry Seymour included; and I do write to
Mr. Hussey to stay so much money as may clear
them.

The four great ships—the Triumph, the Elizabeth Jonas, the Bear, and the Victory—are in most
royal and perfect state; and it is not seen by them,
neither do they feel that they have been at sea,

more than if they had ridden at Chatham. Yet there be some in them that have no goodwill to see the coast of Spain with them, but cast many doubts how they will do in that seas. But, my good Lord, I see no more danger in them, I thank God, than in others. The Bear one day had a leak, upon which there grew much ado; and when it was determined that she should be lighted of her ordnance, her ballast taken out, and so grounded and searched, and that my Lord Admiral would not consent to send her home, the leak was presently stopped of itself; and so the ship proceedeth with her fellows, in good and royal estate, God be thanked. I was bold to trouble your Lordship with these few words touching these four ships, because I know there will be reports as men are affected ; but this is the truth.

The strength of the ships generally is well tried ; for they stick not to ground often to tallow, to wash, or any such small cause, which is a most sure trial of the goodness of the ships when they are able to abide the ground. My Lord Admiral doth not ground with his ship, but showeth a good example, and doth shun charges as much as his Lordship may possible. And so I leave to trouble your good Lordship. From Plymouth, the 17th of July, 1588.

Your honourable Lordship's humbly to command,

JOHN HAWKYNS.

July 17.—ESTIMATE OF CHARGES.

[ccxii. 61, I.—Enclosure in Hawkyns' letter to Burghley of same date. Signed.]

An estimate of the charge of the wages growing for the companies serving under the charge of the Lord High Admiral of England, viz. :—

The last pay was made to the companies serving

in the Narrow Seas under the Lord Admiral to the
11th of February last; since which time there hath
been a pay made to the Treasurer, of those ships
for those companies, to end the 5th of May last, for
2,990 men, being 3 months, amounting unto 6,279*l.*

For the four great ships, being 1,900 men, there
is paid to the Treasurer three months' pay, to end
the 13th of July, which amounted to the sum of
3,990*l.*

	£	s.	d.
To bring the pay of the first number of 2,990 men to end the 28th of July, is 84 days, which is three months' pay, and amounteth to the sum of	6,279	0	0
To bring the 1,900 men serving in the four great ships to the 28th of July, is 15 days' pay, and amounteth unto the sum of .	712	10	0
For grounding, tallowing, sea-store, carpentry, masts, repairing of boats and pinnaces; for cordage, canvas, and such like emptions [1]	2,500	0	0
For conduct in discharge of 1,000 sick men, that were discharged out of the fleet, and for the prest and conduct of others taken up to serve in their places, by estimation. . .	700	0	0
Summa . .	10,191	10	0

This sum is to be sent to Plymouth.

The ships that were under the charge of Sir
Francis Drake :—   .

There is received for the 2,900 men that were

[1] Purchases, things bought.

in Sir Francis Drake's charge, by the Treasurer,
two months' pay, from the 24th of April to the
19th of June, saving there is yet to pay above 800*l.*
(as I think) of the last warrant for the charge ;
which is 4,060*l.*

	£	*s.*	*d.*
To bring the pay of this number of 2,900 men to the 28th of July, is 39 days' pay, and doth amount of the sum of	2,827	10	0
The ships will have been in pay for tonnage, to the 28th of July, 236 days; of which there is allowed by the warrants for 4 months, which is 112 days ; so rest to pay for 124 days, which is 4 months 12 days, and amounteth to	1,771	8	8
For grounding and tallowing of all those ships that were under Sir Francis Drake's charge, sea-store for them, carpentry, re-forming of masts, boats and pinnaces, cordage, canvas, and such like, for her Majesty's ships in that company . .	2,500	0	0
More, for the wages of 700 men entertained by Sir Francis Drake, Knight, for the space of four months in ships of Sir Richard Greynvile's and others, to the number of eight ships taken up to serve with the fleet of her Majesty, which were appointed to continue, by the Council's letters, ending the 28th of July, 1588, amounting to the sum of .	1,960	0	0

For the tonnage of the said ships, being by estimation 800 ton, the sum of . . . . . £ *s.* *d.*
320 0 0
9,378 18 8

This sum is to be sent to Plymouth.

How the 6,000*l.* that was imprested to be carried with my Lord Admiral is defrayed :—

£ *s.* *d.*

Imprimis, there was sent to Sir Francis Drake, Knight, to Plymouth, for the provision of victual, by Mr. Secretary his order, the sum of 2,000 0 0

Item, there is imprested to Mr. Darell, by my Lord Admiral's order, for the victualling of all the navy 2,900 0 0

Item, paid by my Lord Admiral's warrant, for one month's pay to 1,000 soldiers entertained by Sir Francis Drake, Knight, the sum of 500 0 0

Item, more, by like warrant to relieve certain captains likewise entertained by Sir Francis Drake, Knight, the sum of . . . 100 0 0
.5,500 0 0

So as there resteth in my hands of this 6,000*l.*, only the sum of . 500 0 0

An abstract of the money that is now to be paid and sent to Plymouth :—

£ *s.* *d.*

First, for the charge growing upon the ships that served under the

charge of the Lord Admiral in the Narrow Seas &c., as appeareth by the first estimate	£	*s.*	*d.*
	10,191	10	0

Item, for the charge growing upon the ships that served under the charge of Sir Francis Drake, Knight, westward, as by the second estimate appeareth .

	9,378	18	8
	19,570	8	8

Of which there remaineth in my hands of the 6,000*l.*, as appeareth by the account above written . . . . .

	500	0	0

Which being taken out of the former sum, there will remain to be paid from her Majesty . . . 19,070 8 8

C. HOWARD.   JOHN HAWKYNS.

July 17.—*THOMAS FENNER TO WALSYNGHAM*

[ccxii. 62.—Signed. Addressed. Sealed with the arms of the Sussex Fenners—Between 4 eagles displayed, a cross charged with a cross [1] potent.]

My letter of the 12th of July with the advertisements therein enclosed, I hope are come unto your Honour's hand, by Sir Edward Hoby. I was commanded at the sea upon the sudden, to go for the coast of Brittany, moved thereby to send your Honour letters and advertisement by a pinnace to Plymouth, delivered as before, assureth my hope that your Honour have received the same. Since that time I intercepted three great flyboats which

[1] In Burke's *General Armoury* the charge on the cross is given as ' a cross formée.' The device on the seal is, however, perfectly distinct.

came from San Lucar the 7th of June. Their
advertisements which I gathered, I send your
Honour herein enclosed.

Understanding by them of seventeen hulks and
flyboats more, coming after within some three or
four days by their supposition ; as also I gathered,
by very politic means and liberality, a great secret
in one of those ships ; which the name of the ship
being a Hollander, which had my Lord of Leicester
his pass, which ship is sold unto Spaniards in San
Lucar, and now bound for Dunkirk, laden with
wools, and secretly in her, two tons of silver. If the
wind and spring serve him not to put in with
Dunkirk, he makes no care to put for England or
Flushing, in that he hath pass, and is a Hollander.

The Sweden captain which your Honour wrote
unto Sir Francis Drake to let pass is one of the
company of that fleet.

The ship's name that hath the silver is called
the Golden Rose of Enkhuysen. A rose painted in
her stern and in her head.

I write your Honour thus largely in that, if it
please, you may advertise with speed Sir William
Russell to have regard to these points. As also
advertise (as your Honour think meetest) her
Majesty's ships in the Narrow Seas.

There is a very great Hollander also in company,
laden with Spanish goods. By conference with
divers other of the three flyboats, I understood the
said ship to be one of the company ; but sifted not
the secret ; yet found by them that she was sold to
the Spaniards.

I am appointed as this day to put over, if wind
serve, with the Galleon Leicester in company, for
the coast of France, to check [1] with this fleet. God

---

[1] To clash, fight. In this sense it is always followed by 'with.'

send me the happiness to do some effectual service for my gracious mistress and country. There never happened the like opportunity to beat down the Spanish pride, if it be effectually followed. If not, I would to the Lord I had not been one of the company, for our reputations thereby is overthrown. I would I were one of the thirty sail to put it in execution.

This, I betake[1] your Honour to the Almighty, most humbly craving pardon for tedious writing. From aboard the Nonpareil, this 17th of July, 1588.

Your Honour's in all duty to command,

THOMAS FENNER.

Since my letters of the 12th to your Honour at my being at the sea, I spake with three English ships of Dartmouth, who came from Rochelle, bringing certain intelligence of the dispersion of the Spanish fleet into the Passage,[2] the Groyne, and divers other places thereabouts. Withal a pinnace of Rochelle, taking two of their victuallers, within two hours after met with two of the galleons with their mainmasts overboard. They reported further, that many of them were beaten with a wonderful storm in the north part of Ireland.

This present morning a little caravel of Sir Francis Drake arrived which was sent for the coast of Spain for discovery, who met with two French which came from Lisbon the 6th of this month, who confessed six of the Spanish fleet came back into Lisbon before their departure, full of sick men ; the rest of the fleet, some in Bayona, some in the Groyne and in Passage, and in great sickness and mortality. Now is the time, I beseech God move your Honour

---

[1] With this, I commit.
[2] Los Pasages, about four miles to the east of San Sebastian ; formerly a good harbour, but now almost silted up.

to further and hasten our departure.   If not all, yet
some.

The King of Navarre hath good success upon
the river of Bordeaux.

July 18.—*SEYMOUR TO WALSYNGHAM.*

[ccxii. 64.—Signed, and autograph postscript.   Addressed.]

Sir :—I find no manner of difference between
winter and summer, saving that the days be now
longer, and to deliver our hard water works [1] most
stormy and tempestuous the same will hardly be
credited to fall out such in the season.

Being informed from Calais, the 15th of this
month there should come from Rosco 50 sails to
join with them of Dunkirk, I laboured, as much as
wind and weather would give me leave, to attend
them by intercepting their shipping, which was
given me to understand should repair either to
Calais or Dunkirk the next day.

The 16th of this present, I observed the full
tides where they might harbour themselves, but
lost my labour and returned to the Downs.

The next day, the 17th of this instant, I plied
up the former course and anchored between Calais
Cliffs [2] and Blackness, where no usual road was, as
it appeared after by the great storm that happened.
In the interim came Gourdan's ships with two
Rosco flyboats under sail, which I made strike and
ride at anchor with me.

The storm arose presently most outrageous, and
such as, during my [being [3]] aboard the seas, this
winter, I never saw greater.   These sails seemed

---

[1] This may perhaps mean :—For the performance of our hard
work upon the water, stormy &c. to a degree that will hardly &c.
[2] MS. Cleives.   [3] Omitted in the MS.

deep laden, and certainly came from Lisbon, but the extremity of weather was such as I could not send any boat aboard. Yet did Gourdan, with a very nimble sail of shallop, covet to send aboard his ship; but I waved him to come unto me first, which he little regarded; whereby I was enforced to discharge a fair[1] shot over him, and so [he] came room unto me.

Upon further examination of Gourdan's men, they confessed their master's ship full freighted with merchandise at Lisbon, and so gave him leave to go aboard to work the best advantage for his master in this extremity of storm. The other two smaller vessels of Rosco which came in company, I took better care to look unto them, hoping that some of them may answer the charge of the storm which hath scattered many of our fleet, if they be well searched. This, because our navy is not yet gathered together, whereby I cannot yet advertise our fortunes, with my very loving commendations, do betake you to God. From aboard the Rainbow, the 18th of July, 1588, at anchor in the Downs, in most foul weather.

Your very loving assured friend ever,
H. SEYMOUR.

To move the Lord Treasurer.

Sir, You shall do very well to help us with a pay for our men, who are almost 16 weeks unpaid; for what with fair and foul means, I have enough to do to keep them from mutiny. Our coast men likewise would be resolved whether their pay and other necessaries shall be defrayed at her Majesty's charges, as their victuals now are.

[1] MS. fayre.

July 19.—*BURGHLEY TO WALSYNGHAM.*

[ccxii. 66.—Holograph.   Addressed.]

Sir :—I find my mind as much troubled to write
as now I do, as commonly my stomach is against
purging [1] ; but I cannot conceal from you the causes
which will shortly bring forth desperate effects.

' I have received letters from my Lord Admiral
and Mr. Hawkyns, with a schedule declaring that
they have great lack of money for wages, besides
victuals ; for [2] Mr. Quarles hath 6,000*l.* this last
week, and now Mr. Hawkyns' declaration that, to
make a full pay to the 28th of this month, there
must be paid 19,070*l.* ; and of that 6,000*l.* which he
had, there remaineth with him but 500*l.* I marvel
that where so many are dead on the seas the pay is
not dead with them, or with many of them.

And how the reckoning for victuals will fall out
I know not, but I fear that 6,000*l.* will not serve ;
and yet, as I perceive, my Lord Admiral's company
are victualled until mid August, and if Sir Francis
Drake was victualled, his Lordship might go to the
sea without delay. At this time also is demanded
by the office of the admiralty, for to pay an old
debt for provisions, 7,000*l.* ; and to restore their
lacks 6,000*l.* ; *in toto*, 13,000*l.* ; and I have moved
them to content the creditors for the 7,000*l.* with
one-third now, one other third in the end of August,
and the later at Michaelmas ; which is a charitable
relief, and so there might [be [3]] leisure in paying the
other 6,000*l.* for new provisions. There is also paid
to Quarles for one month's victual for the ships in
the Narrow Seas, 1,854*l.*

----

[1] The meaning seems to be :—The writing this letter is as
sickening as the swallowing a nauseous potion would be.

[2] As though he had said :—Which seemeth to me strange,
for &c.   [3] Omitted in MS.

The office of the ordnance demandeth for furniture of habiliments &c., for to serve an army by land, about 8,000*l.* There is also, beside 2,700*l.* lately paid to the creditors, the sum of 2,379*l.* to be paid. I know that the towns and the army have also great need of money.

A man would wish, if peace cannot be had, that the enemy would not longer delay, but prove, as I trust, his evil fortune : for as these expeditions do consume us, so I would hope, by God's goodness, upon their defeat we might have one half year's time to provide for money.

I have had conference with Palavicino and with Saltonstall[1] how 40,000 or 50,000 might be had for 10 per cent. ; but I find no probability how to get money here in specie, which is our lack, but by exchange, to have it out of the parts beyond sea, which will not be done but in a long time; yet there is some likelihood that our merchants of Stade might practise for 20,000 or 30,000, for which there shall be some profit very secretly. I shall but fill my letter with more melancholy matter if I should remember what money must be had to pay 5,000 footmen and 1,000 horsemen for defence of the enemy landing in Essex.

Yours most assured,
W. BURGHLEY.

July 20.—*SEYMOUR TO WALSYNGHAM.*

[ccxii. 69.—Holograph. Addressed.]

Sir :—Your last received letter of the 18th of this month doth in manner answer your two former

[1] Richard Saltonstall, Governor of the Merchant Venturers ; Sheriff of London 1588-9 ; Lord Mayor 1597 ; knighted 1617.

letters of the 17th of this instant; for the flat
bottomed boats meant to be transported from
Gravelines to Dunkirk or Nieuport, the same doth
very well agree with many my letters heretofore
written, declaring the Duke intent only to employ
them for Wakerland [1]; for otherwise they be no
boats to be hazarded to the seas, no more than
wherries or cockboats; and assuredly the Flushingers
reinforcing their strength by sea doth confirm my
opinion. I am very glad likewise that Sir William
Wynter doth concur with me in judgment touching
the Isle of Wight, which heretofore he did not so
well regard, and which in my letters last sent unto
you I remembered the same a special place for a
rendezvous, wishing besides hoys instead of sconces
for defence of the Thames and the City of London.[2]
Also I mistrust Sandwich, which is a strong situation
by nature.

These two places, the Isle of Wight and Sandwich, will very hardly be recovered of the enemy,
being once obtained. But I fear them not this year
nor the next, if her Majesty will not still be entertained with peace, but rather to proceed to intercept
the India fleet which is shortly to return. This,
having due regard to your last advertisements of
Mr. Thomas Fenner's, do take my leave. From
aboard the Rainbow, the 20th of July, 1588, returned to the Small Downs, where we may daily
[espy [3]] any sails upon the coasts of Calais.

Your assured friend to command,
H. Seymour.

There is wanting of our fleet by reason of this
storm, the George, a old hoy of her Majesty's; the
Sun, her Majesty's pinnace; the ship of Yarmouth,

---

[1] Walcheren. [2] Cf. *ante*, p. 207.
[3] Word omitted in MS.

the ship of Rye, the pinnace of Feversham, the flyboat which I stayed, and five of my company in her,
and two Bretons of Rosco, which I stayed in that
distress, and in which one of them[1] are 6 or 7
English mariners of our fleet. These, without
question, are either put to Flushing or Harwich,
hoping[2] by the next fair weather to hear of them.
The galley and the men within her, being 280[3]
persons, may thank God I stayed her going out at
that time, for there is no question but she had
perished.

July 21.—*NOTE OF CHARGES.*

[ccxii. 79.—Endorsed :—The charge of certain works[4] to be done
upon the Thames.]

21st of July, 1588.—Richmond. £

120 masts, at 6*l.* the piece	720
Anchors to moor the same : 20, of 6 and 7 hundred weight, at 26*s.* the hundred .	180
20 smaller anchors, of 5 hundred weight .	140
Ironwork for chains to lock them together, 1,000 weight at 25*s.*	250
Cables to moor the masts, of 9 inches : 20, at 13*l.* the cable	267
Workmanship of the masts	50
6 lighters and 6 ships or hoys, to serve for wages according to the rate of tonnage : Workmanship for this proportion of shipping, at 40*l.* a ship	480
Sum of this, besides the ships . .	2,087

[1] In one of which. [2] So that I hope.
[3] So in MS. Her complement was 250.
[4] The construction of a boom at Tilbury. See *post*, p. 298,
Leicester to Walsyngham, July 22.

July 21.—*HOWARD TO WALSYNGHAM.*

[ccxii. 80.—Signed, and autograph postscript.   Addressed.]

Sir :—I will not trouble you with any long letter ; we are at this present otherwise occupied than with writing.   Upon Friday, at Plymouth, I received intelligence that there were a great number of ships descried off of the Lizard ; whereupon, although the wind was very scant, we first warped out of harbour that night, and upon Saturday turned out very hardly, the wind being at South-West ; and about three of the clock in the afternoon, descried the Spanish fleet, and did what we could to work for the wind, which [by this] morning we had recovered, descrying their f[leet to] consist of 120 sail, whereof there are 4 g[alleasses] and many ships of great burden.

At nine of the [clock] we gave them fight, which continued until one.   [In this] fight we made some of them to bear room to stop their leaks ; notwithstanding we durst not adventure to put in among them, their fleet being so strong.   But there shall be nothing either neglected or unhazarded, that may work their overthrow.

Sir, the captains in her Majesty's ships have behaved themselves most bravely and like men hitherto, and I doubt not will continue, to their great commendation.   And so, recommending our good success to your godly prayers, I bid you heartily farewell.   From aboard the Ark, thwart of Plymouth, the 21st of July, 1588.

Your very loving friend,
C. Howard.

Sir, the southerly wind that brought us back from the coast of Spain brought them out.   God blessed us with turning us back. Sir, for the love of God and our country, let us have with some speed some great shot sent us of all bigness ; for this service will continue long ; and some powder with it.

July 21.—*THE MAYOR¹ OF PLYMOUTH AND MR. DARELL TO THE COUNCIL.*

[ccxii. 81.—Copy. Endorsed.]

Our last intelligence² that we gave to your Lordships was that the Spanish fleet was in view of this town yesternight, and that my Lord Admiral was passed to the sea before our said view, and was out of our sight. Since which time we have certain knowledge, both by certain pinnaces come from his Lordship, as also by plain view this present morning, that my Lord being to the windwards of the enemy, are in fight, which we beheld. As for that we suppose that his Lordship will find in this action great want of men, we have thought most meet to send such forth as the town and country will yield, and in that behalf we have provided divers ships and bottoms to carry them so fast as they come. And so &c.

July 21.—*DRAKE TO SEYMOUR.*

[ccxii. 82.—Signed, and autograph postscript. Addressed :—To the Right Honourable the Lord Henry Seymour, Admiral of her Majesty's Navy in the Narrow Seas ; or in absence, to Sir William Wynter, Knight, give these with speed. Haste, post, haste.]

Right Honourable and my very good Lord :—I am commanded by my very good Lord, the Lord

¹ William Hawkyns, John's elder brother.
² This letter is missing.

Admiral, to send you the caravel in haste with this letter, giving your Lordship to understand that the army of Spain arrived upon our coast the 20th of this present. The 21st we had them in chase, and so coming up unto them, there hath passed some cannon shot between some of our fleet and some of them, and as far as we perceive they are determined to sell their lives with blows. Whereupon his Lordship hath commanded me to write unto your Lordship and Sir William Wynter, that those ships serving under your charge should be put into the best and strongest manner you may, and ready to assist his Lordship for the better encountering of them in those parts where you now are. In the meantime, what his Lordship and the rest here following him may do shall be surely performed.

His Lordship hath commanded me to write his hearty commendations to your Lordship and Sir William Wynter. I do salute your Lordship, Sir William Wynter, Sir Henry Palmer, and all the rest of those honourable gentlemen serving under you with the like; beseeching God of his mercy to give her Majesty, our gracious sovereign, always victory against her enemies. Written aboard her Majesty's good ship the Revenge, off of Start, the 21st, late in the evening, 1588.

> Your good Lordship's poor friend
> ready to be commanded,
> FRA. DRAKE.

This letter, my honourable good Lord, is sent in haste. The fleet of Spaniards is somewhat above a hundred sails, many great ships; but truly, I think not half of them men-of-war. Haste.

> Your Lordship's assured,
> FRA. DRAKE.

July 22.—*JOHN POPHAM*[1] *TO WALSYNGHAM.*

[ccxiii. 1.—Holograph.[2] Addressed.]

My duty unto your Honour most humbly remembered :—It may please you to understand that
upon Friday last the Spanish fleet was discovered
towards the west parts, and upon Saturday they
were all, to the number of eight score and two sail,
over against Falmouth ; and yesterday, being more
easterly, towards Dartmouth. I am advertised
from my Lord Chief Justice Anderson[3] that my
Lord Admiral continued in fight with them from
nine of the clock in the forenoon until three in the
afternoon, and the Spanish fleet is said to endeavour
themselves what they can towards the east. Whereupon my Lord Chief Justice hath written unto me
to understand my opinion what were fit to be done
touching our journey towards Ireland, whither we
resolved to take our voyage upon Monday next in
the morning, and do so resolve still, unless we
receive contrary directions from your Honour. And
for my Lord Chief Justice's better satisfaction therein, I have thought good with all expedition to
despatch this bearer, Cottrel, my servant, to your
Honour to receive your directions whether it shall
be convenient for us to hold on our journey, or
otherwise to make stay thereof until her Majesty's
pleasure be further known in that behalf; which I
pray your Honour I may be advertised of by this

[1] Second son of Alexander Popham, of an old Somerset
family. A successful and unscrupulous lawyer ; became Attorney-
General in 1581, and in 1592 Lord Chief Justice and was knighted.
See Hall, *Elizabethan Society*, pp. 142–6, 277.
[2] A very difficult scrawl.
[3] Sir Edmond Anderson, Chief Justice of the Common
Pleas.

bearer, so as it may be with me here by Sunday next. My Lord Chief Justice doth advertise me that the course towards Ireland is very full of pirates, in respect whereof he saith it behoveth us to pursue somewhat strongly.

I have herewithal sent unto your Honour a letter[1] written out of St. Sebastian by one Redbird, of the date of the 18th of this July,[2] by their account. It came from St. John de Luz, whither it was conveyed by the same Redbird the 12th of this July, by our account. The bark that brought it to Bridgwater arrived there the 21st of this July, and upon Wednesday last discovered the most part of the Spanish navy 25 leagues west the headland of France, holding their course towards England.

With the same letter this other note[3] enclosed was sent. The man I take to be honest, and your Honour can best discern what good is to be collected by the knowledge of what is comprised in them. But with your favour I may write thus much : that these forces of themselves are not fit, as I think, to enter England until they adjoin themselves to greater aids ; and whatsoever the forces were (with good assistance) they are not to be doubted, the country I find everywhere so readily and willing.

I beseech[4] God, her Majesty, in this so dangerous a time, may, with the good advice of my Lords, have a special care of herself ; which being had, we have such an united strength through her Highness, as her enemies, being never so many, they can never prevail against so gracious a Queen. I beseech[4] you, Sir, to pardon me, in that the abundance of my loyalty and dutiful affection to her

---

[1] This letter is missing.
[3] Also missing.
[2] July 8.
[4] MS. beseke.

Majesty hath moved me to write thus much to your Honour, and so do most heartily take my leave. At Wellington, the 22nd of July, 1588.

Your Honour's humbly at commandment,

Jo. POPHAM.

July 22.—DARELL TO BURGHLEY.

[ccxiii. 2.—Holograph. Addressed. Endorsed :—Mar. Darell, from Plymouth. Rd. the 12th of August.]

My duty unto your Honour most humbly remembered :—I did receive yesterday a letter from your Lordship with direction to provide a month's victual for 1,340 men serving under my Lord Admiral in the ships of London, who are already victualled by the city but till the 10th of August; and that the city will allow for the same after the rate of 14*s.* a man, as her Majesty doth; which money, how it may best be conveyed hither, your Lordship doth refer unto me.

The month's victual shall be prepared in a readiness for them, God willing, in due time; and for the money, I wish them of London to deal with some merchant of Exeter for delivery of it there by exchange; a course most easy for them and very convenient for me, in that I do make sundry provisions in places near thereabouts. If any of the coast towns that have set forth ships in this service shall require, in like sort, to have them victualled here, it shall be also performed according to your Lordship's commandment.

Your Honour writeth[1] that the note I sent last of the number of ships and men in service under my Lord Admiral did seem very unperfect, and

[1] See *ante*, p. 270.

disagreeable from my former presentments; and therefore your Lordship requireth to be further certified thereof in some more plain and direct sort than before. It may please your Lordship, I trust it hath been and always shall be most far from me to abuse your Honour with any untrue information. I might well omit the setting down of some ships and men with whom, being not set forth at her Majesty's charge, I had not to do; but I do greatly hope your Honour shall not find I have erred wittingly in any material point concerning the charge committed here unto me. And therefore, until by proof the contrary shall appear, I do most humbly beseech your Lordship not to condemn me.

I do now send unto your Lordship herewith two several notes[1]: the one importing the state of the whole navy, both for the number of ships and men, according to the allowance given, as also for the time of their victualling, which is now reduced to end all together, in all the ships at her Majesty's charge, upon the 10th of August. Only the haste of my Lord Admiral was such in his setting forth upon Saturday morning, by reason he had then received some intelligence of the Spanish fleet, as that divers of his ships had not leisure to receive the full of their last proportions. And the other note containeth an estimate what money will remain of the last warrant towards the victualling of the 7,079 men now at her Majesty's charge from the 10th of August forwards. In both which notes I have not (I hope) set down anything but what your Lordship shall find to be true.

Touching the sparing of the ordinary allowance of victuals in the ships by placing of more than 4

---

[1] These notes (ccxiii. 2, I. and III.) are omitted, as merely repeating, in imperfect detail, the statements here made.

men to a mess, and also by the mortality which
hath been indeed amongst them, as your Lordship
writeth,—what in all this time it hath amounted
unto, the captain and officers of every ship do only
know, who (that notwithstanding) have been from
time to time furnished by me with their due proportions, as if that had not been.   Only, by that
means, they have all in them a store, which no
doubt will serve them a good time after their
ordinary victualling be expired.   And yet this
sparing hath been only at such times when there
hath been fear of want; otherwise the mariners will
hardly endure to be abridged of any part of their
allowances.

I did become a suitor unto your Honour and
the rest of the Council, for nine hundred pounds
which is owing upon my former reckoning; which
it pleased you, by your next letters, to promise me
should be sent hither soon after.   I do humbly
beseech your Honour to have the same in remembrance; and in the meantime I will presume to
disburse so much out of this last money granted,
because I know it is not your pleasure the country
shall be unpaid.   And so I humbly take my leave,
beseeching God to send your Lordship long life
with increase of much honour.   From Plymouth,
this 22nd of July, 1588.

Your Honour's most humble,

MAR. DARELL.

July 22.—*MEMORANDUM OF CHARGES.*

[ccxiii. 3.—Rough notes in Burghley's hand.   Endorsed by
Burghley :—Memorials for money.   The navy : the provision
for the storehouse : for the office of the ordnance.]

A computation of the numbers as Mr. Hawkyns
accounteth to be paid until the 28th of July :—

For 2,990 men from the 5th of May,
to the day they were paid, until
the 28th of July, being 84 days : 6,279*l.*
3 months . . . . . To be
For 1,900 serving in four great paid.
ships, which was paid to the 13th
of July, now for 15 days, that is 712*l.*
to the 28th of July . . .
The numbers total to be paid are . 4,890 men ;
whereof
There are serving in the Narrow
Seas under the Lord Henry
Seymour . . . . . 1,471 men.
So are serving under the Lord
Admiral on the Broad Seas . 3,419
But yet by Darell's book there are 3,770
So misreckoned 351

An account of the pay due to the ships serving
under Sir Fr. Drake :—

The number certified by Mr. Hawkyns are . . . . . 2,900 men.
Which number was paid until the
19th of June, saving 800 ; so as
there was answered with the 800 4,060*l.* pd.
Item, to bring the pay of these from
the 19th of June until the 28th of 2,827*l.* to be
July, which is 39 days, requireth . paid.

Total to be paid to the 28th of July
for wages .   .   .   .   . 9,818*l.*
Total 7,790 men.
As thereto certified by Hawkyns,
serving in ships of Sir Richard
Greynvile's &c., 700
Total 8,490 men, which cometh by
the month, after 28*s.* a man, to
11,890*l.*, besides tonnage, and
about 705*l.* a month, grounding,
tallowing, carpentry.
Add for wages of 700 men, newly
increased in 8 ships with the Lord
Admiral and Sir Fra. Drake, to
the 28th of July .   .   .   . 1,960*l.*
Total of wages due at the 28th of
July for 8,490 men .   .   .   11,778*l.*

Other demands of Mr. Hawkyns :—

For grounding, tallowing, sea-
store, carpenter, masts, repair
of boats, cordage, canvas &c.,
for the ships under my Lord } 2,500*l.*
Admiral and Lord Henry's   } 5,000*l.*
charge   .   .   .   .   .
For the like charges for the ships
with Sir Fras. Drake .   .   . 2,500*l.*
For tonnage for the ships for 236 [1]
days, until the 28th of July, which } 1,771*l.*
is 4 months [1] .   .   .   .   } 3,731*l.*
For tonnage of the 8 ships taken up
in the west country, for 4 months, } 1,960*l.*
ending the 28th of July   .   .
Item, for conduct in despatching of
1,000 men, and in presting of men   700*l.*
                                               21,209*l.*

[1] So in MS. Burghley's arithmetic is frequently inexplicable.

But Hawkyns summeth the
same to be but .   . 19,570l.
So varieth .   . 1,779l.[1]

The Office of the Admiralty.

There is a debt   . 7,000<i>l</i>. for provision⎫
There is a demand   ⎬ 13,000<i>l</i>.
for new provisions. 6,000<i>l</i>.   .   . ⎭

Office of the Ordnance.

There is a demand for provisions for
	£	s.	d.
to serve for an army :			
The sum of	8,049	0	0
Whereof in emptions presently	2,700	13	4
There is a debt in the said office .	5,211	15	1½
Whereof is already imprested .	2,761	11	3

Notanda.

Mr. Quarles hath had from his beginning in Feb.
1587, until the last of June, 1588, 49,808<i>l</i>. 2s. 3½<i>d</i>.
And in July now presently 6,000<i>l</i>. for the west,
and for the Lord Henry Seymour, 1,854<i>l</i>.

July 22.—*LEICESTER TO WALSYNGHAM.*

[ccxiii. 9.—Signed.]

Abstract.

[He has conferred with Peter Pett about the
lighters and chain to be sent down to stop the river
at Tilbury.   He finds that these will not be
sufficient, ' unless they may be strengthened with a
competent number of masts before them ; for otherwise, if two or three ships made of purpose should
come against it with a full tide and a good strong

¹ So in MS.

gale of wind, no doubt they would break all and pass through.' He has taken Pett to view the place, so that he knows what should be provided. He begs that the lighters and barges to be employed may be sent down with all expedition.]

July 22.—*HOWARD TO SUSSEX* (?).

[B.M. Cott. MS. Otho E. ix, f. 185*b*.—Copy. Fragment, damaged by fire.]

. . . . them by Sunday in the morning about . . . them and continued it until one of the clock in the . . . . did some good, and I dare say they think some harm. I pray [you send] out unto me all such ships as you have ready [for sea at] Portsmouth, with all possible speed, and though they have not ab . . . two days' victuals, let not that be cause of their stay, for they shall have victuals out of our fleet. They shall find us bearing East-North-East after the fleet. We mean so to course the enemy as that they shall have no leisure to land. I pray your Lordship to send in those ships from Portsmouth as many tall men as you can get in so short a time. And so I bid your good Lordship most heartily farewell. From aboard her Majesty's good ship the Ark, the 22nd of July, 1588.

Your Lordship's very loving friend,

C. HOWARD.

The ships you send shall find me East-North-East, following the Spanish fleet.

Since the making up of my letter there is a galleass of the enemy's taken with 450 men in her; and yesterday I spoiled one of their greatest ships, that they were fain to forsake it.

I pray your Lordship send her Majesty word hereof with speed, as from me. The captain's name is, as I hear say, Don Pedro de Alva, general of the field.

The messenger saith that there is an hundred gentlemen in the galleass which was taken, who for the most part were noblemen's sons.

July 23.—SEYMOUR TO THE COUNCIL.

[ooxiii. 12.—Signed.   Addressed.]

May it please your Lordships :—I mean not to trouble you with many lines, because I do send your Lordships the original, Sir Francis Drake's letter,[1] by the which you shall understand the state of the Spanish army, how forward they be ; and to [2] our opinions here, we conjecture still their purpose may be to land in the Isle of Wight, to recover[3] the same—which God forbid.   Thus humbly praying your Lordships to send us powder and shot forthwith, whereof we have want in our fleet, and which I have divers times given knowledge thereof, I humbly take my leave.   From aboard the Rainbow, at anchor a quarter seas over against Dover, the 23rd of July, 1588, at 11 of the clock at night.

Our victuals do end the last of this month ; yet upon extremity, now we know the enemy at hand, we will prolong that little we have as long as we can.

Your Lordships' humbly to command,

H. SEYMOUR.

I do send forthwith to the fleets of Zealand and Holland, to wish [4] them to repair unto us.   Also I have made the Lieutenant of Dover acquainted therewith, to the end he may have a better care thereof.

---

[1] See *ante*, p. 289.

[2] As to.

[3] Gain possession of.

[4] Desire.

July 23.—*NIC. OSELEY*[1] *TO WALSYNGHAM.*

[coxiii. 13.—Holograph.   Addressed.]

Right Honourable, my duty remembered, &c. :—
Presently after your Honour gave me license to
follow my Lord Admiral, with all expedition I
followed the fleet; whereas[2] presently Sir Francis
Drake requested him I might go in the Revenge,
where Sir Francis hath now found all to be of most
truth, that I advertised your Honour at my coming
out of Spain.   And for that I do know he doth
write your Honour of that we past with the Spanish
fleet the 21st, and this day, 23rd of July, as well of
the fights, as the taking of the gallega wherein was
Don Pedro de Valdes, who is third person in this
army of the Duke, and Juan Martinez de Recalde,
vice-admiral, I do think it not needful to repeat.
Neither of the other ship which we have also of
theirs, who spoiled herself with her powder.   Both
of them, so Don Pedro saith, are of their principal
ships.   Of that we found aboard them, I refer me
to Sir Francis, assuring your Honour they are not
in such good order in their putting themself in
battle[3]; but aboard they have as much evil[4] order,
as I did see, who by Sir Francis' commandment was

[1] He had apparently been settled in Spain as a merchant, but
had of late years acted as a spy for the Government, sending such
intelligence as he could pick up.   On January 5, 1588-9, Lord
Howard wrote to Burghley concerning him:—' It hath pleased
her Highness, in respect of his good service heretofore in Spain,
in sending very good intelligence thence, and now since, in our
late fight against the Spanish fleet, to grant unto him a lease of
the parsonage of St. Helens in London.   These are therefore to
pray your Lordship to stay the same parsonage, that no lease be
in the meantime granted out of the Exchequer which should
prevent the reward of one that hath so well deserved in adventur-
ing his life so many ways in her Majesty's service.'—*Lansdowne
MS.* lix. 4; Ellis's *Original Letters*, 3rd S. iv. 67.
[2] Where.   [3] Sc. order of battle.   [4] MS. yevell.

the first went to them.   They have reported to me
they are now left a hundred and fifty sail, divided,
as I do see, twelve in squadron, and do keep such
excellent good order in their fight,[1] that if God do
not miraculously work, we shall have wherein to
employ ourself for some days.

The desire I have to do my duty unto your
Honour hath emboldened me to do this.   If I may
have your Honour's license, from time to time as
we do proceed in this action, I will show myself of
no inferior to any, in hope to serve your Honour ;
most humbly beseeching your Honour to have your
obedient servant in remembrance, so that I be not
the first and only man denied that hath put himself
unto your Honour's protection, but that there may
be consideration of the long time I was prisoner for
a spy, for writing the letters to London that came
to your Honour's hands ; which being proved, could
not I have [2] release but with great expenses and
bribes ; as also the three months I spent in riding
to most ports where this army was made, whereof
I have given true relation unto your Honour ; anything that your Honour shall think convenient for
me, either in England or Ireland,[3] I shall willingly
receive wherewithal, and my person to serve your
Honour wheresoever it shall please your Honour to
use [4] of me ; assuring myself God will give me
grace to do my duty towards your Honour, for
whose long life and increase of honour I daily do
and will pray for.   From the Revenge of her
Majesty's, right against Portland, the 23rd of July,
1588.   Your Honour's obedient servant,

NICHOLAS OSELEY.

[1] So in MS.   It seems to contradict the previous sentence,
which must be supposed to refer only to the prizes, the evil order
of one of which is described *ante*, p. 9.

[2] Sc. I could not have.   [3] MS. Yerlande.
[4] MS. yowse.

July 24.—*REQUISITION FOR POWDER
AND SHOT.*

[ooxiii. 59, I.—Copy.]

Whereas I have received letters from the Right
Honourable the Lord High Admiral of England,
advertising unto me that his Lordship hath taken
two great carracks or ships from the enemy, sent to
the shore, wherein is great store of powder and shot
in either of them; and requireth that all the said
powder and shot be sent unto his Lordship with all
possible expedition, for that the state of the realm
dependeth upon the present supply of such wants :—
These are therefore, in her Majesty's name, straitly
to charge and command you, forthwith, upon receipt
hereof, you make diligent enquiry to what place the
said carracks or ships are gone; and if they shall
arrive near you, to cause the said powder and shot
to be conveyed to his Lordship with all good speed ;
further charging and commanding you to take the
like order by giving intelligence hereof from port to
port, until his Lordship's command shall be therein
performed. Whereof fail you not upon your allegiance. Weymouth and Melcombe Regis, this 24th
of July, 1588.

RICHARD PITT, Mayor.

You shall find the English fleet on the seas,
between this place and the Isle of Wight or eastwards.

To the Mayor of Lyme Regis, and in his
absence to her Majesty's officers in that place.

Received this same day by 9 of the clock in
the morning, and have sent out for the same pur-

pose to seek out the same ships; and we see one great ship alone to lie in sight of this town of Lyme, and we think it is one of the ships.

JOHN JONES, Mayor.

Received the said 24th day at two of the clock in the afternoon.   ROBERT DENYS.

Mr. Upton, repair I pray you forthwith to Dartmouth, and despatch away the powder and shot according to the contents of this direction, with all haste.

JOHN GILBERTE.   GEORGE CARY.

Received the 24th of July about 9 of the clock.

July 24.—PALAVICINO¹ TO WALSYNGHAM.

[ccxiii. 19.—Holograph.   Italian.   Addressed.]

Right Honourable:—If I err, I beseech your Honour to pardon me and to be a mean that her Majesty and the rest of the Lords may likewise pardon me—especially my very good Lord, the Earl of Leicester, to whom I was a suitor to serve a-land under his charge.   But the greatness of my zeal, which desireth to be amongst those who do fight for her Majesty's service and for the defence of her kingdom, doth constrain me, with an honourable company, to depart as this night toward Portsmouth, there to embark and join the Lord Admiral, where I hope to be present in the battle, and thereby a partaker in the victory or to win an honourable

¹ Sir Horatio Palavicino, a Genoese banker settled in England, where he had made a large fortune, and was largely employed in the financial business of the Government.   He was knighted in 1587.

death, thus to testify to the whole world my fidelity to her Majesty. Especially do I commend my affairs to your Honour, and pray God to give you every happiness. From the Court, the 24th of July, 1588.

Your Honour's most assured friend to command,
HORATIO PALAVICINO.

July 25.—*LEICESTER TO WALSYNGHAM.*

[ocxiii. 27.—Holograph. Addressed.]

Mr. Secretary :—We have here news commonly spread abroad that my Lord Admiral hath taken either admiral or vice-admiral and the great galleass, besides one great ship sunk. The Almighty God be praised therefor, and to give further victory, to his glory and the comfort of his poor church, as no doubt it must be, with the greatest renown and perpetual fame to her Majesty that ever came to any prince. And this being true,[1] I would gladly know what her Majesty will do with me. I have here now assembled in camp 4,000 footmen, as gallant and as willing men as ever was seen ; with the horse yet only of this shire. The lying in camp will do them much good, though it be but for a short time ; and in my poor opinion, not good to dismiss them over suddenly, though the fleet be defeated, till ye see a little also what Parma will do. I am here cook, cater and hunt[2] ; for as[3] I myself have not only set the men a-work here about the forts, and was present among them all the first day, but also did peruse[4] and made choice of the ground fittest for the encamping of the soldiers ; and yesterday went to Chelmsford, to take order

---

[1] If this be true.
[2] Caterer and huntsman.
[3] That.
[4] Did examine.

I.
X

for the bringing of all the soldiers hither this day ;
and this day came with the most part of them
hither by 10 a-clock this morning, with very good
provision for them, through the care and diligence
of sundry the justices of peace here, which hath
deserved great thanks, if their pains had been seen
to[1] others as to[1] me. But if the news be true of
this good beginning, which[2] I cannot but suspend
till I hear from you, and be sorry that all men shall
receive them before myself, yet I pray you be
not forgetful to resolve what shall be done here,
and let me know it as soon as may be, for many
respects.

I assure you I am angry with Sir John Norreys[3]
and Sir Roger Williams. They were both appointed
by mine own[4] desire, as well as otherwise, to offices
of great charge ; Mr. Norreys, as marshal of our
companies, the other of the horsemen. Sir John,
at his arrival yesterday morning at 3 a-clock, told
me that in respect of[5] the Spanish fleet were passed
hitherward and not impeached, as now we hear it
is, he was willed to go to Dover to see if the Lord
Admiral did pass that way, to relieve him with men
and to assemble the forces there ; which I did like
very well, albeit altogether without anybody to

---

[1] By.   [2] My belief in which.
[3] Second son of Lord Norreys, and grandson of Sir Henry
Norreys, executed on a charge of adultery with Anne Boleyn.
He had served with great distinction in command of English
volunteers in the Low Countries, afterwards in Ireland, and again
in the Low Countries under Leicester, who conceived a special
hatred for him, possibly because he was a competent soldier,
which Leicester was not. The feud had been patched up by
Walsyngham's good offices, but, if we may judge from this letter,
the reconciliation was very hollow. In the following year Norreys
was with Drake, in joint command of the expedition to Portugal.
He was afterwards Lord-General in the Low Countries, and, later
on, in Ireland, where he died in 1597.
[4] MS. my none.   [5] Seeing that the Spanish fleet.

supply his place, being marshal; but for a day or two content to travail the more myself as I have done; willing him and Sir Roger Williams both in any wise to return this day early to me again, for that all our forces would be assembled at the place for our camp; which they promised faithfully, especially Sir John Norreys. But yet neither of them both do I hear of, myself returning this morning with most of our men; nor anybody to order the camp, either for horse or foot, but only Edmund Yorke [1] and myself. Which manner of dealing, I assure you, doth much mislike me in them both; for, except my Lords of the Council did give Sir John such special order, as he saith, to go to Dover, I am ill used, having so many men to take charge of, and not one officer here, but only my cousin Leighton [2] and myself; and that the country must now needs see me so hardly accompanied as I am; for it is now 4 a-clock, but hears not of them. If they come not this night, I assure you, for my part, I will not receive any of them into office, nor bear such loose careless dealing at their hands. If you saw how weakly I am assisted, you would be sorry to think that we here should be the front against the enemy, that is so mighty, if he should land here. But I see the mighty God doth behold his little flock, and will do all things to his glory, not regarding our sins. And seeing her Majesty hath appointed me her Lieutenant-General, and numbers of men to govern, and officers accordingly, I look [3] that respect to be used toward me that is due to my place.

I am herein somewhat to entreat you to consider

[1] A brother of Rowland Yorke (see *ante*, p. 85), but seems to have remained true to his allegiance. His son, also Edmund, preferred to follow in the footsteps of his uncle.

[2] Sir Thomas Leighton, knighted in 1579; afterwards Governor of Guernsey.   [3] Look for.

of this service, and albeit her Majesty hath sum-
moned all her Lords to attend her person, yet were
it meet in so great a conference as this is, wherein
her surety and the whole realm doth consist, that as
much countenance as may be, be given thereto.
Among other, though he be no man of war, yet I
find the country doth much respect and love him,
especially that he is a true faithful subject to her
Majesty and known to be zealous in religion.   His
presence with me would do much good.   It is my
Lord Rich,[1] whom I pray you send back, with her
Majesty's good liking to me.   You have all the rest
of [the][2] nobility and their forces ; and if you could
procure my Lord Wentworth's[3] coming also, I
would think they should well further this service.

Even as I had written thus much, being
5 a-clock, I received this letter[4] from Mr. Norreys.
You will see whether there be such necessity of his
special journey for that he writeth of, but I could
have directed by my letters to the lieutenants there.
But surely, Mr. Secretary, he makes me conceive
that there is other matter in it, that having an
honourable place under me and no authority elsewhere, for aught I know, more than as a supervising
muster master, should deliver himself thus from me
to command apart, without commission, rather than
with me, in the honourable place appointed him.

---

[1] Robert, Lord Rich, a justice of the peace for Essex : was
created Earl of Warwick in 1618 and died the same year.   He
married the Lady Penelope Devereux, sister of the Earl of Essex,
whom he divorced for adultery ; and was, by her, the father of
that Earl of Warwick who was Lord High Admiral for the Parliament during the Civil War.

[2] Omitted in MS.

[3] Thomas, 2nd Lord Wentworth, was deputy of Calais when
it was taken by the French in 1558.   For that loss he was tried
and acquitted.   He sat as one of the judges of the Duke of
Norfolk in 1572 and of the Queen of Scots in 1586.   He died
in 1590.   [4] Missing.

And where[1] he promised faithfully to be here with me this morning early, it appears by his letter that he means to stay longer to receive my further opinion. Before God, I am much troubled with this dealing ; you knowing how well I have dealt with him since our reconcilement. But I pray you judge evenly whether this be not cause to think strangely of his doings, to leave me thus to myself, being my principal officer. If my Lords did appoint him to this, I must say they do me the more wrong, to alter and change in these cases without acquainting me with the matter. And albeit I do complain to you in this matter, yet mean I not but to use it well, and hear what he can say ; but that I must deal frankly with you, for you were a doer between us, and this is a time you know for all officers under me to show their care and love, if the matter were of less moment. I have little backing or countenance enough beside, and therefore we ought to join the better together in so needful a service. And so, with my paper, at this time to end my letter. In hot haste going to our camp again, this 25th of July.   Your assured,
                                                    R. Leycester.

July 25.—SEYMOUR TO WALSYNGHAM.

[ccxiii. 30.—Holograph. Addressed.]

Sir :—I am most glad of this most happy beginning of victory obtained of her Majesty's enemies, but most sorry I am so tied I cannot be an actor in the play. But if the Duke be as good as his threats, he will now show his courage, for hitherto he hath only played with surprises of towns

[1] Whereas.

more undirectly than directly. I pray God it may be my fortune to light upon himself, the same being so given out, but I fear me this matter will daunt him.

We are here very carefully cared for by Sir John Norreys, for munition, men, and powder, which is not yet come unto us. In the mean [time] [1] we are assisted with the presence of worthy gentlemen that are of purpose come to serve her Majesty with the venture of their lives ; which I thought necessary to acquaint you therewith, to the end her Majesty may give them thanks. Their names be Sir Charles Blount,[2] Francis Carey,[3] Richard Lee,[4] Brute Brown.[5]

[1] Omitted in MS.

[2] Second son of the 6th Lord Mountjoy, born in 1563. On coming to the Court in 1583, his good looks attracted the Queen's notice and won for him her favour. He is described as then ' of a brown hair, a sweet face, a most neat composure, and tall in his person.' He was knighted by Leicester for service in the Low Countries in 1587, and succeeded as 8th Lord Mountjoy on the death of his elder brother in 1594. He commanded the Lion at Cadiz in 1596, and the land forces, under Essex, in the Islands' Voyage in 1597. In 1600 he was appointed Lord Deputy of Ireland, and Lord-Lieutenant in 1603, when he was created Earl of Devonshire. Died in 1606, leaving no legitimate issue, but several children by Lady Rich (see *ante*, p. 308), whom he afterwards married.

[3] The spelling of the name is uncertain, and there is no other mention of him. He may have been a son of Sir Francis Carew, then in command of the Surrey militia (ccxvii. 75). It does not appear that he was any relation of Lord Hunsdon, whose youngest son, Robert, joined the E. Bonaventure with the Earl of Cumberland (*Memoirs*, ed. 1759, p. 18).

[4] He may have been a younger cousin of Sir Henry Lee, afterwards Master of the Ordnance ; or the name may have been Leigh. It is impossible to identify him.

[5] Brute seems to have been a common Christian name in a family of Browns of Tavistock. The parish register shows the birth of John son of Brute Brown in 1616 ; also the burial of Brute son of Brute Brown in 1620. This particular Brute Brown was probably the man slain by a great shot at Porto Rico in 1595, as he was sitting at supper with Drake, who, as he started up, exclaimed, ' Ah ! dear Brute, I could grieve for thee, but now is no time for me to let down my spirits.'

Thus preparing myself for the service, do commit you to God. From aboard the Rainbow, a pretty way in the sea, in Dover Road, but shifting further forth, the 25th of July, 1588.

Your assured friend &c.

H. SEYMOUR.

Post.—Sir, upon this extremity I am bold to retain certain ships for this service, which can not be long ; hoping, if you will, a means to see the charge answered ; for by intelligence we daily look for them. I have sent Monsieur Gourdan of these news.

July 25.—MEMORANDUM BY BURGHLEY.

[ccxiii. 34.—Endorsed, in Burghley's hand :—Memorial at Richmond.]

Nich. Gorges :—That Holstok and Mr. Hawkyns' deputies may take care for preparing and setting forth to the seas the 8 ships hereafter following, to be sent the Lord Henry Seymour :—

George Bonaventure, Violet, Vineyard, Anne Francis, Jane Bonaventure, Samuel, Susan Parnell, Solomon.

The number of the men are 530.

That some money be delivered in prest to Hawkyns' deputy for this purpose.

For 14 days' wages, 185*l.* 10*s.*

For 1 month's victuals, 371*l.* } 556*l.* 10*s.*

Every ship to have 20 barrels of powder.

For other furniture, as calivers &c. for [1] tonnage.

Bellingham :—To choose out 12 more strong ships above 100 tons out of the Stade fleet.

For men in the same, for 14 days.

For victual for one month.

[1] According to.

July 25.—*ED. BURNHAM*[1] *TO WALSYNGHAM.*

[**S.P. Holland, lv.**—Holograph.   Addressed.]

Right Honourable:—According to your Honour's commandment by your last letters I have informed myself of the price of all sort of armours here in Middelburg, which differeth something from that it is worth in Holland, being somewhat better cheap there than here, but not much. The musket with the band-roll and rest, 22*s.* sterling ; the caliver and furniture, 12*s.* and 13*s.* sterling. The horseman's armour complete, with cuissants, the breast petronell proof, and the backpiece proof, 3*l.* and 3*l.* 6*s.* 8*d.* sterling. There is one Finch[2] that hath bought 30 for Sir Thomas Heneage at 3*l.* sterling the piece ; but since they are grown dearer, for that he bespake them a good while ago. Powder is here at 4*l.* 10*s.* sterling the quintal, which is a hundredweight. In England is 8*l.* more than this. There is no great quantity to be had here ; but the greatest store that is for these countries is in Amsterdam. By some of our merchants I do understand that there is good quantity at Hamburg and Stade,[3] and better cheap than in these parts. . . .

We understand here that the great galley which the enemy hath made at Sluys, going out before the last tempest, was forced to put in to the Texel, wherein there is a hundred Italian soldiers and 200 *forçats.*[4] Yesternight here arrived a drum from the

---

[1] An agent of Walsyngham's. He was back in England in September. Probably the Mr. Burnham named by the Queen in October 1591, when ' it was her pleasure to have some honest person sent to Brittany to view and report on the forces there.'

[2] If Sir Moyle Finch (see *post*, p. 320), it is strange that Burnham should speak of him as an unknown man.

[3] MS. Stoades.   [4] MS. forsats.

enemy about certain prisoners of theirs which be here, who saith that the galley hath been long missing and they cannot tell what is become of her, which makes us think to be true. They of Enkhuysen have of late taken a Scots pirate who had 94 men aboard of him and 25 pieces of ordnance. It is thought that they will execute most part of the men. I have, since my last to your Honour, spoken to Monsr. de St. Aldegonde,[1] who telleth me that he can do nothing with the Count Maurice, and that he is altogether led by Villiers the marshal, Monsr. de Famars,[2] and Villiers the preacher. By reason of my sickness which hath held me long, I could not as yet go into Holland, but I sent my despatches to Mr. Kyllygrew, of whom I have answer that he had received the same, and since that time I have received letters from him, by the which he writeth me that the Count Maurice would have me to come, which I will not fail to do, as soon as it shall please God to send me health. I find St. Aldegonde to be in a very bare estate, and was resolved if the Princess[3] had gone in France, to have gone with her, and to have presented his service to the King of Navarre. Her stay is the cause of his. He desired me to write to your Honour to know your Honour's advice whether he should proceed in this determination of himself, since that now the Princess doth not go, but findeth many difficulties. Among the rest, the lightness and unconstance of that nation ; want of means to provide himself for such a journey ; the small means that the King hath now in this time to do for him.

[1] Had been the confidential minister of the Prince of Orange, and on repeated missions to England.
[2] MS. Famasse.
[3] The Princess of Orange. See *ante*, p. 100 *n*. She was still at Middelburg in the end of August.

This last tempest forced all the ships of war of these countries, that lay before Dunkirk and Nieuport, to come in. The like hath not been seen by any at this time of the year. But this day it is thought they will all go forth again. The corn of this island is in danger to be spoiled by reason of the great store of rain that is fallen of late.

By others I know your Honour shall be advertised of the pacifying of the mutiny in Gertruidenberg.[1] The States, they have paid their money; assurance they have none but the honesty of the mutineers. They have railed very much against all the States, especially against Barnevelt, whom they name Barrabas, and Brasser of Delft. They advised Count Maurice, who lay before the town, to take heed of them all, and that they would betray him as they had done his father. Sir John Wingfeild[2] they have been content to accept for their governor. Herewith I send your Honour a pacquet which I received yesternight from Mr. Kyllygrew, with my most humble duty ; and as I am bound, I beseech the Almighty long to bless and preserve your Honour. Flushing, the 25th of July, 1588.

Your Honour's most humble
and obedient servant,
EDW. BURNHAM.

[1] MS. Gettenbergen. With many others, the garrison of Gertruidenberg had revolted in February on much the same grounds as Colonel Sonoy (see *ante*, p. 83), declaring that they recognised no authority but that of the Queen of England, and would not treat except with Lord Wyllughby. By his mediation, an agreement was come to, by which they were to return to their duty on being paid 216,000 fl. The money was paid, but the garrison mutinied again and delivered the town to the Prince of Parma. See De Thou (Fr. edit. of 1734), x. 162–3.

[2] In 1591–2 Master of the Ordnance in the expedition to Brittany ; slain at the storming of Cadiz in 1596

•

July 26.—SHIPS TO BE SENT TO SEYMOUR.

[ccxiii. 35.]

A note of the 8 ships appointed to be sent to the Lord Harry Seymour into the Narrow Seas the 25th July, 1588, under the command of Mr. Nicholas Gorges, Esquire.

The names of the ships and their number of men after :

	Men
The Susan Parnell of London .	80
Solomon	80
George Bonaventure . .	80
Anne Francis . . .	70
Vineyard	60
Violet	60
Samuel	50
Jane Bonaventure . .	50
Sum of the men	530

The 26th of July the ships and men entered into pay, and from that day was victualled for one whole month.

	£	s.	d.
The victualling of 530 men for one month, after 14s. the man, amounteth to	371	0	0
For prest of 530 men at 12d. per man	26	10	0
For the pressers due at 4d. per man	8	16	8
Sum	406	6	8

July 26.—WINCHESTER[1] *TO THE COUNCIL.*

[ccxiii. 36.—Signed. Endorsed.]

Right Honourable :—Having according to the tenor of your Lordships' late letters signified your Honours' pleasures unto the deputy lieutenants of Dorset for the present dispatch and sending of one thousand men to be employed in Essex, do find by answer returned from the said deputies that the strength of that county, being of itself very small, to be thereby greatly weakened and the present state thereof to require all places of danger to remain fortified, having the enemy so near them at sea and in sight, as besides, advertisement being given them of the great preparations of the French, likewise ready to put to the sea in assistance of the Spaniard. There is already drawn out of the said county, by warrant from the Lord Admiral, for his better supply, 400 men. With all which I have thought it my part to acquaint your good Lordships, leaving the same to your Honours' considerations, humbly praying your further pleasures to be returned touching the said 1,000 men so required, to be either supplied out of Wilts, Somerset, or Devon, or otherwise to be stayed at home for the present guard of that county, for the causes before alleged. And even so do leave your good Lordships to the tuition of the Almighty. Basing, this 26th of July, 1588.

Your Lordships' at commandment,

WINCHESTER.

[1] William Powlett, Marquis of Winchester, Lord Lieutenant of Dorset and Hampshire, married Agnes, Lord Howard's half-sister.

•

July 26.—THE COUNCIL TO HOWARD.

[**B.M. Addl. MS. 33740, f. 2.**—Signed. Addressed.]

After our right hearty commendations to your Lordship :—Forasmuch as the Queen's Majesty is informed that the enemy is very well provided of shot,[1] and it may be that your Lordship is not at this present furnished with such a number to answer them as is meet, her Highness, being very careful that your Lordship should be supplied with all the provisions that may be had, hath given order that in the county of Kent a good number of the best and choicest shot of the trained bands in the said county should be forthwith sent to the seaside, to the intent that upon any notice to be given from your Lordship they may be brought unto you to double man the ships that are both with your Lordship and the Lord Henry Seymour, which her Majesty hath thought good to signify unto your Lordship by this bearer, Sir Thomas Gorges, Knight, who is of purpose dispatched unto your Lordship for that cause. And so beseeching Almighty God to send your Lordship a happy and honourable end of this service, we bid you right heartily farewell. From Richmond, the 26th of July, 1588.

Your assured loving friends,

CHR. HATTON, Canc.	W. BURGHLEY.
F. KNOLLYS.	T. HENEAGE.
A. POULET.	J. WOLLEY.

[1] Musketeers.

July 26.—LEICESTER TO WALSYNGHAM.

[ccxiii. **38.**—Holograph.   Addressed.]

Mr. Secretary :—The 4,000 men of Essex are all come together and lodged here together at West Tilbury upon a very good ground for aptness for the defence of this coast.   They be as forward men and all willing to meet with the enemy as ever I saw. Some want, their captains showed in themselves, that being suddenly removed to this place, brought not so much as one meal's provision of victual with them, so that at their arrival here there was not a barrel of beer nor loaf of bread for them.   Enough after 20 miles' march to have been discouraged and to have mutinied, but all with one voice, finding it to be the speediness of their coming, said they would abide more hunger than this to serve her Majesty and the country.

I did send to have Robert Arderne [1] come down and to bring a hundred tuns of beer, and to be here this day ; but I hear not of him yet, and if he fail it will be the greater ill hap, seeing all this part, on this side and the other, within 4 miles of the water, cannot yield drink enough for them.   And for that I hear the 1,000 men from London will be here this night also, I have sent presently to stay them till we may provide for them here, except they have provision with them.

And touching the resolution of my Lords for their captains to continue their leadership I am sorry for it ; because it must now light upon me, their displacing ; but rather than I will hazard her Majesty's safety and the whole realm's service, I

---

[1] Officially styled 'Assistant to the Clerk of the Acatery'— i.e. the office of buying provisions for (catering for) the Sovereign.

would displace my brother or any man. As for the account of the regiments, I do yet scarcely see how I shall bring it to pass without getting other manner of persons than goldsmiths and mercers are ; and yet if it may be so there is not place for half such captains as so great a service requires. And for that it hath pleased God to begin graciously with us and to give hope of comfortable victory, yet let us not be too secure when the substance of their forces remain yet whole, and being so resolutely bent as they be ; but that we continue our defensive preparations, rather more than less, against them.

And because I see and find many causes now to increase my former opinion of the dilatory wants you shall find upon all sudden hurly-burleys, for which respect I am in duty bound to move her Majesty and humbly to beseech her, that as these cases that touch her honour, life, and state, that there may be such due regard had for all provisions as in times past hath been. But in no former time was ever so great cause as at this time. And albeit her Majesty hath appointed on shore an army to resist her enemies if they land, yet how hard a matter it will be to gather the men together, I find it ; and may judge, if it will be 5 days to gather the very countrymen,[1] what will it be and must be to look in short space for those that dwell 40, 50 and 60 miles off ; and this must be warning that considerations of victuals as well as anything else be provided at the place of assemblies &c. I did two whole days before the coming of these make proclamation in all market towns for victuallers to come to the place where the soldiers[2] should encamp, and to receive ready money for it ; but there is not one victualler come in to this hour. I have sent to all

---

[1] The men of the immediate neighbourhood.
[2] MS. soldyers.

the justices about it from place to place; but I speak it to this end, that timely consideration is to be had of all these things, and not to defer and put off in hope, till the worse come and the time do [1] overpass.

And that it may please her Majesty, of her princely magnanimity, now above all other former times, to show herself careful and provident not only for her own person, which is the stay of us all, but also of all her whole realm and people, whom God hath committed to her protection. And were she secured, and all about her did counsel her to have presently a convenient force both of horse and foot about her, that she will not defer the time upon any supposed hope both to assemble them in time, and to appoint some special nobleman about her to govern and direct them; for her Majesty cannot be strong enough too soon; and if her navy had not been strong and abroad, as it is, whatsoever cost hath been bestowed, what case had herself and her whole realm been in by this time? Or if God do [1] not miraculously give her victory there, what case will she be in, if her forces be not, not only assembled, but an army perfectly dressed, with all the officers appertaining, to withstand that mighty enemy that is to approach then her gates? I pray you, Mr. Secretary, with humble pardon, deliver thus much to her Majesty; for God doth know I speak it not to bring you to charges. I would she had less cause to spend than ever she had, and her coffers fuller than they be; but I will prefer her life and safety, and the defence of the realm, before all sparing and charges, being in the present danger it is in.

There is a portion of money appointed I perceive to the charge of Sir Moyle Finch [2] to be

---

[1] MS. to.

[2] Eldest son of Sir Thomas Finch, of Eastwell in Kent, by right of his wife Katharine, daughter and heiress of Sir Thomas

brought hither. I am glad of it, and do desire the gentleman may be our Treasurer here ; and whether the extraordinary charges, as for platforms, fortifications and such like, shall be paid by him or no, and Peter Petts' charge. And so with my paper I end. At Gravesend this 26th of July.

Your assured friend,

R. LEYCESTER.

July 26.—*LEICESTER TO WALSYNGHAM.*

[ccxiii. 39.—Holograph. Addressed :—For her Majesty's affairs.]

Mr. Secretary :—After the writing of my other letters, here is arrived Sir Roger Williams, and perceive Mr. Norreys will be this night with me. In the meanwhile, they have put me to more travail than ever I was in before. I perceive by Sir Roger, that my Lord Henry Seymour is departed toward Rye, to assist my Lord Admiral, but doth want both men and powder. Good Lord, how is this come to pass, that both he and my Lord Admiral is so weakened of their men ? I hear their men be run away, which must be severely punished, or else all soldiers will be bold. He saith also that the Prince [1] is looked to issue out presently. He hath suffered no stranger this seven or eight days to come to him, or to see his army and ships, but he hath blindfolded them.

I beseech you assemble your forces, and play not away this kingdom by delays, and hasten our

Moyle of Eastwell. He was, at this time, officially styled 'Treasurer at Wars.' He married Elizabeth, daughter and heiress of Sir Thomas Heneage, Chancellor of the Duchy of Lancaster, Vice-Chamberlain of the Household, and one of the Lords of the Council.

[1] Of Parma.

horsemen hither and footmen, if you hear not that
the fleet [1] is scattered or beaten ; for surely if they
come to the Narrow Seas, the Prince will play
another manner of part than is looked for.   I have
written enough already.   God send care with expedition with you there, and good success with us here ;
specially with our sea forces.   In all haste, 26th of
July.

Yours assured,

R. LEYCESTER.

There is no hope of a thousand men furnished,
more than we have, out of Berkshire.

July 26.—SUSSEX [2] *TO WALSYNGHAM.*

[ocxiii. 40.—Signed.   Addressed.]

It may please your Honour :—I received a letter
this day at two of the clock in the morning from Sir
George Carey, the copy whereof I have sent unto
your Honour herein enclosed, and also a letter from
my Lord Admiral, which I received at six of the
clock this morning, wherein he writeth for powder
and shot, and saith he hath very great want thereof,
by reason of three great fights which he hath had
with the Spanish fleet.   Whereupon I have sent
him so much as that I have altogether unfurnished
myself, as may appear by a note to your Honour
herein sent ; which I shall desire your Honour to be
a mean that it may be supplied, for that I shall have
great want thereof if any attempt be offered.   And

[1] The Spanish fleet.
[2] Henry Ratcliffe, Earl of Sussex, Constable of Porchester
Castle, Warden and Captain of the town, castle, and isle of
Portsmouth, joint Lord-Lieutenant of Hampshire.   K.G. in 1589,
and died in 1593.   He was Howard's first-cousin.

so, hoping in my next letters to send your Honour some certain news of good success, I commit your Honour to God. From Portsmouth the 26th of July, 1588.

Your Honour's to his power,

SUSSEX.

Postscript.—I have considered of the proportion of powder and shot which is to come from the Tower, which is but five last of powder; and if I shall take out (as I must of force) so much as I have sent unto my Lord Admiral, there would none be left. Wherefore it were very requisite that there should be more sent hither, or into some place in Sussex where my Lord Admiral is like to come, or might have knowledge of it; for else it will be wanting.

July 25.—*SIR GEORGE CAREY TO SUSSEX.*

[ocxiii. 43.—Vera Copia. Endorsed.]

May it please your Lordship to understand that, finding by yours the copy and direction of the Lords' letters for supplying the Lord Admiral's wants, touching that, I have thus far proceeded. Two days since I sent his Lordship 4 ships and a pinnace sufficiently furnished with mariners and soldiers; from whom I have not yet heard any news; but sending yesterday another pinnace unto him with an hundred men, he returned them unto me this afternoon with great thanks, willing the captain to tell me that he had as many men as he desired or could well use. For your Lordship's news I humbly thank you.

This morning began a great fight betwixt both

fleets, south of this island 6 leagues,[1] which continued from five of the clock until ten, with so great expense of powder and bullet, that during the said time the shot continued so thick together that it might rather have been judged a skirmish with small shot on land than a fight with great shot on sea. In which conflict, thanks be to God, there hath not been two of our men hurt

The news in the fleet are my Lord Harry Seymour is hardly laid unto by the Dunkirkers, and that Scilla[2] is taken by the French or the Spanish.

The fleets keep the direct trade[3] and shot into the sea out of our sight by three of the clock this afternoon ; whereupon we have dissolved our camp wherein we have continued since Monday. And so praying your Lordship to send this enclosed by the post, I humbly commit you to God. From Carisbrooke Castle, this 25th of July, at 8 hours in the night. Your Lordship's to command,

GEORGE CAREY.

July 26.—ROBERT SALMAN[4] *TO BURGHLEY.*

[ccxiii. 41.—Signed.   Addressed.]

Right Honourable, my duty considered :— Whereas I unworthy am chosen for this year to be Master of the Trinity House of Deptford Strond,

---

[1] As the fleets were well in sight at the time, the distance is enormously exaggerated ; but down to the beginning of this century there was no way in use to measure the distance of a ship, and the guesses were often extremely wild.

[2] Silly.

[3] The fairway of the Channel.

[4] Of Leigh, in Essex, where the family had been settled for upwards of two hundred years. A brass plate in Leigh Church records that ' he took to wife Agnes, with whom he lived thirty-

as I am a subject, my duty is to use all the means I can for the preservation of her Majesty and our country; [and]¹ my place doth require me, in my opinion, to be more careful for my duty. If it may please your Honour, as I do understand, my Lord Admiral could be content to have some supply of ships and men at this time. If it be so, your Honour shall hear my poor opinion : that is, there may be within this 4 days near 30 sail of serviceable merchant ships ready to set sail, who are so furnished with ordnance and artillery of their own that some small supply beside will suffice. As for their men, they have 20 men a-piece, which they now brought home with them; I mean those ships that be come from Stade now. If they may have 5 or 6 mariners more a-piece, and 20 soldiers, every ship to² those mariners, they may do very good services, as they are easily to be had now, and very willing too in this needful service.

As for victuals,³ if the victualler³ can provide for them in so small a time, he may be commanded with all expedition to do it for some 14 days or three weeks ; if they shall tarry longer, they may have some more provided to send after them. If he cannot provide for them in so short a time, if it please your Honour to give me authority⁴ and provision,⁵ and to command them that I will take to me, your Honour shall see what haste there shall be made. If there be not beef enough ready, then

---

two years, and had issue by her six sons and four daughters.'
He died September 6, 1591, in his 58th year. One of the sons, Robert, was also Master of the Trinity House from 1617 till his death, June 18, 1641, at which time he was Sheriff of London. His monument is in Leigh Church. Barrett's *The Trinity House of Deptford Strond*, pp. 135-8.

¹ MS. has *it*, apparently a slip of the pen.
² In addition to.   ³ MS. vetals, veteler.
⁴ MS. atoryte.   ⁵ Sc. of money.

they shall have fish and peas, butter or cheese, and let them go. The brewer and baker will provide hastily for some 14 days or more; if it may be within this time done, it will be some good en couragement[1] to my Lord Admiral and those that be in service with him, and a discouragement to the enemy.

And thus I crave your Honour's pardon for my boldness, it wishing well to her Majesty and our country, if I could any ways do any services therein. And here I leave your Honour to the safekeeping of the Almighty. From Tower Hill, this 26th of July, 1588.

Your poor vassal to command,

ROBERT SALMAN, Master.

July 26.—SIR JOHN GILBERTE[2] AND GEORGE CARY, DEPUTY LIEUTENANTS OF DEVON, TO SIR FRANCIS WALSYNGHAM.

[ccxiii. 42.—Signed.   Addressed :—For her Majesty's affairs.]

Our humble duties to your Honour remembered:—Whereas the Roebuck hath brought into Torbay one of the Spanish fleet, Jacob Whiddon being captain of the said Roebuck, and these two gentlemen appointed by Sir Francis Drake for the conducting of the said Spanish ship into some safe harbour, but the present necessity of her Majesty's service so requiring for the speedy dispatch of the said Roebuck again to her Highness' navy, they have requested us to take the care for the safe harbouring of the said ship; which, by God's grace, we will take so good care of as possible we may.

[1] MS. incorydgment.
[2] Brother of Sir Humphrey Gylberte, and half-brother of Sir Walter Ralegh.

And for the better furnishing of her Majesty's navy with munition, we have taken out of the said ship all the shot and powder, and sent the same to her Highness' navy. There is also taken out of the said ship one piece of ordnance for the better furnishing of a ship to join with the navy, wherewith we hope your Honour and the rest of my Lords will not dislike. We have also sent to the seas all the shipping and mariners in all our county, to be employed as my Lord High Admiral shall appoint. And touching the ordnance and the residue of the goods that do remain in the said ship, there shall be a true and perfect inventory made, and the goods laid in safety as soon as the same shall be brought into Dartmouth, which we will forthwith do our best endeavours to perform ; and so acquaint your Honour and the rest of my Lords with the particularities thereof. And so in haste we humbly [take] [1] our leave. From Torbay this 26th of July, 1588.

Your Honour's to command,

JOHN GILBERTE. GEORGE CARY.

July 26.—WALSYNGHAM TO BURGHLEY (?).

[Otho E. ix. f. 214 *b.*—Holograph. A fragment, damaged by fire.]

I find by a letter written from my Lord Admiral unto her Majesty that, for lack of powder and shot, he shall be forced to forbear to assail and to stand upon his guard until he shall be furnished from hence. There is 23 last of powder sent unto him with a proportion of bullet accordingly.

I hope there will be an 100 sail of Hollanders and Zealanders at the least to assist the Lord Admira' within these three days.

[1] Omitted in MS.

There are letters sent to the Lord Wyllughby, and in his absence to Sir William Russell, to send over 1000 of their best shot for the furnishment of the ships. [This,] in haste, I most humbly take my leave. The 26th of July, 1588.

Your Lordship's to command,

FRA. WALSYNGIIAM.

July 27.—SIR JOHN GILBERTE AND GEORGE CARY TO THE COUNCIL.

[ocxiii. **43.**—Signed.   Addressed :—For her Majesty's affairs.]

Our humble duties to your good Lordships :— Whereas there is one of the Spanish fleet brought into Torbay (as your Honours have been heretofore advertised of), in which ship there is almost four hundred soldiers and mariners, all which for divers respects we have taken out of the ship and brought them under safe guard unto the shore, some 20 or 30 mariners only excepted, which we have left in the said ship to be the better help to bring the said ship into safe harbour,[1] being at this present, through the occasion of her Majesty's service, great want of mariners of our own country.

If it may so stand with your Lordships' pleasure, we desire to know your resolutions, what shall become of these people, our vowed enemies. The charge of keeping of them is great, the peril greater, and the discontentment [of][2] our country greatest of all, that a nation so much disliking unto them should remain amongst them. To her Majesty's commandment and your Honours' direction we refer this action, and likewise ourselves. Eftsoons praying your Lordships' resolved determinations, we are thus

[1] MS harborowe.   [2] Omitted in MS.

bold, under your Lordships' correction, to give them their maintenance, touching [1] their sustenance of such provision as remaineth in the said ship.

There is one thing more that giveth us occasion to desire your Lordships' direction, for that the French King (as your Honours well know) being entered into the Holy League (as they term it) and vowed the extirpation of all others which are of the contrary, there are yet [2] divers French boats and vessels, that under pretence of transporting of passengers and other things, come into our ports and creeks. We greatly suspect and are much afraid lest their coming be rather to give intelligence, and understand her Majesty's proceedings in these perilous times ; and therefore do humbly pray your Lordships' directions herein, where [3] we shall stay them, or otherwise give them leave in peaceable manner to depart. And so very humbly take our leave from further troubling your Lordships. From Torbay this 27th of July, 1588.

Your Lordships' to be commanded,
JOHN GILBERTE.   GEORGE CARY.

Mr. Carew Ralegh [4] hath requested us to move your good Lordships that it would please you to give him warrant for some six pieces of ordnance which are in this Spanish ship to be placed in her Majesty's fort or castle of Portland, for the better strength thereof ; for that your Honours (as he saith) hath been heretofore informed of the want of artillery which is to be required for the defence of the said castle.

[1] Taking.   [2] MS. yeat.
[3] Whether.   [4] Elder brother of Sir Walter Ralegh.

[ccxiii. 50.—Signed. Addressed.]

May it please your Lordships :—I have received three letters in a packet of the 25th of this month, and with the same a single letter of the same date from Mr. Secretary, wherein is signified that by reason of advertisement that came after the making up of the packet from the Lord Admiral, her Majesty's pleasure was, notwithstanding all former directions from your Lordships, I should bend myself to stop the issuing of the forces of the Duke of Parma from Dunkirk. How easily [1] the lying of our ships against Gravelines, much more Dunkirk, I can say no more than I have many times written. But seeing it is her Majesty's pleasure we will endeavour to perform it as near as wind and weather will give us leave.

Our victualling doth end the last of this month ; and for that your Lordships, by your writing, do reckon the galley to be in the Thames mouth for the guarding of the river, I have therefore taken order for Mr. Borough in the galley for the Thames, and [this] [2] was the only cause of the saving her and all the men's lives the last great storm.

I have besides to signify unto your Lordships that our fleet being from the first promised to be 78 sail, there was never yet, when the same was most, 36 ; and now we have not above 20 ; and of them, of her Majesty's shipping, as I have always written, but 8 sails besides pinnaces ; and for the

---

[1] So in MS., meaning, in fact, uneasily, or difficult. The following sentence shows this as well as the postscript, and Sir W. Wynter's letter of the same date.

[2] Omitted in MS.

coast men, I think[1] more than the hoys of Ipswich, the ships of Dover and Sandwich, the ships of Yarmouth and Lynn ; few also of the coast that were set down for service,[2] little available. So giving your Lordships to understand that the Hollanders are not with us, and that I think they desire more to regard more their own coast than ours, do humbly take my leave. From aboard the Rainbow, the 27th of July, 1588, at anchor in the Downs.

I have also seen by experience, which I have likewise advertised, that our merchants' ships are not able to abide that stress upon these coasts which her Majesty's are able to endure, which is to be considered of.

Your Lordships' humble to command,

H. SEYMOUR.

So long as the wind holdeth West-South-West, your Lordships may not look to have us on the other coasts, neither can the enemy come out.

To make it more plain to your Lordships :—

Whensoever we ride upon the other coasts, if the wind come without the land our merchants' ships are enforced to forsake us, as not able to ride ; so that our trust for this service is only upon her Majesty's ships, in number 8, besides pinnaces, which are not able to ride it out. I am driven to write this much, because, in my former letters,[3] your Lordships, having many matters, do forget them.

---

[1] There seems to be a ' no ' omitted.
[2] ' And those ' is perhaps omitted.
[3] Sc. though I have written it before, in my former letters.

July 27.—WYNTER TO WALSYNGHAM.

[ccxiii. 49.—Signed.   Addressed.]

Your Honour's letter of the 25th of this present I received this last night at 12 of the clock, being then within 4 miles of Calais, and according to your Honour's commandment I have dealt with Mr. Borough, who is most ready to obey your Honour's commandment, and will, I dare undertake, most faithfully perform it. The long staying to the westwards of the King of Spain's army, which might have been here 4 days past if they had been disposed to have come so low, doth confirm the opinion which I have held that their intention is to surprise Portsmouth and to possess the Isle of Wight ; for if that were had, in my poor conceit [1] it were the only degree [2] to bring to pass their desires. And truly, I have ever loved and honoured my Lord Admiral ; but now, in respect of the wise and honourable carriage of himself in preventing of the army, that they gain not that place which, I do assure myself, is the only thing that they hunger for, doth double my service towards him ; and under your Honour's correction, speaking as to my honourable good friend, I do not think it wisdom nor discretion for my Lord with his army to put it to a journey, [3] for that were the hazarding of all.   Sir, these huge ships that are in the Spanish army shall have but a bad place to rest in, if they come so low as to the eastward of Portsmouth.

And now, Sir, you must look to the Thames mouth, which you may easily do by placing of shipping at the Nore-head ; which will serve two

[1] MS. concayht.   [2] Step.
[3] MS. jornaye : a day's fight, a pitched battle (*Fr. journée*).

turns, both touching Sheppey, and also the Thames.
For those, how many so ever*they be, you may
victual and furnish them daily and hourly; and
then if we, serving here, may be remembered in
time with victuals and things needful (which hath
been sent for), I doubt not but her Highness
shall lie quietly at Greenwich in despite of any he
whatsoever.

I humbly pray you that ye will so consider of
your commandment there, as you do not danger us
here. I mean, for riding afore Dunkirk. For if we
should ride where you would have us, and as my
Lord Admiral advises, I dare assure your Honour it
is ten to one that we shall be put to Flushing or at the
least to Yarmouth, as divers of us were of late ; and
of some of them no news is heard as yet. And if
we should be so put from thence, then we shall leave
the gap open to our enemy. What danger and
hurts our fleet incurred and sustained in the last
storm which did put us from the other coast, I do
think is not made known to your Honour and the
rest of my Lords. I know there hath been such as
hath promised and took upon him to make warrants
to your Honour and the rest of my Lords, that he
would ride thwart of Dunkirk all weathers, to avoid,
to impeach, and let [1] all passengers in and out ; but I
assure your Honours, his judgment and skill for that
matter is neither grounded upon skill or reason, as I
will be ready to prove it at all times.

I humbly beseech [2] your Honour to let me know
whether your Honour did send away my letter to my
Lord Admiral which I wrote of late to his Lordship,
and sent the same open to your Honour to peruse
by my servant Roger. Thus in haste I most humbly
take my leave, praying God to preserve your Lordship. Written in the seas midway between Folke-

[1] Hinder. [2] MS. beseek.

stone and Boulogne, the 27th of July at 6 of the clock in the [evening],[1] *anno* 1588.

Your Honour's most faithful to command,

W. WYNTER.

The best store of victuals that I and Sir Henry Palmer have at this time is your Honour's venison, for the which we humbly thank you.

July 27.—THE COUNCIL TO GEORGE TREN-CHARD AND FRANCIS HAWLEY.

[ccxiii. 47.—Copy. Endorsed.]

After our hearty commendations :—Whereas we are informed that the Spanish ship lately taken and brought into Portland hath good store of powder, bullets, and other munition and furniture, fit to be employed in her Majesty's service, we have thought good to require you, calling unto you for your as-sistance, Francis Hawley, esquire, Vice-Admiral of those parts, to take a diligent view and perfect inventory of all such powder, bullets, and other things of worth that shall be found in the said ship, and carefully to be kept until you receive our further direction ; but for the powder, you may not fail, with all the speed possible, to convey the same to Dover on some little bark fit for that purpose. And touch-ing the doubts delivered unto us by Captain Wye, we have sent our answer thereunto by way of apos-tilles [2] to your several demands. And so we bid you heartily farewell. From the Court at Richmond the 27th of July, 1588. Your loving friends,

CHR. HATTON, Canc.   W. BURGHLEY.
FRA. WALSYNGHAM.   A. POULET.
J. WOLLEY.

---

[1] Torn off.   [2] Marginal notes.

July 28.—*THE COUNCIL TO SEYMOUR.*

[ccxiii. 53.—Rough draft.[1]   Endorsed.]

After our hearty commendations unto your Lordship:—Where[2] you were directed by letters written by me, the Secretary, in her Majesty's name upon an advice given unto her Majesty by the Lord Admiral that you should presently repair and lie before the town of Dunkirk:—Forasmuch as her Majesty seeth how greatly it importeth her service to have somewhat done to distress the Spanish navy before they shall join with the Duke of Parma's forces by sea, her pleasure is that you should join with the Lord Admiral to do your best endeavour, being joined together, to distress the said army, to be executed in such sort as upon conference between our very good Lord the Lord Admiral and you shall be agreed on. And further her Majesty's pleasure is that we should signify unto you that there is order given for the supply of your wants of powder, men, and munition, which shall be so sufficiently performed as you shall find no lack that way. And so we bid your Lordship heartily farewell. At the Court the 28th of July, 1588.

Your Lordship's loving friends.

And further her Majesty hath especially commanded us to signify unto your Lordship that she nothing doubteth, with the assistance of Almighty God, that when both your forces shall be joined together but that he will bless you with a most happy and glorious victoty, so as it be attempted before

[1] A difficult scrawl, full of erasures and corrections, (?) in Walsyngham's hand.
[2] Whereas.

the Spanish navy shall join with the Duke of Parma,
and that upon conference between the Lord Admiral
and you, you shall see no just cause to stay or delay
the fight.

July 28.—BOROUGH TO WALSYNGHAM.

[ccxiii. 57.—Signed.   Addressed :—For her Majesty's service.
Much stained and partially obliterated by damp.]

Right Honourable :—The Lord Henry [Seymour
hath] appointed me [yesterday] in the forenoon to
come with the galley to the mouth of Thames, for
guarding the river; and his Lordship told me it
was meant that certain ships should come speedily
from London furnished in warlike manner for like
purpose, whereof I should have the charge.

That day in the afternoon, as I purposed to have
come from the Downs hitherwards, news was brought
that the two armies were between Folkestone and
Boulogne near the other coast; whereupon with the
ebb, the wind South-West, the Lord Harry with
all his fleet plied to windwards, and before night for
as high up as Scales Cliffs,[1] where I suppose they had
sight of the fleets.   I followed with the galley; but
ere I came half seas over, the wind forced me back
into the Downs, where I remained all night; and
this morning, being little wind, I plied over towards
Calais, in hope to have done some service if it had
proved calm.   When I was three parts of the seas
over, I perceived the English fleet at anchor against
Scales Cliffs,[1] and the Spanish at anchor between
them and Calais.   I could not fetch our [fleet] by
[cause] of the leeward tide of flood, and therefore

[1] MS. Skaels Cleefes : so called from the village of Escalles.
Now Calais Cliffs.

anchored ; but the wind at South-South-West increased so as we could not ride; whereupon I weighed anchor, set sail and came room without the Goodwin Sand, to the North Foreland, and so longst up hither, where I anchored at 10 of the clock at night.

The pinnace that lately carried the Council's letters to Flushing returned back this day, and is gone to my Lord Harry with letters of answer to his. The master of her told me that the Lord Governor of Flushing willed him to tell my Lord Harry that there should be 30 or 40 sail of good ships sent to him from thence very shortly. The said master supposed they would be ready this day or to-morrow ; but there was not one of their vessels abroad at sea. He told me further that he heard the mariners there use speeches that they would have their pay ere they went to the seas ; but I hope they will not stick upon it now.

If it shall be thought good to appoint me to farther charge, to command any of the ships that shall guard the river, what shall be directed me therein [I will] observe and perform dutifully, with God's help, whilst life lasteth. I do send herewith a rough plot of this river's mouth, with the channels and shoals in it, to the end I may be appointed in the same plot where the ships should remain. The channels for shipping to come into this river, I have signified in the same with the red lines,[1] by which your Honour may perceive how they concur at the east end of the Nore. And therefore I think it were good they should be placed on each side of the ⊙ where I now ride with the galley. Bylanders[2] and small hoys and boats may come in at half flood, as I have drawn the double lines with black lead.[3]

[1] Here shown by dotted lines.
[2] MS. binlanders ; cf. *ante*, p. 2 *n.*
[3] The double lines drawn east from the position at the Nore.

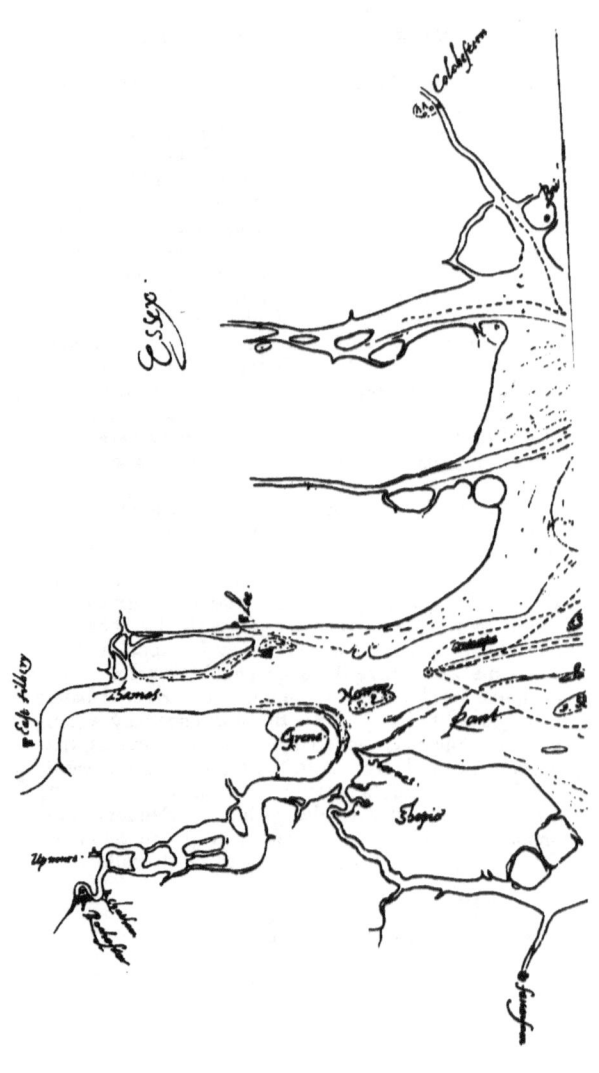

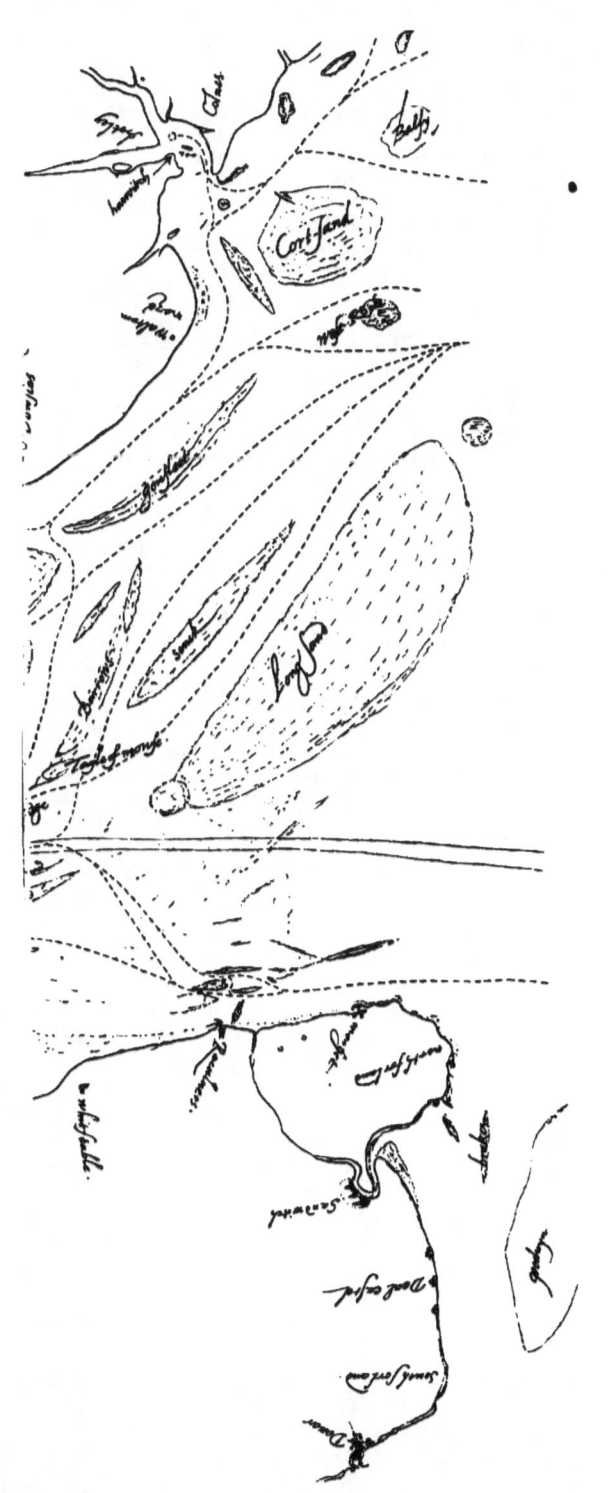

I send my servant of purpose herewith, to return
me your Honour's pleasure where I shall attend,
and in what order; and so with my duty to your
Honour humbly acknowledged, commit you to the
Almighty. From aboard the galley, in the Thames
mouth, by east the Nore-head, this Sunday, the 28th
of July, 1588, at 11 of the clock at night.

Your Honour's humbly at command
and most ready always,
W. Borough.

July 29.—GILBERTE TO THE COUNCIL.

[ccxiii. 59.—Signed. Addressed.]

My duty unto your Honour most humbly remembered :—I have received your Honour's letters
of the 26th of July, for the sending away of 300 or 400
barrels of powder to the Earl[1] of Sussex out of the
Spanish ship taken by her Majesty's fleet, all which
powder and shot that could be found in her was sent
away to my Lord Admiral, for that his Lordship sent
to Weymouth this direction for powder and shot, and
also sent a pinnace from the fleet of purpose for the
powder and shot that was in the ship, which was but
88 barrels of powder and 1,600 shot that I could by
any means learn of after I came to her ; and if I find
any in unloading of the ship, I will with all speed
send it to the Earl of Sussex, according to your
Honour's directions, and will have special care for
the putting in safety of the ordnance, and other
munitions and goods in the ship whatsoever. Having no farther to trouble your Honour withal at this
present, most humbly I take my leave. From
Greenway, this 29th of July, 1588.

Your Honour's most humbly to command,
John Gilberte.

[1] MS. Earell.

July 29—*ARMAMENT OF THE LONDON SHIPS.*

[ccxiii. 63.—Endorsed :—29th of July, 1588. The number of men, ordnance and powder in the ten ships of the Merchants Adventurers. They are victualled for twenty days from the last of July.]

Ten ships, to be set out by the Adventurers for her Majesty's service, are to be furnished, as under followeth :—

Tons	Men		Demi-culverin	Sakers	Minions	Falcons	Fowlers	Round shot	Cross bar, langrell, and cloven	Culivers	Muskets	Powder: Barrels: every barrel containing 100 lbs.
								For every piece				
100	50	The Pansy of London. William Butler, Master		2	5	3	4	20	40	12	8	9
110	55	The Dolphin of Leigh William Hare,[1] Master		0	9	2	4	20	40	14	8	10
110	55	The Salamander of Leigh William Goodlad,[2] Master		2	6	4	4	20	40	14	8	10
120	60	The George Noble of London Richard Harper, Master		2	8	4	4	20	50	14	10	11
120	60	The Antelope of London Abraham Bonner,[2] Master		1	7	5	2	20	50	14	10	10
110	55	The Jewel of Leigh . Henry Rawlyn, Master		2	7	4	4	20	40	14	8	10
100	50	The Anthony of London Richard Dove,[3] Master		1	7	4	2	20	40	12	8	9
120	60	The Toby of London . Robert Cuttle, Master	1[4]	1	9	2	3	20	50	14	10	11
100	50	The Rose Lion of Leigh Robert Duke, Master		2	6	2	4	20	40	12	8	9
120	60	The Prudence of Leigh Richard Chester,[2] Master		2	6	4	4	20	50	14	10	11
	555											100

[1] The MS. here has 100*, that is 100 cwt. or 5 tons: obviously a clerical error.

[2] All of Leigh. William Goodlad, presumably the son of the Master of the Salamander, was Master of the Trinity House in 1638, and died in 1639, aged 62. The family of Bonner was connected by marriage with that of Robert Salman, the Master of the Trinity House in 1588. Richard Chester's tombstone in the church of Leigh records that he was Master of the Trinity House in 1615 : that he lived in marriage with Elizabeth his wife about 49 years, by whom he had issue four sons and a daughter ; and that he died April 6, 1632 (Barrett, *The Trinity House of Deptford Strond*, pp. 135-37, 140-41).

[3] A shipowner of London in 1597 (*ib.* 140).

[4] The Toby's demi-culverin is written in later, by the same hand, but in different ink. Whether it had the same allowance of shot as the other guns does not appear.

Z 2

Besides this furniture, these ships are to have pikes, bills and swords sufficient, with convenient fireworks. As part of the great ordnance is impressed by warrant, so doth there want to furnish this proportion of small shot, 100 muskets, whereof it is humbly prayed they may be furnished out of her Majesty's store. It is purposed, if it may be, that all the men for these ships shall be mariners. But because thereof is no appearance, it is humbly prayed that Mr. Captain Bellingham may have warrant to furnish the want by press.

July 29.—HOWARD TO WALSYNGHAM.

[ccxiii. 64.—Signed ; first postscript, autograph ; the second postscript, on a separate scrap of paper, is in the same writing as the letter. Addressed.]

Sir :—I have received your letter wherein you desire a proportion of shot and powder to be set down by me and sent unto you ; which, by reason of the uncertainty of the service, no man can do ; therefore I pray you to send with all speed as much as you can. And because some of our ships are victualled but for a very short time, and my Lord Henry Seymour with his company not for one day, in like[1] to pray you to dispatch away our victuals with all possible speed, because we know not whether we shall be driven to pursue the Spanish fleet.

This morning we drove a galleass ashore before Calais, whither I sent my long boat to board her, where divers of my men were slain, and my lieutenant[2] sore hurt in the taking of her. Ever since we have chased them in fight until this evening late,

---

[1] I have also, or in like manner, to pray you.
[2] Amyas Preston.

and distressed them much ; but their fleet consisteth
of mighty ships and great strength ; yet we doubt
not, by God's good assistance, to oppress them ;
and so I bid you heartily farewell. From aboard
her Majesty's good ship the Ark, the 29th of July,
1588.

Your very loving friend,

C. HOWARD.

Sir :—I will not write unto her Majesty before
more be done. Their force is wonderful great and
strong ; and yet we pluck their feathers by little and
little. I pray to God that the forces on the land be
strong enough to answer so present a force. There
is not one Flushinger nor Hollander at the seas.

Sir, I have taken the chief galleass this day before
Calais, with the loss of divers of my men ; but Monsieur Gourdan doth detain her, as I hear say. I
could not send unto him, because I was in fight ;
therefore I pray you to write unto him, either to deliver her, or at leastwise to promise upon his honour
that he will not yield her up again unto the enemy.

July 29.—DRAKE TO WALSYNGHAM.

[ccxiii. 65.—Holograph. Addressed.]

Right Honourable :—This bearer came aboard
the ship I was in in a wonderful good time, and
brought with him as good knowledge as we could
wish. His carefulness therein is worthy recompense, for that God hath given us so good a day in
forcing the enemy so far to leeward as I hope in
God the Prince of Parma and the Duke of Sidonia
shall not shake hands this few days ; and whensoever they shall meet, I believe neither of them

will greatly rejoice of this day's service. The town
of Calais hath seen some part thereof, whose Mayor
her Majesty is beholden unto.   Business commands
me to end.   God bless her Majesty, our gracious
Sovereign, and give us all grace to live in his fear.
I assure your Honour this day's service hath much
appalled the enemy, and no doubt but[1] encouraged
our army.   From aboard her Majesty's good ship
the Revenge, this 29th of July, 1588.
    Your Honour's most ready to be commanded,

FRA. DRAKE.

There must be great care taken to send us
munition and victual whithersoever the enemy goeth.

Yours,
FRA. DRAKE.

July 30.—*ROBERT CECILL TO LORD BURGHLEY.*

[ccxiii. 66.—Holograph.   Addressed.]

My duty remembered to your Lordship :—
Although this bearer's letter to Mr. Secretary will
thoroughly advertise your Lordship, yet with remembrance of my duty, I thought good to acquaint
you with that which I have heard of a Spanish
gentleman taken yesterday in one of the galleasses,
which was run ashore at Calais, and there is seized
by Monsr. Gourdan.   The captain of this ship,
named Moncada, one of the greatest personages in
the fleet, was killed with a small shot of a musket
that pierced both his eyes.   The second of account
in that ship is taken and kept in one of the ships in
her Majesty's fleet.   This man that is here is a
proper gentleman of Salamanca, who affirmeth that

[1] It hath.

there is great lack imputed to the Duke of Parma,
in that he hath not joined with this fleet which hath
lingered about Calais and Gravelines of purpose for
him, and would not have stirred from those roads, if
the device of the fireworks on Sunday had not
forced them to slip their anchors and so make head
away, in which instant my Lord Admiral gave them
that fight which we saw upon the land yesterday ;
where, as terrible as it was in appearance, there was
few men hurt with any shot, nor any one vessel
sunk. For, as this man reporteth, they shoot very
far off ; and for boarding, our men have not any
reason.

It is to be thought that Monsr. Gourdan will
hardly part with this ship to her Majesty's use ; and
if he do not relieve her, and send them her again,
yet it is the less harm. He sent, they say, a kind
message to my Lord Admiral concerning it, which
I am sure your Lordship is advertised of.

The opinion of this gentleman is that from
Scotland they shall have aid ; and for their own
parts, he told me, they would think it sufficient if
they could but draw away our fleet to the northward, thereby hoping *tenere il mare netto*, whereby,
without impeachment, the Duke of Parma's men
might land here ; who, as he understandeth, is not
in readiness ; for his soldiers are yet unshipped, and
as it is thought the Zealanders lie in the mouth of
the haven to impeach their putting forth.

The powder your Lordship sent hither yesterday is gone now to our fleet in the Roebuck, which
Sir W. Ralegh built, which is a fine ship and well
furnished. Of my Lord of Derby I can hear
nothing ; wherefore I have determined to leave
order here to be advertised immediately upon his
arrival, that I may meet his Lordship from London
upon the way, where I think to be to-morrow or

next day, if the wind turn not to bring the ships upon this coast again. From Dover this 30th of July, 1588, at 12 of clock. I most humbly take my leave of your Lordship. In haste,

Your most obedient son,

ROBT. CECILL.

July 30.—*RICHARD TOMSON*[1] *TO WAL-SYNGHAM.*

[ccxiii. 67.—Holograph.]

Since our first meeting of our enemies, which was on Sunday the 21st of this present, we have had four encounters such as, the Lord be praised, hath not a little daunted the minds of our enemies, but much impaired their great and unexpected forces, and to very little or no detriment of our English navy. At our first meeting of them, which was within two miles of Looe in Cornwall, they were 136 sail of ships and pinnaces, whereof 90 were very great ships, and the rest of smaller account ; and at that time our English navy was not above 67 sail. By God's goodness and the good working of our commanders, we got the wind of

---

[1] Lieutenant of the Margaret and John of London ; not improbably a brother of Lawrence Tomson, Walsyngham's servant or secretary. He had been for some years engaged in the Mediterranean trade, which, in 1582 and following years, had brought him into litigation with the Turkey Company. In 1583 he had made a voyage to Algiers to ransom captives. In September 1588 he was employed in arranging the ransom of the Spanish prisoners. At the end of the century he was living in London, writing occasional letters to Sir Robert Cecyll, then Secretary of State. He appears to have been a man of some education, conversant with French and Spanish, and may possibly have been a son of that Robert Tomson of Andover and Seville mentioned in the Introduction, though other indications seem to connect him with Norfolk.

them, which is a very great advantage and a special
safety for the weaker part ; and ever since, God
hath so blessed us that we have kept the same, to
the great annoyance of our enemies ; and by that
means, we have so daily pursued them at the heels,
that they never had leisure to stop in any place
alongst our English coast, until they came within
two miles of Calais, where in the evening, very
politicly, they came all upon a sudden to an anchor,
being Saturday the 27th day, purposing that our
ships with the flood should be driven to leeward of
them ; but in happy time it was soon espied, and
prevented by bringing our fleet to an anchor also in
the wind of them.

The same night sent [1] ashore to Calais and forthwith to the Duke of Parma, advertising of their
being there ; and one received answer that he with
his forces would be in readiness upon Tuesday
following, and come and join with them, with intent
to come over and land their forces in England,
about Margate [2] in Kent, as since I have thoroughly
learned of the Spaniards that were taken in the
chief galleass that the King had, hard under the
jetty head at Calais. It hath appeared by many
arguments that they Spaniards were not evil welcome to Monsieur Gourdan and the rest of his government, by permitting their messengers to go so
speedily between the Duke and that place, as also
by suffering the boats to go to and from the shore
so usually, all Sunday the 28th of July, as they did ;
and most of all, by sending his kinsman and lieutenant aboard the Duke of Medina with a great
present ; whereof no semblance was made at all
unto our Lord Admiral.

It pleased my Lord Admiral to appoint certain
small ships to be fired on Sunday about 12 of the

---

[1] They sent.   [2] MS. Margarett.

clock at night, and let drive with the flood amongst
the Spaniards; which practice, God be thanked,
hath since turned to our great good; for it caused
they Spaniards to let slip their anchors and cables,
and confusedly to drive one upon another; whereby
they were not only put from their roadstead and
place where they meant to attend the coming of the
Duke of Parma, but did much hurt one to another
of themselves; and[1] now by the earnest pursuit of
our Englishmen, very much weakened and dispersed,
the Lord be praised; so that of the 124 sail that
they were in Calais Road, we cannot now find by
any account above 86 ships and pinnaces; so that I
cannot conjecture but by the furious assault that my
Lord and his associates gave them early on Monday
morning, and did continue in vehement manner 8
hours, hath laid[2] many of them in the bottom of the
sea, or else run with the coast of Flanders to save
their lives, though unpossible to save their great
ships, by reason of their evil harbours.

At the break of day upon Monday morning, my
Lord and all the fleet setting sail after our enemies,
we espied riding within shot of the town of Calais
the greatest of the King's galleasses, the rest of the
Spanish fleet being two leagues to leeward of her.
My Lord Admiral began to go toward the galleass
with his ship, the Ark, but finding the water to be
shallow, other ships of less draught bare in with her
and shot at her; whereupon she let slip and run the
galleass aground hard before the town.

In our ship, which was the Margaret and John
of London, we approached so near that we came on
ground also; but afterwards came safely off again
with the flood, being damaged by nothing but by
the town of Calais, who, off the bulwarks, shot very

[1] Are.
[2] Sc. Many of them have been laid . . . or else forced to run.

much at us, and shot our ship twice through. And
the like powder and shot did Monsieur Gourdan
bestow upon sundry of our countrymen, and make
us relinquish the galleass, which otherwise we had
brought away, being masters of her above two hours,
and gotten by hard assault, to the great credit of
our country, if Monsieur Gourdan herein had not
showed his affection to the Spaniards to be greater
than our nation, or seemed by force to wrest from
us that which we had gotten with bloody heads.

My Lord Admiral, seeing he could not approach
the galleass with his ship, sent off his long boat unto
her with 50 or 60 men, amongst whom were many
gentlemen as valiant in courage as gentle in birth,
as they well showed. The like did our ship send
off her pinnace, with certain musketeers, amongst
whom myself went. These two boats came hard
under the galleass sides, being aground; where
we continued a pretty skirmish with our small shot
against theirs, they being ensconced within their ship
and very high over us, we in our open pinnaces and
far under them, having nothing to shroud and cover
us; they being 300 soldiers, besides 450 slaves, and
we not, at the instant, 100 persons. Within one half
hour it pleased God, by killing the captain with a
musket shot, to give us victory above all hope or
expectation; for the soldiers leaped overboard by
heaps on the other side, and fled with the shore,
swimming and wading. Some escaped with being
wet; some, and that very many, were drowned.
The captain of her was called Don Hugo de
Moncada,[1] son to the viceroy of Valencia. He
being slain, and the most part of their soldiers fled,
some few soldiers remaining in her, seeing our
English boats under her sides and more of ours
coming rowing towards her, some with 10 and some

[1] MS. Moncalla.

with 8 men in them, for all the smallest shipping were
the nearest the shore, put up two handkerchiefs [1]
upon two rapiers, signifying that they desired truce.
Hereupon we entered, with much difficulty, by
reason of her height over us, and possessed us of
her, by the space of an hour and half as I judge ;
each man seeking his benefit of pillage until the
flood came, that we might haul her off the ground
and bring her away.

It may please your Honour to understand that
during our fight to get her, the men of Calais stood
in multitudes upon the shore hard by us and
beholding all things, showing themselves at that
instant indifferent lookers-on ; but so soon as they
saw us possessed of so princely a vessel, the very
glory and stay of the Spanish army, a thing of very
great value and strength, as was well known to them
of Calais, for that they had been on board twice or
thrice the day before ; I say, Monsieur Gourdan,
seeing us thus [2] possessed, sent aboard to us that
were in her, in which boat came his kinsman and
another captain, desiring to parle [3] with us. None
being then in place that either understood or spake
French but myself, I asked them from whom they
came. They [4] answered, from Monsieur Gourdan,
the Governor of Calais. I demanded to know what
his pleasure was. They answered that he had stood
and beheld our fight and rejoiced of our victory,
saying that for our prowess and manhood showed
therein we had well deserved the spoil and pillage
of the galleass, as a thing due unto us by desert ;
and that he willingly consented that we should have
the pillage of her ; further requiring and commanding us not to offer to carry away either the ship or
ordnance, for that she was on ground under the

---

[1] MS. handkerchers.   [2] MS. this.
[3] Speak, confer.   [4] MS. the.

commandment of his castles and town, and therefore did of right appertain unto him. I answered
unto them that, for our parts, we thanked Monsieur
Gourdan for granting the pillage to the mariners
and soldiers that had fought for the same ; ac-
knowledging that without his leave and good will
we could not carry away anything of that we had
gotten, considering it lay on ground hard under his
bulwarks ; and that as concerning the ship and
ordnance, we prayed it would please him to send a
pinnace aboard my Lord Admiral, who was here in
person hard by, from whom he should have an honourable and friendly answer which we all are to obey
and give place unto. With this answer, to my
seeming they departed well satisfied ; but since I
have understood that some of our rude men, who
make no account of friend or foe, fell to spoiling the
Frenchmen, taking away their rings and jewels as
from enemies ; whereupon[1] going ashore and com-
plaining, all the bulwarks and ports were bent
against us, and shot so vehemently that we received
sundry shot very dangerously through us. If this
have not incensed Monsieur Gourdan, I suppose that
he will easily, upon request made, either surrender
all or the better part of all things unto her Majesty ;
for the ship cannot be so little worth, with her
ordnance, as eighty thousand crowns ; having in her
four whole cannons, 8 demi-cannons, 12 culverins
and demi-culverins, 16 sakers and minions, all of
brass, 200 barrels of powder, and of all other things
great provision and plenty ; but very little or no
treasure that I can learn to be in her.

This is the substance and very truth of all that
passed in this action. Being thus departed from
the galleasses, my Lord with all the fleet pursued
the enemy, with all violent pursuit that our ordnance

---

[1] The Frenchmen.

and small shot could yield; little to our hurt, the
Lord be praised, but greatly to the detriment of the
enemy, as the bearer hereof, Mr. John Watts[1] of
London, can amply inform your Honour; for he was
present at the doing of most of these things happened
within these two days, not without danger enough
of his person both of cannon and musket shot,
whereof his apparel beareth some tokens, although
it pleased God to spare his life. At this instant we
are as far to the eastward as the Isle of Walcheren,
wherein Flushing doth stand, and about 12 leagues
off the shore; and the wind hanging westerly, we
drive our enemies apace to the eastward, much
marvelling, if the wind continue, in what port they
will direct themselves. Some imagine the river of
Hamburg, which is a bad place for the receipt of ships
of such charge; others suppose, because they have
yet provision of victuals for three months, they will
about Scotland, and so for Spain. I trust her Majesty may, by God's help, little fear any invasion by
these ships; their power being, by battle, mortality,
and other accidents, so decayed, and those that are
left alive so weak and hurtless, that they could be
well content to lose all charges to be at home, both
rich and poor. There is want of powder, shot and
victual, amongst us, which causeth that we cannot
so daily assault them as we would. God grant the
want may in time be supplied that so necessary a
service be not neglected thereby. Thus I take my
humble leave of your Honour, to whom Almighty
God send all continuance of health and increase of
happiness.   Subscribed,   RICHARD TOMSON.

---

[1] A merchant who, in connection with his partner, John Byrd,
is repeatedly mentioned in the State Papers as exporting wheat,
trading with Spain, sending intelligence, and, in 1590, capturing two
Spanish ships. He seems (Lediard's *Naval History*, 277) to have
been the owner of the Margaret and John.

•

July 31.—*KYLLYGREW TO WALSYNGHAM.*

[**Holland, lv.**—Signed, and autograph postscript. Addressed.]

It may please your Honour :—I could not let
your Honour's own servant pass without some
few lines, having at this present no great matter
to write.

My Lord Governor of Flushing sent me of late
a letter from my Lords of the Council unto him for
the soliciting of the States of Holland to furnish out
what shipping they could withal spare ; wherein, as
his Lordship hath moved them there, so here I
have also done the like ; and I understand the
Admiral Justinus is gone out already with thirty
sail from Flushing, besides some other which are
presently to follow from those parts and North
Holland, so as I doubt not her Majesty's ñeet will
be strong enough, especially the merchants being
now returned from Stade and St. Nicholas,[1] as we
understand. But, as I have signified unto your
Honour heretofore, for any great assistance to be
had from hence, it is not to be looked for at their
hands. Their troubles and mutinies here have
brought them so low, especially this last of Gertruidenberg, which hath cost them 215,000 fl., for
the supplying whereof they have been fain to
stretch their credits to the uttermost. So having
moved them (according to your Honour's instructions sent unto me by Burnham) for the raising of
some extraordinary contributions, I find no means
to effectuate the same, considering as they say their
extraordinary charges this year arise, through their
preparations at sea, to a greater sum than many
years heretofore, and that especially her Majesty's

[1] In the White Sea.

letter to them of Gertruidenberg was very accept-
able to these men, as assuring them of her Highness'
honourable meaning towards them ; but coming now,
as it did, too late, they think it not convenient to
deliver it.

For your Honour's letter to my Lord General[1]
touching the articles[2] of peace, it was also very good
news unto them, and my Lord hath dealt for the
publishing thereof : but for the finding out of the
authors of such malicious slanders, they have no
other means than to learn of the Count William[3]
(who sent the same out of Friesland to the Count
Maurice) and of my Lord Governor of Flushing
(from whom also I received a like copy) from
whence they came into their hands. To the Count
William, the Council of State will write to that
effect ; and to my Lord Governor of Flushing, I
have done the like. They are in hand to dispatch
away Sir Martin Schenk[4] towards Bergen with
some horse and foot for the relief thereof, and to
furnish him with a bond of 30,000 fl. upon their
credit, to be paid after the enterprise is achieved.
Some of our horsemen lying thereabout in the
garrisons adjoining are to be drawn out to this
service.

The controversies of Utrecht are not yet ended,

---

[1] Lord Wyllughby.

[2] Certain articles, alleged to be the basis of the negotiations
for the treaty, had been published. They excited great indignation in Holland and Zealand, and were now vehemently denied
on the part of the Queen.

[3] Stadholder of Friesland, and brother-in-law of Maurice.

[4] A distinguished soldier of fortune, born in 1549, who after
serving with the Spaniards for several years, changed sides in
1585, in a pique with the Duke of Parma. He was knighted by
Leicester in 1586, and after many valiant deeds was drowned by
the sinking of his boat in 1589. A lively, but perhaps highly
coloured, picture of the man and his exploits is given by Motley
in the second volume of his *History of the United Netherlands.*

and rather grow worse and worse by reason of a request presented by the gentlemen of late, which hath made those of Utrecht more backward than before. In mine opinion it were not amiss if it might please her Majesty to address her letters unto them, requiring them in regard of the common cause to lay down their particularities.[1] For the 1,000 shot[2] to be sent over, my Lord General is very careful to dispatch them away presently, and to that end doth now repair into Zealand. Thus in haste, I most humbly recommend myself to your Honour's good remembrance, craving pardon for my rudeness. At the Hague, the 31st of July, 1588.

Your Honour's most assuredly
to be commanded,
H. KYLLYGREW.

I can but pray to God against the power and malice of Satan, for here there will be little more aid come than you have had. They make duty[3] to suffer any of her Majesty's people to return, because they stand in so great need themselves. Yet have they been dealt withal by all manner of persuasion. Their anchor hold is the treaty, and their towns in her Majesty's possession and the inability[4] they stand in to furnish Bergen and Ostend with any of theirs, who cashier[5] of their own daily, for want of means to keep them; and sure if there come no money over to pay our companies their lendings, there will fall out great inconvenience, for here I see no relief to be had for them, unless some letters be written to our merchants at Middelburg to supply their needs at a pinch. My Lords may do well to advise upon this point, and under correction, the drawing of so

---

[1] Their personal interests or quarrels.
[2] Musketeers.
[3] Sc. but not willingly.
[4] MS. unhabillytye.
[5] MS. cassire : to break, disband.

many out of Flushing may prove more dangerous than by taking the whole number from Ostend.

I hear of great preparation in England to fight, but if London were trenched about as Paris was, it were a retreat in all events, and the only[1] way thought by good soldiers to break all the enemy's designs to his utter ruin. Many hands will make light work. The Lord of all power show us mercy.

These men are moved to set forth more ships, by name one that came from carrying[2] the Count Hohenlo to Hamburg [and][3] the wafters of the herring fleet newly come home. We have also moved the Count Maurice and the Council to go into Zealand, but yet the matter is in dispute, and will not be resolved this week by the States General who be here yet assembled.

I heard nothing out of England since the 11th of this present. Sir Thomas Morgan doth come over with the 2,000 shot, and hath been able to prevail in nothing here ; yet have I done for him what I could, though small thanks for my labour. I thank your Honour for remembering of Mr Gilpin ; I trust her Majesty shall receive good service by him. I write to no man at this time but to your Honour, and therefore it may please you to impart what your Honour shall think good.

July 31.—*MEMORIAL FOR RICHARD DRAKE.*

[ccxiii. 69.]

St. James, the last of July, 1588.

A memorial for Richard Drake, Esquire, being sent to the Lord Admiral, of such things as her Majesty doth desire to be informed of.

---

[1] We have heard something of this kind, even in our own time.
[2] MS. caring.   [3] Omitted in MS.

To be enquired :—

What number of ships are in service with my Lord Admiral, and of what burden?

How many are of the Queen's own ships? how many of them are ships of good bulk? how many are pinnaces, and how many of the country's charge?

What number of soldiers and of mariners serve in the Queen's ships?

How the Queen's ships are victualled?

How the other ships are victualled?

What powder and shot every ship hath?

How much powder and shot doth the navy use to spend in the fights with the enemies upon one day?

What quantity of powder and bullet hath been brought to the navy since the Lord Admiral met with the Spanish fleet near Plymouth? And from what places hath it been brought to the navy?

What losses of men and ships hath been on the Spanish side? and where were the losses? and where are the prisoners? And what powder, munition and any treasure hath been taken upon them?

What losses hath happened to the Queen's army of ships and men?

What men hath been lost since the beginning of the services at Plymouth?

What causes are there why the Spanish navy hath not been boarded by the Queen's ships? And though some of the ships of Spain may be thought too huge to be boarded by the English, yet some of the Queen's ships are thought very able to have boarded divers of the meaner ships of the Spanish navy.[1]

And if his Lordship, upon good advice there

---

[1] This query is doubtless the explanation of Ralegh's celebrated defence of Howard's policy, quoted in the Introduction.

taken, shall find it more necessary to have those ten ships[1] to be used upon the coast of Flanders to imbarke[2] the Duke of Parma's shipping there, then, upon his commandment, the said ten ships shall repair to such place for that service as he shall appoint.

The Queen's Majesty would have Pedro de Valdes, that was the captain of the galleon distressed, to be sent safe into England; and such other Spaniards as have been taken and are now kept on seaboard; for that she thinketh very inconvenient to have any such kept upon any English ship, where either they may practise some mischief, or else come to understanding of the secrets of the services intended.

To inform the Lord Admiral that some Englishmen, and Spaniards also that are taken, do say that the intent of the Spanish navy is to draw along the English navy from the coast of Flanders; that the sea being clear, the Duke of Parma might come out with his forces to invade the realm, and namely to come to London. Some also do think that if this navy of Spain cannot prevail against the English, that they will sail to the river of Emden; whereof the Lord Admiral may see well to inform himself what may be probable to think thereof.

The Lord Steward,[3] who was at Dover the 29th of July, saith that a Hollander came to Dover declaring that he came in company with 30 or 40 sail of Hollanders, and came to the Spanish fleet in the night unawares, the night before when the fire was put by English boats, and that in the morning those Hollanders came to the Lord Admiral and joined with his navy. But by reason the Lord Admiral's

---

[1] The London ships under Bellingham. See *ante*, p. 339.
[2] So in MS. To embargo, embar, stay.
[3] The Earl of Leicester.

letters [1] written the 30th of this month reporteth that there was no Hollander nor Londoner upon the sea, it is to be enquired what may be thought thereof, and to enquire how the mouth of the Sluys is kept by any ships of Zealand, where it is said the Duke mindeth to set out a number of his by-landers.

You shall seek to learn the state of our commissioners at Bourbourg, whether they be come thence, and to what place, and with what surety they may come into England.

If any words can be sent to Sir Wm. Russell, to require him to send away 20 lasts of powder, and that if he may, some 8 or 10 lasts thereof may, in the way, be sent to the Lord Admiral.

Ex^m per W. WAAD.[2]

Ex^m per W. Waad. [2]

/

July 31.—*GORGES TO WALSYNGHAM.*

[coxiii. 70.—Signed.   Addressed.]

Right Honourable :—According to your direction have done my endeavour, all that might be, for the coming to my Lord Henry Seymour with the eight ships of London ; and on the 30th of July, passing through the sands, we were becalmed and forced to anchor the same night in the New Channel. The next morning, being the last of this month, we had the wind at South-East and blew very

---

[1] No letter of Howard's, of this date, is now known. It may be that it was read and re-read and handed about till it fell to pieces ; but the reference is, more probably, to the letter to Walsyngham of the 29th (*ante*, p. 341), which says no Hollander nor Flushinger. And in fact, there were, within Howard's knowledge, many London ships at sea—the Margaret and John among others—though Gorges was still in the river.

[2] William Waad, Clerk of the Council.

much, so that by no means we could recover the
North Foreland. And thus riding in the New
Channel we understood by a ketch that both the
fleets weighed anchor on Sunday at night, and fell
presently into fight, and so continued till they were
out of sight of land plying to the North-East; but
what course they have taken, as yet we cannot learn.
But I mean with all diligence to ply into the Narrow
Seas, to understand whether my Lord Henry hath
left any order what I shall do; and if there be order
left for my service there, I mean to ply after the
fleet with all possible means I can make. And thus,
with my humble duty, I wish you increase of honour
with all happiness. From aboard the Susan Parnell, at ten of the clock, this last of July.

Your Honour's most readiest to command,

NICHOLAS GORGES.

July 31.—*HAWKYNS TO WALSYNGHAM.*

[ccxiii. 71.—Signed and autograph postscript. Addressed.]

My bounden duty humbly remembered unto
your good Lordship:—I have not busied myself to
write often to your Lordship in this great cause, for
that my Lord Admiral doth continually advertise
the manner of all things that doth pass. So do
others that understand the state of all things as well
as myself. We met with this fleet somewhat to the
westward of Plymouth upon Sunday in the morning, being the 21st of July, where we had some
small fight with them in the afternoon. By the
coming aboard one of the other of the Spaniards, a
great ship, a Biscayan, spent her foremast and
bowsprit; which was left by the fleet in the sea, and
so taken up by Sir Francis Drake the next morn-

ing. The same Sunday there was, by a fire
chancing by a barrel of powder, a great Biscayan
spoiled and abandoned, which my Lord took up
and sent away.

The Tuesday following, athwart of Portland,
we had a sharp and long fight with them, wherein
we spent a great part of our powder and shot, so as it
was not thought good to deal with them any more
till that was relieved.

The Thursday following, by the occasion of the
scattering[1] of one of the great ships from the fleet,
which we hoped to have cut off, there grew a hot
fray, wherein some store of powder was spent; and
after that, little done till we came near to Calais,
where the fleet of Spain anchored, and our fleet by
them; and because they should not be in peace
there, to refresh their water or to have conference
with those of the Duke of Parma's party, my Lord
Admiral, with firing of ships, determined to remove
them; as he did, and put them to the seas; in
which broil the chief galleass spoiled her rudder,
and so rode ashore near the town of Calais, where
she was possessed of our men, but so aground as she
could not be brought away.

That morning, being Monday, the 29th of July,
we followed the Spaniards; and all that day had
with them a long and great fight, wherein there was
great valour showed generally of our company. In
this battle there was spent very much of our powder
and shot; and so the wind began to blow westerly,
a fresh gale, and the Spaniards put themselves
somewhat to the northward, where we follow and
keep company with them. In this fight there was
some hurt done among the Spaniards. A great
ship of the galleons of Portugal, her rudder spoiled,
and so the fleet left her in the sea. I doubt not but

[1] MS. schateringe : separation. Cf. *ante*, p. 13.

360 DEFEAT OF THE

all these things are written more at large to your
Lordship than 1 can do ; but this is the substance
and material matter that hath passed.

Our ships, God be thanked, have received little
hurt, and are of great force to accompany them, and
of such advantage that with some continuance at
the seas, and sufficiently provided of shot and
powder, we shall be able, with God's favour, to
weary them out of the sea and confound them.
Yet, as I gather certainly, there are amongst them
50 forcible and invincible ships which consist of
those that follow, viz. :—

Nine galleons of Portugal of 800 ton apiece,
saving two of them are but 400 ton apiece.

Twenty great Venetians and argosies of the
seas within the Strait, of 800 apiece.

One ship of the Duke of Florence of 800 ton.

Twenty great Biscayans of 500 or 600 ton.

Four galleasses, whereof one is in France.

There are 30 hulks, and 30 other small ships,
whereof little account is to be made.

At their departing from Lisbon, being the 19th
of May by our account, they were victualled for six
months.   They stayed in the Groyne twenty-eight
days, and there refreshed their water. At their coming
from Lisbon they were taken with a flaw, and four-
teen hulks or thereabouts came near Ushant, and so
returned with contrary winds to the Groyne, and there
met ; and else there was none other company upon
our coast before the whole fleet arrived.   And in
their coming now, a little flaw took them, fifty
leagues from the coast of Spain ; where one great
ship was severed from them, and four galleys, which
hitherto have not recovered their company.

At their departing from Lisbon, the soldiers
were twenty thousand, the mariners and others
eight thousand ; so as, in all, they were twenty-eight

thousand men. Their commission was to confer with the Prince of Parma, as I learn, and then to proceed to the service that should be there concluded ; and so the Duke to return into Spain with these ships and mariners, the soldiers and their furniture being left behind. Now this fleet is here, and very forcible, and must be waited upon with all our force, which is little enough. There would[1] be an infinite quantity of powder and shot provided, and continually sent abroad ; without the which great hazard may grow to our country ; for this is the greatest and strongest combination, to my understanding, that ever was gathered in Christendom; therefore I wish it, of all hands, to be mightily and diligently looked unto and cared for.

The men have been long unpaid and need relief. I pray your Lordship that the money that should have gone to Plymouth may now be sent to Dover. August now cometh in, and this coast will spend ground tackle, cordage, canvas and victuals ; all which would be sent to Dover in good plenty. With these things, and God's blessing, our kingdom may be preserved ; which being neglected, great hazard may come. I write to your Lordship briefly and plainly. Your wisdom and experience is great; but this is a matter far passing all that hath been seen in our time or long before. And so praying to God for a happy deliverance from the malicious and dangerous practice of our enemies, I humbly take my leave. From the sea, aboard the Victory, the last of July, 1588.

The Spaniards take their course for Scotland ; my Lord doth follow them. I doubt not, with God's favour, but we shall impeach their landing. There must be order for victual and money, powder and shot, to be sent after us.

Your Lordship's humbly to command,
JOHN HAWKYNS.

[1] Should.

This is the copy of the letter I send to my Lord
Treasurer, whereby I shall not need to write to your
Honour. Help us with furniture, and, with God's
favour, we shall confound their devices.

Your Honour's ever bounden,

JOHN HAWKYNS.

I pray your Honour bear with this, for it is done
in haste and bad weather.

J. H.

July 31.—*BARREY TO WALSYNGHAM.*

[coxiii. 72.—Signed. Addressed.]

My most humble duty unto your Honour remembered :—Upon Sunday last Sir Henry Palmer
came unto Dover from the Lord Admiral for some
of the boats that were appointed to be laden with
bavens[1] and pitch, and had presently away with him
that night 19 boats of the ports laden with bavens ;
and every boat one barrel of pitch of their own,
besides the 72 barrels sent down by your Honour,
the which were sent in one of those boats. Sir
Henry Palmer embarked himself in one of those
boats, and departed from Dover on Sunday night
last, about 12 of the clock. Before Sir Henry
Palmer's coming unto my Lord Admiral, there was
an attempt made by other vessels for the firing of
the Spanish fleet ; by which means the fleet was
removed from the road before Calais, and so are
passed towards the North Seas, and all her Majesty's
navy in chase of them. And I hope in the Almighty
God, he will give good success unto our navy.

Some of the boats that were sent out with the

---

[1] Faggots, bundles of brushwood.

bavens are returned from my Lord Admiral, who say that my Lord discharged them, But, for that it may be shift of wind may put back the fleet again, I make stay of all the boats that are here, as well of those that are returned as of the rest that were not yet sent forth.

Yesternight, about 6 of the clock, Jasper Swift [1] came unto me and showed me an order from your Honour for certain boats that should come unto Dover, which are not yet come, not above 3 of them ; and if the Spanish fleet return not, here will be no use of them. The ports' men [2] deserve commendation for their willing readiness ; for within one day after they received letters from me, with your Honour's letter, they sent 30 boats into this harbour. If there shall not be any further employment of them, may it please your Honour to signify your Honour's pleasure therein ; for they are most of them fishermen of Rye and Hastings, and lie here at great charges, calling upon me every day to victual them. I gave my bills for victualling those that were sent with Sir Henry Palmer, as also for the bavens that were taken up, and the pitch that they brought in their own boats ; and money also disbursed by me for sending to the ships and for labourers and boats in shipping of the bavens ; most humbly beseeching your Honour that order may be taken by your good means for the satisfying thereof, the particulars whereof by my next I will send unto your Honour ; and so I most humbly cease from troubling of your Honour. At Dover Castle, this last of July, 1588.

Your Honour's always most bounden
at commandment,

RYCHARD BARREY.

---

[1] Sergeant of the Admiralty.
[2] The men of the Five Ports.

July 31.—*DRAKE TO WALSYNGHAM.*

[ccxiii. 73.—Holograph. Addressed.]

Most Honourable :—I am commanded to send these prisoners ashore by my Lord Admiral, which had ere this been long done, but that I thought their being here might have done something which is not thought meet now.

Let me beseech your Honour that they may be presented unto her Majesty, either by your Honour, or by my honourable good Lord, my Lord Chancellor, or both of ye. The one Don Pedro is a man of greatest estimation with the King of Spain, and thought next in his army to the Duke of Sidonia. If they should be given from[1] me unto any other, it would be some grief to my friends. If her Majesty will have them, God defend[2] but I should think it happy.

We have the army of Spain before us and mind, with the grace of God, to wrestle a pull[3] with him. There was never anything pleased me better than the seeing the enemy flying with a southerly wind to the northwards. God grant you have a good eye to the Duke of Parma ; for with the grace of God, if we live, I doubt it not but ere it be long so to handle the matter with the Duke of Sidonia as he shall wish himself at St. Mary Port among his orange trees.[4]

[1] Sc. away from.   [2] Forbid.   [3] MS. wressell a poull.
[4] Cf. Nelson to Addington, 12th of August, 1801 : 'In my command I find much zeal and good humour ; and should Mr. Bonaparte put himself in our way, I believe he will wish himself even in Corsica.' The coincidence is only one of many which occur in Nelson's letters, and raise the suspicion that he had read much more than is commonly supposed.

God give us grace to depend upon him ; so shall we not doubt victory, for our cause is good. Humbly taking my leave, this last of July, 1588,
Your Honour's faithfully to be commanded ever,
FRA. DRAKE.

I crave pardon of your Honour for my haste, for that I had to watch this last night upon the enemy.
Yours ever,
FRA. DRAKE.

END OF THE FIRST VOLUME